CONTENTS

S377

MOLECULAR AND CELL BIOLOGY

1

FROM MOLECULES TO CELLS

prepared for the Course Team by
Mark Hirst, Jane Loughlin, David Male, Radmila Mileusnic and
Sotiris Missailidis

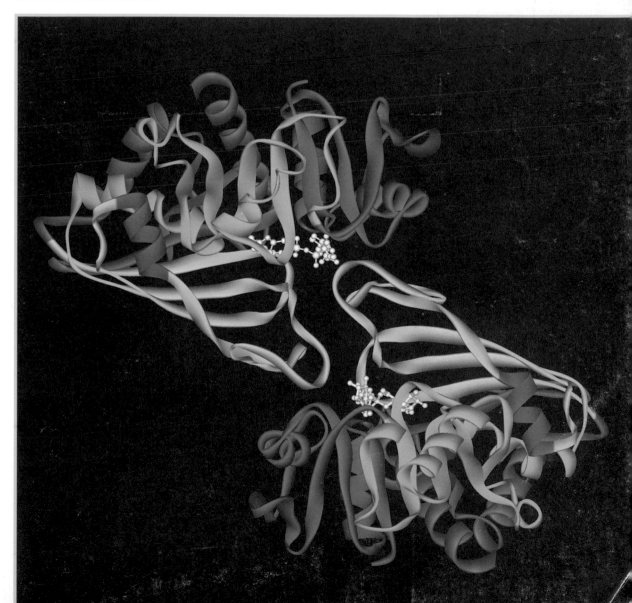

The Open University

The S377 Course Team

Course Team Chair
David Male

Course Manager
Viki Burnage

Course Team Assistants
Rebecca Efthimiou
Lara Knight

Course Team authors
Mark Hirst
Jane Loughlin
David Male
Radmila Mileusnic
Sotiris Missailidis
Ignacio Romero
Jill Saffrey
Robert Saunders

Consultant author
Sally Cowley

Editors
Gerry Bearman
Ian Nuttall
Dick Sharp
Margaret Swithenby

Academic Reader
Christine Gorman

External Course Assessor
Iain Campbell

OU Graphic Design
Roger Courthold
Sara Hack
Jenny Nockles

Video production
Wilf Eynon
Michael Francis

CD-ROM production
Greg Black
Eleanor Crabb
Hilary MacQueen

Rights Executive
Chris Brady

Picture Research
Lydia Eaton

Indexer
Jane Henley

Course website
Patrina Law
Louise Olney

GIFT   571.6

The Open University, Walton Hall, Milton Keynes, MK7 6AA, United Kingdom
First published 2004.

Edited, designed and typeset by The Open University.

Printed and bound in the United Kingdom by The Alden Group, Oxford

ISBN 0 7492 66309

This publication forms part of an Open University course S377 *Molecular and Cell Biology*. Details of this and other Open University courses can be obtained from the Course Information and Advice Centre, PO Box 724, The Open University, Milton Keynes MK7 6ZS, United Kingdom: tel. +44 (0)1908 653231, e-mail general-enquiries@open.ac.uk

Alternatively, you may visit the Open University website at http://www.open.ac.uk where you can learn more about the wide range of courses and packs offered at all levels by The Open University.

To purchase a selection of Open University course materials visit the webshop at www.ouw.co.uk, or contact Open University Worldwide, Michael Young Building, Walton Hall, Milton Keynes MK7 6AA, United Kingdom for a brochure. tel. +44 (0)1908 858785; fax +44 (0)1908 858787; email ouwenq@open.ac.uk

S377 Book 1 i1.1

1 EVOLUTION OF THE CELL

1.1 Introduction

Despite the evident variety in living organisms, at the level of the cell many basic biological processes are common to all of them. Furthermore, we can surmise that cellular processes and systems in present-day organisms are similar to those that operated in evolutionarily distant organisms. Thus, whilst we cannot be sure of the colour of a pterodactyl's wing, we can be confident that the cells in that wing released energy in a similar way to the cells in our own fingers. How is it possible to make such a bold statement, when there is no direct evidence for it? If we examine the biochemical pathways and systems that produce energy in ourselves, other animals, plants or fungi (i.e. eukaryotes), we find striking similarities both in their mechanisms and in the cellular components of which they are composed. Moreover, equivalent, albeit distinct systems operate in many prokaryotes.

A comparison of the structures of many enzymes in biochemical pathways demonstrates little variation across the entire range of eukaryotic organisms (see, for example, Figure 1.1). The conservation of key enzymes in diverse species illustrates that fundamental biochemical pathways are common to virtually all life forms. These common features suggest that all present-day organisms have evolved from common ancestors.

◻ List some structures and functions of cells that are common to all life forms. (Note that viruses are *not* cells.)

● The main common features of cells are as follows:

  ▸ All cells have a plasma membrane which encloses and defines the cell.
  ▸ All cells use DNA (deoxyribonucleic acid) as their genetic material and this is formed from just four nucleotides.
  ▸ Cells transcribe the information from DNA into RNA (ribonucleic acid).
  ▸ RNA is translated into proteins on ribosomes according to a universal genetic code.
  ▸ All cells use the same standard set of 20 amino acids to synthesize their proteins.

There is no reason to suppose that the organization of life as we see it now is the only way it could be. Take, for example, the amino acids that are the building blocks of proteins; would it be possible to use *other* amino acids and still have functional proteins? Most likely it would be possible and indeed, in certain proteins, some of the standard amino acids are modified after synthesis of the protein (see, for example, Figure 1.2). It seems that the universal set of 20 amino acids provides sufficient diversity to create a wide range of proteins, but we cannot tell whether this particular set has any unique property.

Figure 1.1
Note the similarity in the molecular structures of the glycolytic enzyme glyceraldehyde 3-phosphate dehydrogenase in (a) a human (*Homo sapiens*, here excmplified by Charles Darwin), and (b) a spiny lobster (*Palinurus versicolor*), despite the gross physiological differences between these two species. The enzymes are shown with their coenzyme, NAD, bound (the white ball-and-stick structures).

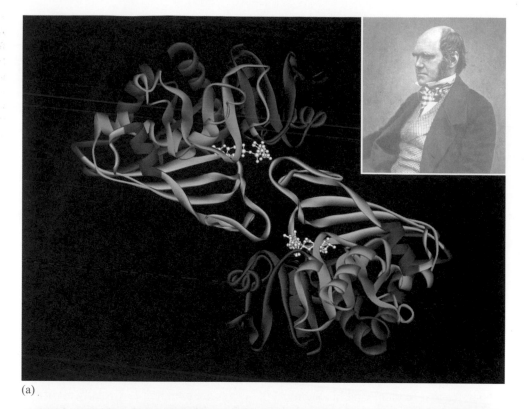

(a)

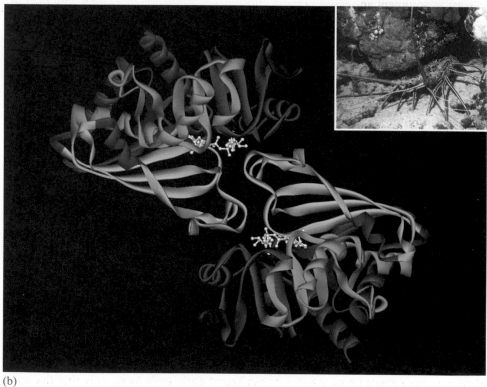

(b)

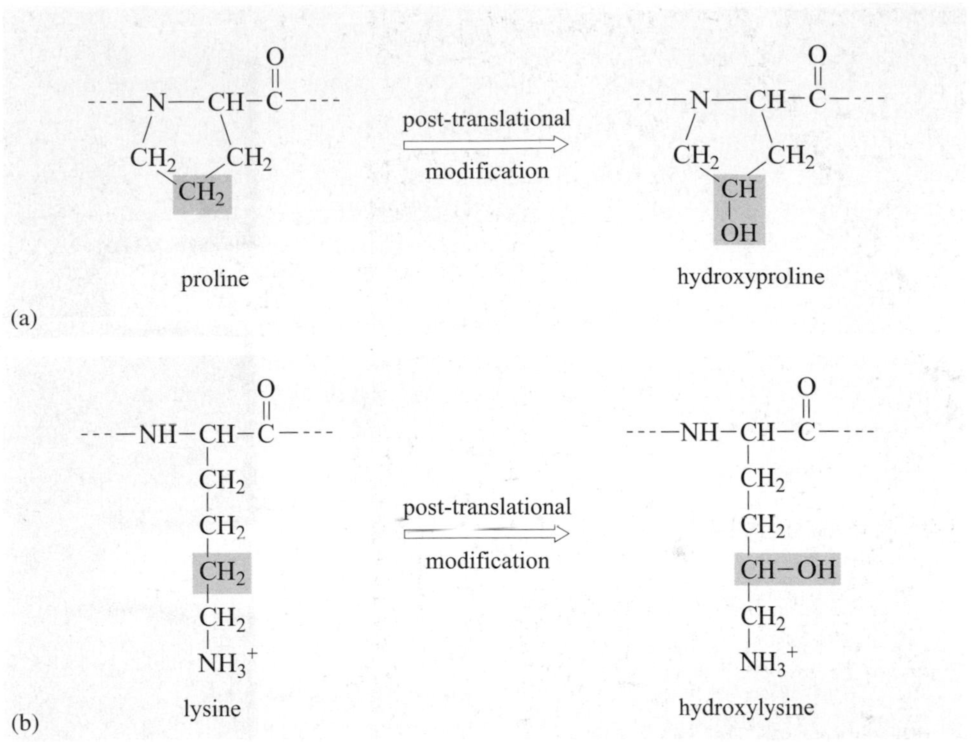

(a)

(b)

Figure 1.2
Amino acids hydroxyproline (derived from proline) and hydroxylysine (derived from lysine) are both found in the protein collagen. They are not directly encoded in the collagen gene but rather are produced by post-translational modification. These modified amino acids contribute to the bonds that form between collagen fibrils and so are essential for collagen function.

A similar argument applies to genetic information. When we look at the key features of living organisms, it is apparent that reproduction, entailing the replication of genetic material, is essential and nucleic acids, as 'self-replicating' molecules, fulfil the role of hereditary information. However, there almost certainly were other earlier prebiotic systems about which we can only speculate. Furthermore, although all present-day organisms use the same genetic code consisting of three consecutive nucleotides to specify each amino acid in a protein, some minor differences do exist in some organisms. For example, the triplet of bases CUA encodes the amino acid leucine in the universal genetic code but, in the mitochondria of yeast, CUA encodes a threonine residue. Such interesting exceptions to the general rules of gene coding and protein synthesis demonstrate quite clearly that the universal genetic code is not the only possible basis for life. Rather, the universality of this coding system most likely arose through its *fixation* within an early replicating/coding system that was perpetuated through natural selection. As a consequence, every living organism on Earth uses DNA to store its hereditary information and encodes this information in the same way.

1.2 Every organism is composed of cells

A key feature of living organisms is cellularity. Every organism we see today, from unicellular amoebae or bacteria to multicellular animals and plants, is composed of cells that are defined by a plasma membrane, invariably a phospholipid bilayer. However, we cannot know what forms different early cells took, only that the most successful primordial cells must have had a physical boundary of this sort.

◯ What characteristics of phospholipids make them suited to the formation of a membrane separating two aqueous compartments?

■ The non-polar (hydrophobic) tail portion acts as a diffusion barrier for water-soluble molecules. The polar phosphoryl groups, orientated towards the inner and outer aqueous compartments, allow stable membranes to form within an aqueous environment.

In this section, we consider some of the features of cells in present-day organisms and question why cellularity is a universal property of life. The conclusion that will emerge is that cells are fundamental to all living organisms because they allowed primordial life to evolve from collections of prebiotic organic molecules.

Most biologists consider the cell to be the smallest unit of life, with the plasma membrane separating living and non-living collections of molecules. A major objective of this course is to understand how and why biological processes are compartmentalized within a cell.

Confining biological molecules within a cell has two important consequences.

1   It provides a controlled environment in which molecules can interact effectively because they do not diffuse away from each other.

2   Cells can be different from each other because they contain distinct sets of molecules.

It follows therefore that compartmentalization permits diversification, a process fundamental to both evolution and the development of complex multicellular organisms.

A further explanation for the cellular nature of all living organisms is suggested in Chapter 4, where living processes are considered from a thermodynamic perspective. One consequence of the laws of thermodynamics is that it is only possible for an ordered structure to develop if the rest of the world becomes more disordered. Seen in this way, development of order and complexity could only occur within a discrete compartment, i.e. in the primitive or **primordial cell**.

1.2.1 The evolution of the first cell

It is not possible to know how life first evolved. However, during early evolution it is thought that primordial cells may have formed by chance, each containing a collection of prebiotic molecules. If the molecules in one of these 'cells' happened to include some that favoured the processes of life (self-replication and the ability to accumulate further organic molecules), then that 'cell' would outcompete others for the available organic molecules, effectively starving any other 'cells' (Figure 1.3). The idea that evolution could occur at such a primitive stage of development may be surprising, but it accords perfectly well with conventional views of evolution. When Charles Darwin proposed the theory of evolution by natural selection, he thought of it as a mechanism by which animals and plants develop and adapt over time to changes in the environment. For evolution by natural selection to occur, there must be variation. We now know that random variation arises as a result of errors in replication of genetic material. Diversification of, and competition between, individuals are the starting points for evolution. Importantly, these evolutionary processes, which apply to all present-day prokaryotes and eukaryotes, would also have applied to developing primordial cells.

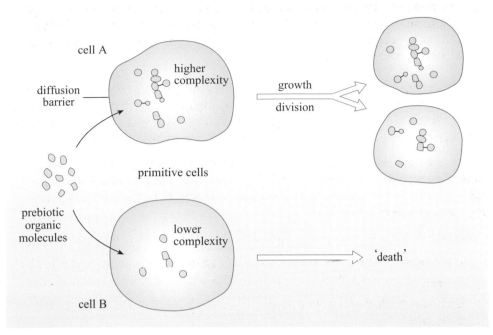

Figure 1.3 A possible scheme for the early evolution of life. Prebiotic organic molecules can accumulate in primitive cells, and may polymerize. The larger molecules diffuse out slowly because of the diffusion barrier provided by a primitive cell membrane. 'Cells' A and B compete for 'nutrients' but, by chance, 'cell' A accumulates these molecules more efficiently than does 'cell' B. 'Cell' A therefore grows and may divide, while 'cell' B is starved. Thus primitive cells provide the basis for diversification, competition and natural selection.

1.2.2 From primordial cells to multicellular eukaryotic organisms

For at least two billion years, unicellular bacteria were the only life form on Earth. It is a common and very easily made mistake to consider the bacteria we see all around us today as the evolutionary ancestors of complex multicellular organisms. This, of course, is not true. All organisms on Earth today have been subject to evolutionary pressures and bacteria living today are just as highly 'evolved' for their environments and lifestyles as are yeasts, algae or, indeed, ourselves. A critical stage in the evolutionary history of life was that at which prokaryotic and eukaryotic lineages became distinct. As much of this course is directed towards the understanding of eukaryotic cells, we will follow this branch of evolutionary history a little further.

A key distinguishing feature of eukaryotic cells is the presence of a specialized compartment in which the cell's hereditary material is located, namely the nucleus. This distinction suggests that subcellular specialization was critically important to the development of eukaryotic organisms. At some point in time, a larger cell is assumed to have incorporated into its cytoplasm the bacterium that ultimately would develop into a mitochondrion. Perhaps this happened just once, perhaps many times; we cannot be sure. A photosynthetic bacterium incorporated in the same way would later evolve into what we see today as the chloroplast. These organelles allowed plants and animals much greater flexibility and efficiency in use of energy sources and are clear examples of subcellular compartmentalization and specialization.

○ Think of a specific type of animal cell and list as many of its subcellular compartments as you can.

● You should have included mitochondria, the nucleus, the nucleolus, endoplasmic reticulum and the Golgi apparatus, since all animal cells have these. Depending on the type of cell you selected, you might also have included lysosomes, endosomes, phagosomes, peroxisomes, secretory vesicles, granules, lipid rafts, basal and apical zones of the plasma membrane, and perhaps others too.

Subcellular compartmentalization is, however, only one stage in the evolution of single-celled organisms, a process that also permitted the development of complex multicellular organisms. In present-day eukaryotic cells (see Figure 1.4) we can identify some of the systems and features that primordial cells must have acquired through evolution, including intracellular compartments, transport systems and a cytoskeleton, as well as the biochemical complexity that is the basis for these systems. However, we cannot know exactly how and in what order these systems were acquired during evolutionary history. Figure 1.5 illustrates a possible scenario by which present-day single-celled and multicellular eukaryotic organisms may have developed from ancestral primordial cells. Bear in mind that this is a highly simplistic and speculative representation that belies the incremental nature of evolution.

Compartmentalization of cells resulted in the specialization of different parts of the cell for different functions.

○ What advantages can you see for a cell that has specialized subcellular compartments? What requirement does this specialization place upon the cell?

● Enzymes required for particular functions can be grouped together, e.g. the enzymes of the citric acid cycle (also known as the Krebs cycle) in the mitochondria. Conversely, incompatible molecules can be segregated from each other; for instance, the degradative enzymes of the lysosomes are kept away from the proteins in the rest of the cell, which they could digest. It is possible to have many different kinds of 'environment' within the same cell; for example, endosomes can be alkaline, neutral or acidic. This specialization leads to the requirement for transport systems within the cell, to take molecules from one place to another.

Several transport systems operate in eukaryotic cells (Figure 1.6). There are the systems of vesicles that transport macromolecules and metabolites between the different membrane-bound compartments, such as the endoplasmic reticulum and the Golgi apparatus. Other transport systems take molecules from one part of the cytoplasm to another or from one zone of the plasma membrane to another. The development of intracellular transport systems is a key evolutionary step (Figure 1.5). It is no coincidence that prokaryotic organisms are much smaller than eukaryotic cells. Although prokaryotes do have simple cytoskeletal components, for the most part molecules move within them by diffusion and this process is relatively slow, especially for larger biological molecules such as proteins. In contrast, proteins produced in one part of a eukaryotic cell are transported quite rapidly to where they are needed. For example in nerve cells (neurons), organelles and proteins that are produced near the cell body are transported down the axon at a speed of up to one metre per day. This means that a mitochondrion could be transported from a cell body in the spinal cord to the tip of the toe within a day, a process that would take several years if mediated solely by passive diffusion.

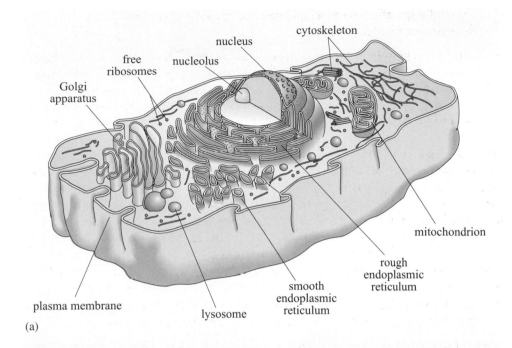

(a)

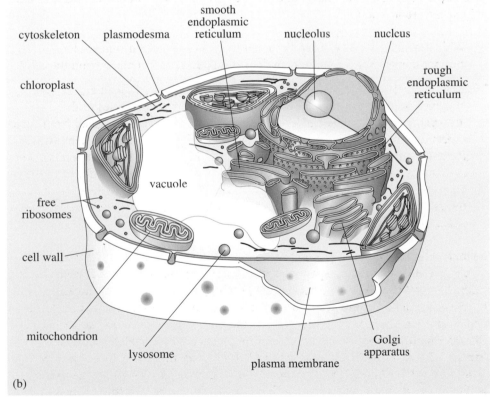

(b)

Figure 1.4   Schematic diagrams of (a) a typical animal cell and (b) a typical plant cell, showing the high degree of intracellular organization.

Figure 1.5
Key stages in the evolution of
(a) single-celled eukaryotes and
(b) multicellular eukaryotes. (a) The
incorporation of early prokaryotic
cells would have advantaged the cell
by providing increasingly versatile
and efficient energy management.
Primordial cells depended on diffusion
of nutrients from their surface to the
interior of the cell. The size of a cell
that could be supported by diffusion
in this way would be limited, since
larger cells would have a lower surface
area : volume ratio. However, the
chance formation of some basic
intracellular compartments and
transport systems would have
conferred an advantage on larger
cells, by accelerating the delivery of
nutrients and removal of wastes. The
development of a cytoskeleton would
have further advantaged cells, offering
structural support and physical
resistance and a framework for
intracellular transport. The
cytoskeleton would also provide a
platform for motility. (b) At some
stage, replicating early eukaryotic
cells, instead of dispersing, must have
formed a cohesive colony. We know
from studying differentiation in
present-day organisms that this
process requires intercellular
communication, and depends on
distinct developmental pathways.
Complex differentiation patterns
require controlled cell division and
even the death of some cells by
apoptosis. In early multicellular
organisms, these regulatory
mechanisms and communication
systems would have developed in an
incremental fashion by chance and
would have persisted because they
conferred an advantage on the
organism. In the same way, as
organisms became larger, selective
pressure would have favoured those
that had some form of transport
system, and such systems would have
been a feature of complex organisms
with many separate organ systems.

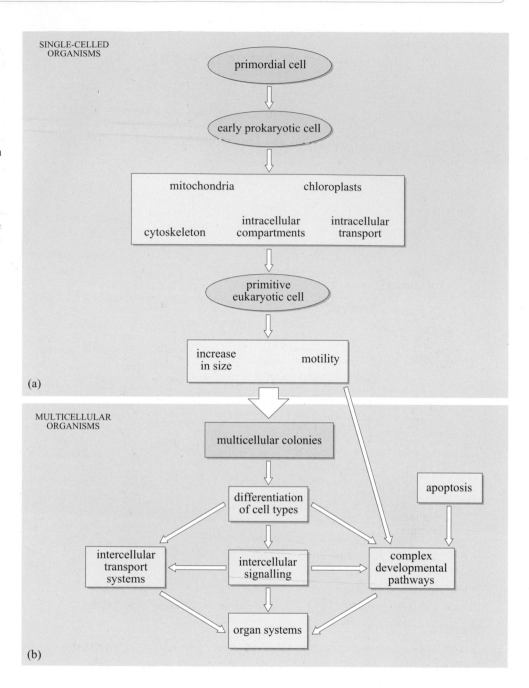

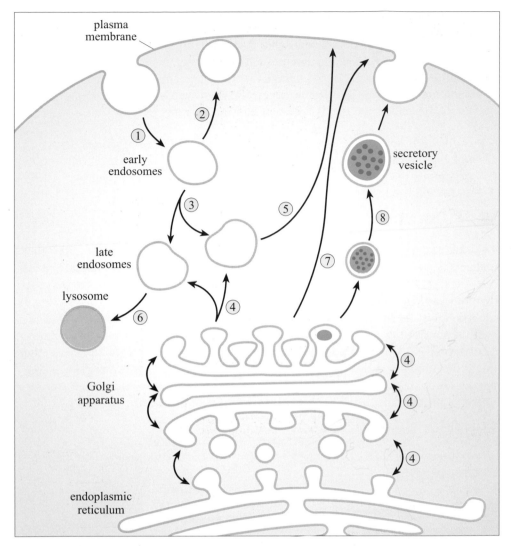

Figure 1.6
Intracellular trafficking pathways. Substances from outside the cell are taken up into early endosomes (1) from where receptors and other molecules can return to the cell surface (2). Many specialist types of late endosome occur (3) and these intersect the pathways of protein production from the Golgi apparatus (4). From here, molecules may be channelled back to the plasma membrane (5) or into lysosomes where they are broken down (6). Proteins synthesized in the endoplasmic reticulum and processed in the Golgi apparatus may be channelled directly to the cell surface (7) or may be stored in secretory vesicles before being released (8).

○ If proteins and organelles are to be moved around a cell from one compartment to another, this intracellular transport requires a further development. What is it?

● A system of 'addressing' is required, so that each protein or organelle is transported to the correct destination or compartment within the cell.

Transport systems, facilitating both internal traffic of molecules and organelles within the cell and exchange of molecules with the extracellular medium, allowed eukaryotic cells to increase in size. As a cell increases in size, its volume increases at a greater rate than its surface area. In prokaryotes, everything that enters the cell does so by crossing the plasma membrane; the process may be assisted by carrier molecules or transporters, but the surface area of the plasma membrane in relation to the volume of the cell limits the size of these cells. In comparison, the endosomes and internal membrane systems of eukaryotic cells give them a much larger effective surface than their size would dictate.

1.2.3 Differentiation of specialized cells

The increased size of eukaryotic cells and their subcellular specialization would have contributed to the development of multicellular organisms with differentiated cells and tissues (Figure 1.5b). Multicellular plants and animals are characterized by a remarkable variety in the different types of cell of which they are composed, and these cells typically have specialized functions and distinct shapes.

▢ Name and sketch a variety of animal cells that have different shapes. Include just the outline (plasma membrane) and nucleus of the cells. Here are some suggestions to get you started: macrophage, gut epithelial cell, neuron, endothelial cell, sperm cell.

◼ See Figure 1.7.

The shape of a cell is determined by its cytoskeleton as well as by its extracellular contacts. Extracellular components, such as collagen in animals and lignin in plants, act as a scaffold to which cells attach via adhesion molecules in their plasma membranes. There are three principal component structures of the cytoskeleton: the microtubules, the intermediate filaments and the microfilaments (Figure 1.8). The basic subunits of the microtubules (tubulin) and microfilaments (actin) are similar in most animal cells, although the intermediate filaments are more variable. Given that the basic subunits are similar, the variety of different cell forms is determined by the way in which the cytoskeleton is assembled, which can be related to the different proteins that associate with the cytoskeleton to stabilize it.

> The basic components of the cytoskeleton are outlined in S204, Book 3 *The Core of Life*, Vol. II, but their functions are considered in more detail in this course.

Figure 1.7
Simple sketches of some different types of animal cells, illustrating the variety of shapes.

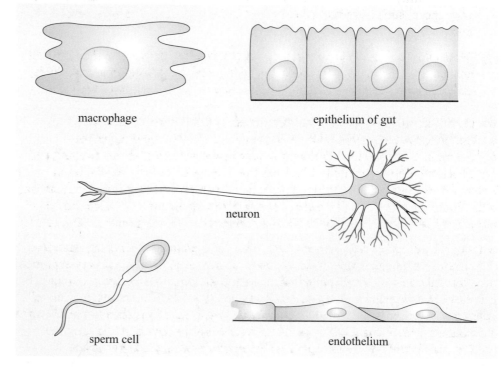

macrophage

epithelium of gut

neuron

sperm cell

endothelium

Figure 1.8
The microfilaments in the cytoskeleton of cultured human astrocytes are stained red using a specific fluorescent label. Nuclei are stained purple. Astrocytes are a type of cell found in the brain of vertebrates.

10µm

The cytoskeleton of a cell is a dynamic structure. As well as affecting the shape of the cell, it plays an essential role in a number of processes, including cell division, endocytosis, secretion and intracellular transport, and is also required for cell movement. Adhesion molecules in the plasma membrane allow cells to bind to other cells or to the extracellular matrix, but they must interact with the cytoskeleton for the cell to develop traction and motility. In higher plants and in adult animals, cell migration is seen in only a very limited range of cell types, but during development animal cells migrate extensively to arrive at their correct final location. For example, during development of the mammalian brain, neurons migrate in successive waves from the central area where they are produced, towards the outside where they form the cerebral cortex.

○ Identify a number of cell types present in adult multicellular organisms that show motility. Be sure to distinguish cells that have their own intrinsic motility from those, such as red blood cells, that are transported passively around the body.

■ Macrophages (wandering phagocytes) are present in most animals; sperm cells are also motile; during wound healing, cells such as fibroblasts and endothelial cells of blood vessels can migrate into the site of damage to initiate repair.

During development, once cells have migrated to their correct position, differentiation results in the selective expression of one group of genes and repression of the remainder. Different sets of genes are expressed in different cell types, determining both the form and functions of the cell. Gene regulation in prokaryotes is important in the control of many cell processes, such as metabolism of different nutrients. In eukaryotes, gene structure and gene regulation are much more complex, as reflected in the greater complexity of their genomes (Figure 1.9).

Although most adult eukaryotic cells contain a full genome, which is replicated in its entirety during cell division, many genes are not used. Some genes are expressed for a limited period during development and are not required in the adult, or they are expressed in a very limited number of cell types. It is this selective expression of genes that determines the behaviour, morphology and functions of individual cells in multicellular organisms. Gene repression occurs at many levels. At the genome level, it may involve the silencing of an entire chromosome, such as occurs in

Figure 1.9
A segment of the human genome from the centre of the major histocompatibility complex on chromosome 6. This segment is 8×10^5 base pairs in length and contains a large number of different genes (indicated by coloured boxes), which are expressed in different tissues. For example TNF (tumour necrosis factor) is a signalling protein produced by macrophages, while the C4A gene (at about 260 kb) is expressed in the liver to produce a serum protein, C4. Each gene contains many separate exons separated by large introns, so that only a small proportion of the region shown (< 5%) actually encodes protein. Expanded below are the genes for lymphotoxin (LTB) and one form of TNF. Each of these genes includes four exons (indicated by coloured boxes), and are transcribed into RNA before being spliced to remove the non-coding regions. The region between the two genes contains several regulatory elements (not individually identified), which control whether the gene will be transcribed or not.

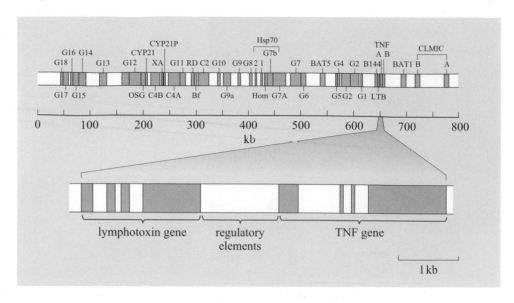

female mammals, where one of the X chromosomes is inactivated in each cell. At the chromosome level, segments of chromosomes may be inactivated by alterations in local chromatin structure or through methylation of the DNA. At the gene level, transcription of individual genes or small sets of genes is controlled by transcription factors which bind to regulatory regions close to the gene. These mechanisms of controlling gene expression are explained in Chapters 5 and 10.

○ It seems very surprising that specialized cells replicate so much DNA that they will never use. Can you think of reasons why this should be so?

● The simple answer is that the genes required by specialized cells are distributed on many different chromosomes, so that a cell requires the full set of chromosomes in order to have those genes that it needs for its functions. However, if we go beyond the simple explanation, this is a very difficult question indeed. Possibly the process of cell division is so fundamental to life, that all cells have retained the absolute requirement to accurately replicate their full set of genes before they can progress through the cell cycle to mitosis.

Of great importance in differentiation is the control and limitation of cell division. In single-celled prokaryotes and eukaryotes, the limits of cell division are set principally by the availability of nutrients, but in multicellular eukaryotes the number of cells required to form an organ is related to the function of the organ and the requirements of the rest of the body. Development in complex multicellular organisms entails the controlled death of certain cells at critical times (Figure 1.10) and the process by which this occurs, known as programmed cell death or apoptosis (see Figure 1.5b), is a central evolutionary advance. For example, more than 90% of lymphocytes that develop in the thymus gland die by apoptosis, without ever leaving that organ. The reason for this apparently wasteful process is that the majority of these cells are not suitable for their function within the body. In other words, unwanted cells die because this is advantageous for the organism. Multicellular organisms most likely evolved because individual cells cooperated rather than competed with each other.

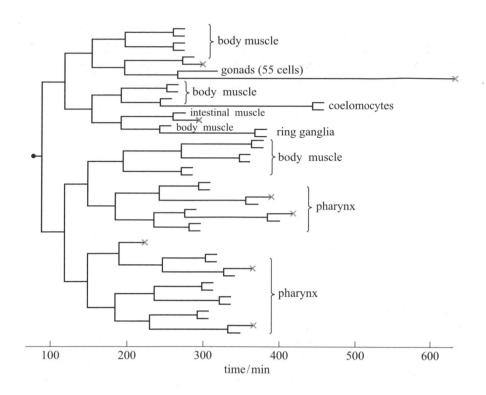

Figure 1.10
Part of the developmental tree of the cells in *Caenorhabditis elegans*, a nematode worm. The length of the horizontal lines is proportional to the amount of time that elapses between each cell division. A single fertilized egg cell gives rise to exactly 558 cells in the newly-hatched worm, which become 959 cells in the adult, each cell going through a defined sequence of development and differentiation. During development, exactly 131 cells die by apoptosis (indicated by the red crosses on the figure), and failure of cells to die produces developmental abnormalities. The whole developmental sequence is genetically programmed down to the fate of every single cell.

1.2.4 Transport systems and intercellular communication

In the same way that subcellular specialization is most effective because of intracellular transport mechanisms, so, in multicellular organisms, differentiation and specialization of tissues are supported by transport systems and communication between different parts of the organism. Generally speaking, the larger the organism, the more complex are its transport systems.

○ Name some of the transport and intercellular communication systems present in individual animals and plants.

● Transport systems include the blood and lymphatic systems in vertebrates, the xylem and phloem of plants, and the haemocoel of arthropods. Intercellular communication systems include: chemical signalling via molecules such as hormones, in both animals and plants, and by cytokines in vertebrates; electrochemical signalling via neurons in the nervous system of animals, and between individual cells in plants.

Intercellular communication systems operate at a more local level compared to the organism-wide transport systems. It is estimated that there are more than 200 different cell types in an adult human. With this level of specialization the requirements for intercellular communication are enormous; hundreds of different hormones, growth factors and cytokines have been described, each with its own unique or shared receptor. In order to respond correctly to signals, the complexity of the intracellular signalling systems has to match that of the intercellular signalling. Many responses require the cell to integrate several different signals, and this involves cross-talk between the second messenger systems that control the cell's response. How this signal integration is achieved is a key theme of this course.

13

1.3 What is life?

We are so familiar with the properties of life (reproduction, respiration, etc.) that we usually think of them as a package, and point out the interesting organisms or biological systems such as viruses, that lack particular properties. However, as we have emphasized in this chapter, the properties of different life forms have emerged successively over billions of years.

For most of human history people have believed that living things and non-living things were fundamentally different. It therefore came as something of a surprise to many scientists in the 19th century that organic molecules and inorganic molecules are assembled using the same basic laws of chemistry. An early demonstration of this fact was carried out in the 1820s when the chemist Friedrich Wöhler synthesized the biological molecule urea from the non-biological chemicals cyanic acid (CNOH) and ammonia (NH_3). As the 19th century progressed, organic synthesis produced increasingly complex molecules. Nevertheless, well into the 20th century many scientists believed that living things contained some essential 'life force' or 'élan vital'. With the rapid progress of molecular and cell biology in the last 50 years, it has become clear that biological systems obey the laws of chemistry and physics – the key difference between living and non-living things is the higher level of order seen in the former. Knowing the laws of chemistry, it would be impossible to predict that self-replicating polynucleotides would form the basis of life. However, we see that the replication of nucleotides conforms fully to the laws of chemistry and physics. There is no special biological principle, just increasing levels of complexity.

1.4 Studying biological molecules and cells

In this chapter we have seen how the evolution of complex organisms has progressed from, and required, increasing complexity and specialization of cells. Although the details of this progression are lost in time, life forms have evolved from collections of prebiotic chemicals through cellular evolution and on to the hugely diverse range of present-day organisms – from single-celled prokaryotes and eukaryotes to multicellular eukaryotes with differentiated tissues. In one way, this course follows a similar path, starting with simple biological molecules, going on to the structure, functions and specialization of cells and finishing with some examples of complex physiology that can only be understood on the basis of molecular and cell biology.

To study different aspects of biology, researchers often use **model organisms,** which shed light on particular aspects of cell biology, physiology or development. These selected species are studied in great depth, not necessarily because the organisms are intrinsically important (to humans) but because their study allows greater understanding of specific biological processes. Since you will encounter several of these organisms during the course, we are introducing them here in relation to their position on an evolutionary tree (Figure 1.11).

In this course, you will be looking at the structures, function and organization of cells. Only by understanding cellular processes and some of the underlying biochemistry is it possible to understand more complex processes, such as ageing or tumour development; this is the way we have organized the course. In Book 1 we examine the building blocks of cells and the composition, organization and

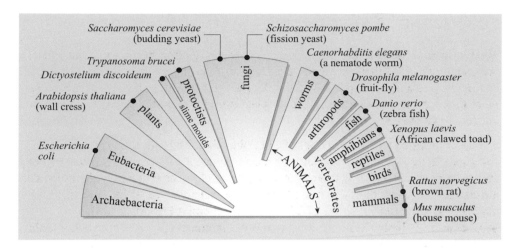

Figure 1.11
A simple schematic in which several model organisms have been plotted onto evolutionary divisions of life forms. Details of these model organisms can be found in the Glossary.

function of different cellular compartments at the molecular level, emphasizing the relationship between structure and function. The dynamic relationship between different components of the cell and how these participate in the life and death of the cell is the subject of Books 2 and 3. This area includes basic cellular processes such as how molecules are grouped together and moved from one compartment to another in the cell and how signals are interpreted by the cell so that it can maintain its integrity and respond appropriately to changes in the external environment or to signals from other cells. In the last book, we present some special cases of how cells differentiate and respond to external signals. Many complex biological phenomena can be related to basic cellular processes. For example, understanding how cancer develops requires knowledge of how cell division is normally controlled. To understand cell division, in turn, requires an understanding of how proteins interact with each other within the cell, which proteins are synthesized and ultimately how the genome determines the fate of each cell. It is the ability to investigate complex biological processes at many different levels that makes this subject so fascinating and rewarding.

Summary of Chapter 1

1   All life forms on Earth are believed to be derived from simple primordial cells that incorporated nucleic acids as the basis of a system of self-replicating molecules.

2   Variation in nucleic acids provided the variation in organisms upon which natural selection could act.

3   The formation of cells provided stable environments for metabolism.

4   The universal genetic code uses a set of 20 amino acids to form proteins and is found in all life forms.

5   The increase in size of eukaryotic cells was possible because of the development of intracellular compartments and transport systems.

6   A major evolutionary step occurred with the emergence of multicellular organisms, cell differentiation and specialization into organ systems. This evolutionary development necessitated intercellular signalling and transport systems.

Learning outcomes for Chapter 1

When you have studied this chapter, you should be able to:

1.1 Define and use each of the terms printed in **bold** in the text.

1.2 Describe some of the properties of living systems and relate these to the biological molecules, cellular subsystems, and biological processes that underlie them.

Questions for Chapter 1

Question 1.1

What cell processes depend on the cytoskeleton? What evolutionary opportunities did the cytoskeleton confer?

Question 1.2

What properties do the cells in a complex multicellular organism have, that are lacking in single-celled eukaryotic organisms?

Further sources

Maynard Smith, J. and Szathmáry, E. (1995) *The Major Transitions in Evolution*, W. H. Freeman and Company Ltd, Oxford.

Alberts, B., Johnson, A., Lewis, J., Raff, M., Roberts, K. and Walter, P. (2002) *The Molecular Biology of the Cell* (4th edn), Chapter 1, Garland Science, New York.

2 THE FOUNDATIONS OF LIFE

Although living organisms are enormously diverse, because of their shared ancestry many of the basic features of life are common to all cells. Despite their complexity, living processes obey the basic laws of physics and chemistry. Whilst one could not predict completely the complex properties of living systems from a knowledge of chemistry, nevertheless, chemistry is needed to explain how biological systems work.

Biochemistry, the chemistry of living things, is concerned with reactions occurring under relatively restricted chemical and physical conditions. Cells maintain a very close homeostatic control on their intracellular milieu, in terms of, for example, pH, ion concentrations and the levels of different organic molecules. For mammals, the extracellular environment and temperature are also tightly regulated. With the exception of extremophiles (organisms that, through evolution, have adapted to survive in extreme environments), the biochemical reactions taking place in all organisms do so within a narrow range of temperature and pressure. Water (H_2O) is the universal solvent in biological systems and is the most abundant molecule in all organisms, comprising 60–80% of a cell by mass. The biochemist is therefore concerned primarily with the chemistry of biological molecules in an aqueous (watery) environment under what are known as *physiological conditions* of temperature and pressure.

Only ten elements together comprise the major part of living organisms. These are detailed in Table 2.1 which shows a breakdown of the chemical composition of the human body. Notice that only four elements – oxygen, carbon, hydrogen and nitrogen – together make up 96% of the human body by mass, the bulk of the hydrogen and oxygen being combined as water. The solid material in a cell or organism (i.e. all the cell contents apart from water) consists largely of the organic macromolecules – proteins, lipids, polysaccharides and nucleic acids – with a relatively small proportion represented by small organic molecules (amino acids, nucleotides, sugars and other metabolites) and inorganic molecules. Despite their rather limited elemental repertoire, biological molecules are very diverse. Importantly, they are also very stable. These properties derive from the chemistry of carbon – the single most important atom in biological molecules.

In this chapter, we will review some of the principles of chemistry that apply to living systems and look more closely at the properties and functions of some of the major chemical components of the cell. Key chemical concepts such as chemical equilibrium, pH and interactions between molecules will be explored in the context of biological systems. We begin by considering the role of water.

Beyond a basic overview of carbon (Section 2.2), there is not space in this course to cover the chemistry of all the elements that are found in a cell and the rules that govern their covalent bonding patterns. A basic knowledge of atomic structure and covalent bonding and familiarity with the terms **valency** and **electronegativity** (found in S103, Block 8 *Building with Atoms*, Chapter 5) will aid understanding of the material covered here.

Table 2.1 The composition of the human body by mass.

Type	Substance	% body mass
Elements	oxygen	65
	carbon	18
	hydrogen	10
	nitrogen	3
	calcium	2
	phosphorus	1.1
	potassium	0.35
	sulfur	0.25
	sodium	0.15
	chlorine	0.15
	iron, manganese, copper, iodine, cobalt, zinc	traces
As water and solid matter	water	60–80
	total solid material	20–40
As types of molecules in the solid matter	protein	15–20
	lipid	3–20
	polysaccharide	1–15
	small organic molecules	0–1
	inorganic molecules	1

2.1 Water

As has already been noted, water is the major molecular constituent of every cell and every organism. It is not only within the cell but also in the extracellular environment that water is critical. In multicellular organisms, individual cells in tissues are bathed in aqueous solution and transport systems are water-based. Similarly, the survival of most single-celled organisms depends on aqueous surroundings. In fact, life as we know it could not exist without water.

Water has a unique role in biological systems, serving a number of critical functions:

▶ as a ubiquitous solvent;

▶ affecting the structure adopted by macromolecules, the interactions between molecules and the assembly of cellular structures;

▶ temperature stabilization;

▶ as a reactant or product in many different reactions.

To understand how water fulfils these roles, we must consider the chemical properties of this molecule.

2.1.1 Water is a polar molecule

The water molecule is triangular in shape, with an O—H bond length of 0.958 Å and an H—O—H bond angle of 104.5°, as represented in Figure 2.1a. The O atom has two electron pairs in its outer electron shell that do not participate in the covalent bonds. These non-bonding electron pairs (sometimes referred to as *lone-pairs*) together with the bonding electron pairs, have an approximately tetrahedral arrangement around the nucleus (Figure 2.1b).

Though the water molecule is uncharged, the distribution of charge within it is asymmetric and water is therefore described as **polar**. Note that the term 'polar' can be used to describe either bonds, groups of bonded atoms, or molecules that have no net charge but have an asymmetric distribution of charge. The polarity of water is due to the asymmetric distribution of the electrons in its two O—H bonds, which create what is known as a **dipole**, with one atom having a slight positive charge (indicated by $\delta+$) and one having a slight negative charge (indicated by $\delta-$). The dipole generated in the O—H bonds in water is represented in Figure 2.1a.

The two shared electrons that form each O—H bond are distributed asymmetrically due to the difference in the relative tendencies of the bonding atoms to attract them, the O atom attracting the electrons more strongly than the H atom. Electronegativity is the term used to describe the tendency of an atom to attract electrons. Thus, having the greater tendency to attract electrons, O is said to be more **electronegative** than H. The degree of polarity in a bond depends on the difference in the electronegativities of the bonding atoms.

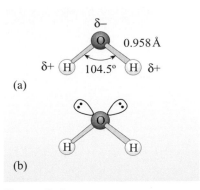

Figure 2.1
(a) Water is a polar molecule.
(b) Representation of a water molecule showing the two pairs of non-bonding electrons on the O atom.

2.1.2 Water molecules associate with each other through hydrogen bonds

The asymmetric distribution of charge in water molecules means that they tend to spontaneously orient themselves such that the strongly electronegative O atom of one molecule is associated with a less electronegative H atom of an adjacent molecule, forming what is known as a **hydrogen bond**. In the hydrogen bond, the O—H group of one water molecule points towards one of the non-bonding electron pairs on another water molecule, as represented in Figure 2.2a.

Hydrogen bonds do not only form between water molecules but can occur when a hydrogen atom that is covalently bonded to a strongly electronegative atom is close to a strongly electronegative atom with an non-bonding electron pair. A generalized hydrogen bond can be represented as D—H---A where D—H is a donor group

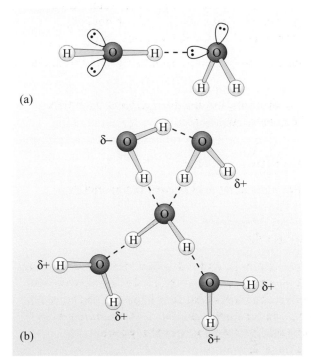

Figure 2.2
(a) A hydrogen bond (red dashed line) between a pair of water molecules. (b) Hydrogen bonds form an extensive network between water molecules.

containing the H atom that participates in the hydrogen bond (such as N—H or O—H) and A is an acceptor atom bearing a pair of non-bonding electrons (such as N or O). All the participating atoms in the hydrogen bond are approximately colinear; thus the interaction is *directional*. Hydrogen is unique in being able to form this type of bond because it is the only atom small enough to allow the strongly electronegative acceptor atom to come close enough to interact with its positive charge.

As you will see throughout this course, the formation of hydrogen bonds between and within molecules is a critically important factor in establishing and stabilizing the structures of many macromolecules as well as the interactions between macromolecules. These interactions will be discussed further in Section 2.7.3.

☐ How many hydrogen bonds can each O atom in a water molecule form?

◼ Since each O atom has two pairs of non-bonding electrons, it can form two hydrogen bonds.

Hydrogen bonds between water molecules can form an extensive three-dimensional network, as shown in Figure 2.2b, with each H atom in a water molecule able to form a hydrogen bond with different adjacent water molecules and each O atom able to form two such interactions.

☐ What is the maximum number of neighbouring water molecules with which a single molecule could associate via hydrogen bonds?

◼ A single water molecule could associate with a maximum of four other molecules in this way.

In fact, in ice, all the water molecules are maximally hydrogen-bonded, forming a regular crystalline array. In the liquid state, the extent of hydrogen bonding between molecules is only slightly less than in ice, each molecule being associated with, on average, 3.5 neighbouring molecules at any one time. Unlike the relatively stable covalent bonds, the hydrogen bonds between water molecules are constantly being broken and reformed, having a half-life of the order of 10^{-6} seconds.

The high level of hydrogen bonding between water molecules in the liquid state gives water a strong internal *cohesiveness*. This property of water is of critical importance in biological systems. For example, the large temperature-stabilizing capacity of water is due to the high level of intermolecular hydrogen bonding. Thus in a cell, in which there are many metabolic processes releasing energy as heat, this energy, instead of elevating the temperature by increasing movement of the water molecules, breaks hydrogen bonds. In this way, the hydrogen bonds in the aqueous environment of the cell help to buffer against large changes in temperature.

2.1.3 The solvent properties of water

For a substance (solute) to be soluble in a particular solvent, the solvent molecules must disrupt the interactions between solute molecules or ions. In other words, the solute molecules or ions must interact more strongly with the solvent molecules than they do with each other. A general rule for solubility is that 'like dissolves like'. Thus polar substances are soluble in polar solvents such as water and non-polar substances are soluble in non-polar solvents such as carbon tetrachloride (CCl_4).

Solutes that readily dissolve in water are described as **hydrophilic** (meaning 'water-loving') and comprise polar and ionically charged substances including salts. Of the many different small organic molecules found in cells, including amino acids, nucleotides, sugars and carboxylic acids, most are hydrophilic. Molecules that are neither charged nor polar do not tend to dissolve well in water and are termed **hydrophobic** (meaning 'water-fearing'). In the cell, hydrophobic molecules include lipids and proteins located in cell membranes.

Why are polar or charged substances soluble in water? If we consider a salt such as sodium chloride (NaCl), in water the attraction between the oppositely charged Na^+ and Cl^- ions can be overcome by the polar water molecules, which interact electrostatically with the ions. The water molecules form what are called **hydration shells** around the ions, orienting themselves so that their appropriate polarized charge faces the ion, i.e. $\delta+$ (on each of the H atoms) towards the anion, and $\delta-$ (on the O atom) towards the cation, as depicted in Figure 2.3. Notice in Figure 2.3 that the outside of the hydration shell has a net charge that has the same sign as that of the ion in the centre. This charge on the outside of the hydration shell in turn tends to orient water molecules in the vicinity, leading to a second concentric hydration shell. The ions are said to be **solvated**, or more specifically in this case, **hydrated**.

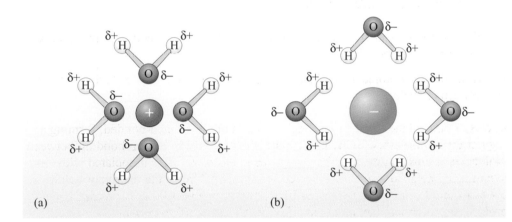

Figure 2.3
Hydration shells. Ions are soluble in water because water molecules form hydration shells around them, thereby neutralizing the attraction of the oppositely charged ions for each other. The polar water molecules orient themselves according to whether the ion is (a) positively charged or (b) negatively charged.

⭕ What effect would dissolving a salt in water have on the hydrogen bond network in the solvent?

⬤ The hydrogen bond network would be disrupted.

⭕ Salt water has a lower freezing temperature than pure water. Why is this so?

⬤ The ions in salt water are hydrated, preventing the water molecules from forming the regular crystalline array of ice.

Some biological compounds, such as those carrying carboxyl (COOH), amino (NH_2) or phosphoryl (PO_3^{2-}) groups, exist as ions under physiological conditions of pH (near-neutral) and such compounds are hydrated in the same way as Na^+ and Cl^- ions. Water molecules also form hydration shells around uncharged polar groups, e.g. hydroxyl (OH), carbonyl (C=O), amino (NH_2) or thiol (SH) groups. The solubility of uncharged polar compounds can be attributed to the bond dipoles in their polar groups. The resulting interactions disrupt the hydrogen bonding between water molecules in the immediate vicinity. Furthermore, if polar and charged solutes carry groups capable of forming hydrogen bonds with water molecules, as depicted in Figure 2.4, then the hydrogen bonding network in water is further disrupted and their solubility is enhanced. Nucleic acids, carbohydrates and many proteins carry many such groups, rendering them soluble in the aqueous environment of the cell.

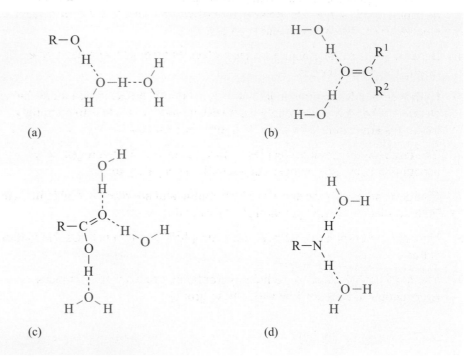

(a)

(b)

(c)

(d)

Figure 2.4   Hydrogen bonding between water molecules and (a) hydroxyl, (b) carbonyl, (c) carboxyl and (d) amino groups.

Hydrophobic molecules, having no polar groups or ionic charge, are unable to interact with water molecules in the way described and cannot disrupt hydrogen bonding between water molecules in an aqueous environment. The tendency of water molecules to associate through a network of hydrogen bonds excludes the hydrophobic molecules (which would otherwise disrupt hydrogen bonding). Thus in an aqueous solvent, hydrophobic molecules tend to coalesce.

Some molecules, such as fatty acids or phospholipids, have both polar (or ionically charged) and non-polar portions and are therefore both hydrophilic and hydrophobic. These molecules are described as **amphipathic** (or alternatively, amphiphilic). In an aqueous environment their hydrophilic portion is hydrated, whilst the hydrophobic portion is excluded. Thus, amphipathic molecules aggregate such that their hydrophilic portions point out into the aqueous environment and their hydrophobic portions, excluded from water, coalesce on the inside of the aggregate. The tendency of water to exclude hydrophobic groups results in weak interactions between these groups, known as **hydrophobic interactions**, which stabilize the aggregates. Hydrophobic interactions are discussed further in Section 2.7.4. The association of amphipathic lipids to form biological membranes is discussed in detail in Chapter 6.

Summary of Section 2.1

1   Water (H_2O) is the major molecular constituent of every cell and every organism.

2   The water molecule is triangular in shape but the electron pairs in the outer electron shell of the O atom have a tetrahedral arrangement.

3   The water molecule is polar, being uncharged but having an asymmetric distribution of charge. The polar nature of water is due to the difference in the electronegativities of the O and H atoms.

4   Because of their polar nature, water molecules associate with each other through hydrogen bonds.

5   Hydrogen bonds are directional and can occur when a hydrogen atom that is covalently bonded to a strongly electronegative atom is close to a strongly electronegative atom with a non-bonding electron pair.

6   The tendency of water molecules to form a network of hydrogen bonds accounts for the large temperature-stabilizing capacity of water.

7   Charged and polar substances are hydrophilic and are readily soluble in water. Water molecules form hydration shells around these solutes.

8   Uncharged non-polar substances are hydrophobic and do not dissolve well in water.

9   The tendency of water to exclude hydrophobic groups results in weak hydrophobic interactions between these groups.

2.2 The chemistry of carbon-containing biological molecules

An appreciation of the chemistry of carbon is crucial to understanding the structure and chemistry of biological molecules. The macromolecules (proteins, nucleic acids, lipids and polysaccharides) and many of the small metabolites that together comprise the major part of the cell after water, all contain carbon. The single most important point to make about carbon is that it has a *valency of four*; that is to say, it lacks four of the eight electrons necessary to fill its outermost electron shell. To fill this shell, and thereby achieve a stable chemical state, carbon atoms form four covalent bonds with other electron-deficient atoms, each atom contributing one electron to the bond. Carbon atoms form covalent bonds most commonly with other C atoms and with H, O, N and S atoms. The four covalent bonds required by carbon atoms to achieve a stable chemical state are not necessarily formed with four different atoms. Thus sometimes two or even three electron pairs are shared by two atoms in, respectively, double or triple bonds.

In this section, we will review some of the general properties of carbon-containing molecules. We begin by examining how the chemistry of carbon determines the shape of the molecules in which it is found. It is important to appreciate that molecules are three-dimensional entities. The term **stereochemistry** is used to describe the three-dimensional shape or conformation of a molecule. The conformation of biological molecules and the relationship between molecular structure and function are central themes running through this course. The representation and interpretation of molecular structures are therefore introduced here.

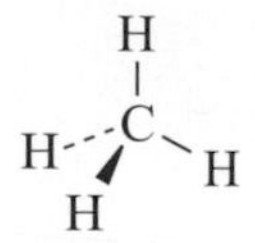

Figure 2.5
Tetrahedral arrangement of hydrogen atoms around the single carbon atom in methane (flying-wedge notation).

2.2.1 The tetrahedral carbon atom

Covalent bonds arise from the sharing of two electrons between two atoms. In a molecule with more than one such bond, the pairs of electrons repel one another if they come too close together, and this repulsion increases dramatically as the electrons get closer and closer. For this reason, the four bonds around a central carbon atom tend to be arranged so that they are as far away from each other as possible, within the limits of a fixed bond length. This is achieved by having the four bonds directed to the four corners of a tetrahedron. The tetrahedral arrangement of H atoms around a central C atom in a methane (CH_4) molecule is shown in Figure 2.5 in what is known as the 'flying-wedge' notation (see Box 2.1). It has been shown experimentally that the angle between any two of the four bonds to the central atom of this molecule is 109° 28′, consistent with a regular tetrahedral arrangement.

In a molecule such as methane, where the C atom is bonded to four identical groups (i.e. four H atoms), the regular tetrahedral geometry, with a bond angle of 109° 28′, is indeed observed. However, if one of the attached atoms or functional groups is larger than the others, this geometry, though still based on a tetrahedron, is distorted. The large atom or group has the effect of 'pushing' the others closer together and reducing the tetrahedral angle. The size of an atom or group is determined by its surrounding electron cloud, described by what is termed its **van der Waals radius** and it is these measurements that provide the basis for 'space-filling' models of biological molecules, of which you will encounter many in this course. Table 2.2 gives values for the van der Waals radii of some atoms and groups of atoms. For comparison, the covalent radii of the atoms are included in this table. The covalent radius of an atom is half the length of a single bond between it and an identical atom (e.g. C—C). Notice that the van der Waals radius of an atom is larger than its covalent radius.

Table 2.2   Van der Waals and covalent radii of common atoms or groups.

Atom or group	Van der Waals radius / pm*	Covalent radius / pm*
C	170	77
H	120	37
N	155	75
O	152	73
P	180	106
S	180	102
methyl ($-CH_3$)	200	
hydroxyl ($-OH$)	140	
amino ($-NH_2$)	150	

* 1 pm = 10^{-12} m = 0.01 Å.

The concept of the tetrahedral carbon atom is so fundamental to our present understanding of structural organic chemistry that it is difficult to believe that until the late 1800s chemists considered molecular shape to be of little importance. In order to have some way of representing three-dimensional structures on a two-dimensional page, and to simplify the representations of molecules, organic chemists use various ways of representing structures (Box 2.1).

Box 2.1 Representations of organic molecules

The simplest way of representing an organic molecule is by its chemical formula. For example, the chemical formula of butane is C_4H_{10}. Whilst its chemical formula tells us that butane has four C atoms and ten H atoms, it does not give us any indication of how these atoms are arranged. In fact, there are two different molecules having the chemical formula C_4H_{10}. The structural formulae of these molecules, known as straight-chain butane and isobutane, are represented below. Having the same molecular formula but different structural formulae, these two molecules are said to be **isomers**. (See also Section 2.2.3 and 2.2.4 for descriptions of other types of isomerism.)

$$CH_3-CH_2-CH_2-CH_3$$

straight-chain butane

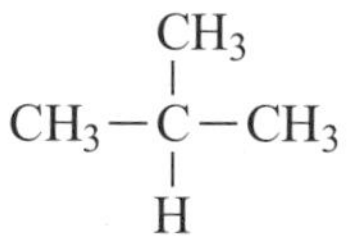

$$CH_3-\overset{\overset{\displaystyle CH_3}{|}}{\underset{\underset{\displaystyle H}{|}}{C}}-CH_3$$

isobutane

Note that the structural formulae of straight-chain butane and isobutane can also be represented in text as, respectively, $CH_3(CH_2)_2CH_3$ and $(CH_3)_3CH$. A shorthand way of representing the same molecules as a carbon skeleton is also shown below. Here the C—C bonds have been represented by straight lines. Unless otherwise indicated, the end of each line or the junction between two lines signifies a C atom. The H atoms are also omitted. In interpreting these simplified representations of organic molecules, it is important to bear in mind the valency of carbon.

straight-chain butane

isobutane

☐ Draw the full structural formulae of the organic molecules (a) and (b) below.

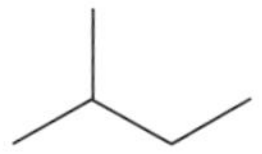

(a)

(b)

● The corresponding formulae showing all the C and H atoms present are as follows:

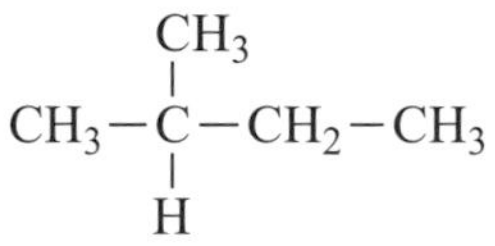

$$CH_3-\overset{\overset{\displaystyle CH_3}{|}}{\underset{\underset{\displaystyle H}{|}}{C}}-CH_2-CH_3$$

(a)

$$\underset{H}{\overset{CH_3}{\diagdown}}C=C\underset{CH_3}{\overset{H}{\diagup}}$$

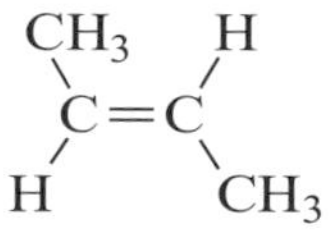

(b)

It is less easy to abbreviate formulae of cyclic compounds in this way. Consider the full structural formula of the cyclic compound α-D-glucopyranose, a monosaccharide (see overleaf, left). Again this structure can be represented by omitting the C atoms and any C—H bonds (overleaf, right).

As in the butane example, in this representation each line represents a C—C bond, unless another atom is inserted. The six-membered ring is therefore shown as a hexagon with one of the members of the ring being an O atom. In interpreting these representations you have to remember that two hydrogens will be attached at every angle in the drawing; where three lines meet at a point, a single hydrogen atom must be added.

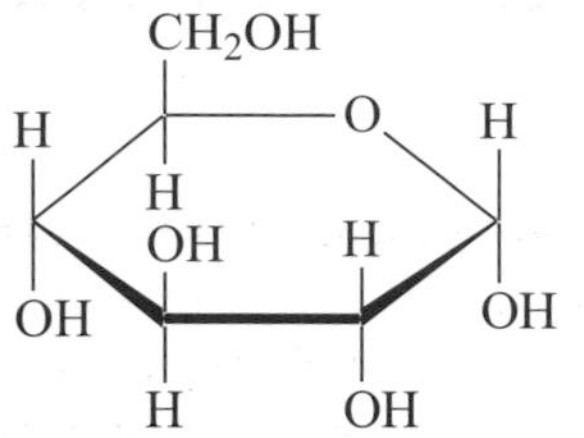

structural formula of α-D-glucopyranose 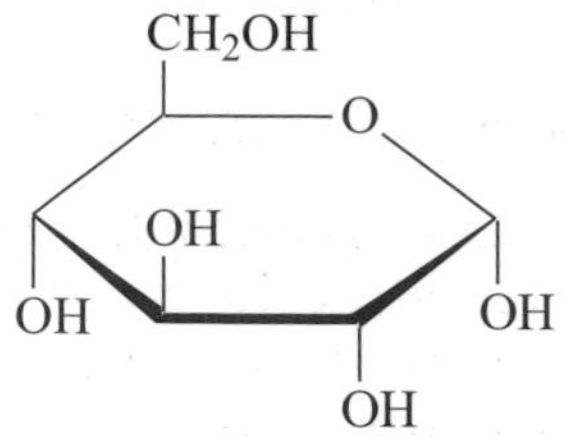   skeleton structure of α-D-glucopyranose

Of course a molecule is not 'flat' and these representations in two dimensions – in the plane of the paper – are not always entirely satisfactory. Frequently, we need more than this, and specifically we need a representation that conveys shape and perspective more accurately. In general, the most useful of the methods available is the picturesquely named **'flying-wedge' notation**. This notation uses three different types of line to represent bond direction: the wedge, the continuous line, and the broken line. A flying-wedge representation of the amino acid alanine is shown below. Note that the central tetrahedral C atom is commonly omitted from such representations.

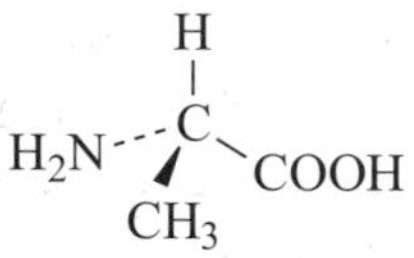

flying-wedge diagram of alanine

The carbon atom at the pointed or thin end of the wedge is assumed to be in the plane of the paper and the atom at the thick end is *above the plane*. The connection between the shape of this wedge and the observed perspective is obvious. A continuous line (—) joins two atoms that both lie in the plane of the paper. A broken line (---) joins two atoms, one of which is in the plane of the paper and the other below it. Any atom at the junction of a broken line with a wedge, or at the junction of two continuous lines, will therefore lie in the plane of the paper.

In the rest of this section, we shall be concentrating on carbon-based compounds, but a slight digression, on compounds containing nitrogen or oxygen, is appropriate at this point. In Section 2.1.1, where we considered the shape of the water molecule, we noted that, though the two single bonds formed by the oxygen atom form a 'V-shape', the electron pairs in the outer shell of the O atom actually are approximately tetrahedral in their arrangement. This is because, in its chemically stable form (in, for example, water, ethers or alcohols), an oxygen atom has a full complement of four pairs of electrons in its outer electron shell, two of which are non-bonding pairs. All four pairs of electrons, bonding and non-bonding, repel each other in the same way that the four pairs of bonding electrons do in the carbon atom. In the case of nitrogen, which forms three single bonds as in the amines ($-NH_2$), the bonds give this atom an apparent pyramidal geometry. However, like oxygen, the N atom has four pairs of electrons, three bonding pairs and one non-bonding pair, and each pair takes up one position in a tetrahedral array. The tetrahedral geometries of the O and N atoms in, respectively, a water molecule and an ammonia molecule are represented in the margin. Note that the non-bonding electron pairs are shown in both cases, completing the tetrahedral structure.

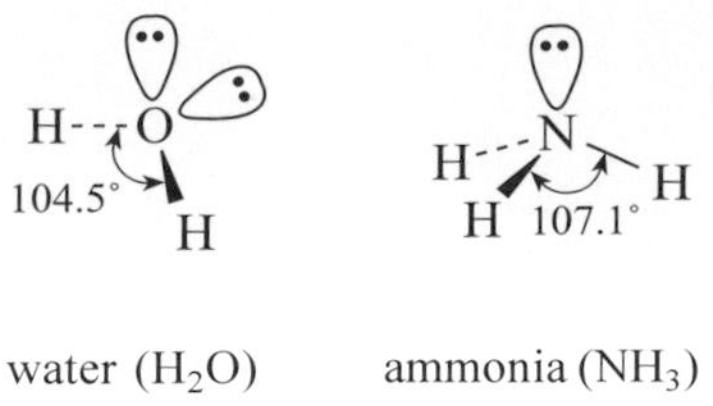

water (H_2O)   ammonia (NH_3)

2.2.2 Molecular conformation

One of the most significant features of the chemistry of carbon is that carbon atoms can be joined together to form long chains and rings of various sizes, without the chemical compounds that are generated becoming unstable. Straight-chain aliphatic hydrocarbons up to $C_{78}H_{158}$ are found in crude petroleum and carbon rings of up to 30 atoms or more can be synthesized. In terms of biological systems, there are carbon-containing compounds containing cyclic structures, as in the amino acid tyrosine, or long carbon–carbon chains, as in the fatty acids. How does the concept of the tetrahedral carbon atom apply when a chain of carbon atoms is involved?

If you consider the molecule ethane (C_2H_6), it is possible to change its overall appearance by rotating one of the CH_3 groups about the carbon–carbon single bond (Figure 2.6). However, there is only one compound 'ethane', a sample of which always behaves in the same way as any other under the same conditions. In open-chain molecules, of which ethane is a simple example, there is practically free, unhindered, **internal rotation** about C—C bonds (and most other single bonds). Thus at room temperature, the two methyl groups in ethane are spinning rapidly relative to each other. The energy for this motion is gained from molecular collision with other molecules and with the walls of the container. Collisions in liquid and gaseous systems are very frequent, and all molecules show rapid internal rotation as they travel and tumble. At room temperature, in a sample of ethane, there are literally hundreds of millions of slightly different arrangements at any given instant.

Arrangements of atoms within a molecule that can be interchanged solely by internal rotation about a single bond are called **conformations**. No covalent bonds are broken or made during a change in conformation. An individual molecule of ethane can change its conformation rapidly. In this sense, there are many different ethanes; but there is only one compound 'ethane', with each molecule behaving in the same way as any other. Note that two, or more, molecules can be assumed to be identical if they can be superimposed; if necessary, *rotations about single bonds may be carried out to achieve this aim.*

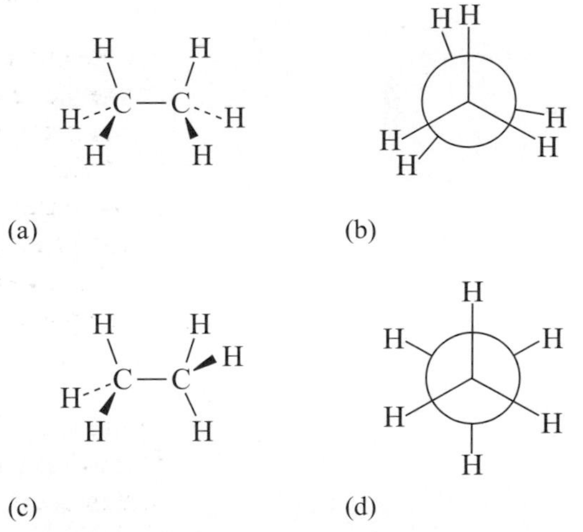

To show differences in the conformation caused by rotation about the C—C bond, we can represent the molecule as it would seem if it is viewed looking down the C—C bond. This is called a Newman projection (Figure 2.6). If one looks at the Newman projection in Figure 2.6b, the hydrogen atoms from the two carbons are superimposed. This is known as an eclipsed conformation (shown as side-on view in Figure 2.6a). If one of the carbons is rotated 60° about the C—C bond, a staggered

Note: You should be familiar with the following terms used to describe organic molecules. Organic compounds that have an open-chain structure are often described as **aliphatic**, e.g. fatty acids. **Aromatic** compounds (e.g. the amino acid tyrosine) are those that contain hydrocarbon rings (typically 6C) that have properties similar to benzene (C_6H_6).

(a)

(b)

(c)

(d)

Figure 2.6
Rotation of the internal C—C bond of ethane.
(a) Side-on view of the eclipsed conformation.
(b) Newman projection of the eclipsed conformation.
(c) Side-on view of the staggered conformation.
(d) Newman projection of the staggered conformation.

conformation is obtained (Figure 2.6c and d). Notice that in the eclipsed conformation, the hydrogen atoms bonded to one C atom are slightly closer to those on the other C atom than when they are in the staggered conformation. This means that there is slightly more repulsion between the hydrogens of the two carbon atoms in the eclipsed form and the staggered form is therefore energetically favoured.

For more complex molecules in which the groups or substituents bonded either side of the single bond are bulky, rotation about the single bond may be limited, i.e. the number of possible conformations would be reduced. Conformations that would require large groups to come close together or to clash would be 'forbidden'. This effect is an example of **steric hindrance** or **steric interference,** where crowding of molecules (or substituents) causes repulsion between electrons in neighbouring bonds and the electron clouds of constituent atoms (defined by their van der Waals radii). As a result of these repulsive forces, certain conformations are energetically unfavourable. You will encounter an example of this effect in Chapter 3, where we discuss protein structure.

2.2.3 Stereoisomers of molecules containing carbon–carbon double bonds

As described above, provided that there are no steric limitations, rotation about a single bond can occur freely. In contrast, rotation about double bonds is restricted under normal conditions. As a result, any molecule or part of a molecule consisting of a carbon–carbon double bond (known as an **alkene** group) with two groups on each C atom is rigid and planar with bond angles of approximately 120° (see margin). The precise geometry varies depending on the nature of the groups involved. Some such compounds can exist as one or more **stereoisomers**, molecular entities that have the same molecular formula but different stereochemical formulae; that is, they differ in the arrangement of their atoms in space. Unlike the isomerism demonstrated by the linear and branched forms of butane (Box 2.1), stereoisomers have identical atom–atom connections.

The principle of stereoisomerism resulting from a double bond in a molecule can be illustrated by considering the generalized molecular formula $R^1CH=CHR^1$, in which R^1 represents a group other than H. Due to the rigid nature of the carbon–carbon double bond, there are *two* quite distinct compounds to which this general formula is applicable, as depicted below.

$$
\begin{array}{ccc}
R^1 \quad\quad R^1 & & R^1 \quad\quad H \\
\diagdown \quad\quad \diagup & & \diagdown \quad\quad \diagup \\
C=C & & C=C \\
\diagup \quad\quad \diagdown & & \diagup \quad\quad \diagdown \\
H \quad\quad\; H & & H \quad\quad R^1
\end{array}
$$

cis $R^1CH=CHR^1$ *trans* $R^1CH=CHR^1$

☐ Draw a structural formula for the molecule $R^1CH=C(R^1)_2$. Does this molecule exist as stereoisomers?

⬤ The structural formula of $R^1CH=C(R^1)_2$ is:

$$
\begin{array}{c}
R^1 \quad\quad R^1 \\
\diagdown \quad\quad \diagup \\
C=C \\
\diagup \quad\quad \diagdown \\
H \quad\quad R^1
\end{array}
$$

No, this molecule does not demonstrate stereoisomerism. There is only one structural formula that corresponds to this molecular formula.

Notice that the stereoisomers arise because the two groups attached to each C atom differ. It is not necessary however for the two C atoms to have the same groups. You can confirm that this is so by trying different substituents in the generalized molecular formula shown on the previous page. To distinguish between the stereoisomers and to specify their configuration, the following system is used. If the same atoms or groups are on the *same side* of the C=C bond, the label *cis* is applied; when the same atoms or groups are on *opposite sides* of the double bond, the designation of the isomer is *trans* (see depiction of stereoisomers).

Stereoisomers are not able to interconvert rapidly, even at temperatures greater than 200 °C; so they are not different 'conformations' of the same molecule. Instead, they are described as two distinct **configurations**. Importantly, one configuration can only be converted into the other by the breaking and remaking of chemical bonds. The type of stereoisomers described here are sometimes referred to as **diastereomers** and are distinct from a very different kind of stereoisomer, **enantiomers**, described in the next section. Unlike enantiomers, diastereomers have distinct physical and chemical properties.

Molecules containing carbon–carbon double bonds are described as **unsaturated**. Many fatty acids that are used to make the lipid components of biological membranes are unsaturated. As you will see in Chapter 6 when we look at biological membranes, unsaturated fatty acids have very different physical properties from saturated fatty acids (which contain no C=C bonds), and crucially affect the properties of the membranes in which they are found. Naturally occurring unsaturated fatty acids are generally of the *cis* configuration (Figure 2.7).

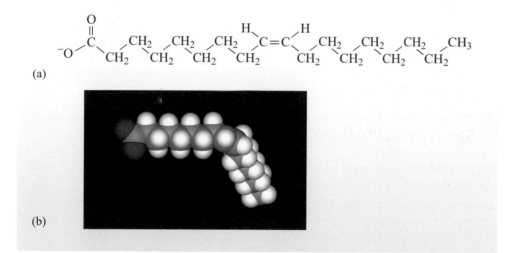

(a)

(b)

Figure 2.7
Oleate, the ionized form of oleic acid, a monounsaturated fatty acid (i.e. containing just one carbon–carbon double bond). (a) Structural formula. (b) Space-filling structure. Note that the double bond is in the *cis* configuration.

2.2.4 Chirality in carbon-containing molecules

A fundamental property of the tetrahedral carbon atom is its potential for chirality. If a carbon centre is asymmetric, i.e. it has four *different* atoms or groups attached, it can exist in two different configurations, which cannot be interchanged without breaking and then remaking bonds in different positions (Figure 2.8). Once again we have a pair of stereoisomers – distinct, separable compounds that have the same molecular formula and have the atoms joined together in the *same sequence*.

Figure 2.8
When four different groups are attached to a tetrahedral C atom, two different spatial configurations are possible. The two configurations, called enantiomers, are mirror images of each other and cannot be superimposed on one another, just as your left and right hand cannot be superimposed.

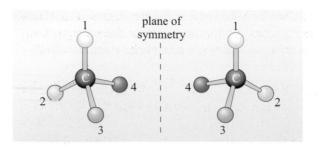

The bonds to the central carbon atom again have different spatial orientation, but unlike the stereoisomers that arise as a result of C=C bonds, these molecules do not differ in 'shape'; they differ only in their 'handedness'. The name given to this handedness is **chirality** and molecules possessing handedness are described as chiral molecules. A carbon atom with four different groups attached, wherever it occurs in a molecular structure, is called a **chiral centre**. A mirror image pair is called an **enantiomeric pair**. Enantiomers can therefore be defined as chiral molecules that exist as *non-superimposable mirror images*.

Unlike diastereomers, enantiomeric compounds cannot easily be distinguished by their physical properties, having exactly the same melting temperature, boiling temperature, solubility and infrared spectrum. There is, however, one special physical property that allows *all* enantiomers to be distinguished: solutions of individual enantiomers rotate plane-polarized light in opposite directions. Molecules that rotate the plane of plane-polarized light are said to be optically active, and so enantiomers are sometimes referred to as **optical isomers**. A pure, optically active substance (that is, a sample containing molecules of only one handedness) rotates plane-polarized light by a characteristic amount. If a quantity of one enantiomer rotates the plane of this light by x degrees, then the same quantity of the other enantiomer under the same conditions will rotate the plane by exactly $-x$ degrees.

Normal light consists of electromagnetic vibrations that occur in all directions at the same time. In plane-polarized light, the electromagnetic vibrations are in a single plane. Plane polarization is achieved by passing monochromatic (single frequency) light through a very thin slit.

○ What does this observation imply about the rotation caused by a mixture containing equal amounts of two enantiomers?

● There will be *no observed rotation*. The effect of one enantiomer is exactly cancelled by that of the other.

A mixture containing equal amounts of two enantiomers is called a **racemic mixture**. Enantiomers are distinguished with a plus (+) or minus (−) sign, according to the direction of rotation of plane polarized light. However, this designation does not tell us anything about the configuration of the enantiomer. There are two systems for naming enantiomers, the Fischer convention and the Cahn–Ingold–Prelog system. The Fischer convention, introduced in 1891 by Emil Fischer, designates stereoisomers a D or an L (both small capitals) prefix according to whether their configuration is consistent with, respectively, the (+) and (−) stereoisomers of glyceraldehyde. The Cahn–Ingold–Prelog system, devised in 1956 by Robert Cahn, Christopher Ingold and Vladimir Prelog, relies upon ranking of the four groups around the chiral centre according to the atomic number of the atom nearest to the centre and designates stereoisomers an **R** or an **S** prefix according to the arrangement of the groups.

The designation of optical isomers can be very confusing, particularly since, for historical reasons, both conventions are used and there is no simple way of relating the two. Chemists most commonly use the Cahn-Ingold-Prelog system, whereas biologists traditionally use the Fischer convention. For the purposes of this course, it is not necessary that you concern yourself with the details of these conventions. But you should appreciate that most biological molecules, such as amino acids, contain chiral centres.

As yet, the D configuration has not been found in any naturally occurring proteins and all amino acids derived from proteins have the L stereochemical configuration. A generalized amino acid structure is represented in the L form in Figure 2.9. If you imagine looking at the central asymmetric carbon atom from the viewpoint of the attached H atom, reading in the clockwise direction, the remaining groups are COOH, R (side-chain) and NH$_2$. (The mnemonic CORN is helpful in remembering this convention.)

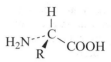

Figure 2.9
Flying-wedge representation of the generalized amino acid structure in the naturally occurring L configuration.

◯ What would be the consequences if both D and L amino acids occurred naturally?

⬤ Protein molecules with the same amino acid sequence would have different shapes/configurations, depending on which amino acid configuration was used at each position.

Because proteins are chiral molecules, it is possible to obtain information about their structure from their ability to polarize light, a property referred to as **circular dichroism** (**CD**; described in Box 2.2 overleaf). In the next chapter, we discuss the structure of proteins in some detail. The standard techniques for analysing protein structure are X-ray diffraction and nuclear magnetic resonance (NMR) imaging, which are mentioned again at the end of this chapter, but CD analysis is particularly useful where these techniques do not yield results.

Though the chemist might struggle to differentiate between enantiomers in the laboratory, the distinction may be made more readily in a biological system. The reason is that most biological molecules themselves demonstrate chirality and therefore discriminate between configurations. For example, the two enantiomers of carvone (Figure 2.10) both occur naturally. The *R* isomer is the principal odour component of spearmint oil, but the *S* isomer has the odour and flavour of caraway seeds.

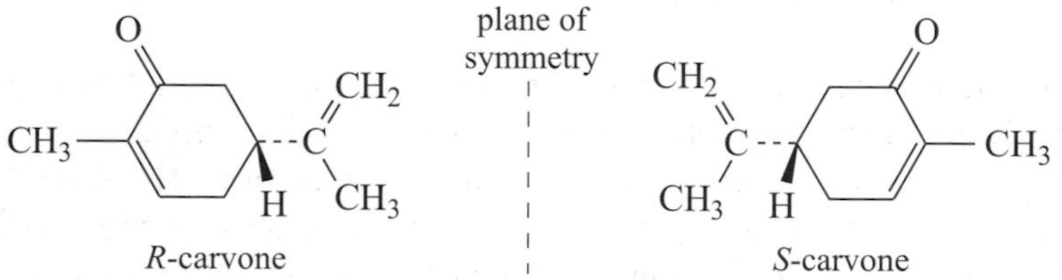

Figure 2.10 Structures of the two enantiomers of carvone.

◯ What does this observation tell us about the olfactory receptors in the nose?

⬤ Receptors respond to only one of a pair of enantiomers. In other words, they involve chiral molecules.

The ability of biological systems to discriminate between enantiomers is an important consideration in the pharmaceutical industry, where some enantiomers show higher toxicity than their optical counterpart (Box 2.3 overleaf).

Box 2.2   Circular dichroism

The phenomenon of chirality has been exploited in the analysis of biological macromolecules. Circular dichroism (CD) is a technique that exploits the chiral nature of peptides, proteins and nucleic acids to determine their secondary and tertiary structure and their interactions. CD is defined as the differential absorption of right from left circularly polarized light. In circularly polarized light, the electromagnetic wave or vibration spirals around its axis rather than remaining in one plane (as plane-polarized light). Circularly polarized light can be either a right-handed or a left-handed spiral.

There are several mathematical methods to correlate the secondary structure of a protein with its CD spectrum in the far-UV region (165–240 nm) and to provide estimates of the fraction of residues in α-helical, β sheet, β turn and unordered conformations (Figure 2.11a). (See Chapter 3 for details of protein structure.) This type of information is useful in the absence of high-resolution data, such as in cases where the protein cannot be crystallized or is too large for NMR. CD can also indirectly provide information about the tertiary structure of proteins from measurements in the near-UV region (320–240 nm), which are related to absorbances of aromatic residues. Furthermore, CD has many applications in the study of nucleic acids. The different conformations of DNA (Figure 2.11b) and RNA (discussed in Chapter 5) have been well characterized by CD, and the various modes of drug binding to DNA have been identified using this technique.

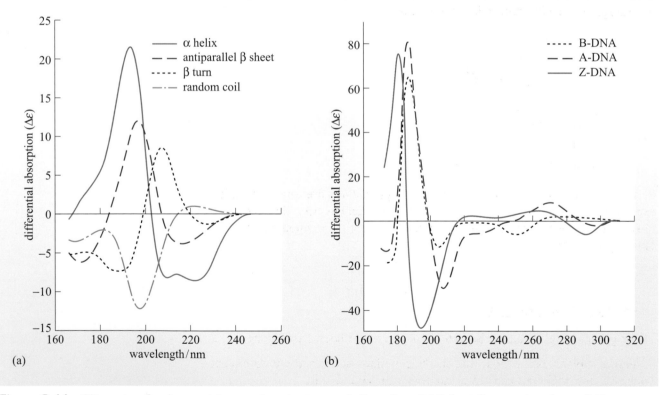

Figure 2.11   CD spectra of various protein secondary structures: α helix, antiparallel β sheet, β turn and random coil (from Johnson, 1990). (b) CD spectra of poly[d(GC)], a synthetic polydeoxyribonucleotide, in three different forms: B-DNA, A-DNA and Z-DNA (from Woody, 1995).

Box 2.3   Enantiomers in pharmaceutical research

Until quite recently, the majority of pharmaceutical products that contain chiral centres were synthesized by processes that generated equal amounts of each configuration (i.e. a racemic mixture). However, there are clear disadvantages in doing this. Most of the substances that participate in biological processes are chiral and are able to distinguish between optical isomers. As a consequence, only one isomer is likely to be bioactive. In the case of pharmaceuticals, the production of a racemic mixture is potentially problematic; whilst one isomer might have the desired biological effect, the other may be excreted unchanged, or potentially have adverse side-effects. That half of a preparation is inactive and excreted may represent a considerable cost in terms of production of the drug. Far more serious, though, is the danger of adverse effects.

The use of thalidomide first drew attention to this problem on an international scale. This versatile drug is almost non-toxic, even to children; provided it is not taken by pregnant women, there is virtually no risk. Indeed, thalidomide is still being manufactured to treat leprosy, and may have potential for AIDS, arthritis and transplant therapy. We now know, however, that whilst the *R* form of the molecule (see below) is effective and safe to use, the *S* form is teratogenic, causing deformity in the fetus.

R-thalidomide, the 'safe' enantiomer

It is possible to separate enantiomers, but the procedures are time-consuming, expensive and wasteful. Consequently much research has been directed towards the development of procedures for synthesizing compounds in an optically pure form.

Summary of Section 2.2

1   Four groups bonded to a carbon atom take up a tetrahedral arrangement.

2   Identical molecules are those that can be superimposed exactly. Rotation about one or more single bonds may be necessary to achieve this.

3   Two or more arrangements that can be made identical by rotation about single bonds are called conformations of the same molecule.

4   At room temperature there is effectively free rotation about a C—C (single) bond.

5   The alkene group, >=<, is planar and rigid and rotation about the C=C (double) bond can not occur.

6   The necessary condition for alkenes to show stereoisomerism is that neither of the two alkene carbon atoms should bear two identical groups. If both carbon atoms bear a single identical group, then stereoisomerism is still possible.

7   A carbon atom that has four different groups surrounding it is called a chiral carbon atom (or centre).

8   Molecules containing chiral centres have two configurations of opposite handedness. The two non-superimposable mirror images are called enantiomers.

9   Equal quantities of each of a pair of enantiomers rotate the plane of polarized light equally, but in opposite directions. There is no correlation between the configuration of the groups about a chiral centre and the way in which that centre will rotate plane-polarized light.

It can be difficult to visualize three-dimensional molecules that are represented as two-dimensional drawings. A major objective of this course is to help you to understand how the structures of biological molecules relate to their functions. To do this, you will be using a sophisticated program called ViewerLite™, which allows you to view, rotate, analyse and model complex biological molecules. This program takes as its data the molecular coordinates and bonding patterns of the atoms in a molecule (expressed as x, y and z coordinates) and can then project them so that you can view the molecules from different angles and at different magnifications. It also allows you to analyse their molecular structures. The data of the molecular coordinates of each molecule are given in files called 'pdb' files. The abbreviation 'pdb' stands for 'protein database', and files of this type have the suffix .pdb, which is recognized by molecular modelling programs. The files may contain just the data for a few atoms in a simple molecule (e.g. ATP) or the data set for a large protein or multimolecular complex. For example, the pictures of glyceraldehyde 3-phosphate dehydrogenase shown in Figure 1.1 in Chapter 1 were produced by taking the molecular coordinates of the proteins which had been isolated from *Homo sapiens* and *Palinurus versicolor* (spiny lobster) and projecting them with ViewerLite™. The data for the molecular coordinates of proteins and nucleic acids are determined by X-ray diffraction, NMR or theoretical modelling. You will find out more about X-ray diffraction and NMR in a video to which you will be directed at the end of this chapter. To teach you how to use ViewerLite™, we have produced a series of molecular modelling activities. The first comes at the end of the next section (Section 2.3). In addition to the specific activities using ViewerLite™, we have provided (on CD-ROM) the pdb files for many of the molecules that we discuss in the course text. When a pdb file is available, its number will be given at the appropriate point in the text. It is not usually necessary to view a structure in order to understand the associated text, but you will find it easier to visualize a molecule's three-dimensional shape if you do so.

2.3 Small organic molecules

The study of carbon-containing compounds is known as organic chemistry. As biologists, we are interested in the chemistry of those organic molecules that occur in biological systems. Having explored, in the previous section, some of the general principles of the chemistry of carbon-containing compounds, we now consider the simple biological molecules that serve as the building blocks of life.

The many different structures in a cell, for example the chromosomes, membranes and ribosomes, are highly ordered assemblies of macromolecules – proteins, nucleic acids, polysaccharides or lipids. These macromolecules are, in turn, manufactured by the cell from a range of small precursors or building blocks (Figure 2.12). More complex macromolecules are formed from units belonging to different classes. For example, most of the proteins that are present on the surface of a mammalian cell have covalently bound sugar chains, making them into glycoproteins. Other examples are the intracellular proteins that are modified by the addition of lipid units. These modifications of proteins will be explained more fully in Section 3.3.3. In addition to their role in forming macromolecules, many of the small organic molecules have important functions in their own right. For example, the monosaccharide glucose is metabolized in the cytosol by glycolysis to provide energy, and adenosine triphosphate (ATP), one of the nucleoside triphosphate precursors of DNA and RNA, also functions as a readily available source of energy.

The structure, variety, synthesis and function of the various macromolecules are discussed in appropriate chapters later in the course. For now we will consider only the building blocks. To better understand the chemistry of these molecules we will begin with a brief review of functional groups.

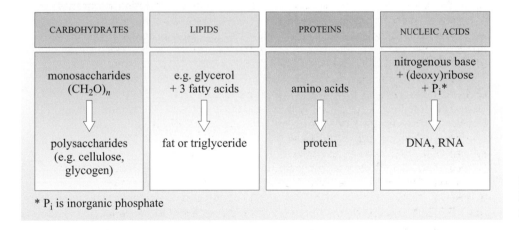

CARBOHYDRATES	LIPIDS	PROTEINS	NUCLEIC ACIDS
monosaccharides $(CH_2O)_n$	e.g. glycerol + 3 fatty acids	amino acids	nitrogenous base + (deoxy)ribose + P_i*
⬇	⬇	⬇	⬇
polysaccharides (e.g. cellulose, glycogen)	fat or triglyceride	protein	DNA, RNA

* P_i is inorganic phosphate

Figure 2.12
Macromolecules are synthesized from simple building blocks.

2.3.1 Functional groups

Organic molecules are often classified according to their specific **functional groups**. This approach is based on the understanding that the chemistry of organic molecules is determined by their reactive groups, such as the hydroxyl group, −OH, found in alcohols. As well as explaining the reactivity of biological molecules, functional groups are also critically important in intermolecular interactions. Table 2.3 lists the most common functional groups.

Table 2.3 Some common functional groups.

Name	Functional group	Example
alkene	$\diagdown C = C \diagup$	isoprene (building block for steroids)
alcohol (hydroxyl)	$-OH$	glycerol
ether	$-O-$	$CH_3-CH_2-O-CH_2-CH_3$ diethylether (an anaesthetic)
aldehyde	$-C\diagup^{O}_{H}$	D-glucose (linear form)
ketone	$\diagdown C = O$	D-fructose (linear form)
carboxyl	$-C\diagup^{O}_{O-H}$	$CH_3-(CH_2)_{14}-C\diagup^{O}_{O-H}$ palmitic acid (a fatty acid)
ester	$-C\diagup^{O}_{O-R}$	triacylglycerol*
amino	$\diagdown N-$	amino acid

* Formed as a result of an esterification reaction between the carboxyl group of each of three fatty acid molecules and the hydroxyl groups of glycerol.

Table 2.3   (continued)

Name	Functional group	Example
amide		peptide bond
thiol	—SH	cysteine
phosphate		ATP

Looking at Table 2.3, you should notice that most of the functional groups contain oxygen or nitrogen atoms, or both.

We can now gather together functional groups with common features and show how these features are important, starting with **carbonyl compounds** (those containing C=O). These compounds include aldehydes, ketones, carboxylic acids and esters.

☐   Which other carbonyl compound can you find in Table 2.3?

⬤   Amides.

As the carbonyl compounds all have the C=O group in common, we may speculate that the presence of such a functional unit would confer a similar reactivity on all members of the series. This sort of generalization is valid up to a point, and helps understanding, but we must bear in mind that some of the carbonyl functions are affected by other nearby functional groups. Note that the ester functional group, —COOR, contains both C=O and —OR groups, but has quite different chemical properties from ethers (R^1OR^2) and ketones (R^1R^2CO). (Make sure you do not confuse esters and ethers; they are completely separate classes of compounds.)

Also, the carboxyl function, —COOH, contains both >C=O and —OH groups, but it *cannot* be thought of as being a ketone or an alcohol separately. The carboxyl group reactions can be understood only by the —COOH group as a whole.

▢ What other way can you suggest for classifying functional groups such as —COOH?

◼ It would also be possible to classify functional groups according to whether they were acidic (as in the case of —COOH) or basic.

The acidity or basicity of a functional group depends very much on its structure, and is expressed as its pK (see Box 2.4). Amines (R$_3$N) are quite strongly basic (pK around 10–11) and react readily with protons to form amine salts (R$_3$NH$^+$). On the other hand, amides (RCONR$_2$) are only very weakly basic (pK about 7.5). This observation illustrates that the whole of the functional group needs to be examined (for example, CH$_3$CONH$_2$ has –CONH$_2$ as the functional group). It is the functional groups rather than the hydrocarbon backbone, or R group, that determines the acidity or basicity of organic acids or bases. Note, however, that the R group can affect the extent of the property.

Box 2.4   Acidic and basic groups and pK

In neutral solutions, acidic groups such as —COOH tend to dissociate, releasing protons into solution:

$$\text{—COOH} \longrightarrow \text{—COO}^- + \text{H}^+$$

In reality this is an equilibrium reaction; if the pH of the solution is reduced, i.e. the concentration of H$^+$ ions is increased, the reaction will reverse. (Note that this effect is a demonstration of the Le Chatelier principle, described in Section 2.5.4.) At some particular acidic pH, half of the carboxyl groups will be ionized and half will not. This pH value is the pK for this functional group.

A similar argument applies to basic groups such as —NH$_2$, which tend to bind protons in neutral solutions to become ionized:

$$\text{—NH}_2 + \text{H}^+ \longrightarrow \text{—NH}_3{}^+$$

If the pH is increased, the concentration of H$^+$ ions is reduced and the reaction reverses. The alkaline pH at which half of the groups are ionized is the pK for this group. Hence pK is a measure of the propensity of these groups to accept or donate protons. You will learn more about equilibria and pK later in this chapter (Sections 2.5 and 2.6).

▢ There is another way in which functional groups can be classified. What might it be? (Hint: What is the structural feature that characterizes the alkene functional group?)

◼ We can classify functional groups as saturated or unsaturated. All the functional groups in Table 2.3 are unsaturated except alcohols, ethers, amines and thiols.

The main centres of unsaturation are double bonds between two atoms of carbon, between carbon and oxygen, or between carbon and nitrogen. There are also carbon–nitrogen and carbon–carbon triple bonds, and nitrogen–nitrogen double and triple bonds. Although compounds containing benzene rings are unsaturated, they are often classified separately as aromatic compounds.

A final contributor to chemical reactivity is one that we have already encountered in relation to water, i.e. bond polarization (Section 2.1.1). Remember that bond polarity arises because one of the bonding atoms is more strongly electronegative than the other. As you will see when we come to consider enzyme mechanisms in Chapter 3 (Section 3.7), the polarity of groups located in the active site of an enzyme is frequently critical to catalytic activity.

A knowledge of the properties of functional groups helps us to understand the various ways in which biological molecules interact, as well as how medicinal drugs exert their biological activity. Ionizable functional groups can, for example, aid the solubility of a particular drug and may determine the specificity of the drug binding to a receptor or a metabolic enzyme. As you study this course, an appreciation of the covalent and non-covalent interactions that any particular biological molecule can undertake will greatly aid your understanding of how such molecules interact. This is particularly true for the molecular interactions between the major biological macromolecules – proteins and nucleic acids – within the cell.

In the following sections we shall look at particular classes of small organic molecules, including the carboxylic acids, sugars, amino acids, nucleic acids, and a range of coenzymes and signalling molecules. Many of these molecules may be familiar to you, but a brief review is appropriate.

2.3.2 Carboxylic acids

The structures of some **carboxylic acids** commonly found in the cell are shown in Figure 2.13. *In vivo* these exist mainly in their ionized form, as the corresponding carboxylate anion; examples include acetate (ethanoate), succinate, fumarate, lactate and pyruvate. The simplest of the carboxylic acids is acetate, which serves as a vital building block in the synthesis of larger and more complex molecules such as the long-chain fatty acids. These fatty acids are themselves carboxylic acids and are building blocks in the synthesis of membrane lipids. Fatty acids are built by the stepwise addition of the acetyl group (see opposite), to the growing carbon chain. To facilitate such reactions, the acetyl group is covalently bound to a sulfur-containing coenzyme, known simply as **coenzyme A** (or CoA for short), to form

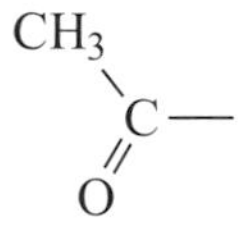

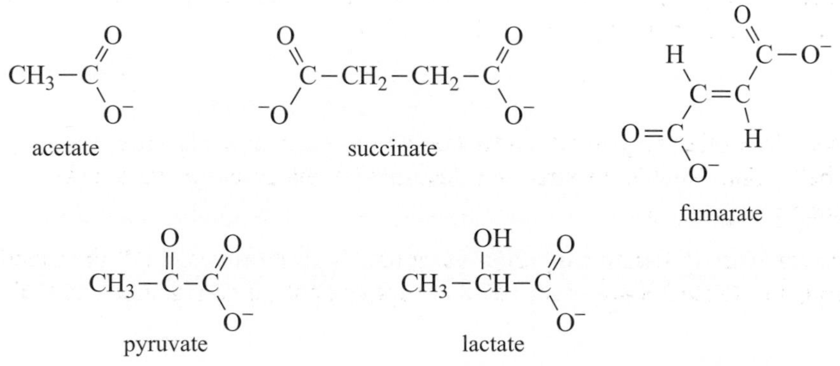

Figure 2.13
Structures of some commonly occurring carboxylic acids (as the ionized forms, in which they exist in the cell).

acetate

succinate

fumarate

pyruvate

lactate

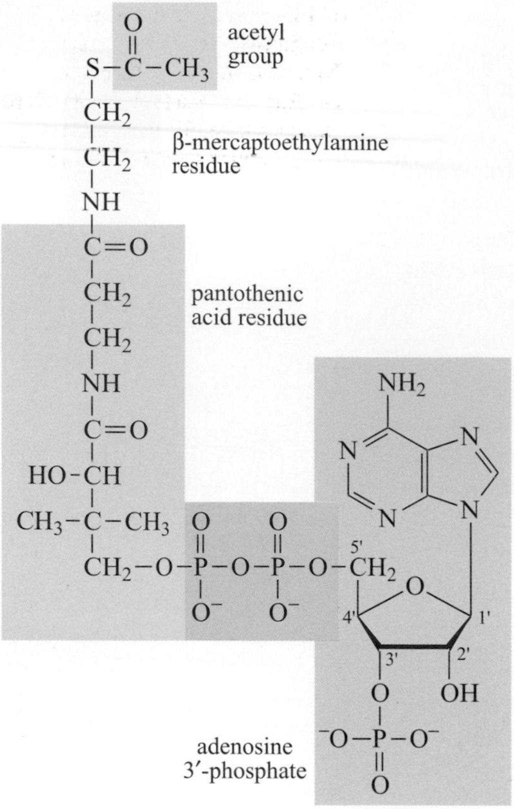

Figure 2.14
Structure of acetyl CoA.

acetyl CoA (Figure 2.14). Conversely, during many catabolic reactions, acetyl groups are split off sequentially from molecules as they are degraded.

Formation of the bond between the acetyl group and CoA requires energy, whilst breaking it releases energy. This linkage, known as a thioester bond, is a 'high-energy' bond.

Amongst the other common cellular carboxylic acids is pyruvate, the end-product of **glycolysis**, which is the first stage of glucose breakdown and occurs in the cytosol. In the absence of oxygen, pyruvate is converted into lactate, which leaks out of the cell into the extracellular fluid. In the presence of oxygen, pyruvate enters the mitochondria where it undergoes a cycle of metabolism known as the **tricarboxylic acid (TCA) cycle**. Elucidated in the 1930s by the biochemist Hans Krebs, this pathway is also sometimes called the **Krebs cycle**. A number of other carboxylic acids feature as intermediates in the TCA cycle (e.g. oxaloacetate, citrate, α-ketoglutarate, succinate, fumarate and malate).

The pathways of glycolysis and the TCA cycle are fully described in S204 Book 3 *The Core of Life,* Vol. I, Chapter 4 and the associated CD, 'Making ATP'. Although we shall cover the energetics of mitochondrial ATP generation in Chapter 4 of this book, you should be familiar with the basic biochemical pathways from your previous study.

2.3.3 Monosaccharides (sugars)

Also present in small quantities in the cell – the concentration depending on metabolic conditions – are **monosaccharides**, simple sugars with the general formula $(CH_2O)_n$ where $n = 3–8$. The most common sugar in animals is the six-carbon glucose. Sugars are the building blocks of complex polysaccharides and, as you know, glucose is a primary source of metabolic energy for both plants and animals. Glucose (or more correctly α-D-glucose) is shown in Figure 2.15a. It exists almost entirely as a six-membered ring, but in aqueous solution the ring form is in equilibrium with a minute proportion of the linear form. Monosaccharides are characterized not only by the number of C atoms that they contain, but also by the type of carbonyl group present, i.e. aldehyde or ketone (see Table 2.3). If the carbonyl is an aldehyde group, as in glucose, the sugar is an aldose. If the carbonyl group is a ketone, as in fructose (a sugar present in a number of fruits), the sugar is known as a ketose (Figure 2.15b). Circularization of monosaccharides occurs as the result of an intramolecular reaction between an alcohol (hydroxyl, —OH) group and a carbonyl (C=O) group, illustrated in Figures 2.15a and b.

In the reactions represented in Figures 2.15, the movement of an electron pair is denoted by a curly red arrow. This is a useful convention and you will encounter it elsewhere in the course. Notice that movement of an electron pair entails bond cleavage.

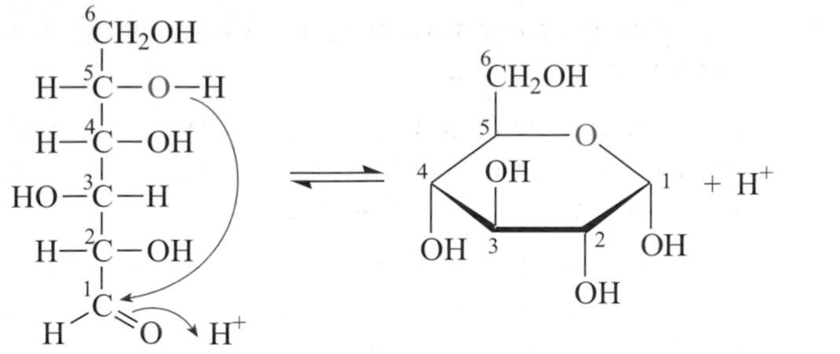

Figure 2.15
(a) Linear and cyclic forms of
α-D-glucose (an aldose sugar).
(b) Linear and cyclic forms of
α-D-fructose (a ketose sugar). Here,
and elsewhere, for clarity, the ring
hydrogen atoms are not shown.

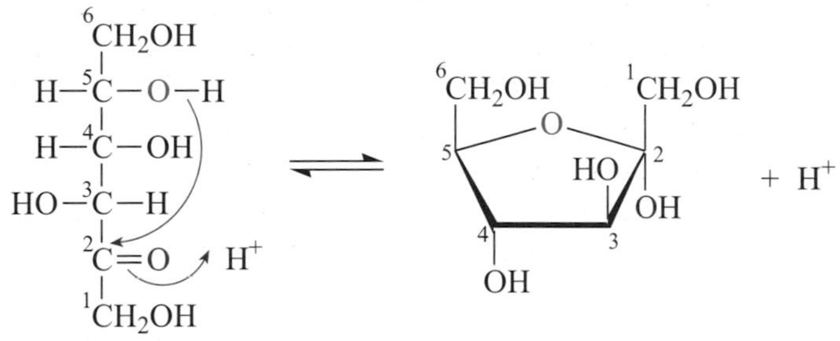

Most biological polysaccharides are built up from monosaccharide constituents of molecular formula $C_nH_{2n}O_n$, where n is usually 6 (hexoses), but sometimes 5 (pentoses). However, there are 24 different ways in which the atoms in a hexose could be arranged, each forming different compounds, all with the molecular formula $C_6H_{12}O_6$.

○ How could you describe these compounds?

● They are isomers; that is, they have the same molecular formula but different structural formulae or stereochemistry.

This large number of potential isomers reflects the many different positions that the hydroxyl (OH) and carbonyl (C=O) groups could occupy on the C atom backbone. The position of these groups in relation to each other and the carbon chain defines a number of isomeric forms. For our purposes, it is not necessary to discuss these different isomers in any detail. However, you should be aware that cells have the ability to discriminate between them and utilize different sugar isomers in different ways.

Covalent linkage of monosaccharide units (or 'residues') occurs as the result of a condensation reaction (i.e. the elimination of water) between two hydroxyl groups. Two monosaccharides linked in this way form a disaccharide (e.g. sucrose comprises a glucose and a fructose residue). Many monosaccharide molecules can be thus linked, forming long chains. The term **oligosaccharide** is used to describe such polymers consisting of up to 15 monosaccharide residues. Larger sugar polymers, called **polysaccharides**, may be used as storage molecules (e.g. glycogen and starch) or structural material (e.g. cellulose in plant cell walls). Box 2.5 details the chemical structure of some monosaccharides, oligosaccharides and polysaccharides. Many proteins that are located on the surface of cells have oligosaccharides covalently attached to them. You will learn more about these *glycoproteins* in Chapter 3.

| Box 2.5 | Monosaccharides, oligosaccharides and polysaccharides |

Monosaccharides

These simple sugars have the general formula $(CH_2O)_n$, where $n = 3$–8. They contain either an aldehyde group or a ketone group:

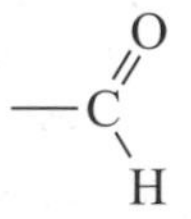

aldehyde group 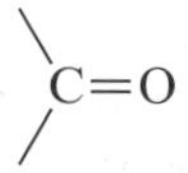   ketone group

In aqueous solution, monosaccharides exist in a ring form. The chemical structures of some of the common monosaccharides are illustrated below. Note that the D prefix refers to the stereoisomer. L sugars are biologically much less abundant that D sugars. The β prefix indicates the position of the highlighted hydroxyl group, i.e. above the ring as represented here. An α prefix is used when this OH group is below the ring (as in Figure 2.15). Monosaccharides can convert between α and β isomeric ring forms via the linear form.

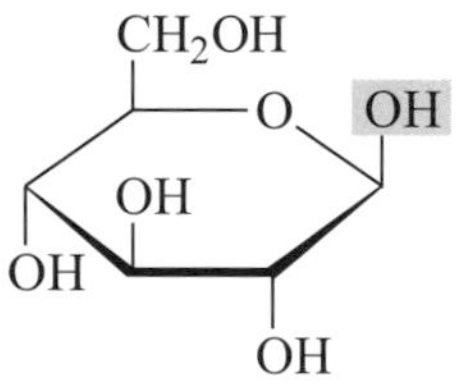

β-D-glucose $(C_6H_{12}O_6)$ 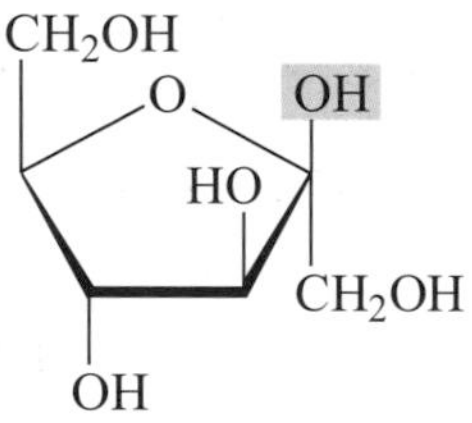   β-D-fructose $(C_6H_{12}O_6)$

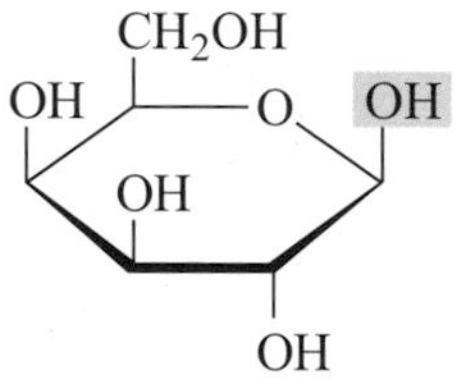

β-D-galactose $(C_6H_{12}O_6)$ 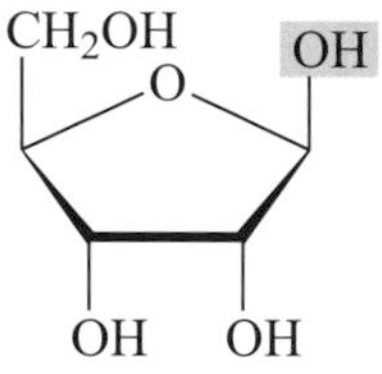   β-D-ribose $(C_5H_{10}O_5)$

Sugar derivatives

The —OH groups on monosaccharides can be replaced by other groups, e.g. an acetylated amino group as in N-acetylglucosamine (NAG):

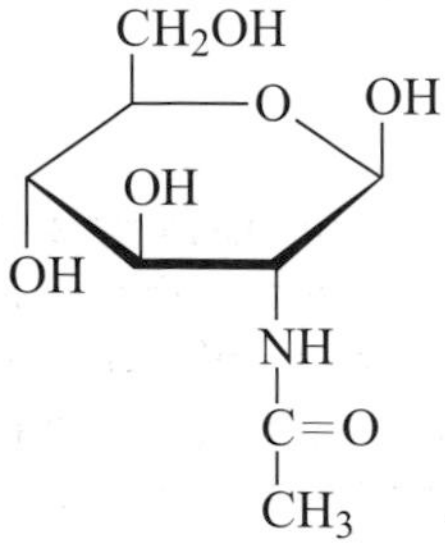

N-acetylglucosamine (NAG)

Oligosaccharides and polysaccharides

Oligosaccharides and polysaccharides are formed by polymerization of monosaccharide units. This process involves a condensation reaction. A disaccharide is two monosaccharide residues linked in this way. Oligosaccharides are short chains of monosaccharide residues and polysaccharides are long chains. Both oligosaccharides and polysaccharides can be branched. For example, glycogen is a polysaccharide composed entirely of glucose units joined together (shown below). Oligosaccharides linked to proteins are varied, often complex and have a non-repetitive sugar sequence. They frequently contain residues that are sugar derivatives, e.g. *N*-acetylglucosamine, as in the example below.

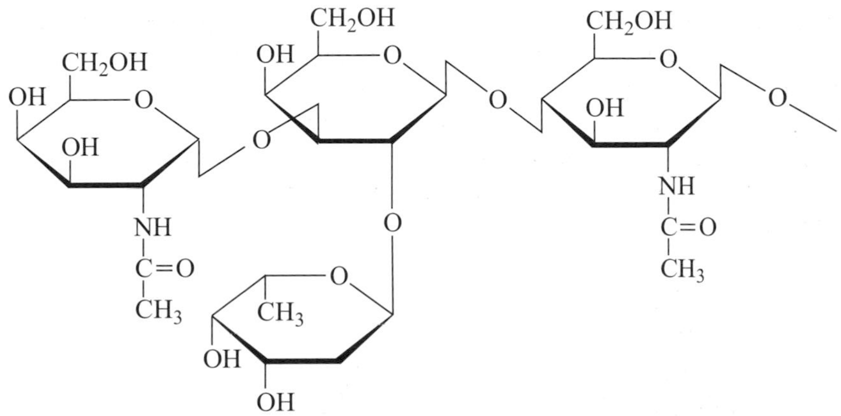

a complex oligosaccharide

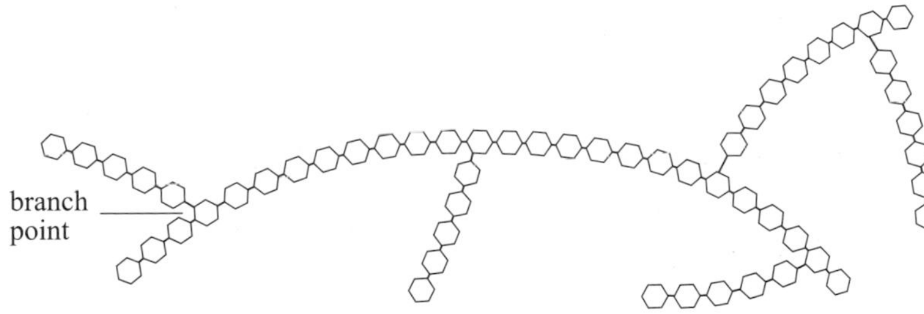

branch point

glycogen

As well as acting as building blocks for polysaccharides, sugar residues are components of many smaller molecules. For example ribose, a pentose sugar, forms part of the structure of ATP and, indeed, the other ribonucleotides (Section 2.3.5).

2.3.4 Amino acids

Although a very large number of compounds containing both amino and carboxyl groups are present in living organisms, the most prominent are the 20 **amino acids** found in proteins. These amino acids have their amino and carboxyl groups attached to the same carbon atom, which is called the α (alpha) carbon; hence they are also commonly called α-amino acids. Amino acids are found in the cell both as free

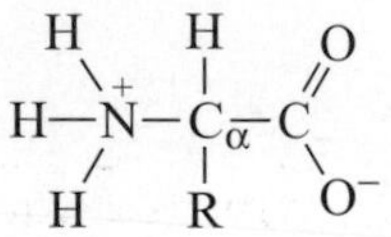

Figure 2.16
General structure of an amino acid. Note the basic amino group and acidic carboxyl group on the same carbon atom (C_α). R denotes the variable side-chain. In the physiological pH range, both the amino and the carboxyl groups are completely ionized, as shown here; hence the amino acid is dipolar.

molecules and as polymers, i.e. proteins. You have already come across the general structure of an amino acid (Figure 2.9). At physiological pH, free amino acids exist in a **dipolar** form, having both a positively and a negatively charged group (Figure 2.16).

The 20 amino acids of which proteins are composed differ only in their side-chain (R) (Figure 2.17). The variable side-chain determines the particular chemical properties of an amino acid and, as you will see in Chapter 3, directly influences the shape and function of the protein of which it is a component. The amino acids in Figure 2.17 have therefore been divided into four categories according to the nature of their side-chains: basic, acidic, uncharged polar or non-polar.

In Section 2.2.4, you learned that asymmetric carbon atoms in organic molecules have a property known as chirality. Remember that *all amino acids derived from proteins have the L stereochemical configuration.*

◻ Looking at the structures of the amino acids in Figure 2.17, explain why alanine may occur as an enantiomeric pair, whereas glycine cannot.

■ The central carbon atom in alanine is linked to four different groups, −COOH, −NH₂, −CH₃ and H. In glycine, there are only three different groups, −COOH, −NH₂ and two H atoms.

◻ Aspartic acid and glutamic acid side-chains have a pK of about 4. What functional group is responsible for their acidity?

■ They both have carboxyl groups which ionize in neutral solutions, releasing hydrogen ions.

Amino acids are frequently given three-letter or single-letter designations (as indicated in Figure 2.17). Thus lysine may be abbreviated 'Lys' or just 'K'. These notations are particularly useful when referring to the sequences of amino acids found in a protein. A **peptide** is formed by linking two or more amino acids by way of a **peptide bond**. In peptide bond formation, water is eliminated in a condensation reaction between the acidic carboxyl group of one amino acid and the basic amino group of another amino acid, as shown in Figure 2.18a.

◻ What is the functional group that includes the peptide bond (highlighted in Figure 2.18a)?

■ An amide group (see Table 2.3).

The term **polypeptide** describes a long chain of amino acids linked in this way (Figure 2.18b). Proteins consist of one or more polypeptide chains. Within a polypeptide, the linked amino acids are frequently referred to as 'residues'. Notice that the two ends of a polypeptide are distinct, one having an amino group, the other having a carboxyl group. When polypeptides are synthesized, amino acid residues are added to the growing chain at the carboxyl terminus (also called the C-terminus) and, by convention, residues are numbered from the amino terminus (N-terminus), as in Figure 2.18b.

Figure 2.17   The 20 amino acids found in proteins, grouped according to the nature of their side-chains. Both the three-letter and the single-letter abbreviations are given for each amino acid. (For simplicity, the amino acids are shown with their C_α amino and carboxyl groups unionized.)

BASIC SIDE-CHAINS

ACIDIC SIDE-CHAINS

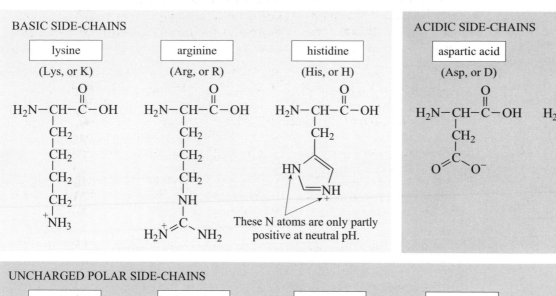

UNCHARGED POLAR SIDE-CHAINS

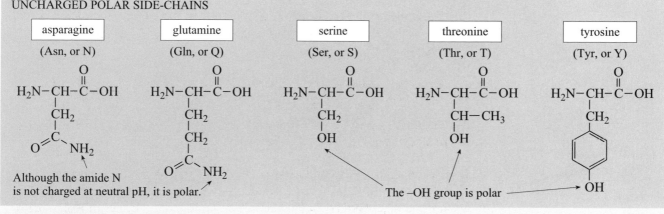

NON-POLAR SIDE-CHAINS

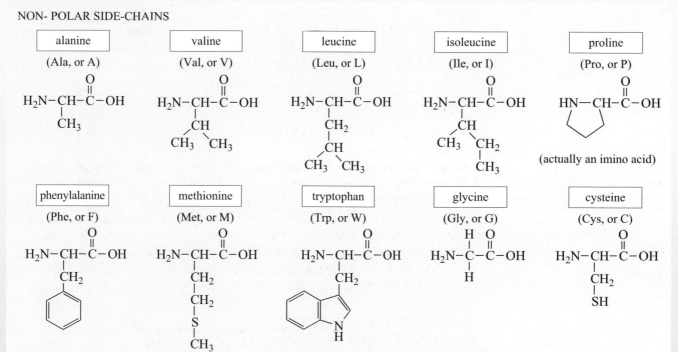

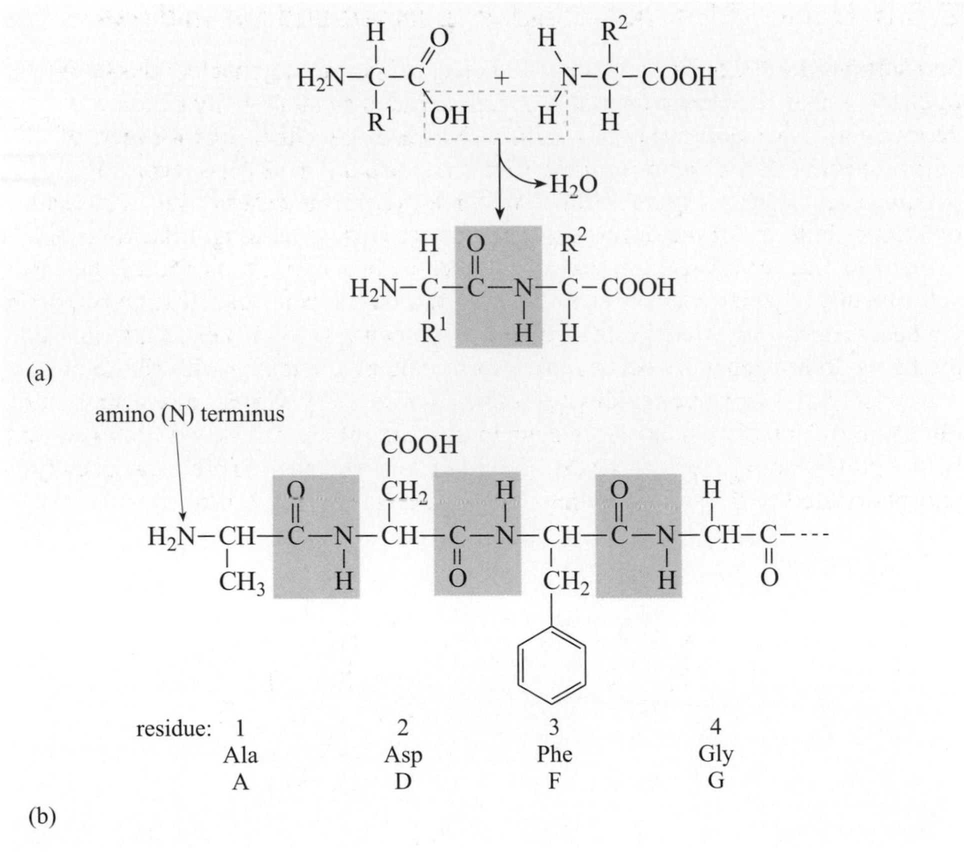

Figure 2.18
(a) Peptide bond formation.
(b) A polypeptide is a long chain of amino acids linked via peptide bonds. This example shows the first four amino acids in a polypeptide chain. Note that polypeptide chains are always listed and synthesized in sequence, starting with the N-terminus.

Table 2.4 lists some of the most common amino acids, and gives the concentration at which they are found in their free form in one particular type of cell, neurons in the brain. Unlike the other precursor molecules that have been described hitherto, many amino acids are present in relatively high concentrations in the cell. This abundance suggests that they may have functions other than simply serving as protein building blocks. And indeed this is the case. Glutamate, for instance, which is present at high concentrations in the brain neurons (and in other body cells), is an important messenger molecule, functioning as a neurotransmitter. Another amino acid, gamma-aminobutyric acid (GABA), which – as you can tell from its name – is not an α-amino acid, is not present in proteins but is a neurotransmitter.

Table 2.4 Amino acid concentrations in the brain.

Name	Three-letter abbreviation	Amount free in brain / μmol per 100 g tissue	Name	Three-letter abbreviation	Amount free in brain / μmol per 100 g tissue
alanine	Ala	50	leucine	Leu	10
aspartate	Asp	200	phenylalanine	Phe	7
cysteine	Cys	4	proline	Pro	9
glutamate	Glu	1000	serine	Ser	100
glutamine	Gln	350	threonine	Thr	20
glycine	Gly	120	tyrosine	Tyr	8

2.3.5 Nucleotides, nucleosides, purines and pyrimidines

Nucleotides are the building blocks of nucleic acids and oligonucleotides (short nucleotide chains). They comprise a phosphorylated sugar (usually ribose or deoxyribose) covalently linked to a **base**. The bases are either **pyrimidines**, of which the commonest are *thymine, cytosine* and *uracil*, or **purines**, typically *adenine* and *guanine* (Figure 2.19a). The three pyrimidine bases differ from each other only in terms of the different substituent groups on the ring. Likewise, the two purines are structurally very similar. As you will see in Chapter 5, it is the ring substituents, together with the shape and orientation of each base, that make possible the base pairing on which the double-helical structure of DNA depends. In the cell, the bases do not generally occur in free form, but are combined with ribose or deoxyribose to form **nucleosides** (**cytidine**, **uridine**, **thymidine**, **adenosine** and **guanosine**). Note that nucleosides containing deoxyribose are sometimes identified by the prefix 'deoxy' (e.g. deoxythymidine) or 'd'. Nucleosides are subsequently phosphorylated to the corresponding nucleotides (see Figure 2.19b).

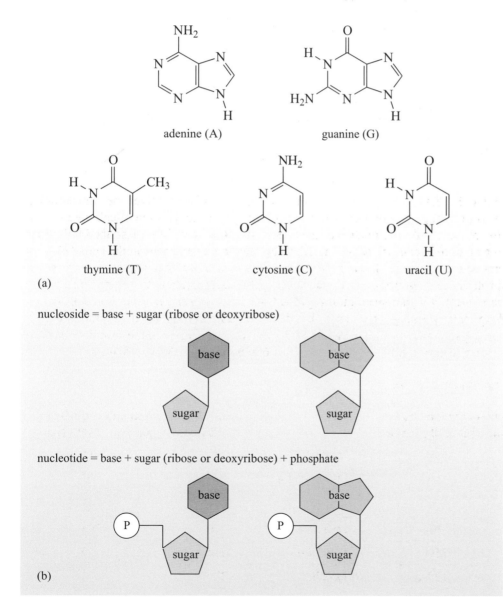

(a)

nucleoside = base + sugar (ribose or deoxyribose)

nucleotide = base + sugar (ribose or deoxyribose) + phosphate

(b)

Figure 2.19
(a) The chemical structures of purines (adenine and guanine) and pyrimidines (thymine, cytosine and uracil). The single-letter code for each base is given in brackets. Notice that the purine skeleton is bicyclic (two fused rings) and the pyrimidine skeleton is monocyclic. (b) Simplified representations of nucleosides (base–sugar) and nucleotides (base–sugar–phosphate). In DNA, the sugar component is deoxyribose; in RNA it is ribose.

Nucleotides are not simply building blocks of nucleic acids. Many metabolic pathways are regulated by nucleotides, such as the different phosphorylated forms of adenosine – ATP, ADP and AMP. A related cyclic form, cyclic AMP (cAMP), and its guanosine analogue (cGMP) are involved in intracellular signalling processes (discussed in Chapter 13). Nucleoside triphosphates, most notably ATP but also guanosine triphosphate (GTP), function as 'energy carriers' (Figure 2.20), being produced as a result of energy-releasing metabolic processes and used to drive energy-requiring processes. The formation of ATP from ADP and inorganic phosphate involves a condensation reaction, as shown below, and requires energy to produce the phosphoanhydride bond.

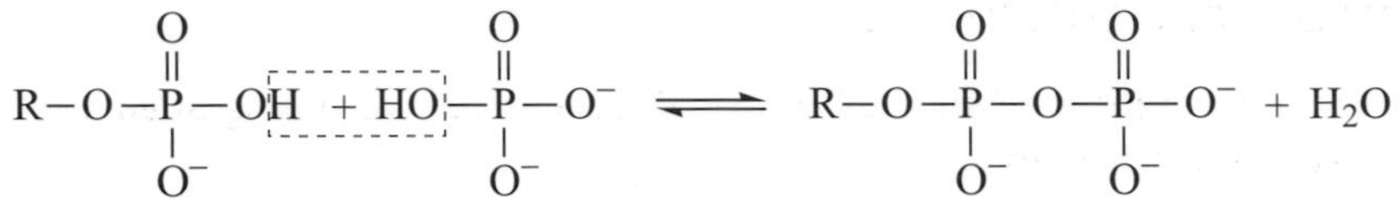

$$R-O-\overset{\overset{\displaystyle O}{\|}}{\underset{\underset{\displaystyle O^-}{|}}{P}}-OH \; + \; HO-\overset{\overset{\displaystyle O}{\|}}{\underset{\underset{\displaystyle O^-}{|}}{P}}-O^- \;\rightleftharpoons\; R-O-\overset{\overset{\displaystyle O}{\|}}{\underset{\underset{\displaystyle O^-}{|}}{P}}-O-\overset{\overset{\displaystyle O}{\|}}{\underset{\underset{\displaystyle O^-}{|}}{P}}-O^- \; + \; H_2O$$

Hydrolysis of this 'energy-rich' bond releases energy which can be used to drive energy-requiring reactions. The bioenergetics of ATP formation are considered in Chapter 4.

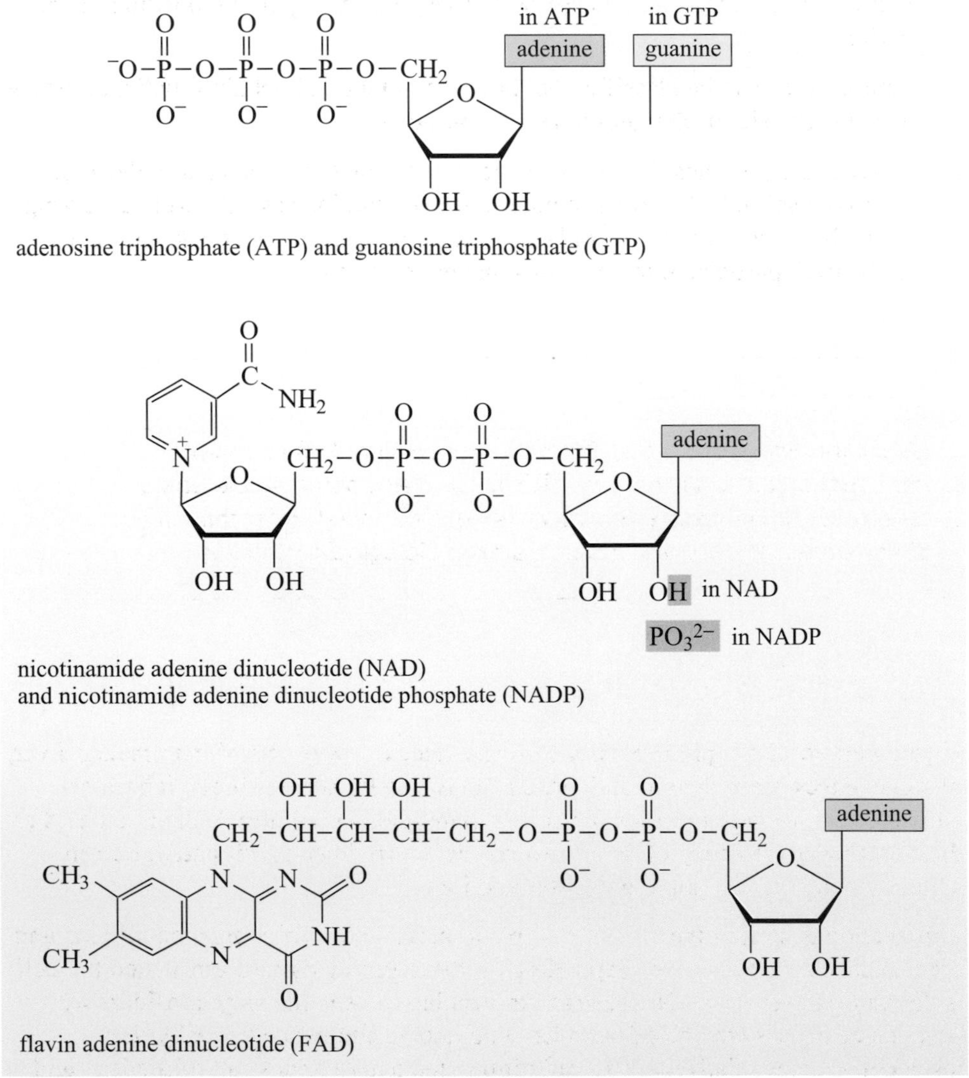

adenosine triphosphate (ATP) and guanosine triphosphate (GTP)

nicotinamide adenine dinucleotide (NAD)
and nicotinamide adenine dinucleotide phosphate (NADP)

flavin adenine dinucleotide (FAD)

Figure 2.20
Structures of some energy-rich nucleotides and adenosine derivatives involved in cellular energy-exchange reactions.

Other derivatives of adenosine function as coenzymes, which are molecules that bind temporarily to an enzyme and are chemically altered by the enzymatic reaction. You have already encountered coenzyme A, a derivative of adenosine. The nicotinamide coenzymes NAD and NADP and the flavin coenzyme FAD are also derived from adenosine (Figure 2.20). NAD, NADP and FAD serve as electron acceptors in metabolic processes; that is, they become reduced. Reduction of these coenzymes effectively stores the energy released on oxidation of a substrate and this energy is released when the coenzyme is oxidized. You will learn more about how NAD and FAD are involved in energy transfer in Chapter 4.

Summary of Section 2.3

1   Macromolecules are formed from small precursors, including sugars, amino acids and nucleotides.

2   The biochemistry of organic molecules can be understood on the basis of their individual functional groups. These groups contribute to the active centres of macromolecules, such as enzymes.

3   Sugars can be classified according to the number of carbon atoms they contain and can be described as aldoses or ketoses, depending on the position of the carbonyl group.

4   Amino acids can be classified on the basis of their side-chain functional groups, as acidic, basic, uncharged polar, or non-polar.

5   Nucleotides are phosphorylated nucleosides, which have a sugar (ribose or deoxyribose) linked to either a purine or a pyrimidine base. As well as serving as the building blocks for synthesis of nucleic acids, nucleotides and their derivatives participate in energy-exchange reactions.

Molecular modelling 1

Go to the Study Skills file: *Molecular modelling 1*. This activity introduces you to ViewerLite™. You will learn some of the basic functions of the program, whilst using it to investigate the three-dimensional structures of some simple biological molecules.

2.4 Ions in biological systems

If you were to take a piece of tissue, for instance a few grams of mammalian liver, or some leaves from a plant, and grind it up with a little water in the laboratory equivalent of a food processor (a process called homogenization), then add acid to the resulting suspension, all the macromolecules would be precipitated. Left in solution would be the small molecules and ions.

This section describes the ions in a 'typical' animal cell. Of course, conditions and constituents vary somewhat, depending on the organ or tissue from which the cell is derived. However, whilst the macromolecular content can vary considerably between cell types (red blood cells have no nuclei, and hence no DNA, for instance), there is relatively little variation in the nature or amount of the ions and small molecules in different cell types. Most of those found in mammalian cells are also found in other animals and even in plants and bacteria, though some important exceptions will be noted in passing. Finally, traces of certain metals such as copper and zinc are found in all living tissues. They are critical components of certain proteins; for example, one group of enzymes, the matrix metalloproteases, which degrade components of the extracellular matrix, all contain zinc.

2.4.1 Ionic composition

The starting point to understanding the biological significance of small molecules and ions lies in the fact that every aspect of a living system's chemistry goes on either in dilute aqueous solution, on the complex surfaces provided by the macromolecules of the cytosol, or in the lipid hydrophobic environment of the cell's membranes. Inorganic ions and small polar or charged organic molecules are dissolved in the cytosol, i.e. they are hydrated, with water molecules forming a hydration shell around them, as described in Section 2.1.3. These ions and molecules are also found in the membranes, where they are often tightly bound to specific sites or sequestered within the lipid and protein matrix.

The other inorganic cations in solution include sodium (Na^+), potassium (K^+), calcium (Ca^{2+}) and magnesium (Mg^{2+}). The anions include hydroxide (OH^-), chloride (Cl^-), bicarbonate or hydrogen carbonate (HCO_3^-) and hydrogen phosphate (HPO_4^{2-}). The intracellular concentrations of these ions in a human cell are shown in Table 2.5. We have chosen a red blood cell as an example, but the picture would be no different for any other cell of the body. Table 2.5 also shows the concentrations of the same ions in the external environment of the cell, which, for the red blood cell, is blood plasma. As you can see, the commonest cations, both inside and outside the cell, are sodium and potassium and the commonest anion is chloride. All the other soluble constituents of cells are present at much lower concentrations. Note that ions can not pass freely through the hydrophobic environment of cell membranes, but the plasma membrane, by virtue of specific channel proteins, is permeable to ions. In fact, it is semipermeable, in that it allows ions to enter and leave in a selective manner. The overall intracellular and extracellular concentrations of the ions must therefore be in balance. In other words, the *total number* of ions is the same on both sides of the membrane, even though the types of ions may differ. This condition, known as **osmotic equilibrium**, ensures there is no net flow of ions between the two environments unless this is required for a particular function. In practice, cells do maintain small differences in the overall balance of ions across the plasma membrane. This imbalance results in a small voltage difference across the membrane; typically, the inside of a mammalian nerve cell is around $-100\,mV$ with respect to the outside.

Table 2.5   Ionic composition of plasma and red blood cells (concentrations in $mmol\,l^{-1}$).

	Cations					Anions		
	Na^+	K^+	Ca^{2+}	Mg^{2+}		Cl^-	HPO_4^{2-}	HCO_3^-
red blood cells	11	92	10^{-4}	2.5		50	3	10
blood plasma	160	10	2	2		100	3	25

2.4.2 Hydronium and hydroxide ions

Whilst protons in biochemical reactions are commonly represented as H^+, they more correctly have the formula H_3O^+, since the proton is not stable in aqueous solution but binds to a water molecule. H_3O^+ is known as the **hydronium ion**. The 'bare' proton, H^+, can be passed rapidly from one molecule of water to the next, giving the hydronium ion an anomalously high effective mobility in solution. Its anionic counterpart, the hydroxide ion (OH^-), demonstrates a similarly high effective mobility in solution when protons are passed between water molecules in the opposite direction.

Protons may also bind to oxygen and nitrogen atoms in other molecules, exchanging sites very rapidly. However, the concentration of H_3O^+, i.e. the pH, is critical for most of the physical and chemical processes taking place within the cell. The *effective* hydrogen ion concentration (i.e. the concentration of 'free' protons bound to water) in the cytosol is normally maintained at about $4 \times 10^{-8}\,mol\,l^{-1}$ (i.e. pH 7.4) and thus the cytosolic pH lies a little on the alkaline side of neutrality. Other compartments, such as the lysosome or the space between the inner and outer mitochondrial membranes, can have quite different pH values.

2.4.3 Sodium and potassium ions

☐ From Table 2.5, what can you observe about the concentrations of sodium and potassium ions in blood plasma compared to their concentrations inside the red blood cell?

◼ The relative concentrations are reversed: whereas the intracellular concentration of potassium is much higher than that of sodium, outside the cell sodium is at a much higher concentration than potassium.

This difference between internal and external sodium and potassium concentrations seems to be true of all cells in multicellular organisms, and a regime of relatively high potassium and low sodium is important in producing an ionic environment that stabilizes DNA. But how does the concentration difference arise, and how is it maintained? Small ions such as sodium and potassium can pass through the lipid bilayer of the cell membrane using specific ion transporter systems, and ions in solution tend to diffuse down a concentration gradient, thereby equalizing concentrations throughout the solution. So it is clear that cells must possess some special features to oppose this diffusion, rendering the membrane only semipermeable and preserving the transmembrane differentials in the concentration of sodium and potassium. A clue to the mechanism is provided by the observation that if a red blood cell, or its energy-generating system, is damaged in any way (or even temporarily put out of action, for instance by cooling to around 4 °C), then sodium enters and potassium leaves the cell. Each of these ions passes across the membrane down its respective concentration gradient. Preserving the normal ratios therefore demands a considerable and continuous expenditure of energy by the cell.

Transmembrane ion concentration differences depend on special properties of particular proteins of the plasma membrane. Ion channels permit selective passage of ions into or out of the cell, according to the prevailing concentration gradient. Importantly, the opening and closing of these ion channels is subject to regulation. In addition, specific ion pumps transport ions against the concentration gradient in an energy-requiring process known as **active transport**. In mammalian cells, the

Na⁺/K⁺ ATPase is principally responsible for maintaining the gradient of these ions across the plasma membrane. It pumps three Na⁺ ions out of the cell and two K⁺ ions in, with the concomitant hydrolysis of an ATP molecule (Figure 2.21). Other ion pumps transport calcium ions and protons.

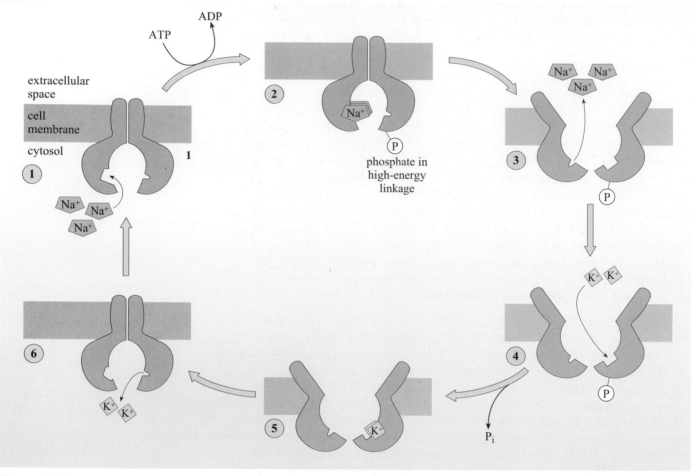

Figure 2.21   A scheme showing the activity of the Na⁺/K⁺ ATPase, which extrudes three Na⁺ ions for every two K⁺ ions taken up.

The Na⁺/K⁺ ATPase and a number of other transport systems are described in more detail in S204, Book 3 *The Core of Life,* Vol. I, Chapter 3. You should also be familiar with the various classes of transport system and the terms **transporter**, **cotransporter**, **facilitated diffusion**, **ion channel**, **symport** and **antiport**.

2.4.4 Divalent cations

As well as monovalent cations, the cytosol contains significant, though much lower, concentrations of two divalent cations, calcium (Ca^{2+}) and magnesium (Mg^{2+}). Many complex metabolic pathways in the cell proceed optimally only in the presence of concentrations of sodium and potassium rather close to those found in the cell as a whole. However, the functions of calcium and magnesium are rather more specific. A number of enzymes require one or other of these ions to maximize their activity. For example, magnesium ions are an obligatory cofactor for a number of enzymes, including several that are involved in the synthesis or utilization of ATP (for instance, in muscular contraction). Magnesium is also firmly bound to the light-absorbing pigment chlorophyll, in which it plays a central role in photosynthesis in all photosynthetic organisms, with the exception of the halobacteria. Furthermore, many of the adhesion molecules, i.e. proteins involved in direct cell–cell contacts, have Mg^{2+} located at the binding site of the molecule.

In addition to its functions in enzymes, calcium has a key role in the regulation of cell metabolism. The normal cytosolic concentration of calcium ions is extremely low. The extracellular Ca^{2+} concentration is several thousand times higher than the intracellular level (see Table 2.5), though some intracellular organelles, such as mitochondria, are able to take up Ca^{2+} ions from the surrounding medium in quite high concentrations. The control mechanisms required to ensure homeostasis against so large a concentration gradient have to be very sophisticated. Because many key processes in mammalian cells are activated by calcium ions, a local change in the intracellular concentration of Ca^{2+}, either by a pulse of the ion entering the cell from the external medium or by release from an intracellular store, can result in a rapid change in enzyme activity. There is evidence that, as organisms age, the mechanisms that ensure calcium homeostasis tend to break down. By interfering with the subtle control of calcium-activated cellular enzymes, this breakdown of calcium homeostasis contributes to some of the characteristic disorders of ageing in humans and other mammals.

Just as intracellular sodium and potassium levels are regulated by the plasma membrane, so too are calcium levels, and the membrane has special calcium-permeable channels and calcium pumps. Whilst the general cytosolic concentration of calcium ions is of the order of 10^{-7} mol l^{-1}, the membrane calcium channels can open to admit as many as 10^7 calcium ions per second, and the Ca^{2+} concentration can rise by a factor of 10^3 within 10 nm from the mouth of the channel, creating a steep gradient of Ca^{2+} concentration. In this way, calcium ions can act as an intracellular signal or messenger. In its role in signalling, it is not the overall Ca^{2+} concentration that is important, but rather the *rapid, localized changes* in that concentration. Such local changes profoundly affect the conformation, and hence the function, of a wide variety of proteins. Embedded in the plasma membrane, in the mitochondrion, or free in the cytosol, are a large number of calcium-binding proteins. Some of these, such as protein kinase C (Figure 2.22), are enzymes that can phosphorylate the amino acid residues of other membrane proteins. Such phosphorylation events may alter the enzymatic activity of some proteins, or cause ion channels in the membrane to open. The role of Ca^{2+} in intracellular signalling is dealt with in detail in Chapter 13 where we look more closely at signal transduction processes.

Another calcium-binding enzyme is calpain, which is a protease, i.e. it hydrolyses the peptide bonds between the amino acid residues of a protein chain. Other calcium-binding proteins are essential components of the cellular framework, or cytoskeleton, and as such, help maintain cell structure; fodrin is one such protein. Yet other calcium-binding proteins participate in the mechanisms of cell motility.

Figure 2.22
The structure of the polypeptide backbone of the C2 domains (Ca^{2+}-binding regulatory modules) of rat protein kinase C (PKC). There are two identical subunits, coloured purple and orange, each with three bound calcium ions (shown in space-filling format in green). PKC is activated on binding of Ca^{2+}. (Based on pdb file 1a25)

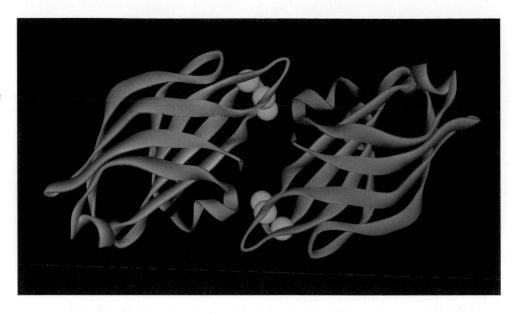

2.4.5 Anions

> In this section, we refer to equilibrium reactions where the reactants and products are present in a dynamic equilibrium and the rate of the forward reaction is equal to the rate of the reverse reaction. The principles of equilibrium reactions are discussed in, for example, S103 Block 8 *Building with Atoms*. At this stage, you just need to understand the notation of reversible reactions (i.e. the double-headed arrow) and understand that the reaction can proceed in either direction. We return to the ideas of equilibria and biological buffering in Section 2.5.

Table 2.5 lists key anions present in the cell. Hydrogen phosphate (HPO_4^{2-}) and hydrogen carbonate (HCO_3^-) fulfil a particularly important role in maintaining the concentration of H_3O^+ at the value required for cellular processes. The process of stabilizing the pH of a solution or of a cell is called **buffering**. It is carried out jointly by these anions and by anionic groups present on protein molecules, all of which share the property, when protonated, of being weak acids. This means they are proton donors; that is, they can dissociate to produce H^+, which in its hydrated form is H_3O^+. An example of a buffer is hydrogen carbonate, HCO_3^-, whose reaction with H_3O^+ at equilibrium is weighted in favour of the right-hand side of the equation:

$$H_3O^+ + HCO_3^- \rightleftharpoons H_2O + H_2CO_3 \tag{2.1}$$

H_2CO_3 (carbonic acid) is, in turn, in equilibrium with dissolved carbon dioxide and water:

$$H_2CO_3 \rightleftharpoons CO_2 + H_2O \tag{2.2}$$

An increase or decrease in H_3O^+ concentration is therefore buffered by the responses of the above equilibria. Analogous equations can be written for the buffering action of hydrogen phosphate.

○ Write an equilibrium equation showing the response of the dihydrogen phosphate ion, $H_2PO_4^-$, to the introduction of hydroxide ions, OH^-, in aqueous solution.

● $H_2PO_4^- + OH^- \rightleftharpoons HPO_4^{2-} + H_2O$ (2.3)

Equations 2.1 and 2.2 are important in other respects in most organisms. CO_2 is generated during the oxidation of nutrients such as glucose and must be removed from the cell and ultimately released into the atmosphere. By means of the reversible reactions in Equations 2.1 and 2.2, the hydrogen carbonate ion effectively carries CO_2 in dissolved form. In multicellular organisms, it therefore plays a major role in the regulation of CO_2 levels, as well as the pH of both intra- and extracellular fluids.

In solution, phosphate ions (as HPO_4^{2-} and $H_2PO_4^-$) serve many cellular functions apart from helping to buffer the intracellular medium. In particular, a multitude of coenzymes and metabolic intermediates are phosphorylated, the most notable of these being ATP. The special feature of inorganic phosphate that makes it so important in biological chemistry lies partly in its capacity to combine with organic acids and partly in the fact that it can form not only mono- but also di- and triphosphates (as in ATP). Whilst the amount of energy required to synthesize adenosine monophosphate (AMP) from adenosine and inorganic phosphate is relatively small, that required to phosphorylate AMP, first into ADP and then, in a second phosphorylation step, into ATP, is large. The addition of these terminal phosphoryl groups to AMP thus becomes a convenient way of 'storing' the energy released in the oxidation of glucose. Phosphate is also incorporated in other important compounds such as nicotinamide adenine dinucleotide phosphate, NADP (see Figure 2.20).

2.4.6 Trace elements

All elements other than those discussed above exist in the cell in only very small concentrations; the metals include iron, copper, manganese, cobalt, zinc, molybdenum and, in some organisms, traces of others such as vanadium. Amongst the anions, the most significant is iodide. Small though their concentrations may be, these trace elements are essential to life. Iodine, for instance, occurs in the mammalian hormone thyroxine (Figure 2.23), and the absence of this element from the human diet leads to thyroid deficiency, in which the metabolic rate is reduced and most bodily functions are impaired.

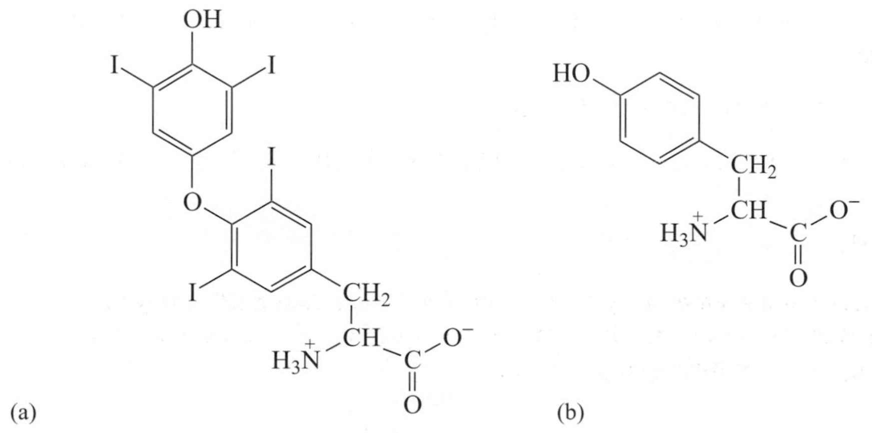

(a)

(b)

Figure 2.23
(a) The iodine-containing hormone thyroxine. Note its structural similarity to the amino acid tyrosine (b), from which it is formed.

In the cell, the metal ions occur almost always bound to particular proteins, where they often play a crucial role in maintaining the protein's three-dimensional shape. If the protein is an enzyme, the metal may be needed for catalytic activity. A good example is the role of iron and copper ions in cellular oxidation processes. Metal ions like iron and copper can each exist in two oxidation states. Fe(II) and Fe(III) correspond to the cations Fe^{2+} and Fe^{3+} respectively, and Cu(I) and Cu(II) correspond to Cu^+ and Cu^{2+} respectively. Fe(II) can be readily oxidized to Fe(III), and Fe(III) can be reduced to Fe(II) under appropriate conditions. A number of enzymatic processes take advantage of this capacity. For example, during the oxidation of glucose, iron bound to a class of mitochondrial proteins known as cytochromes is alternately oxidized to its Fe(III) state and reduced to its Fe(II) state (Figure 2.24). Another of the cytochromes utilizes the oxidation and reduction of its copper (Cu(I) and Cu(II)) component in a similar way.

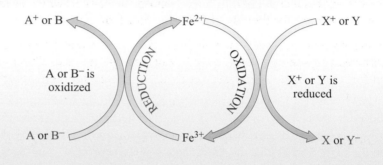

Figure 2.24
Reduction and oxidation (redox) processes promoted by iron cations.

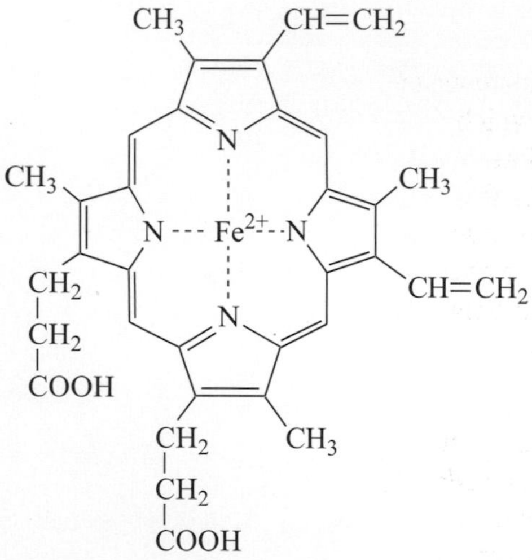

In the iron-containing cytochromes, and in the protein haemoglobin, iron is bound in the form of a complex known as haem, illustrated in Figure 2.25. Haem is an example of a **coordination complex**, a compound with a central metallic atom or ion which is held by **coordinate bonds** with surrounding groups, four N atoms in this case. The Fe^{2+} in haem can form a further two coordinate bonds when the haem complex is in situ in haemoglobin – one with a histidine side-chain and one with an oxygen molecule (see Figure 3.24 in Chapter 3). Haemoglobin in vertebrate red blood cells acts as a carrier of oxygen, which binds reversibly to the haem complex. Thus oxygen, obtained by breathing, binds to haemoglobin and circulates via the blood to the tissues where it is discharged to be used by the cells for metabolism.

Other metals ions, such as manganese (Mn), molybdenum (Mb) and zinc (Zn) also contribute to protein function. The concentrations of metal ions are often of considerable importance and excessive amounts can be toxic. Metals that are not usually found in cells or tissues can also be toxic if, for example, they have ionic properties similar to those of a naturally occurring metal ion that serves some biological function. In such cases, toxicity can be a result of competition between the naturally occurring and the foreign metal ion, e.g. for binding at an enzyme active site. Lead (Pb) is a good example of such a toxic metal.

Figure 2.25
Structure of the haem coordination complex showing the planar ring structure with four N atoms forming coordinate bonds to the central Fe^{2+}.

Summary of Section 2.4

1 There are substantial differences between the intracellular and extracellular concentrations of ions. Most strikingly, the intracellular concentration of K^+ is relatively high and that of Na^+, relatively low. In mammals, these ion gradients are maintained principally by the Na^+/K^+ ATPase.

2 Both magnesium and calcium are activators for key enzymes; Ca^{2+} concentrations are also regulated by transport processes across the membrane and changes in the cytosolic concentration of the ion serve as a signal for many vital intracellular processes.

3 Hydrogen carbonate (bicarbonate) and phosphate ions help buffer intracellular pH to around pH 7.4. Hydrogen carbonate is also a carrier for carbon dioxide.

4 Several key small organic molecules occur as phosphates (ATP is an example), and the cell makes use of short di- and triphosphate chains (which require considerable energy for their synthesis) for short-term energy storage.

5 Trace ions present in the cell include those of metals such as iron (in the cytochromes and haemoglobin), copper, zinc, manganese, etc. These ions are crucial for many enzyme-catalysed reactions, and almost always occur tightly bound to proteins.

2.5 Reversible reactions and chemical equilibria

When we considered how the pH of a cell is buffered by bicarbonate ions, the importance of the equilibrium between bicarbonate, carbonic acid and carbon dioxide was apparent (Equations 2.1 and 2.2, Section 2.4.5). In this section, we are going to look a little more deeply into **equilibrium reactions**.

In principle, all chemical reactions are reversible, so the direction in which we write a chemical reaction (i.e. which components are considered reactants and which products) is arbitrary. For example, in the equilibrium reaction represented in Equation 2.3, one could consider the HPO_4^{2-} ion to be either the reactant or the product, depending on whether one started with HPO_4^{2-} or $H_2PO_4^-$. In this case, we refer to the reagents as 'components' of the equilibrium. The essence of an equilibrium reaction is that whether one starts with the components from the right- or the left-hand side of the equation, the reaction yields the same mixture of components.

In practice, however, many reactions run almost completely in one direction. For example, if ATP is left for a long time, it will spontaneously break down into ADP and phosphate, before breaking down further into AMP. However, if one places pure ADP and phosphate together in solution, they will not produce significant amounts of ATP. A reaction of this type, which essentially runs in one direction only, is said to be *complete* when the equilibrium mixture contains no significant amount of one of the components. In this case, the reaction equation is often written in one direction only and the reverse reaction is said 'not to occur'. Although the reaction *is* reversible, the reverse reaction is very slow by comparison with the forward reaction.

2.5.1 The law of mass action

The equilibrium point of any reaction is determined by the relative rates of the forward reaction and the reverse reaction. When a reaction is at equilibrium, the rates of these two reactions are identical, so no net (macroscopic) change is observed, although individual components are actively being transformed at the microscopic level. Guldberg and Waage showed that the rate of the reaction in either direction is proportional to what they called the 'active masses' of the various components.

If we apply this principle to the equilibrium between HCO_3^- and H_2CO_3:

$$H_3O^+ + HCO_3^- \rightleftharpoons H_2O + H_2CO_3 \tag{2.1}$$

then:

$$\text{rate of forward reaction} = k_f [H_3O^+][HCO_3^-]$$

and

$$\text{rate of reverse reaction} = k_r [H_2O][H_2CO_3]$$

where the constants k_f and k_r are called the rate constants for, respectively, the forward and reverse reaction and, in each case, the square brackets denote the concentration of the reaction component. (Note the use of 'k' in the lower case for rate constants.)

If we start with just water and carbonic acid, the reverse reaction starts immediately, but, with the formation of bicarbonate, the forward reaction also gets underway. As the reaction proceeds, the rate of the reverse reaction diminishes while that of the forward reaction increases. Eventually the two processes are proceeding at the same rate, and the reaction is at equilibrium:

rate of forward reaction = rate of reverse reaction

$$k_f [H_3O^+][HCO_3^-] = k_r [H_2O][H_2CO_3]$$

If we now change the composition of the system by adding some acid (H_3O^+) or withdrawing some carbonic acid (carbonic acid is removed by the reaction in Equation 2.2; Section 2.4.5), thus changing their 'active masses', the forward rate will exceed the reverse rate and a change in composition will occur until a new equilibrium composition is achieved. Thus the equilibrium composition of a reaction mixture varies according to the quantities of components that are present. This fundamental principle is known as the **law of mass action**.

2.5.2 The equilibrium constant

The **equilibrium constant**, K_{eq}, for a reaction is defined as the ratio of the concentrations of products and reactants (components) when that reaction has reached equilibrium.

$$K_{eq} = \frac{[\text{products}]}{[\text{reactants}]} \tag{2.4}$$

(Note the use of 'K' in the upper case for the equilibrium constant.)

This relationship takes account of the stoichiometry of the reaction, i.e. the *quantitative* relationship between the reactants and the products. Thus the molar concentrations of each of the products of the reaction are multiplied together above the line and are divided by the molar concentration of each of the reactants (below the line). If a reaction equation has two or more molecules of one type on one side of the equation, then the concentration of that component must be multiplied an appropriate number of times. So, for example, in the reaction:

$$A + B \rightleftharpoons 2C$$

$$K_{eq} = \frac{[C][C]}{[A][B]} = \frac{[C]^2}{[A][B]}$$

Thus for the equilibrium

$$H_3O^+ + HCO_3^- \rightleftharpoons H_2O + H_2CO_3$$

$$K_{eq} = \frac{[H_2O][H_2CO_3]}{[H_3O^+][HCO_3^-]}$$

where the concentrations of reaction components are those at equilibrium.

At equilibrium

$$k_f[H_3O^+][HCO_3^-] = k_r[H_2O][H_2CO_3] \quad \text{(see above)}$$

Rearranging this equation

$$\frac{k_f}{k_r} = \frac{[H_2O][H_2CO_3]}{[H_3O^+][HCO_3^-]}$$

It follows therefore that

$$K_{eq} = \frac{k_f}{k_r}$$

Thus the equilibrium constant for a reaction is related directly to the *rate constants for the forward and reverse reactions*, as well as to the *equilibrium concentrations of the reaction components*.

2.5.3 Reaction kinetics

The hydrolysis of ATP occurs spontaneously, but in the absence of a catalyst this reaction is not very fast. Such a reaction is **thermodynamically favourable** because it releases energy, but it is **kinetically inhibited**, meaning that it is slow. Since the uncatalysed reverse reaction (the synthesis of ATP from ADP and phosphate) is extremely slow, the equilibrium point is still well over towards ADP. It is important to distinguish the **kinetics** of a reaction (how quickly it happens), from the **thermodynamics**, which determine whether it happens at all and to what degree. Enzymes are biological catalysts and can affect the kinetics of a reaction, but they do not affect the thermodynamics or the equilibrium point of a reaction. We will return to this subject in Chapter 4.

The term 'stoichiometry' can be applied to both chemical reactions and molecular interactions and is also used to describe the quantitative relationship between the atomic constituents of a compound.

In living biological systems, very few reactions ever reach equilibrium, because the components are continually being resupplied or removed by other reactions, and the rate at which this addition or removal occurs depends on the activities of enzymes. However, such dynamic systems may reach what is called a **steady state**, where overall changes are negligible even though many individual reactions are not at equilibrium. Despite the fact that biological reactions rarely reach equilibrium, it is still important to understand the principles of equilibrium reactions, because this tells us how changes in the concentration of a component will affect a reaction.

> In Chapter 4 we will deal with thermodynamic aspects of enzyme activity, and different catalytic mechanisms are discussed in Chapter 3 (Section 3.7). However, the kinetics of enzyme-catalysed reactions are not dealt with in this course. S204, Book 3 *The Core of Life*, Vol. I, Chapter 2 covers this subject in some depth and provides useful background reading for this course.

2.5.4 The Le Chatelier principle

If a reaction is at equilibrium and we alter the conditions so as to create a new equilibrium state, then the composition of the system will tend to change until that new equilibrium state is attained. (We say 'tend to change', because if the reaction is kinetically inhibited, the change may be too slow to observe or it may never take place.) In 1884, the French chemical engineer and teacher Henri Le Chatelier (Figure 2.26) showed that, in every such case, the new equilibrium state is one that partially reduces the effect of the change that brought it about. This law is known as the **Le Chatelier principle**. His original formulation was somewhat complicated, but a reasonably useful paraphrase of it reads as follows:

> If a system at equilibrium is subjected to a change in pressure or temperature or the concentration of a component, there will be a tendency for a net reaction in the direction that reduces the effect of this change.

Figure 2.26
Henri Le Chatelier (1850–1936).

As far as biologists are concerned, the overall temperature and pressure of living systems (cells, organisms) change very little as biochemical reactions take place, so we do not normally concern ourselves with these parameters. However, the Le Chatelier principle is very relevant for understanding how changes in the concentrations of molecules and ions can affect a reaction and its equilibrium point.

Let us look at how this principle applies to a physiological reaction, the buffering of blood. To simplify this, we shall use an equation that emphasizes the role of carbonate ions (CO_3^{2-}) as a carrier of CO_2:

$$H_2O + CO_2 + CO_3^{2-} \rightleftharpoons 2HCO_3^- \tag{2.5}$$

CO_2, generated by metabolic activity, acts as a weak acid which would cause the blood pH to fall to dangerous levels if it were not promptly removed by excretion from the cells. This CO_2 removal is accomplished by combining it with carbonate ion through the reaction in Equation 2.5. In the tissues, the high local CO_2 concentration forces the reaction to the right. Once the hydrogen carbonate ions reach the lung tissues, where the CO_2 partial pressure is much lower, the reaction reverses, producing CO_2 which is then expelled. Thus, in accordance with the

Le Chatelier principle, the increase in CO_2 concentration in the tissues causes a net reaction such that CO_2 is removed, whilst lower CO_2 levels in the lungs cause a net reaction, the effect of which is to produce CO_2. Because many biochemical reactions are potentially reversible, the Le Chatelier principle is widely applicable in biology (Box 2.6).

Box 2.6   The Le Chatelier principle in biology

Many of the chemical reactions that occur in living organisms are regulated through the Le Chatelier principle. Consider, for example, the binding of oxygen (O_2) to haemoglobin, a process that occurs in vertebrate red blood cells.

The partial pressure of O_2 in the air is 20–26 kPa, sufficient to allow these molecules to be bound by haemoglobin to give a complex known as oxy-haemoglobin:

$$\text{haemoglobin} + O_2 \rightleftharpoons \text{oxy-haemoglobin}$$

In the capillaries, which deliver the blood to the tissues, the O_2 concentration is reduced by about 50% owing to its consumption by the cells. This O_2 removal shifts the equilibrium to the left, releasing the oxygen which can then diffuse into the cells. Carbon monoxide is toxic because it also binds to haemoglobin and so blocks the uptake and transport of O_2. Carbon monoxide binds to haemoglobin 200 times more tightly than does O_2. This sets up a competing equilibrium reaction, which reduces the concentration of free haemoglobin available for the O_2 binding reaction above.

Summary of Section 2.5

1   All reactions are potentially in equilibrium. As a chemical change proceeds, the quantities of the components on one side of the reaction equation decrease, and those on the other side increase. Eventually the reaction reaches an equilibrium state, when no further overall change occurs.

2   The equilibrium composition is independent of the direction from which equilibrium is approached; the labelling of substances as 'reactants' or 'products' is arbitrary.

3   Some reactions effectively go to completion because thermodynamic considerations mean that either the forward reaction or the reverse reaction is negligible.

4   Some reactions take a long time to reach equilibrium, because they are kinetically inhibited. The overall rate of a reaction and its equilibrium position are independent. Enzymes can alter a reaction rate, but not its equilibrium position.

5   The rates of the forward and reverse reaction are governed by the concentrations of the substances reacting, according to the law of mass action; as the reaction proceeds, the magnitudes of these rates approach each other and at equilibrium they become identical.

6   The equilibrium constant for a reaction is related directly to the rate constants for the forward and reverse reactions, as well as to the equilibrium concentrations of the reaction components.

7   Biological systems are rarely at equilibrium, but in a dynamic steady state.

8   If an equilibrium is disturbed by subjecting the system to a change of pressure, temperature, or concentration of a component, then a net reaction will tend to take place that moves the system to a new equilibrium state. The Le Chatelier principle says that this net reaction will occur in the direction that opposes the change.

2.6 pH and pK

pH is a very important parameter in biology. Biological macromolecules, especially proteins, are significantly affected by pH changes, which may result in loss of both their structure and activity. Similarly, the interactions between biological macromolecules, particularly proteins and DNA, as well as the interactions of drugs that bind to such molecules, are dependent on pH. Though the cytosol generally has a pH of about 7.4, there are intracellular compartments in which the pH differs significantly from this value. For example, lysosomes contain hydrolytic enzymes that are optimally active at a pH of about 5 and this pH is maintained inside the organelle by a proton pump in the lysosomal membrane. Finally, in multicellular organisms, certain parts of the body may have a pH that differs from 7.4. An obvious example is the interior of the mammalian stomach, though it is strictly outside the organism (being continuous with the outside environment). Here the pH normally ranges from 1–3, but may be higher in some pathological conditions.

In this section, we will revise briefly the meaning of pH, its relationship with pK and the significance of these two parameters for biological molecules such as proteins. The equations that relate these quantities are given in Box 2.7.

Box 2.7   The relationship between pH, pK and K_{eq}

pH is defined as:

$$pH = \log_{10} \frac{1}{[H^+]} = -\log_{10} [H^+] \tag{2.6}$$

The ionization equilibrium of a weak acid is given by:

$$HA \rightleftharpoons H^+ + A^-$$

Note that HA and A$^-$ are described as a conjugate acid and base pair.

The equilibrium constant, K_{eq}, for the ionization of HA is:

$$K_{eq} = \frac{[H^+][A^-]}{[HA]} \tag{2.7}$$

By analogy with Equation 2.6, the pK of an acid is defined as:

$$pK = \log_{10} \frac{1}{K_{eq}} = -\log_{10} K_{eq} \tag{2.8}$$

From Equation 2.7, we can see that:

when $[A^-] = [HA]$, $K_{eq} = [H^+]$

Substituting $[H^+]$ for K_{eq} in Equation 2.8, we get:

$$pK = -\log_{10} [H^+] = pH$$

In other words, the pK of an acid is the pH at which it is half dissociated ($[A^-] = [HA]$).

Rearranging Equation 2.7:

$$\frac{1}{[H^+]} = \frac{[A^-]}{K_{eq} [HA]} \tag{2.9}$$

Taking the logarithm of both sides of Equation 2.9 gives us:

$$\log_{10} \frac{1}{[H^+]} = \log_{10} \frac{1}{K_{eq}} + \log_{10} \frac{[A^-]}{[HA]} \tag{2.10}$$

Substituting pH for $\log_{10} \frac{1}{[H^+]}$ and pK for $\log_{10} \frac{1}{K_{eq}}$ into Equation 2.10 yields:

$$pH = pK + \log_{10} \frac{[A^-]}{[HA]} \tag{2.11}$$

Equation 2.11, which relates pH to the concentrations of acid (HA) and base (A^-), is known as the **Henderson–Hasselbach equation**.

The parameter pK, which you encountered briefly in Section 2.3, is fundamental to an understanding of the behaviour of biological molecules in solution, since the degree of ionization or dissociation of a molecule or functional group at a given pH is determined by its pK. To illustrate the significance of this relationship, we shall start by considering the carboxyl group in acetic acid, which ionizes to form acetate ions according to the following equilibrium and which has a pK of 4.77:

$$CH_3COOH + H_2O \rightleftharpoons CH_3COO^- + H_3O^+ \tag{2.12}$$

○ If we have a solution in which exactly half of the acetic acid has dissociated into acetate ions, i.e. $[CH_3COOH] = [CH_3COO^-]$, what can you say about the pH of that solution?

● When the acid is half dissociated, pH = pK = 4.77 (as deduced in Box 2.7). Alternatively, we could use the Henderson–Hasselbach equation (Equation 2.11) to answer this question:

$$pH = pK + \log_{10} 1$$

$$\log_{10} 1 = 0, \text{ therefore pH = p}K.$$

If we disturb the dynamic equilibrium in Equation 2.12 by lowering the pH (i.e. adding H_3O^+) to say 2.0, the equilibrium is shifted to the left so that most of the acid is in the undissociated form, as acetic acid molecules. Conversely, raising the pH to say pH 7.4 shifts the equilibrium to the right, so the predominant species is acetate. Thus in mammalian blood, which has a pH of 7.4, any acetic acid present exists predominantly as acetate rather than acetic acid.

The pK rule for predicting the ionization of a carboxyl group is as follows:

▶ When the solution pH is *below* the pK of the molecule, then the *undissociated* (unionized) form predominates.

▶ When the solution pH is *the same as* the pK of the molecule, then [*undissociated*] = [*dissociated*].

▶ When the solution pH is *above* the pK of the molecule, then the *dissociated* (ionized) form predominates.

Similar considerations apply to compounds containing amino groups. Consider the ionization of methylamine, for which the pK is 10.66.

$$CH_3NH_2 + H_3O^+ \rightleftharpoons CH_3NH_3^+ + H_2O \tag{2.13}$$

Above pH 10.66, the equilibrium in Equation 2.13 is shifted to the left and the non-ionized form predominates; below pH 10.66, the equilibrium is shifted to the right and the positively charged, ionized form predominates.

Thus if we know the pH of a solution and the pK of a molecule or group, then we can calculate the relative concentrations of the ionized and unionized forms of the molecule in that solution. This is a very useful thing to know since many properties of molecules, including reactivity, structure, solubility and interactions with other molecules, are affected by ionization and charge.

2.6.1 The effect of pH on proteins

Now let us look at how these factors affect a large molecule, such as a protein in solution. Most proteins have a free carboxyl group at the C-terminus and a free amino group at the N-terminus. In addition, the side-chains of aspartic acid and glutamic acid also have carboxyl groups, while those of arginine and lysine have amino groups. (Refer back to Figure 2.17 to see the structures of these amino acids.) The overall charge on any one protein depends on the proportion of acidic and basic amino acids and on the structure of that protein, and varies with pH. At pH 7.4, both the carboxyl groups and the amino groups are predominantly ionized. (Note that, in these circumstances, aspartic acid and glutamic acid are more correctly referred to as aspartate and glutamate, respectively.) At other pH values, the charge on the acidic and basic groups are different (Figure 2.27).

☐ At pH 7.4, what will be the net charge on a protein that has more acidic amino acid residues than basic residues?

◼ It will be negative. The large number of negatively charged acidic amino acid residues will outweigh the smaller number of positively charged basic amino acid residues.

☐ What will happen to such a protein if the pH falls?

◼ The net negative charge will be reduced, as fewer carboxyl groups and more amino groups will be ionized.

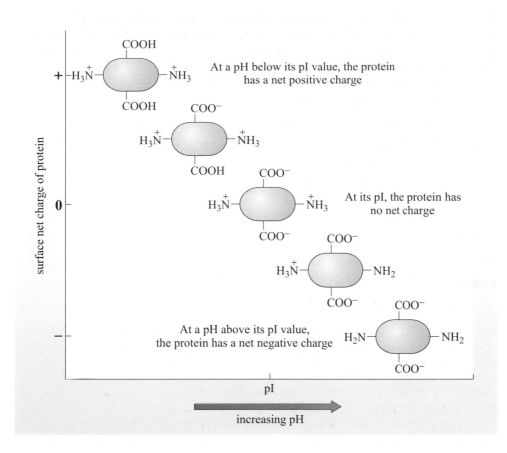

Figure 2.27
The influence of pH on the net charge of a protein. Proteins have a number of free carboxyl and amino groups. The ionization of each of the groups depends primarily on the pH of the solution, but may be affected by surrounding groups. In this example, a protein is illustrated with just two free amino and two free carboxyl groups. In alkaline solution it has a net negative charge, and in acid solution it carries a net positive charge. At some pH in between, the positive and negative charges cancel each other out and the protein has no net charge. This pH is called the isoelectric point of the protein (pI). pI varies from one protein to another, depending on the amino acid composition and the protein's structure.

The three-dimensional shape or conformation of a protein in an aqueous medium depends both on the pH and the ionic composition of the medium surrounding it. Changing either of these variables can alter the shape of the protein dramatically. Some changes have reversible effects, while others are irreversible. In order to know the form and function of any given macromolecule in the cell, it is necessary to specify its environment and know its relationship to neighbouring molecules. Whether a particular protein is part of a supramolecular complex, embedded in a membrane, or relatively freely dissolved in the cell cytosol will profoundly affect how it behaves.

2.6.2 Buffers maintain the pH within cells and extracellular fluids

Most biological systems will function only within a quite narrow range of conditions, and their activity can vary widely within that range. Maintenance of the correct pH inside the cell, and outside the cell too in multicellular organisms, is vital because pH alters the ionization and charge on molecules such as amino acids. A change in charge disturbs protein structure, and leads to malfunction. In humans, for example, only a small change in blood pH can be tolerated (pH 7.4 ± 0.3) and variations outside this range lead to coma and death as vital proteins lose their structure and function. **Buffers**, consisting of a weak acid and its conjugate base or a weak base and its conjugate acid, resist changes in pH and prevent dangerous extremes of pH in biological systems.

To illustrate how a buffer works, we will consider the bicarbonate buffer system, H_2CO_3 / HCO_3^- (Equations 2.1 and 2.2, repeated below), which is a common *extracellular* buffer.

$$H_3O^+ + HCO_3^- \rightleftharpoons H_2O + H_2CO_3 \qquad (2.1)$$

$$H_2CO_3 \rightleftharpoons CO_2 + H_2O \qquad (2.2)$$

This buffer system is responsible for maintaining a stable pH in extracellular fluids and in vertebrate blood plasma. Two activities tend to disturb the pH of blood.

1   Protons (H^+) produced during metabolism tend to lower blood pH.

2   Exhalation of carbon dioxide and water from the lungs tends to remove protons, and so increase blood pH.

☐   Explain in terms of Equations 2.1 and 2.2, how breathing out carbon dioxide disturbs blood pH.

◼   Exhaling CO_2 causes a shift in the equilibrium in Equation 2.2, so that the level of carbonic acid (H_2CO_3) in the blood falls. Reduction in carbonic acid shifts the equilibrium in Equation 2.1 so that the levels of hydronium ions and bicarbonate fall. A lowering of H_3O^+ concentration equates to a rise in pH.

How is this effect countered? The pK of carbonic acid is 6.1, i.e. lower than the prevailing blood pH of 7.4. Consequently, at pH 7.4, the dissociated species (i.e. the bicarbonate) predominates, and in fact the ratio of $[HCO_3^-] : [H_2CO_3]$ is 20 : 1. The large excess of hydronium and bicarbonate ions compared to carbonic acid means that when water and carbon dioxide are exhaled, the resultant decrease in the concentration of carbonic acid does not greatly disturb the $[H_3O^+]$ and $[HCO_3^-]$ in the blood.

The most common *intracellular* buffer is $H_2PO_4^- / HPO_4^{2-}$, though organic phosphates such as ATP also have a buffering role inside cells.

☐   What other component of cells could potentially buffer against changes in pH?

◼   Proteins can absorb and release protons on their acidic and basic groups and therefore act as buffers.

Although not their primary function, the buffering capacity of proteins can be significant, as they are present at high concentrations both in the cytosol and in extracellular fluids such as vertebrate blood plasma.

The ability of a molecule to buffer pH is most significant around its pK. Hence bicarbonate (pK 6.1) is useful for buffering at pH values around neutral. A carboxyl group on a protein (pK 4–5) is not so useful for buffering at neutral pH; however, the pH of some subcellular compartments varies significantly from neutrality. As mentioned already, the environment inside lysosomes is acidic (around pH 5) and at this pH, the buffering capacity of the proteins becomes increasingly important.

Summary of Section 2.6

1 pH affects the degree of ionization of different groups, particularly carboxyl and amino groups, and thus affects the charge of molecules containing these groups.

2 The pK value of a particular group is the pH at which 50% of the groups are ionized or dissociated.

3 The charge of a protein at neutral pH depends principally on its amino acid composition and its structure. Alterations in pH affect protein charge, structure and function.

4 A buffer consists of a weak acid and its conjugate base (or vice versa) and resists changes in pH in a solution. In vertebrates, the extracellular pH is buffered principally by the bicarbonate system, whilst the pH of the cytosol is buffered principally by the hydrogen phosphate system. Proteins can also contribute to intracellular buffering in some circumstances.

2.7 Intermolecular and intramolecular interactions

The chemical bonds shown in the molecular structures in Box 2.1 are all covalent bonds. In this section, we turn our attention to what are collectively called 'non-covalent bonds'. This general term encompasses several different types of interatomic interaction that are particularly important in the structural conformation and function of macromolecules. These interactions can occur between different molecules (intermolecular) or within an individual molecule (intramolecular). They are involved in practically every biological process, including the folding of proteins, DNA structure, protein–protein and protein–DNA interactions, assembly of membranes, enzyme–substrate complexes, catalysis and interactions between macromolecules and small ligands.

Covalent bonds are individually much stronger than non-covalent bonds and consequently are more stable. To make or break covalent bonds, it is necessary to overcome an activation energy barrier, and in biological systems enzymes function by lowering this energy barrier. In contrast, non-covalent bonds are individually weak and transient (Table 2.6). However, the formation of many non-covalent bonds can often result in an overall interaction that is strong. In Chapter 3, you will be looking at the conformation of proteins (their secondary and tertiary structure), which depends on multiple non-covalent bonds and is just as much a feature of the protein as its primary structure, which depends on covalent bonds.

Table 2.6 The bond energies of different bond types.

Bond type	Bond energy / kJ mol^{-1}
covalent	170–460
ionic	21
hydrogen bond	4–29
hydrophobic	4
van der Waals	2–4

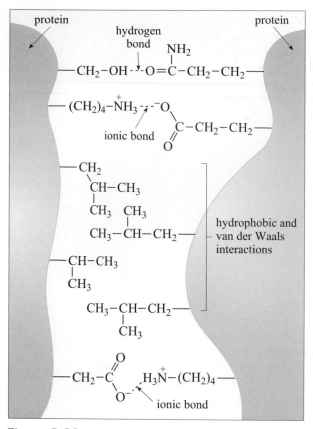

Figure 2.28
Schematic of two hypothetical proteins illustrating the four types of non-covalent interaction.

We shall consider four classes of non-covalent bond that can form between molecules in aqueous solution: ionic bonds, van der Waals interactions, hydrogen bonds and hydrophobic interactions. These interactions have been represented schematically, at the interface between two hypothetical proteins, in Figure 2.28 and are dealt with in turn below. Of these four types of non-covalent interaction, all but hydrophobic interactions depend in some way on **electrostatic** forces, i.e. the attraction that occurs between parts of molecules that have opposite charge (sometimes partial and/or transient).

2.7.1 Ionic bonds

As we noted in Section 2.6, some functional groups carry a charge. For example, at pH 7.4, carboxyl and amino groups are predominantly ionized (i.e. $-COO^-$ and $-NH_3^+$). Electrostatic interactions can occur between these oppositely charged groups. The association of a positively charged group and a negatively charged group constitutes an **ionic bond**, also sometimes referred to as an **ion pair** or **salt bridge**.

○ What can you say about the pK of the groups commonly involved in an ionic bond?

● The pK of one of them will be lower than the pH of the solution and the pK of the other one will be higher.

Ionic bonds are potentially quite strong (see Table 2.6), but in aqueous solution the strength of these interactions is less than might be expected. This is because the charged groups are highly solvated (see Section 2.1.3). The hydration shell formed around the ion by water molecules has the effect of spreading the ionic charge over the volume of the solvated complex, and reducing the strength of the interaction. In proteins, some ion pairs are buried deep within the folded protein. Here, water molecules may be excluded and a strong electrostatic interaction forms between the unsolvated ions.

2.7.2 Van der Waals forces

Van der Waals forces are weak interactions between molecules, and were first described by Johannes Diderik van der Waals (1837–1923), a Dutch physicist who won the Nobel Prize for Physics for his work on attractive forces between molecules. Van der Waals forces arise between electrically neutral molecules when the atoms are very close together, such that they disturb the distribution of the electrons in nearby atoms. Although uniform over time, the distribution of electrons in a molecule varies slightly and at any one moment there may be a slight excess negative charge in one region. This asymmetric distribution of electrons results in a dipole, where one area of a molecule has a slight negative charge and the other a corresponding positive charge. The presence of a region with negative charge on an atom induces a net positive charge in an atom in a neighbouring molecule, resulting in an attractive force. Thus van der Waals forces arise from electrostatic interactions between induced dipoles. Unlike the permanent dipole that exists in water molecules (described in Section 2.1.1), in van der Waals forces the dipoles are very transient and they oscillate between the neighbouring molecules.

Van der Waals forces are generated only when molecules approach sufficiently closely to disturb the electrons of the neighbouring molecule. However, molecules cannot approach each other too closely because when the electron clouds overlap a repulsive force is encountered. This means that two molecules will only be attracted by van der Waals forces if they have highly complementary shapes. When attraction occurs, many weak van der Waals forces are produced, without the repulsion that occurs if protruding atoms start to impinge on the other molecule. This is why the shapes of, for example, polypeptide hormones and their receptors are complementary.

2.7.3 Hydrogen bonding

Refer back to Section 2.1.2 to refresh your memory on the subject of hydrogen bonding.

As discussed previously, a hydrogen bond can occur when a hydrogen atom that is covalently bound to a strongly electronegative atom (the donor group), is close to another strongly electronegative atom bearing a non-bonding pair of electrons (the acceptor atom). The attractive force is electrostatic in nature, arising because of the proximity of the permanent dipole in the donor group and the non-bonding pair of electrons on the acceptor atom. As explained in Section 2.1.2, only hydrogen is small enough to permit the necessary close approach of the acceptor atom.

Hydrogen bonds are a particularly strong type of intermolecular interaction, though still much weaker than covalent bonds (Table 2.6). In biological molecules, the electronegative atoms of the donor group and the acceptor are usually oxygen and/or nitrogen atoms and the distance between these atoms is in the range 260–310 pm (Table 2.7).

Table 2.7   Lengths of some hydrogen bonds.

Bond	Length / pm*
O—H---O	270
O—H---O$^-$	263
O—H---N	288
N—H---O	304
N$^+$—H---O	293
N—H---N	310

*1 pm $= 10^{-12}$ m $= 0.01$ Å.

○ Looking at Table 2.7, compare the length of the hydrogen bond between N—H and O with that between N$^+$—H and O. Explain the difference.

● The positive charge on the N means that the dipole in the N$^+$—H group is greater than that in N—H. As a result the partial positive charge ($\delta+$) on the H atom is greater and exerts a stronger attractive force on the acceptor O atom, making the hydrogen bond shorter (293 pm compared to 304 pm).

An important feature of hydrogen bonds is that they are highly directional, with the hydrogen atom sandwiched between the two electronegative atoms in a linear array. However, slight deviations from this linear geometry can occur. Hydrogen bonds are critically important for the base pairing of DNA and RNA (described in Chapter 5) and in stabilizing the secondary structure of proteins (discussed in the next chapter). Indeed proteins tend to fold such that internal hydrogen bonding is maximized. Of course, soluble macromolecules may also form hydrogen bonds with water molecules, via groups that are exposed to this solvent.

2.7.4 Hydrophobic interactions

In Section 2.1.3, when we discussed the solvent properties of water, we noted that hydrophobic molecules do not dissolve readily in water. This is because hydrophobic molecules or groups are neither charged nor polar and therefore cannot interact with the polar water molecules. In aqueous conditions, hydrophobic molecules would tend to disrupt the network of hydrogen bonds between the water molecules. Since formation of the hydrogen bond network in water is energetically favourable, hydrophobic molecules are 'excluded' and coalesce to minimize contact with water molecules. Associations between hydrophobic groups are therefore 'driven' by the need to adopt an energetically favourable state.

Hydrophobic interactions result from the tendency of water to exclude hydrophobic groups and molecules and they are unique to an aqueous environment. These interactions are comparable in strength to van der Waals forces but weak compared to hydrogen bonds (Table 2.7) and, unlike hydrogen bonds, they lack directionality.

In the aqueous environment of the cytosol, proteins and nucleic acids, which have many different hydrophobic and hydrophilic groups, automatically adopt a conformation such that their hydrophobic groups become tucked away towards the interior of the molecule, out of contact with the water. Here they interact with one another, thereby strengthening the three-dimensional shape of the polymer molecule. Van der Waals forces between the buried groups can also stabilize the structure. The hydrophilic groups are exposed on the surface of the molecule, and are either solvated or form hydrogen bonds with individual water molecules, further enhancing the stability of the folded molecule. Figure 2.29a shows a model of a soluble protein molecule (myoglobin) in which the hydrophobic side-chains have been highlighted to show their location at the centre of the folded structure. In contrast, hydrophilic side-chains decorate the exterior surface of the protein (Figure 2.29b).

Most importantly, hydrophobic interactions are responsible for the structural integrity of biological membranes. The lipid bilayer that gives membranes their overall structure is formed from amphipathic lipid molecules (see Section 2.1.3). This bilayer, essentially an aggregate of lipid molecules, is stabilized by hydrophobic interactions between the hydrophobic parts of the lipid molecules, which form its core. The hydrophilic parts of the lipids are presented on the membrane surfaces, where they interact with each other and with the surrounding water molecules. In Chapter 6 you will learn about the structure and composition of membranes.

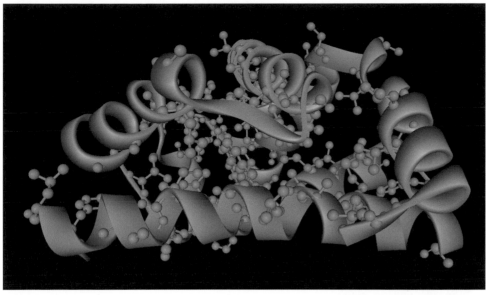

(a)

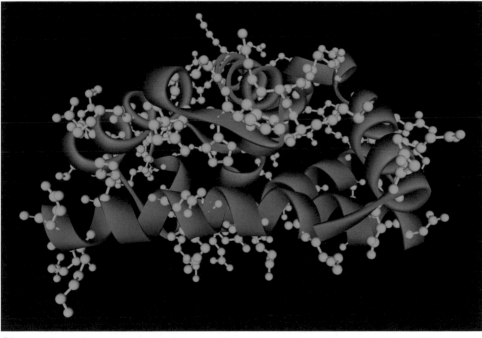

(b)

Figure 2.29 Myoglobin (pdb file 1azi), a globular protein, is shown with the polypeptide backbone in purple. Strongly hydrophobic amino acid side-chains (coloured orange) are buried in the centre of the protein (a), whilst hydrophilic residues (side-chains coloured green) are predominantly exposed on the outer surface of the folded protein (b).

2.7.5 Molecular interactions and binding affinity

As we noted above, a number of weak non-covalent bonds may together produce a strong interaction between two molecules. The interactions between different molecules (proteins, nucleic acids, hormones, etc.) control almost all cellular events and we frequently need to know how strongly one molecule binds to another – a property known as **binding affinity**. For example, if we were trying to design a drug to displace a hormone from its receptor, it would be necessary for the drug to bind to the receptor with a similar affinity to the hormone; otherwise it would not be able to compete effectively for the binding site. In such an example, both the drug and the hormone are **ligands** for the receptor in question. Below we look at how the affinity of ligand binding to its receptor can be determined. However, the general approach outlined here can be applied to the interaction between any two molecules.

One of the more frequently encountered measures used to determine the ability of a ligand to bind to a receptor is the ligand's **equilibrium dissociation constant**, K_D. (Note that this is a similar idea to the equilibrium constant for a reaction, K_{eq}.)

When a ligand, L, interacts with a receptor protein, R, it forms a complex, RL. These three species are in dynamic equilibrium:

$$R + L \rightleftharpoons RL$$

The extent of formation of the receptor–ligand complex depends on the strength of the molecular interactions between the ligand and the receptor; the stronger the interactions, the more RL is formed. The dissociation constant, K_D, is a measure of the extent to which the ligand–receptor complex dissociates to free ligand and free receptor and is defined as:

$$K_D = \frac{[R][L]}{[RL]}$$

where [R], [L] and [RL] are the concentrations of receptor, ligand and receptor–ligand complex, respectively.

At a purely qualitative level, it can be seen from the above that the weaker the binding of ligand to the receptor, the smaller the value of [RL], and the larger the values of [R] and [L]. Thus, *large* values of K_D represent *weak* binding of the ligand to its receptor, whereas *small* values represent *strong* binding. Values of K_D for binding of biological ligands to their receptors range from 10^{-7} to 10^{-12} mol l^{-1}.

Values of K_D are usually determined by incubating, in separate experiments, a constant amount of receptor with increasing, known concentrations of a radio-labelled version of the ligand. In each experiment, a different amount of receptor–ligand complex is formed, which can be measured accurately via its radioactivity. These experiments are almost always carried out under conditions in which the concentration of ligand used is vastly greater than that of the receptor (i.e. the ligand is *in excess*). In this situation, the amount of bound ligand is minimal compared to the total drug concentration used. So, the concentration of free ligand, [L], in the incubations can be assumed to be equivalent to the total ligand concentration used in the experiment. Thus, both [L] and [RL] are known.

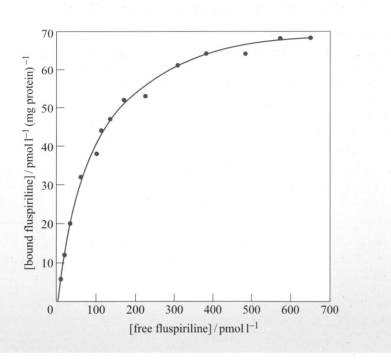

Figure 2.30
A plot of bound drug concentration against free drug concentration for the antipsychotic agent fluspirilene binding to a dopamine receptor preparation.

Figure 2.30 shows a typical plot of bound ligand concentration, [RL], versus free ligand concentration, [L]. The plot shown is for binding of a drug, the antipsychotic agent fluspirilene, to a dopamine receptor.

All that remains, in order to calculate K_D, is to determine [R]. As it turns out, it is not necessary to know this value, because the concentration of receptor used in each experiment, $[R]_{tot}$, is kept constant, and in each case is equal to the sum of [R] and [RL]. Using this relationship, together with the equation for K_D, it is possible to derive (though we won't do so here) the Scatchard equation, which is:

$$\frac{[RL]}{[L]} = -\frac{[RL]}{K_D} + \frac{[R]_{tot}}{K_D} \qquad (2.14)$$

A plot of bound ligand concentration divided by free ligand concentration, against bound ligand concentration, i.e. [RL]/[L] against [RL], is known as a **Scatchard plot** and gives a straight line. The slope of the line equals $-1/K_D$ and the intercept on the y-axis is $[R]_{tot}/K_D$. Figure 2.31 shows a Scatchard plot of the data for fluspirilene, from Figure 2.30. Thus K_D and $[R]_{tot}$ can be determined from a knowledge of [RL] and [L].

It is important to appreciate that since values of K_D are determined *in vitro*, not in whole cells, they are purely a measure of the chemical interaction between a ligand and its receptor. No measure of biological activity or response is involved. Nevertheless, a comparison of K_D values for, for example, a number of different drugs may provide a useful means of identifying those drugs that bind strongly to a receptor.

Figure 2.31
Scatchard plot for the binding of
fluspirilene to its receptor.

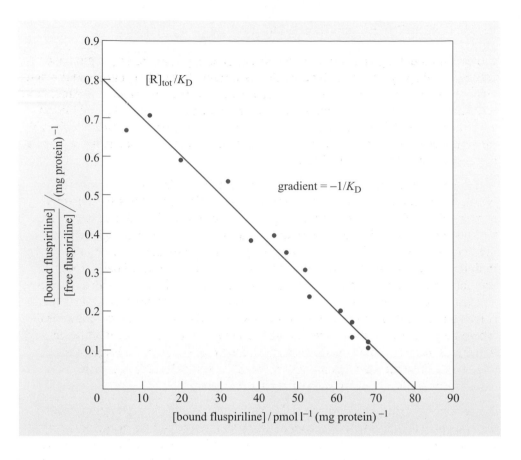

Summary of Section 2.7

1   Non-covalent bonds are extremely important in biology; they stabilize
    macromolecules, and are involved in all intermolecular interactions.
    Although individually weak, non-covalent bonds can collectively produce
    a strong interaction.

2   Ionic bonds are formed between groups with opposite charge in aqueous
    solutions.

3   Van der Waals forces are created by oscillating dipoles on closely apposed
    atoms. For these forces to be significant, the interacting molecules must have
    complementary shapes.

4   Hydrogen bonds are formed by a hydrogen atom positioned in an
    approximately colinear conformation, between two electronegative atoms.
    They are very important in water and in stabilizing the structures of proteins
    and nucleic acids.

5   Hydrophobic interactions occur between non-polar groups, as such groups
    are excluded from the aqueous environment and seek energetically more
    favourable conformations. Hydrophobic groups are typically folded into the
    interior of proteins.

6   The dissociation constant, K_D, is a measure of the binding affinity between two
    molecules. A large K_D value indicates a low binding affinity.

2.8 Molecular modelling

Molecular modelling is a very diverse subject, ranging from the acquisition and subsequent display of molecular coordinates through to highly accurate simulation using theoretically derived values. A related area described as 'molecular simulation' uses molecular modelling techniques to describe the behaviour and properties of collections of molecules on a macroscopic scale. 'Molecular dynamics' deals with the time-dependent properties of collections of molecules. The latter two methods are beyond the scope of this discussion.

A number of experimental techniques, such as X-ray diffraction and structural NMR, have been partnered with powerful computational methods to construct accurate three-dimensional models of proteins, nucleic acids and their complexes with various ligands. In such cases, molecular modelling is not being used to predict a structure on the basis of properties of the atoms that make up the individual macromolecules, but, in conjunction with experimental data, it allows accurate calculation of parameters and representation of those experimental data to construct the structure of the macromolecule. A number of structures have been solved and their details are deposited in data banks (such as the Protein Data Bank) where they are accessible to the scientific community through the worldwide web. At various stages in this course, you will use the molecular modelling program ViewerLite™ to view and manipulate many different molecules and molecular assemblies that have been retrieved from such a source.

There is no substitute for practical laboratory experience, but computer modelling methods play an important role both as an aid in interpreting experimental results and as a means of explaining these results. Molecular modelling is now as widely used by biologists as it is by chemists. Figure 2.32, for example, shows a computer model of the protein interleukin-8.

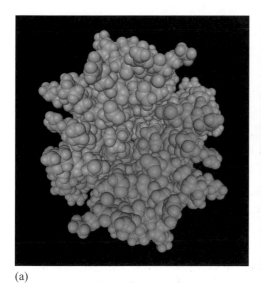
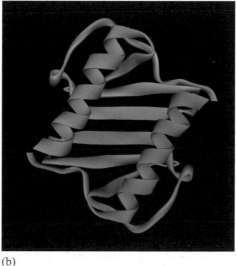

(a) (b)

Figure 2.32   The structure of human interleukin-8 (pdb file 1il8), a homodimer. The molecular modelling program ViewerLite™ has been used to create these representations, in which the two identical subunits have been differently coloured. In (a) the protein is presented in space-filling format, i.e. all atoms are included and defined by their van der Waals radii. In (b) the polypeptide backbone is represented as a solid ribbon and it is possible to identify elements of secondary structure.

> **Molecular modelling 2**
>
> Go to the Study Skills file: *Molecular modelling 2*. You have already started to learn how to use the molecular modelling programme ViewerLite™, and later in this course you will use this programme to investigate increasingly complex molecules, including proteins and nucleic acids. In this activity, however, you will watch the video 'Probing proteins', which explains how the data on protein structure are derived using X-ray diffraction and NMR techniques.

Learning outcomes for Chapter 2

When you have studied this chapter, you should be able to:

2.1   Define and use each of the terms printed in **bold** in the text.

2.2   Explain the properties and function of water in biological systems in terms of the chemistry of this molecule.

2.3   Represent and interpret simple molecular structures, including use of the flying-wedge notation.

2.4   Explain the different types of stereoisomerism and how they arise.

2.5   Describe the basic composition of a typical cell and the different types of molecules and macromolecules found in cells.

2.6   Describe the ionic composition of cells and the roles played by the different ions.

2.7   Define the equilibrium constant for a reaction, relate this to rate of reaction and apply the Le Chatelier principle.

2.8   Explain the relationship between pH and pK, and how pH is buffered in biological systems.

2.9   Explain how binding affinity is determined and describe, with examples, the different kinds of non-covalent interactions that occur between and within molecules.

2.10 Use the ViewerLite™ package to view and manipulate electronic three-dimensional models of simple molecules.

2.11 Describe the principles of X-ray diffraction and NMR and how these techniques are applied to the study of protein structure.

Questions for Chapter 2

Question 2.1

Describe the hydrogen bonding network that exists in water. How does it arise? Give an example of how this hydrogen bonding affects the physical properties of water.

Question 2.2

How many chiral carbon atoms are there in leucine and isoleucine? Draw a representation of L-leucine, using the flying-wedge format.

Question 2.3

(a) What is a buffer and why are buffers important in biological systems?

(b) Describe the biological importance of bicarbonate ions (HCO_3^-) and hydrogen phosphate ions (HPO_4^{2-}).

Question 2.4

What will be the charge of the following tetrapeptides at pH 7.4? Explain your answers.

(a) Ala-Asp-Gln-Tyr; (b) Arg-Glu-Lys-Gly.

Question 2.5

Draw the structure adopted by glutamic acid in aqueous solution at pH 7.4.

Question 2.6

A hormone dissociates from its receptor with $K_D = 10^{-9}$ mol l^{-1}. Suppose you have a small peptide inhibitor (M_r 1200), which interferes with hormone–receptor binding and binds to the receptor with $K_D = 10^{-8}$ mol l^{-1}. Which of these two molecules binds with the higher affinity to the receptor?

In a mixture of the inhibitor and the receptor, 50% of the receptor has inhibitor bound. What is the concentration of free (unbound) inhibitor in this mixture? Give your answer in µg l^{-1}.

References

Johnson, W. C. (1990) Protein secondary structure and circular dichroism: A practical guide, *Proteins: Structure, Function and Genetics*, **7**, pp. 205–214.

Woody, R. W. (1995) Circular dichroism, *Methods in Enzymology*, **246** (Biochemical Spectroscopy), pp. 34–71.

3 PROTEINS

3.1 Introduction

Proteins are the 'doers' of the cell. They are huge in number and variety and diverse in structure and function, serving as both the structural building blocks and the functional machinery of the cell. Just about every process in every cell requires specific proteins.

Let us begin by listing some of the basic cellular processes and the role that proteins play.

▶ *Chemical catalysis*   Enzymes, which are responsible for catalysing biological reactions, are the largest functional group of proteins. Whilst there are thousands of different enzymes, all catalysing different reactions, they do have some features in common and can often be identified as members of a particular family of enzymes.

▶ *Mechanical support*   Typically, support is provided by proteins, e.g. the cytoskeletal proteins inside the cell and the extracellular matrix proteins outside the cell.

▶ *Communication*   The signals within and between cells (e.g. cytokines) and the apparatus for recognizing and interpreting or reacting to signals (receptors and transducers) are mainly proteins.

▶ *Adhesion*   Cell surface proteins mediate contact between cells and between a cell and the extracellular matrix (which is also made up of proteins).

▶ *Movement*   Proteins generate movement in a cell (motor proteins).

▶ *Defence*   Antibodies (immunoglobulins) are proteins that recognize specific targets (usually proteins themselves). This facility is critical for an immune response.

▶ *Transport*   Proteins are key molecules in the transport of substances both within a cell and to and from the cell.

▶ *Storage*   A number of proteins serve to store small molecules or ions; for example, ferritin binds iron and stores it in the liver.

You will come across many examples in this course of proteins performing the functions outlined above, and the molecular basis for various cellular processes will be examined in some detail. The basic principles of protein structure and function, which are reviewed in this chapter, are crucial to understanding how proteins perform their various roles.

The huge diversity in the functions of proteins is reflected in the specialization of these molecules. As you will see in this chapter, every protein optimally performs a particular job and the key to how it does so is its structure. The refinement of protein structure and optimization of protein function are driven by evolutionary pressures. Mutations at the DNA level that result in a change in protein structure and function will persist if they enhance survival or are not detrimental to the organism.

Proteins come in as many different shapes and sizes (Figure 3.1) as they have functions. A broad distinction is made between **globular proteins** and **fibrous proteins**. Globular proteins are a particularly diverse group that includes enzymes, receptors and transport proteins, and are characterized by a roughly spherical compact shape. Fibrous proteins are elongated and rod-like (e.g. collagen, represented in Figure 3.1) and often have a structural role. Most of the proteins discussed in this chapter are globular proteins, which reflects both their number and the fact that they lend themselves to structural analysis by X-ray diffraction and NMR (described in the activity *Molecular modelling 2* at the end of the previous chapter).

In this chapter, we will consider aspects of the structure of proteins and illustrate how, through their interactions with other cellular components, they can function as dynamic molecular machines. We will begin by exploring the three-dimensional nature of proteins, reviewing some of their biochemistry and the biophysical rules that determine their structure and studying key structural elements that are common to many proteins. The molecular modelling program ViewerLite™ is used to help you study proteins in three dimensions, in three molecular modelling activities. You will encounter these activities as you progress through the chapter. The relationship between protein structure and function is explored using as examples a variety of different proteins, including enzymes, signalling proteins and transport proteins. All proteins bind other substances, often other proteins or organic molecules or inorganic ions. These interactions are integral to a protein's function and their specificity and affinity are critically determined by the protein's structure. This aspect is discussed at some length. The chapter finishes with a consideration of some of the techniques employed in studying protein–protein interactions.

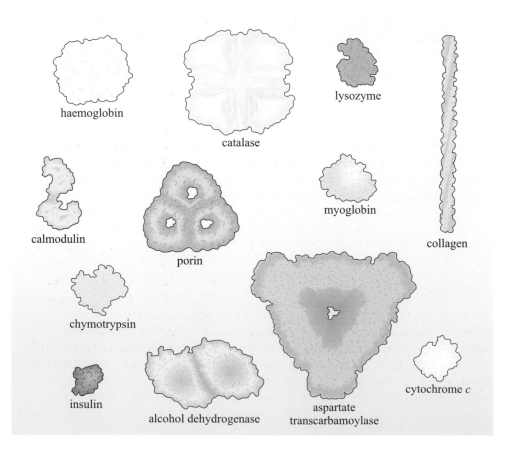

Figure 3.1
A few of the many different proteins represented in a highly schematic form and according to their relative sizes.

3.2 The three-dimensional nature of proteins

Proteins are made up of one or more polypeptide chains, polymers of amino acid residues. In Chapter 2, you encountered the 20 amino acids found in all proteins. The structure that a polypeptide adopts is determined by the component amino acid units – both their chemical properties and the order in which they occur in the polymer – and by the structure of the peptide bond that links them.

Protein structure is described in terms of four levels of organization: primary, secondary, tertiary and quaternary. The linear sequence of amino acids in the polymer is its primary structure and the conformations that the polypeptide adopts are described as secondary structure. The arrangement of elements of secondary structure in a folded polypeptide defines its tertiary structure, and, finally, the quaternary structure describes the association of two or more folded polypeptides in multisubunit proteins. In this section, we will begin by considering the structure of the peptide bond, and then go on to look at each of the levels of protein structure in turn.

3.2.1 The peptide bond and primary structure of proteins

The **primary structure** of a protein is defined as the sequence of amino acids of which it is composed. This sequence ultimately determines the shape that the protein adopts, according to the spatial limitations on the arrangement of the atoms in the protein, the chemical properties of the component amino acid residues, and the protein's environment.

The peptide bonds that link amino acid residues in a polypeptide are formed in a condensation reaction between the acidic carboxyl group of one amino acid and the basic amino group of another amino acid, as described in Chapter 2 (Section 2.3.4). In the context of a peptide, the amide group (CO—NH) is referred to as the **peptide group**.

Crucial to an understanding of protein structure is a knowledge of the structure of the peptide bond. Linus Pauling, in the 1930s, used X-ray diffraction to examine the nature of the peptide bond formed between two amino acids. He reported that the peptide group (CO—NH) has *a rigid planar structure*. This structure is due to interactions between electrons of the double bond of the carbonyl group and those of the C—N bond (Figure 3.2) such that the latter acquires partial (about 40%) double-bond properties. This effect is an example of **resonance** which can be thought of as a sharing of electrons between bonds. Since single bonds between two atoms are longer than double bonds between the same two atoms, the lengths of the C—N and C=O bonds in the peptide group differ from those observed for these bonds in other contexts where resonance does not occur. Thus the partial double bond character of C—N in the peptide group means that this bond is shorter than would be predicted for a C—N single bond, whilst the C=O bond, having a partial single bond character due to resonance, is longer than would be predicted for a C=O double bond. The bond lengths in the peptide group are indicated in Figure 3.3. Compare the C—N bond of the peptide group with that between N and C_α (the C atom to which the amino group and carboxyl group are attached).

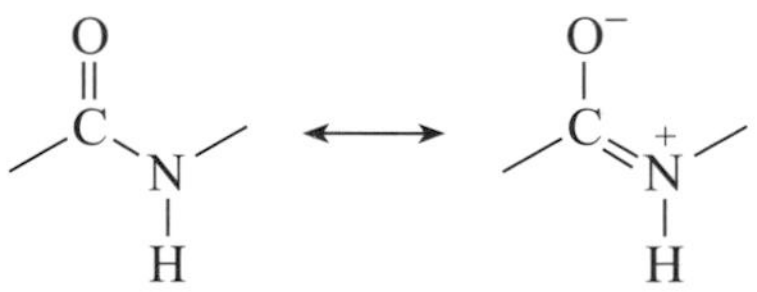

Figure 3.2
Resonance interactions between electrons in the C=O bond and the C—N bond of the peptide group mean that there is 'sharing' of electrons between these bonds. Note the charges on the N and O atoms.

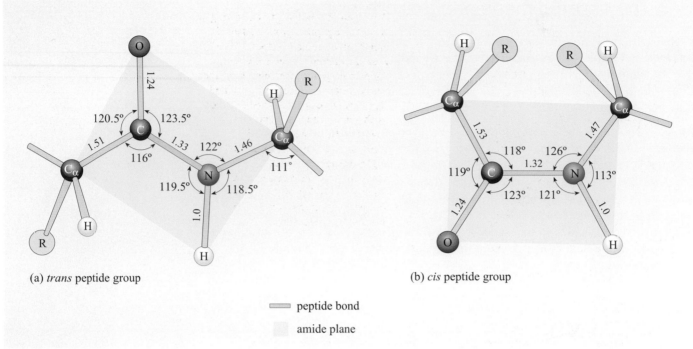

(a) *trans* peptide group

(b) *cis* peptide group

═══ peptide bond

▒▒ amide plane

Figure 3.3
The average dimensions
in angstroms, Å
(10 Å = 1 nm = 1000 pm), and
degrees, of the planar peptide group
in (a) the *trans* conformation and
(b) the *cis* conformation. *Note*: in
this and other representations of
the configuration of polypeptides,
there is no indication of bond order
(i.e. single or double bonds).

There are two possible conformations of the planar peptide bond: in the *trans* peptide group, the C_α atoms are on opposite sides of the peptide bond (Figure 3.3a) and in the *cis* peptide group, the C_α atoms are on the same side of the peptide bond (Figure 3.3b).

▢ Considering the spatial arrangement and the proximity of the atoms in the *cis* and *trans* conformations of the peptide bond, and bearing in mind what you learned about steric hindrance in Chapter 2 (Section 2.2.2), which conformation do you think would be favoured?

▣ The *trans* conformation would be energetically more favourable than the *cis* conformation, since it minimizes steric hindrance.

Generally speaking, peptide bonds are in the *trans* conformation. However, *cis* forms can occur in peptide bonds that precede a proline residue. In such cases, the *cis* form is more stable than usual since the proline side-chain offers less of a hindrance. Nonetheless, *cis* peptide bonds occur only in approximately 10% of instances of peptide bonds preceding proline residues.

Bearing in mind the planar nature of the peptide group, a polypeptide chain can be seen to have a backbone that consists of a series of rigid planar peptide groups linked by the C_α atoms. Figure 3.4 shows part of a polypeptide with two planar peptide groups in the *trans* conformation. Note that though rotation is not permitted about the peptide bonds, there is potential for rotation around the C_α—N and C_α—C bonds. The angles of rotation, termed **torsion angles**, about these bonds specify the conformation of a polypeptide backbone. The torsion angles about the C_α—N and C_α—C bonds are referred to as ϕ (phi) and ψ (psi), respectively and they are defined as 180° when the polypeptide is in the extended planar conformation, as illustrated in Figure 3.4.

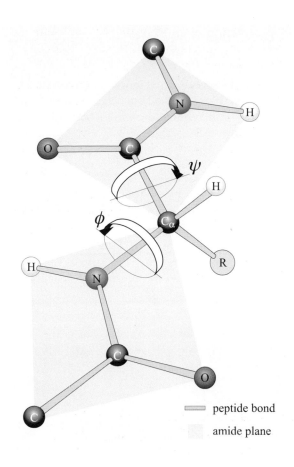

Figure 3.4
A portion of a polypeptide showing two planar peptide groups (shaded areas) joined at the C_α atom. There is little freedom of movement within the peptide group, but rotation of the peptide groups about the C_α—N and C_α—C bonds can occur and is defined by the torsion angles ϕ and ψ respectively. In the extended conformation shown here, both these angles are defined as 180°. By convention, ϕ and ψ increase with clockwise rotation of the peptide group when viewed from C_α, as indicated by the arrows.

—— peptide bond

▨ amide plane

You will not be surprised to learn that steric constraints apply to ϕ and ψ.

○ From what you learned about steric restriction in Chapter 2, what are the constraints on ϕ and ψ?

● Firstly, there is the repulsion between electrons in the bonds of neighbouring atoms (i.e. between those of C_α and those of the adjoined N and C). Secondly, the atoms of the neighbouring peptide groups and side-chains must not conflict; in other words, their van der Waals radii must be accommodated.

As a result of these steric constraints, only certain values of ϕ and ψ, and hence conformations of the peptide, are permitted whilst others are not.

It is possible to calculate these permitted values for a given residue in the context of a polypeptide. This calculation is performed by first determining the distances between all the non-bonding atoms in two neighbouring peptide groups (such as those in Figure 3.4) at all the possible values of ϕ and ψ. It is most readily done for a polypeptide containing just one kind of amino acid. A conformational plot of ϕ against ψ for a particular residue is known as a **Ramachandran plot** (after its inventor, G. N. Ramachandran). Such a plot allows us to identify those conformations (i.e. for a particular value of ϕ and ψ) that are sterically favourable or unfavourable (as in Figure 3.5), according to the following criteria:

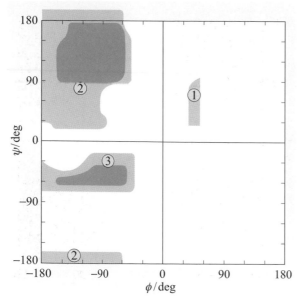

Figure 3.5
A Ramachandran plot showing the sterically allowed ϕ and ψ angles for a peptide chain containing only L-alanine residues (poly-L-alanine). 'Allowed' conformations are within the blue or green areas, with those that are 'outer limit' conformations in the latter. The remaining conformations, in the white area, are 'forbidden'. Note that there are only three discrete regions (numbered 1–3) corresponding to allowed conformations. (Data from Ramachandran and Sasisekharan, 1968).

▶ Where there is no conflict between the van der Waals radii of non-bonding atoms, a conformation is 'allowed'. These conformations lie in the blue areas in Figure 3.5.

▶ Conformations requiring interatomic distances at the limit of that which is permissible are defined as 'outer limit' conformations. They lie in the green areas in Figure 3.5.

▶ Theoretical conformations that require any two non-bonding atoms to be closer to each other than their van der Waals radii allow are sterically 'forbidden'. These lie in the white areas in Figure 3.5.

Notice that the values of ϕ and ψ in Figure 3.5 range from $-180°$ to $+180°$. Turning the peptide group through 360° will of course bring it back to its starting position, and $-180°$ and $+180°$ correspond to the same position. Thus the green strip at the bottom left corner of the plot in Figure 3.5 is contiguous with the field at the top left corner.

○ Use Figure 3.5 to determine whether the following values of ϕ and ψ are sterically favourable or unfavourable: (a) $\phi = 90°$ and $\psi = 90°$; (b) $\phi = -90°$ and $\psi = 90°$.

● (a) Unfavourable; (b) favourable.

Ramachandran plots can be constructed for polymers of each of the 20 amino acids. It is significant to note that the Ramachandran plots for many amino acid residues are generally very similar, having only three regions with favourable or tolerated conformations (labelled 1–3 in the plot for poly-L-alanine in Figure 3.5). Differences do occur, however. For instance, where the side-chain (R in Figure 3.4) is branched near C_α, as in the case of threonine (Chapter 2, Figure 2.17), it occupies more space close to the peptide backbone and restricts the approach of atoms in the neighbouring peptide groups. As a result, allowed conformations (ϕ and ψ angles) are more restricted for polypeptides of branched amino acids.

○ Proline is also quite different from other amino acids in terms of allowed conformations and for polyproline only ϕ values from $-85°$ to $-35°$ are tolerated. Looking at the structure of proline (Figure 2.17), how can you explain this relatively narrow range of permitted ϕ values?

● The side-chain of proline is covalently bonded to the N of the amino group, so in polyproline, there will be less freedom of rotation about the C_α—N bond than with other amino acids. Consequently, allowed ϕ values will be relatively limited compared with other amino acids.

○ Figure 3.6 shows the Ramachandran plot for glycine residues in a polypeptide chain. The regions are colour-coded as in Figure 3.5. What can you say about the conformations that glycine adopts? Consider the structure of glycine (Figure 2.17). Why does glycine differ from the other residues with respect to its conformations?

● Glycine has much greater conformational freedom than do other amino acid residues, because it has only an H atom as its side-chain, and is therefore less sterically hindered.

The Ramachandran plots in Figures 3.5 and 3.6 have been generated for, respectively, L-alanine and L-glycine on the basis of allowed and outer limit distances for interatomic contacts, determined from known values for van der Waals radii of the atoms (Table 3.1). They are therefore *predictive* rather than actual conformational plots. We can, of course, use X-ray diffraction to determine experimentally the 'real' values of ϕ and ψ for residues in a polypeptide. In Figure 3.7, the ϕ and ψ values for all the residues (with the exception of glycine and proline) in a number of different structures have been determined by high-resolution X-ray diffraction and plotted on a Ramachandran plot. We can see that there is a striking correspondence between predicted and actual conformations. Notice, however, that there are some residues whose conformations map to the 'forbidden' areas. Most of these residues map in the region between 'allowed' regions 2 and 3, around $\psi = 0$.

○ Look again at Figure 3.4 and imagine that you can twist the topmost peptide group through 180° so that $\psi = 0$. What groups are likely to conflict in this conformation?

● The N—H groups of adjacent peptide groups will conflict with each other, being forced into close proximity.

The conflict associated with these conformations can be accommodated by a *small* degree of twisting of the peptide bond. Thus, in such conformations the peptide group is twisted out of its usual planar conformation.

Table 3.1 Van der Waals distances for interatomic contacts.

Contact type	Normally allowed / Å	Outer limit / Å
H···H	2.0	1.9
H···O	2.4	2.2
H···N	2.4	2.2
H···C	2.4	2.2
O···O	2.7	2.6
O···N	2.7	2.6
O···C	2.8	2.7
N···N	2.7	2.6
N···C	2.9	2.8
C···C	3.0	2.9
C···CH$_2$	3.2	3.0
CH$_2$···CH$_2$	3.2	3.0

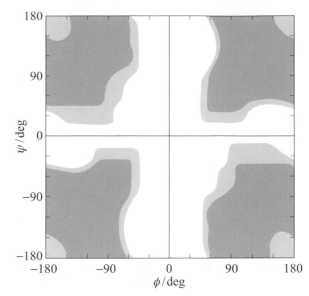

Figure 3.6 A Ramachandran plot for poly-L-glycine. Regions of 'allowed', 'outer limit' and 'forbidden' conformations are coloured as in Figure 3.5. (Data from Ramachandran and Sasisekharan, 1968)

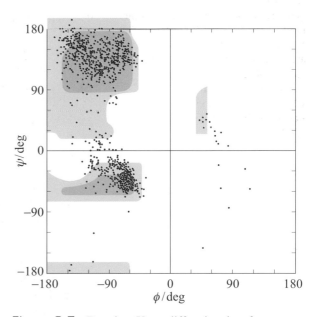

Figure 3.7 Based on X-ray diffraction data for a number of polypeptide structures, the ϕ and ψ values for all amino acid residues (with the exception of glycine and proline) have been superimposed on a predicted Ramachandran plot of 'allowed' and 'outer limit' conformations. Predictions were based on van der Waals distances for interatomic contacts as described in the text. Notice that the majority of actual values correspond to predicted permissible conformations.

A limited number of 'forbidden' conformations of particular residues can be tolerated in a polypeptide if the adopted conformation, as a whole, is energetically favourable. A polypeptide will tend to *fold* such that it adopts the most stable conformation. In this conformation, the polypeptide minimizes its *free energy*, a concept that is discussed in detail in Chapter 4. In the next sections, we shall look at this higher level of protein structure.

Molecular modelling 3

Go to the Study Skills file: *Molecular modelling 3*. This activity involves using ViewerLite™ to study the geometry of the peptide groups in a simple tripeptide. It should help you to understand the steric constraints that apply to torsion angles.

3.2.2 Protein secondary structure

From our consideration of the steric constraints that apply to peptide bonds and amino acid residues in a polypeptide, we have already begun to discuss some of the factors that determine how the backbone of the polypeptide folds. The conformation adopted by the polypeptide backbone of a protein is referred to as **secondary structure**. Whilst it is true to say that all proteins have a unique three-dimensional structure or conformation, specified by the nature and sequence of their amino acids, there are certain structural elements, or types of secondary structure, that can be readily recognized in many different proteins. These secondary structural elements include **helices**, **pleated sheets** and **turns**.

◻ Table 3.2 lists the torsion angles, ϕ and ψ, for the residues in some common secondary structures. Using the Ramachandran plot in Figure 3.5, what can you say about these structures?

● They all fall within the 'allowed' conformation areas.

Table 3.2 Torsion angles, ϕ and ψ, for some secondary structures.

Secondary structure	ϕ / deg	ψ / deg
right-handed α helix	−57	−47
parallel β sheet	−119	113
antiparallel β sheet	−139	135

As well as conforming to allowed torsion angles for component residues, secondary structures are stabilized by non-covalent interactions between atoms and groups in the polypeptide, namely hydrogen bonds and van der Waals forces (described in Chapter 2, Section 2.7.2). The polypeptide may fold and turn many times, and such interactions are often between residues some distance apart in terms of the primary structure.

Roughly half of an average globular protein consists of regular repetitive secondary structures (helices and pleated sheet) whilst the remainder has an irregular so-called coil or loop conformation.

Helices

A variety of helical structures can be identified in proteins using X-ray diffraction. A helix can be described by the number of units (amino acid residues) per turn (n) and by its **pitch** (p), which is the distance that the helix rises along its axis per turn. These parameters are indicated in Figure 3.8 for a number of helices. In proteins, n is rarely a whole number.

An important point to note is that a helix has a 'handedness'; that is, if viewed along its axis, the chain turns either in a clockwise direction (right-handed helix) or in an anticlockwise direction (left-handed helix). For example, helices (b) and (d) in Figure 3.8 are, respectively, right- and left-handed. By convention, the number of repeating units (n) is positive for right-handed helices and negative for left-handed helices. A number of different helical structures have been identified in proteins. The most common is the α **helix**, depicted in Figure 3.9a with details of its conformational parameters.

The α helix was discovered by Linus Pauling in 1951, using a model-building approach. It was later identified experimentally in α-keratin, a protein component of skin, hair and nails. The α helix structure is stabilized by hydrogen bonds between peptide carbonyl groups (C=O) and the peptide amino (N—H) groups that are four residues along (Figure 3.9b). In this way, the full hydrogen bonding capacity of the polypeptide backbone is utilized. Note that the side-chains (R) all project outwards and backwards from the helix as it rises; thus steric interference with the backbone or with other side-chains is avoided. The helix core is tightly packed and stabilized by van der Waals interactions.

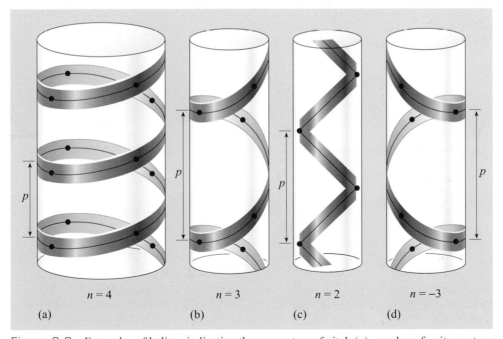

$n = 4$ $n = 3$ $n = 2$ $n = -3$

(a)   (b)   (c)   (d)

Figure 3.8   Examples of helices indicating the parameters of pitch (p), number of units per turn (n) and handedness (+ or −). The black circles denote amino acid residues.

Figure 3.9
(a) The right-handed α helix, first described by Linus Pauling in 1951, showing hydrogen bonds between peptide carbonyl groups (C=O) and peptide amino (N—H) groups that are four residues along. There are 3.6 residues per turn ($n = 3.6$) and the helix has a pitch (p) of 5.4 Å.
(b) An extended polypeptide chain illustrating the groups that form hydrogen bonds in the right-handed α helix.

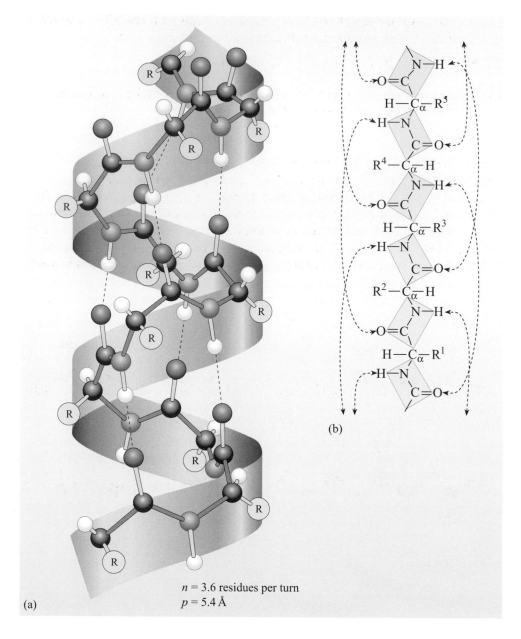

$n = 3.6$ residues per turn
$p = 5.4$ Å

(a)

(b)

In globular proteins, a helical stretch will, on average, include 12 residues although some proteins include α helices that contain up to 50 residues.

○ If a 12-residue stretch of polypeptide adopts an α helix structure, how many turns will it contain and how long will it be? You can answer this question using the values for n and p for the right-handed α helix in Figure 3.9a.

◼ It will contain 3.3 turns and will be 18 Å long.

Since the hydrophilic polypeptide backbone is optimally hydrogen-bonded to itself and hidden away at the core of the α helix, such regions of secondary structure are commonly seen in proteins that traverse the cell membrane, such as transmembrane receptors and transport proteins. In such cases, the side-chains, which project into the lipid environment, are typically non-polar.

○ Looking back at the amino acid structures in Chapter 2 (Figure 2.17), which residues might form a transmembrane helix?

■ Ala, Val, Leu, Ile, Pro, Phe, Trp, Gly and Cys.

The structure of membrane proteins and their interaction with the hydrophobic interior of membranes will be explored in detail in Chapter 6.

β pleated sheets

Another common secondary structure is the β pleated sheet, which contains extended stretches of polypeptide chain with hydrogen bonds between neighbouring strands. In **parallel β pleated sheet**, polypeptide strands run in the same direction (i.e. from N- to C-terminus) whereas in **antiparallel β pleated sheet**, neighbouring strands extend in opposite directions (Figure 3.10). Strands are not fully extended but have a zig-zag shape, which gives the sheet formation, in both parallel and antiparallel structures, a pleated appearance when viewed edge-on

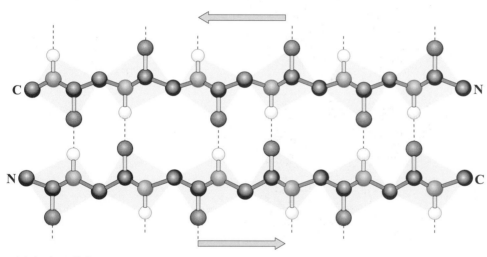

(a) Antiparallel

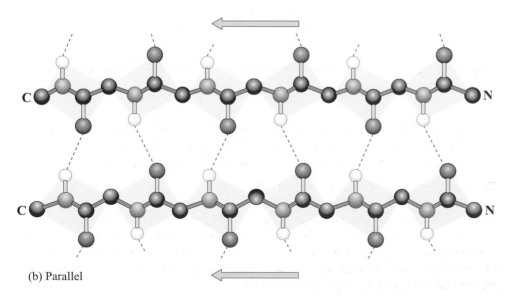

(b) Parallel

Figure 3.10
Hydrogen bonding between neighbouring stretches of polypeptide in (a) antiparallel and (b) parallel β pleated sheet structures. Note a difference in the hydrogen bonds, which are offset in the parallel sheet. The side-chains have been omitted for clarity.

(Figure 3.11). The C_α atoms of successive residues are at, alternately, the top and bottom of each pleat, with the side-chains pointing away from the sheet. Thus there is a two-residue repeating unit, as indicated in Figure 3.11a, which spans 7 Å. For simplicity, β pleated sheets are often represented as ribbons with arrowheads pointing in the direction of the C-terminus (Figure 3.11b).

In globular proteins, antiparallel pleated sheets can contain from two to 15 polypeptide strands, with the average being six strands. A sheet containing six strands is approximately 25 Å wide. Each individual strand can contain up to 15 amino acids, with the average being six.

○ What would be the length of a β pleated sheet in which the strands contained six residues?

■ The length of the sheet would be 21 Å (3 × 7 Å).

Parallel β sheets appear to be less stable that antiparallel sheets and rarely contain fewer than five chains. The relative instability of parallel β sheets may be due to the offset in hydrogen-bonding groups between neighbouring strands (Figure 3.10b). This offset causes some distortion, and hence weakening, in the hydrogen bonds compared to those between antiparallel strands. Mixed parallel and antiparallel β sheets also occur.

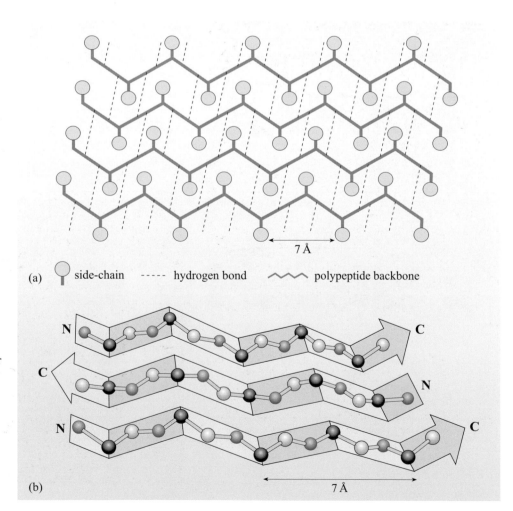

(a) side-chain ----- hydrogen bond 〰 polypeptide backbone

Figure 3.11
(a) Side-chains of residues in parallel or antiparallel β pleated sheet point away from the sheet, with successive side-chains alternately above and below. The two-residue repeating unit indicated spans 7 Å. (b) A three-stranded antiparallel β pleated sheet, showing the polypeptide backbone only, drawn to emphasize its pleated appearance.

Within the context of the entire peptide chain, regions of β sheet are connected by linking peptide. Figure 3.12 illustrates the different kinds of connection that can occur between adjacent strands in pleated sheets. In antiparallel β pleated sheet, a simple hairpin turn links successive strands (Figure 3.12a). There are two options for linking neighbouring parallel strands: the connection can be either a right-handed crossover or a left-handed crossover (Figure 3.12b and c respectively), but the latter rarely occurs. The connections between strands in β pleated sheet can be very long and can themselves contain elements of secondary structure, such as helices.

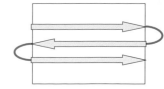

(a) Hairpin connection between antiparallel strands

When viewed along its length, a polypeptide strand in a pleated sheet can be seen to also have a slight helical twist to the right. This twist arises from the conflict between conformational stability within chains and that derived from hydrogen bonds between chains. As a consequence, the sheet as a whole is seen to have a right-handed twist. These twisted sheet structures often form the core of globular proteins (Figure 3.13).

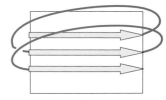

(b) Right-handed crossover connection between parallel strands

○ Looking at the structures in Figure 3.13, are the β pleated sheets parallel, antiparallel or mixed?

● Carboxypeptidase A contains a mixed parallel and antiparallel β pleated sheet structure and triose phosphate isomerase contains a parallel β pleated sheet structure.

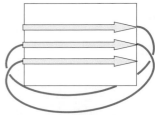

(c) Left-handed crossover connection between parallel strands

Figure 3.12 Types of linkage between adjacent β sheet strands. (a) Simple hairpins in antiparallel structures. (b) and (c) Crossover connections in parallel β pleated sheets.

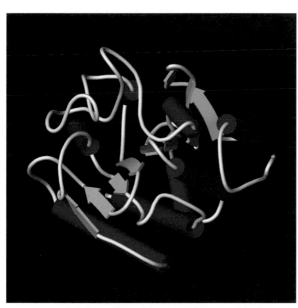

(a)

Figure 3.13 The polypeptide backbones of (a) bovine carboxypeptidase A (pdb file 2ctb) and (b) chicken triose phosphate isomerase (pdb file 1tim). Strands of the β sheets are represented as ribbon arrows, pointing in the direction of the C-terminus, and α helices are shown as cylinders. Note the pronounced right-handed twist of the β sheets in these two enzyme structures. Note also the location of the β sheet structures at the core of the proteins.

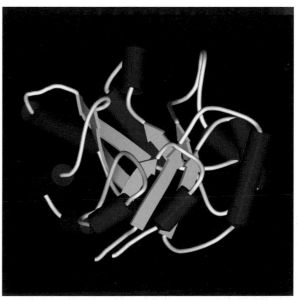

(b)

Reverse turns and loops

In compact globular proteins, a polypeptide often makes a sharp turn called a **reverse turn**. For instance, these turns often link adjacent strands in antiparallel β pleated sheet (as represented in Figure 3.12a). Also known as β **bends**, reverse turns involve four amino acid residues with a hydrogen bond between the C=O group of the first residue and the N—H group of the fourth (Figure 3.14a and b). Type I and type II β bends differ in respect of the torsion angles for the residues. Looking at the $C_{\alpha 3}$—N bond in Figure 3.14a and b, you should be able to confirm that there is a difference of 180° in the torsion angle about this bond (ϕ_3) in the type I and type II bends. Notice also that the β bends are tighter than the turn in the α helix structure. The second residue in the turn is frequently proline, which readily adopts the required conformation for such a turn. Another type of turn is the **omega loop**. This loop contains between six and 16 residues in a compact structure with a pinched-in shape resembling the Greek upper case character Ω (omega) (Figure 3.15). The side-chains of omega loops fill the inside of the loop.

Reverse turns and omega loops tend to be located at the surface of proteins where they play an important part in the recognition role of proteins, such as the recognition of specific antigens by antibodies.

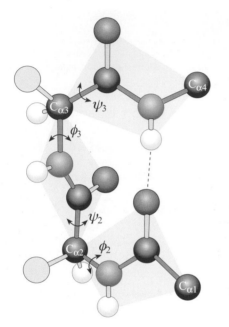

(a) Type I β bend

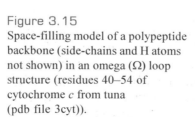

(b) Type II β bend

Figure 3.14
Reverse turns (β bends).
(a) Type I β bend.
(b) Type II β bend.

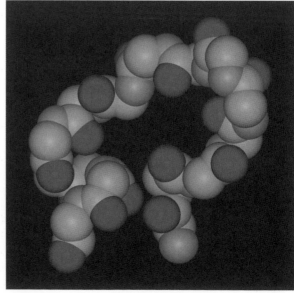

Figure 3.15
Space-filling model of a polypeptide backbone (side-chains and H atoms not shown) in an omega (Ω) loop structure (residues 40–54 of cytochrome *c* from tuna (pdb file 3cyt)).

Coil conformations

In addition to the repetitive helical and pleated sheet structures, there are other non-repetitive, and therefore more varied, elements of secondary structure called **coil conformations**. The lack of regular repetitive order in coil conformations does not, however, mean that these structures are disordered or unstable. In fact, it is clear from X-ray diffraction studies of proteins that these regions are consistent in the conformation that they adopt.

Regions of disorder do exist, however, in some proteins. Sometimes referred to as **random coil**, such regions may play an important part in the protein's function. For instance, random coil may be involved in the binding of a ligand, with consequent changes in the conformation and activity of the protein.

3.2.3 Protein tertiary structure

The term 'tertiary structure' when applied to a protein refers to the three-dimensional arrangement of the polypeptide as a whole, i.e. the spatial relationship between its elements of secondary structure. Though it may not be immediately obvious from the protein structures that you have already encountered in this course, proteins do follow certain recognizable folding patterns.

Examination of protein structures resolved by X-ray diffraction and NMR has revealed a variety of folding patterns common to many different proteins. However, even within these folds, distinct substructures or structural **motifs**, i.e. distinctive arrangements of elements of secondary structure, have been described. The term **supersecondary structure** has been coined to describe this level of organization, which is intermediate between secondary and tertiary. The observation that these motifs and protein folds occur in many different proteins, with quite distinct amino acid sequences, indicates that they are not strictly sequence-dependent. Nonetheless, the chemical nature of the component residues (charged, polar or non-polar) is critical in many cases, and your attention is drawn to these.

Motifs and supersecondary structures

Supersecondary structures or motifs are particular arrangements and combinations of two or three secondary structures, often with defined topology (or connectivity). Table 3.3 (overleaf) describes some of the most common of these.

The **coiled-coil** structure, in which α helices wrap around each other, is found in some structural proteins, such as myosin and α-keratin. The α helices have a strip of non-polar side-chains along one side, and formation of the coiled-coil is driven by interactions between these residues on the two α helices, causing them to twist around each other. In this way, the hydrophobic residues are buried and the hydrophilic groups extend into the aqueous environment. Although the specific amino acid sequences of myosin and α-keratin are quite different, in each case we can identify patterns of hydrophobic and hydrophilic residues in the linear sequence, which specify the coiled-coil conformation.

Table 3.3 describes two different motifs that have been identified in DNA or RNA binding proteins and which interact directly with the nucleic acid. Protein–DNA interactions will be examined in more detail in Chapter 5, but at this point we will consider briefly some of the features of these motifs. The **helix–turn–helix** motif is one of the most common DNA-binding motifs. The C-terminal helix fits into the major groove of the DNA and its side-chains interact with the nucleotides in a

The term 'motif' is also used to describe a consensus sequence of amino acids, i.e. a partial sequence common to a number of different proteins, which may or may not adopt similar conformations in the different proteins.

Table 3.3   Examples of common supersecondary structures/motifs.

Motif	Schematic	Description	Comments	Examples
βαβ		An α helix connects parallel β strands in β sheets. Hydrophobic surfaces on the helix and β sheet interact.	Residues in the first loop (C-terminal end of the β strand) often contribute to the active site in enzymes.	triose phosphate isomerase (a glycolytic enzyme) (pdb file 1tim)
β meander		Antiparallel β sheets are linked sequentially by short loops or hairpins consisting of two, three or four residues.	Basic antiparallel β pleated sheet.	
helix–turn–helix		In the simplest arrangement, two helices lie antiparallel, connected by a short loop.	Energetically favourable interactions between side-chains are accommodated by the relative positioning of the helices (usually at ~20° to each other).	Rop (an RNA binding protein) (pdb file 1rop)
Greek key		Antiparallel β sheet with longer loop connections between some strands.		gamma crystallin (a protein of the eye lens) (pdb file 1gcs)
coiled-coil		Two α helices are wrapped around each another. Strips of hydrophobic side-chains along the length of each helix interact with each other.		myosin (a motor protein); α-keratin (a structural protein, e.g. in skin and hair)
zinc finger		An α helix and two short antiparallel β strands are held together by a zinc ion, which forms coordinate bonds with side-chains in the polypeptide.		Xfin (*Xenopus* DNA binding protein with a role in embryogenesis) (pdb file 1znf; single zinc finger from this protein)

sequence-specific manner. Thus different DNA-binding proteins will recognize different DNA sequences depending on the amino acid side-chains presented by this helix. The **zinc finger** motif is another motif commonly found in proteins that bind RNA and DNA. This finger-like structure consists of an α helix and two short antiparallel β strands all held together by a zinc ion, coordinated between two conserved cysteine and two histidine side-chains. Some forms of zinc finger have four cysteine residues bound to the zinc ion. This motif can be repeated many times in a DNA binding protein, with each finger folding independently. It is amino acids in the α helix that interact with the major groove of the DNA duplex. A third DNA-binding motif, not shown in Table 3.3, is the **leucine zipper**. In this motif, two identical subunits interact via α helices, forming a short stretch of coiled-coil. The interaction is mediated by hydrophobic interactions between side-chains, notably those of leucine residues.

Protein folds

Protein folds are often very extensive arrangements, combining elements of secondary and supersecondary structure. Some of the most common protein folds are described in Table 3.4 with examples of proteins that contain them. Notice that proteins can be conveniently divided into three classes, on the basis of the elements of secondary structure that they contain: all α helix, all β sheet, or mixed α helix and β sheet (α/β).

Protein domains

An important concept in protein structure is that of the **protein domain**. In many cases, a single polypeptide can be seen to contain two or more physically distinct substructures, known as domains. Often linked by a flexible hinge region, these domains are compact and stable, with a hydrophobic core. Domains fold independently of the rest of the polypeptide, satisfying most of their residue–residue contacts internally. Typically, two or more layers of secondary structural elements effectively screen the hydrophobic core from the aqueous environment. A minimum size of 40–50 residues is required, though some domains can consist of up to 350 residues. It is estimated empirically that the number of different domain-folding arrangements is limited to approximately 2000 and, to date, half of these have been described.

The physical resolution of different portions of a polypeptide is often indicative of distinct functions for these domains. For example, Src (pronounced 'sark'), a kinase that has a key role in intracellular signalling, has four domains: the catalytic activity of the protein resides in two domains (*kinase domains*) and the other two domains are important for the regulation of this activity (*regulatory domains*). The functional division of responsibility that domains permit will be examined in relation to some specific proteins later in this chapter and you will encounter many examples throughout this course.

Table 3.4   Examples of common protein folds.

	Fold	Schematic	Description	Comments	Examples
All α	four-helix bundle		Helix–turn–helix motifs. Comprise four antiparallel helices with short connecting loops.	Polar side-chains on exposed surfaces interact with the aqueous environment; hydrophobic residues are towards the centre.	myohaemerythrin, uteroglobin, ferritin (pdb file 1h96)
	globin fold		Usually 6–8 α helices. Variable arrangements. Two C-terminal helices adopt a helix–turn–helix conformation; remaining helices pack with greater angles between their axes (~50°).	Helices wrap around an active site (e.g. a haem molecule).	myoglobins (e.g. pdb file 1az1), haemoglobins (e.g. pdg 1gzx), phyocyanins
All β	up-and-down β barrels		Antiparallel β sheet with β meander connections wraps around to form a barrel structure.	The inner surface of the barrel is rich in hydrophobic side-chains.	retinol binding protein (carries retinol, which is hydrophobic, inside the barrel) (pdb file 1aqb)
	Greek key barrels		Greek key motifs wrap around to form a barrel structure.	The inner surface of the barrel is rich in hydrophobic side-chains.	prealbumin (pdb file 1bmz), gamma crystallin (eye lens)

Table 3.4 (continued) Examples of common protein folds.

	Fold	Schematic	Description	Comments	Examples
α/β	α/β barrels		Parallel β strands alternate with parallel α helices and these components are linked by surface loops. (Thus helices are antiparallel to strands.) The β strands are arranged on the inside, forming the barrel shape, with α helices around the outside of the barrel.	The inner surface of the barrel is rich in hydrophobic side-chains. The loops between the of C-terminus of the β strands and the N-terminus of the α helices form active sites and ligand binding sites.	The α/β barrel structure is common in enzymes of the glycolytic pathway, oxidases, isomerases and hydrolases. Example: triose phosphate isomerase (pdb file 1tim)
	α/β sheet		Alternate α and β components with connecting loops, as in the α/β barrel. β strands are hydrogen-bonded to each other and form a β sheet and the helices are alternately above and below the plane of this sheet.	This arrangement often creates a crevice at the C-terminal edge of the sheet, and it is here that substrates bind.	flavodoxin (redox protein) (pdb file 1ahn)
α/β	Rossman fold		Two βαβαβ units. Mostly parallel β strands connected via loops with helices. Helices run antiparallel to β strands.	This motif is also known as a dinucleotide binding fold.	Different dehydrogenases have variations on this type of fold, e.g. the NAD binding domain of glyceraldehyde 3-phosphate dehydrogenase (an enzyme of the glycolytic pathway) (pdb file 4gpd).

Protein domains in recently evolved proteins are frequently encoded by individual exons within their genes. This observation suggests that such proteins have arisen during evolutionary history by exchange and duplication of exons coding for simpler individual **protein modules**, structural or functional units that are common to many different proteins. This powerful evolutionary process has been termed 'domain shuffling'. Figure 3.16 illustrates how domain shuffling has resulted in the evolution of specialized serine proteases such as factor IX, which is a component of the cascade that produces blood clots in vertebrates, and urokinase and plasminogen, both of which are involved in the lysis of blood clots. Compared to an evolutionarily older serine protease such as the digestive enzyme chymotrypsin, these 'modern' proteases have been refined by the acquisition of additional regulatory domains, such as the epidermal growth factor (EGF) domain, a calcium binding domain or so-called 'kringle' domains.

Domains that have been particularly mobile in protein evolution tend to be smaller (40–200 residues) than the average domain, most likely reflecting physical limits on gene duplication. Typically, they have a core of β strands linked by large loops which often form binding sites for regulatory molecules or substrates. The structures of some such modules are illustrated in Figure 3.17. Notice that, in the growth factor and immunoglobulin modules, the N- and C-terminal ends are at opposite sides of the structure. This arrangement is quite common among protein modules and facilitates the linking of modules in extended series.

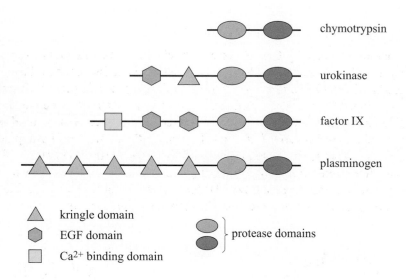

Figure 3.16   Domain shuffling in the evolution of serine proteases. Evolutionarily related domains are represented by the same symbol. Two protease domains are common to all four enzymes represented in this schematic. Compared with chymotrypsin, the other kinases have additional domains that are associated with more specialized function and a higher degree of regulation. These domains include one that is homologous to a domain found in epidermal growth factor (EGF), a Ca^{2+} binding domain and a kringle domain (so called because, with its three looped-out stretches, it resembles a Scandinavian pastry of the same name).

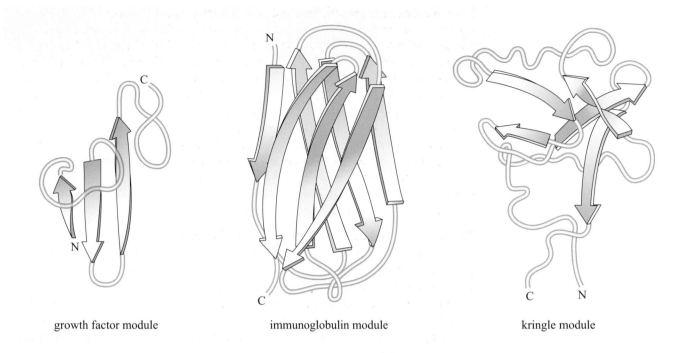

growth factor module   immunoglobulin module   kringle module

Figure 3.17   The structures of three protein modules that are common to many different proteins.

Covalent cross-linkages stabilize protein structure

Proteins that are secreted by the cell, or are attached to the extracellular surface of the plasma membrane, can be subject to more extreme conditions than those experienced by intracellular proteins. Often, covalent cross-linkages stabilize these proteins by connecting specific amino acids within a polypeptide or between polypeptide chains in multisubunit proteins (see below). Typically such a linkage will be a covalent sulfur–sulfur bond which forms between the —SH groups of two cysteine residues that are in close proximity in the folded protein (Figure 3.18). Called **disulfide bonds**, these covalent linkages do not affect the conformation of the protein, and are only formed when the folding is complete. They act, therefore, to secure the conformation and increase the stability of the protein.

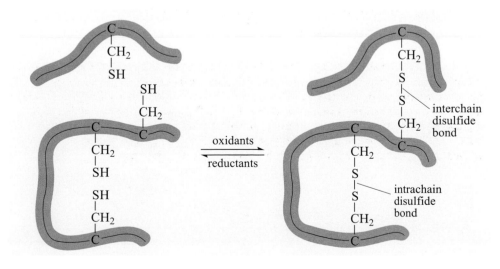

Figure 3.18
An example of how the formation of a disulfide bond between cysteine side-chains stabilizes existing structures in a polypeptide. These bonds can form between two polypeptide strands or between residues in the same polypeptide.

3.2.4 Quaternary structure

This level of protein structure applies only to those proteins that consist of more than one polypeptide chain, termed **subunits**. In such proteins, sometimes referred to as multisubunit proteins, the same kinds of non-covalent interaction that stabilize the folded polypeptides also specify the assembly of complexes of subunits. Quaternary structure refers to the way in which the subunits of such proteins are assembled in the finished protein.

Multisubunit proteins can have a number of identical (**homomeric**) or non-identical (**heteromeric**) subunits. The simplest multisubunit proteins are homodimers – two identical polypeptide chains that are independently folded but held together by non-covalent interactions. An example of a homodimeric protein is the Cro repressor protein from bacteriophage lambda (Figure 3.19), which turns off expression of specific genes in its bacterial host. Haemoglobin, the red blood cell protein responsible for carrying molecular oxygen, contains two each of two different subunits, termed α and β globin (Figure 3.20). Note the symmetry of the two subunits in both these quaternary structures.

Some proteins can assemble to form long filaments. Two such proteins are actin and tubulin. These proteins exist in a soluble globular form that can assemble into long helical filaments called microfilaments (actin) and microtubules (tubulin) (Figure 3.21). Both these proteins are important components of the cytoskeleton, and the filaments that they form can extend from one end of a cell to another (Figure 3.21c). As you will see later in the course, the dynamic assembly and disassembly of microfilaments and microtubules is integral to the responsive nature of the cytoskeleton during many cell processes such as cell division, intracellular transport, and cell movement and adhesion.

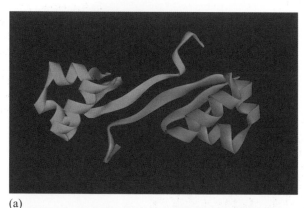

(a)

Figure 3.19
Bacteriophage lambda Cro repressor protein is a homodimer. It is represented here in three ways.
(a) Ribbon format, with the subunits coloured differently.
(b) Space-filling format with the subunits coloured as in
(a). (c) Ribbon format with the polypeptide backbone coloured according to secondary structure: α helix, red; β sheet, cyan; turn, green; random coil, white. (Based on pdb file 1cop)

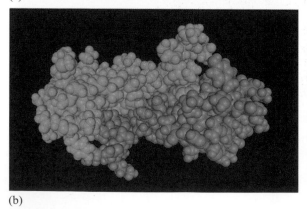

(b)

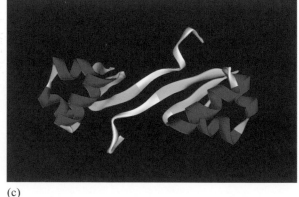

(c)

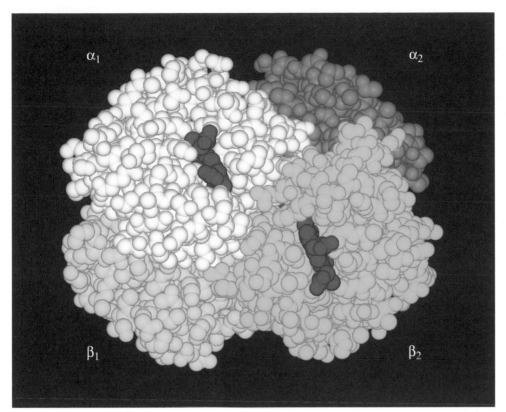

Figure 3.20   Space-filling model of human haemoglobin in its deoxygenated form (deoxyhaemoglobin). The two α and two β subunits are indicated and are coloured differently. The haem complexes (coloured red) that associate with each subunit are only visible in the α_1 and β_2 subunits in this representation. (Based on pdb file 1a3n)

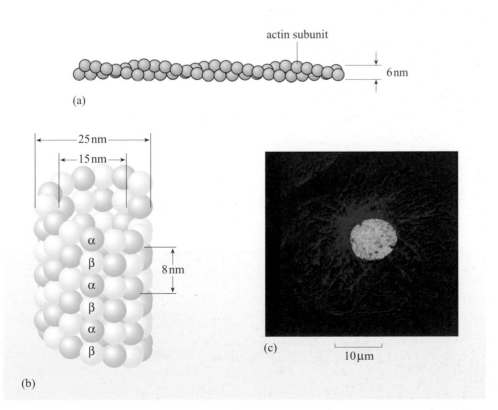

Figure 3.21
(a) Actin subunits can assemble into helical filaments called microfilaments. (b) Microtubules consist of repeating tubulin heterodimers (α and β subunits). (c) Microtubules (stained red) in a cultured mammalian cell during interphase; chromosomes are stained blue.

3.2.5 Fibrous proteins

Most of the proteins described so far have been globular proteins. There are, however, some distinctive features that characterize fibrous proteins and we present here a general overview of these. Elongated fibrous proteins frequently play a structural role in the cell. They do not readily crystallize but tend to aggregate along their long axis to form fibres. X-ray diffraction studies of these fibres, in contrast to analysis of protein crystals, provides only very limited information on the structure of the protein.

The overall shape and structure of fibrous proteins are determined principally by their secondary structure. α-keratin is an intracellular globular protein comprising two long subunits, the α-helical portions of which form a coiled-coil structure as already described (Table 3.3). Through interactions between globular domains at either end of the helical region, this protein can form long filaments. These structures are termed intermediate filaments and, along with microtubules and microfilaments, comprise a cell's cytoskeleton. Notice that the basic building blocks of microtubules and microfilaments are globular proteins, whilst intermediate filaments are composed of fibrous units.

The extracellular matrix (connective tissue), which can be thought of as the glue that holds cells together in a tissue, contains many fibrous proteins. Principal among these is collagen, which consists of a triple helix of three polypeptide chains (Figure 3.22). A single collagen molecule is 300 nm long and these units can assemble into many long overlapping strands to form strong cable-like structures that support and protect cells. The extracellular matrix derives much of its strength from collagen. In contrast, other extracellular matrix components such as elastin contribute elastic qualities. Elastin's polypeptide constituents are covalently cross-linked, creating a non-rigid net-like structure, which permits a degree of distortion or deformation in the tissue.

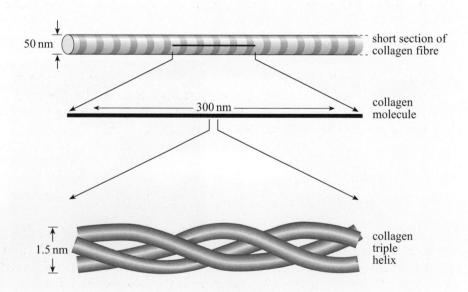

Figure 3.22   The triple helix structure of collagen. Collagen is a long (300 nm) rod-like protein consisting of three polypeptide chains wound together in a triple helix. Many such molecules are cross-linked in long fibres in the extracellular matrix. These collagen fibres are very strong and can not be extended, giving strength and resistance to the extracellular matrix.

Summary of Section 3.2

1   Protein structure is described in terms of four levels of organization: primary, secondary, tertiary and quaternary.

2   The primary structure of a protein is the sequence of amino acids of which it is composed and ultimately determines the shape that the protein adopts.

3   The peptide group formed between two amino acid residues has a rigid planar structure and these planar groups can rotate around the C_α—N and C_α—C bonds. In a polypeptide, the angles of rotation about these bonds (ϕ and ψ respectively) specify the conformation of the backbone. A Ramachandran plot of ϕ versus ψ, based on 'allowed' and 'outer limit' distances for contact between atoms, identifies those conformations that are sterically favourable or unfavourable.

4   A polypeptide will tend to fold in such a way as to give a conformation that minimizes its free energy (i.e. the most stable conformation).

5   Secondary structure refers to the conformation adopted by the polypeptide backbone of a protein and includes helices, pleated sheets and turns. Secondary structures are stabilized by non-covalent interactions between atoms and groups in the polypeptide, namely hydrogen bonds and van der Waals attractions. Supersecondary structures or motifs are particular arrangements and combinations of two or three secondary structures, often with defined topology and three-dimensional structure.

6   Tertiary structure describes how the polypeptide folds as a whole. There are certain distinct folding patterns common to many different proteins. Discrete independently folded structures within a single polypeptide are called domains. Domains are compact and stable, with a hydrophobic core, and frequently have distinct functions.

7   Quaternary structure applies only to those proteins that consist of more than one polypeptide chain (subunit) and describes how subunits associate with each other.

Molecular modelling 4

Go to the Study Skills file: *Molecular modelling 4*. This activity entails using ViewerLite™ to examine the structure of some of the proteins discussed in Section 3.2. You will be able to identify some of the common structures and folds described in this section.

3.3 Assembling a functioning protein

Polypeptides are synthesized by **translation** of messenger RNA (mRNA) on the ribosome, either in the cytosol or in association with the endoplasmic reticulum (rough ER). This process will be described in some detail in Chapter 11. The polypeptide starts to adopt elements of secondary structure and to fold even as it is being synthesized, and certain covalent modifications of the polypeptide can also occur while translation is ongoing. Initial folding is rapid (of the order of a few seconds). Some proteins require **cofactors**, which are non-protein components essential for their function that associate with the polypeptide, via non-covalent interactions, as it folds.

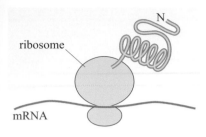

(a) Polypeptide begins to fold as it is being synthesized (non-covalent interactions).

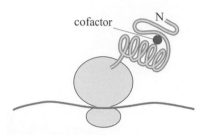

(b) Cofactor binds to polypeptide as it folds (non-covalent interactions).

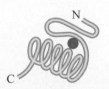

(c) The partially folded polypeptide is released from the ribosome.

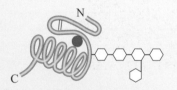

(d) Fine-tuning of the conformation; covalent modification occurs (disulfide bond formation and glycosylation in this case).

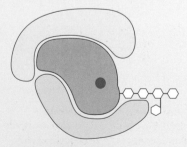

(e) Other subunits bind to give the mature functional protein.

The structure that results from this initial rapid folding is more open and flexible than the final folded polypeptide and is referred to as a **molten globule**. When synthesis is complete, the structure is precisely adjusted and refined and any further covalent modifications of the protein occur at this stage. Fine-tuning of the polypeptide conformation is a much more lengthy process than the initial folding and in many cases is facilitated by specialized proteins called chaperones. For multisubunit proteins, assembly of the subunits occurs after the individual polypeptides have folded.

The result of all these processes is a mature functional protein (Figure 3.23).

3.3.1 Chaperones help polypeptides to fold

We have seen how steric restrictions and energetic considerations specify preferred polypeptide conformations and ultimately determine a protein's three-dimensional structure. It is possible, of course, that there may be more than one energetically favourable conformation for a polypeptide. This is particularly true for large polypeptides. For a protein with a specific function in the cell, misfolding will affect its activity. Indeed, the misfolded protein may actually have some aberrant undesirable activity. To counter any damaging effect of misfolded proteins, mechanisms exist to facilitate correct folding or refolding of proteins and the removal/degradation of misfolded proteins.

Chaperones are proteins whose function it is to ensure correct folding of other proteins. There are two main families of chaperones in eukaryotic cells – hsp60 and hsp70 proteins – with different forms occurring in the cytosol, mitochondria and the endoplasmic reticulum, where they are responsible for refolding different proteins. The hsp nomenclature derives from the term 'heat-shock protein' which reflects the role of these proteins in the cellular response to elevated temperature. Incidences of protein misfolding increase when the cell experiences modest increases in temperature, and the cell responds by increasing expression of hsps to facilitate refolding.

○ Why might an increase in temperature encourage the misfolding of proteins?

● Increased temperature would disrupt hydrogen bonds and increase molecular movements, thereby increasing the risk of incorrect folding.

Despite the presence of chaperones, misfolded proteins do occur and recognition and degradation of these aberrant molecules is essential for the health of the cell. Experimental evidence suggests that up to one-third of newly synthesized polypeptides are degraded rapidly. The protease responsible for degrading these

Figure 3.23 Assembly of a functional protein. As it is being synthesized on the ribosome, the nascent polypeptide starts to fold, and rapid formation of secondary structures occurs (a). As the polypeptide folds, cofactors become incorporated (b). Some covalent modifications can also occur at this stage. With release of the newly synthesized polypeptide from the ribosome (c), further covalent modifications, such as glycosylation and formation of disulfide bonds, occur and the polypeptide undergoes the relatively lengthy process of fine-tuning of its structure (d). This process is facilitated by chaperones and involves many small adjustments of the amino acid side-chains in the structure. Finally, for multisubunit proteins, when the correct tertiary structure of the polypeptide is achieved, it assembles with other subunits to give a mature functional protein (e).

proteins is the **proteasome**, a large multisubunit protein that can chop up protein substrates into small peptide fragments. You will learn more about the role of chaperones in protein folding and about the degradation of proteins by the proteasome in Chapter 11, when we look at protein synthesis and turnover in some detail.

3.3.2 Some proteins require small-molecule cofactors

Cofactors are non-protein substances that complex with particular proteins and are essential for their activity. They include prosthetic groups and coenzymes.

Coenzymes are organic molecules that bind only temporarily to an enzyme. They are often derivatives of a mono- or dinucleotide, e.g. nicotinamide adenine dinucleotide (NAD; Chapter 2, Section 2.3.5), and may serve as a vehicle for a chemical group generated or required in an enzyme-catalysed reaction. In contrast to coenzymes, **prosthetic groups** are *permanently* associated with a protein to give a functional complex.

The activity of up to a third of all enzymes depends on the presence of a metal ion. In some cases, the ion associates loosely with the protein and in others it remains tightly bound for the lifetime of the enzyme (i.e. as prosthetic groups). The latter group of enzymes are referred to as **metalloenzymes** and in these the prosthetic group is typically a transition metal ion such as Cu^{2+}, Fe^{2+}, Fe^{3+}, Zn^{2+} or Mn^{2+}. Other enzymes are activated on binding metal ions. Such interactions are usually weaker than those in metalloenzymes and generally involve ionic forms of the alkali and alkaline earth metals such as Na^+, K^+, Mg^{2+} and Ca^{2+}.

Many respiratory pigments contain more complex prosthetic groups. An example is the haem porphyrin ring in haemoglobin, which contains eight heterocyclic rings (i.e. rings comprising one or more atoms other than carbon) (Figure 3.24). The haem ring structure is a derivative of porphyrin and has four N atoms arranged around an iron atom in the Fe(II) oxidation state. Together with a fifth N from a histidine side-chain of the protein, these N atoms serve to coordinate the Fe^{2+} ion. O_2 binds to the Fe^{2+} on the opposite side of the porphyrin ring from the histidine residue. Each of the four subunits of haemoglobin has an associated haem group, and it is this group that gives haemoglobin its red colour.

There are a number of different types of haem groups (Figure 3.24 shows one example) and several genetic defects affect their biosynthesis, resulting in diseases known as porphyrias. Famously, King George III of England (1738–1820) is believed to have suffered from such a disease. Porphyrias are characterized by the accumulation of porphyrin and/or its biosynthetic precursors. Excretion of these compounds in individuals suffering from a porphyria gives their urine a characteristic red colour. Other symptoms include psychiatric disturbance caused by neurological dysfunction.

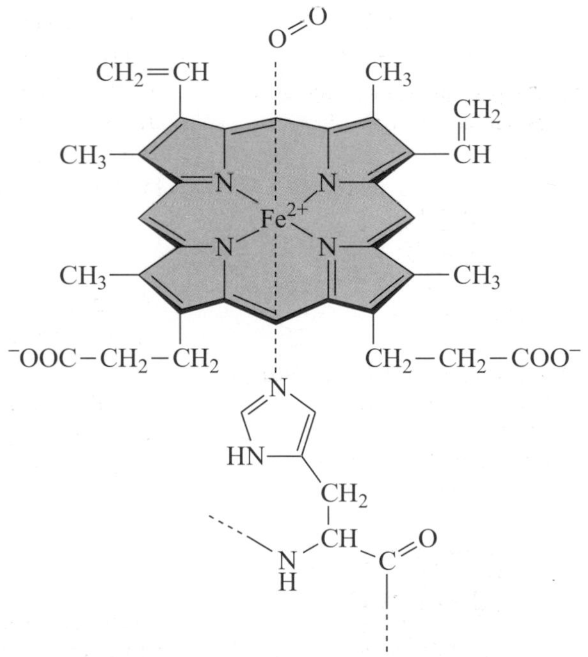

Figure 3.24 One type of haem porphyrin ring (ferroprotoporphyrin IX). This prosthetic group is tightly bound to each of the four subunits of haemoglobin. The iron atom, in the Fe(II) oxidation state, is coordinated by four N atoms in the ring structure, and an N atom in a His side-chain of the protein. An O_2 molecule binds to this prosthetic group as shown.

3.3.3 The covalent modification of proteins

Many proteins are modified by the covalent linking of groups that can affect their function and/or localization in the cell. Such **covalent modifications** occur after synthesis and folding of the polypeptide component. The main types of covalent modification and their functions are listed below.

1   Methylation/acetylation of amino acids at the N-terminal tails of histone proteins in eukaryotes can affect the structure of chromatin and ultimately gene expression. Prokaryotes also use methylation as a means of directly regulating protein activities. For example, the methylation of specific proteins controlling flagellar movement is an important mechanism for the regulation of bacterial chemotaxis.

2   Phosphorylation of proteins (catalysed by specific kinases) is a key regulatory mechanism in eukaryotic intracellular signalling and in metabolic pathways.

3   Lipidation of proteins (i.e. addition of lipid tails) targets them to cell membranes (plasma membrane and cell organelles).

4   Glycosylation is a feature of many extracellular proteins, whether secreted or on the cell surface, and may offer the protein some protection against proteases.

These modifications are catalysed by specific enzymes and can be reversed, permitting regulation of the protein's function. This reversibility is particularly significant with respect to protein phosphorylation (discussed further in Section 3.6.2).

Throughout this course, you will encounter many examples of regulation of protein function by these types of covalent modification. The control of gene expression through modification of histone proteins is discussed in detail in Chapter 5, and the importance of phosphorylation as a means of regulating signalling proteins will be evident in Chapter 13. For now, we will look in more detail at the consequences for protein function of glycosylation and lipidation.

Glycosylation

Glycosylation of a protein entails the covalent attachment of carbohydrate groups (typically oligosaccharides) and the resulting modified protein is called a **glycoprotein**. Covalent attachment of sugar residues to proteins occurs in the endoplasmic reticulum (ER) and Golgi apparatus. The oligosaccharide chains usually contain less than 15 sugar residues but are very diverse and are often branched (refer to Chapter 2, Box 2.5). They are linked to the protein component via either the $-OH$ groups of serine and threonine, termed **O-glycosylation**, or the $-NH_2$ group of asparagine, termed **N-glycosylation**.

Few proteins ultimately destined for the cytosol are glycosylated. However, many proteins that are either secreted into the extracellular space or localized to non-cytosolic membrane surfaces (e.g. the extracellular surface of the plasma membrane or the lumenal surface of the Golgi or lysosomes) are glycosylated. Generally these proteins are synthesized in the rough ER. Glycosylation of newly synthesized polypeptides actually affects their folding and this effect is discussed further in Chapter 11.

How does glycosylation affect the protein and what is the function of this type of modification? Glycosylation may increase the protein's resistance to proteases.

The oligosaccharide chains do not fold up into compact structures in the way that proteins do; they tend, therefore, to occupy more space and restrict access of proteases. In the same way, at the cell surface, glycosylated proteins may offer some protection to the cell. They also mediate cell–cell adhesion and specific molecular interactions involved in cell–cell recognition. For example, the recognition of carbohydrate groups by a family of proteins called selectins is essential for cell–cell adhesion, a process that will be explained in more detail in Chapter 16.

Lipid-linked proteins and lipoproteins

Lipid-linked proteins are proteins that have been covalently modified by addition of one or more lipid groups. Note that the term **lipoprotein**, though sometimes used to describe lipid-linked proteins, is strictly applicable only to those proteins that associate with lipids non-covalently. These proteins have quite distinct functions. Lipoproteins serve to transport triacylglycerols and cholesterol in the blood plasma. We will not be discussing them any further at this point.

In lipid-linked proteins, the lipid component serves to anchor the protein in membranes. Some membrane-associated proteins are initially synthesized as soluble proteins in the cytosol before covalent addition of a lipid group.

◯ Why does the addition of a lipid group cause proteins to locate to membranes?

⬤ The lipid groups are hydrophobic, so readily insert into membranes.

Proteins form covalent attachments to three different types of lipid, which are listed below. The structures of these lipid groups and the nature of their attachments to proteins are indicated in Figure 3.25. (Lipid structure and nomenclature will be discussed further in Chapter 6.)

▸ **Isoprenoid** groups such as farnesyl and geranylgeranyl residues: the modified protein is described as 'prenylated'.
▸ **Fatty acyl** groups such as myristoyl and palmitoyl residues: the modified protein is described as 'fatty acylated'.
▸ **Glycoinositol phospholipids** (**GPIs**): the modified protein is described as 'GPI-linked'.

Prenylation and fatty acylation localize proteins to the *cytosolic surface* of the plasma membrane or, in the case of myristoylated proteins, to membranes of the endoplasmic reticulum and the eukaryotic nucleus. In contrast, GPI linkages anchor proteins to the *extracellular surface* of the plasma membrane. Prenylation of proteins in the nucleus can target them to the inner surface of the nuclear membrane. Such is the case with lamins, components of the nuclear lamina, discussed in Chapter 8.

The most common site of prenylation in proteins is via a thioether linkage ($-S-$) to a cysteine residue near the C-terminus of the polypeptide chain (Figure 3.25a). This critical Cys is the fourth from last residue at the C-terminus and is followed directly by two aliphatic (non-polar) residues. Thus the terminal sequence is given by CaaX, where 'a' denotes an aliphatic residue and 'X' is any amino acid residue.

◯ Which amino acids have an aliphatic side-chain? (Refer back to Figure 2.17 for side-chain structures.)

⬤ Gly, Ala, Val, Leu and Ile.

Figure 3.25
Lipidation of proteins. Some proteins are modified by the covalent attachment of
(a) isoprenoid groups,
(b) fatty acyl groups or
(c) glycoinositol phospholipids (GPIs).

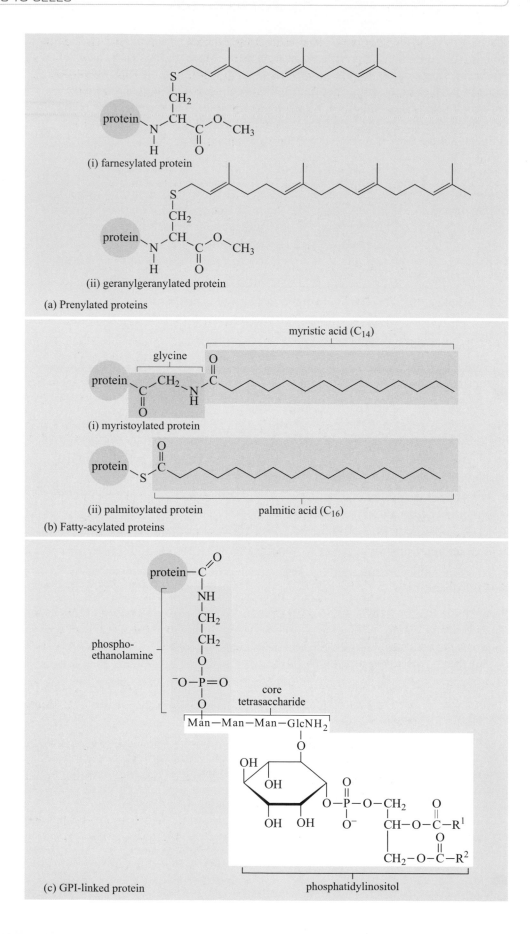

(i) farnesylated protein

(ii) geranylgeranylated protein

(a) Prenylated proteins

myristic acid (C_{14})

glycine

(i) myristoylated protein

(ii) palmitoylated protein

palmitic acid (C_{16})

(b) Fatty-acylated proteins

phospho-ethanolamine

core tetrasaccharide

Man—Man—Man—GlcNH$_2$

(c) GPI-linked protein

phosphatidylinositol

The type of isoprenoid group that is linked to the protein depends on which amino acid X is. Thus, if X is Ala, Met or Ser, a farnesyl group is added at the Cys, whereas, if X is Leu, a geranylgeranyl group is added. With addition of the isoprenoid group, the aaX tripeptide is proteolytically removed and the terminal carboxyl group (belonging to the Cys) is esterified with a methyl group. The isoprenoid group, as well as anchoring the protein to a membrane, also seems to facilitate interaction of its attached protein with other membrane-associated proteins.

In fatty acylated eukaryotic proteins, the fatty acid groups that are covalently linked to the protein component are either myristic acid, a saturated C_{14} fatty acid, or palmitic acid, a saturated C_{16} fatty acid. An amide linkage connects myristic acid to the amino group of the protein's N-terminal glycine residue, whereas palmitic acid is connected to a specific Cys residue via a thioester bond ($-CO-S-$; Figure 3.25b). Myristoylation occurs during protein synthesis (translation) and this modification tends to remain for the lifetime of the protein. In contrast, palmitoylation occurs in the cytosol after the protein has been synthesized, and is reversible.

As well as serving to anchor the protein in membranes, palmitoylation affects protein–protein interactions and activity; the reversible nature of this modification permits regulation of a specific protein in, for example, intracellular signalling.

The complex chemical structure of the GPI anchor is illustrated in Figure 3.25c, in which the molecular components are identified. A phosphatidylinositol unit, which contains two fatty acyl chains, is linked via a glycosidic bond to one end of a tetrasaccharide and the other end of the tetrasaccharide is linked via a phosphoester bond to phosphoethanolamine. This whole structure is linked to the protein by means of an amide linkage between the amino group of phosphoethanolamine and the C-terminal carboxyl group of the protein. The fatty acyl groups and the sugars of the tetrasaccharide vary depending on which particular protein is modified in this way. The GPI anchor is added to newly synthesized proteins in the rough endoplasmic reticulum. In Chapter 11, you will learn more about how lipid modification occurs during protein synthesis and processing.

Summary of Section 3.3

1   A newly synthesized polypeptide can undergo a number of modifications and adjustments before it has the structure and activity of a mature functional protein. Some proteins require non-protein components, termed cofactors, for their function.

2   A newly synthesized polypeptide undergoes rapid initial folding. Fine-tuning of the conformation is much slower and is often facilitated by specialized proteins called chaperones.

3   Covalent modifications of proteins include glycosylation, addition of lipid groups, methylation or acetylation, and phosphorylation. Most covalent modifications of proteins occur after translation; however, myristoylation occurs during translation.

4   Glycosylated proteins are generally destined for secretion or are localized at the extracellular surface of the cell membrane. Lipid modifications serve to anchor proteins in membranes.

3.4 Protein domains

That proteins contain functionally and physically discrete modules or domains is an important principle, one that will be reinforced throughout this course as we examine the roles of specific proteins in a variety of different cellular processes.

There are several advantages conferred by multidomain protein architecture:

1   *Creation of catalytic or substrate-binding sites*   These sites are often formed at the interface between two domains, typically a cleft. Movement of the domains relative to each other allows the substrate to bind and excludes the solvent to create the environment necessary for catalysis.

2   *Segregation of function*   Different domains of a protein often have distinct functions. Figure 3.26 shows a single subunit of the glycolytic enzyme glyceraldehyde 3-phosphate dehydrogenase. The subunit consists of two domains, one that binds the substrate (glyceraldehyde 3-phosphate) and one that binds the NAD coenzyme. Segregation of function in this way permits the swapping of function by swapping of domains. Thus numerous NAD-dependent dehydrogenases share similar domains for binding of NAD, whilst having distinct substrate-binding domains.

3   *Multifunctional proteins*   A multidomain protein may have more than one function, often related, and each function is performed by a distinct domain. For example, *E. coli* DNA polymerase I has both polymerase activity, and two kinds of exonuclease activity, all of which are required for DNA replication (see Chapter 9) and all of which reside on distinct domains of this protein.

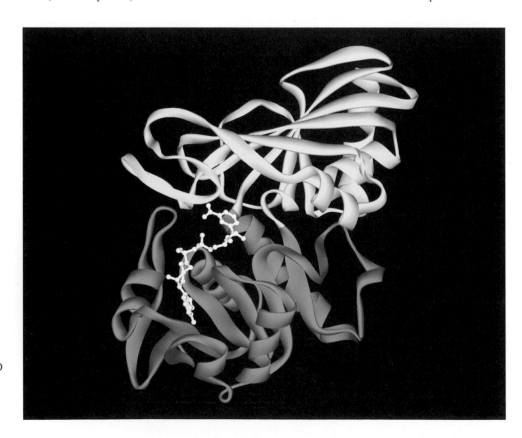

Figure 3.26
A single subunit of human glyceraldehyde 3-phosphate dehydrogenase showing the substrate binding domain (yellow) and the NAD binding domain (green) with an NAD molecule bound in the latter (white). (pdb file 4gpd)

○ Why might it be advantageous to have two enzyme activities on the same protein?

● Where two activities are required at the same time and in the same place, as in the case of the polymerase and exonuclease activities in DNA polymerase I, it is advantageous to have them on the same protein. The cellular process in which they are involved (DNA replication in this case) will be more efficient as all the necessary activities are 'on hand' and are present in equivalent quantities.

Broadly speaking, domains have a structural, catalytic or binding/regulatory function. Catalytic function in proteins will be discussed in detail later in this chapter.

3.4.1 Structural domains

Structural domains can serve as spacers, which position other domains in an appropriate orientation or location, or they may permit movement of domains relative to each other. Examples of domains that function as spacers are the heavy and light immunoglobulin constant domains which 'present' the working end of the immunoglobulin, i.e. the variable domains, for binding to target antigen (Figure 3.27).

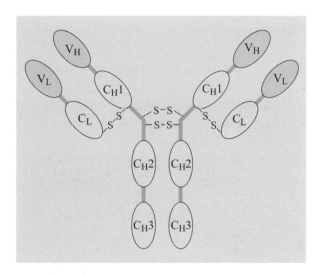

Figure 3.27
Immunoglobulin domains. The heavy and light chains of the immunoglobulin molecule both contain variable (V_H and V_L) and constant (C_H and C_L) domains. The variable domains make up the antigen binding site.

3.4.2 Binding domains in intracellular signalling proteins

The study of intracellular signalling pathways has highlighted the importance of multidomain architecture in protein function and some of the best-characterized binding/regulatory domains are those of signalling proteins.

Signalling pathways serve to communicate extracellular signals, usually recognized and transduced by specific membrane proteins, to effector proteins inside the cell and hence to elicit an appropriate response. Proteins in a signalling pathway are therefore required to interact with both upstream and downstream components via their specific binding domains. Many such interactions are regulated by covalent modification of the interacting proteins, usually phosphorylation. The modular nature of such proteins means that a single signalling protein might bind to a number of other mediators and there is increased potential for modulation of signalling. Table 3.5 details some of the key binding domains of signalling proteins and the motifs that they recognize.

Table 3.5   Binding domains in signalling proteins and the motifs that they recognize.

Domain	Full name	Binds to:
SH2	Src homology 2 domain	phosphorylated tyrosine (phosphotyrosine)
SH3	Src homology 3 domain	proline-rich motif
PTB	phosphotyrosine binding domain	phosphotyrosine
PH*	pleckstrin homology domain	phosphorylated inositol phospholipids
PDZ	(None; the name derives from three proteins in which the domain was first identified.)	specific (~5-residue) motifs at C-terminus or at the end of β hairpin loops

* Note that the PH domain does not recognize another protein but binds to phosphorylated lipid components of the plasma membrane on the cytosolic surface.

Though these binding domains recognize certain motifs, the specific interaction between individual proteins is determined by the special context of the motif within the peptide. PDZ domains are often found in so-called 'scaffold' proteins. Typically a scaffold protein has several such domains, each of which recruits a specific protein to the complex.

As well as domains that specify interactions with other proteins, many signalling proteins also contain domains with enzyme activity (e.g. kinases, phosphatases). These enzymatic domains may act on proteins recruited by binding domains, thereby regulating their activity. Enzyme activity in one domain of a protein may also be directed at another domain in the same protein (e.g. autophosphorylation).

In these ways, a complex network of interactions can build up in which there is potential for manipulation of activities and integration of several signalling pathways. You will learn more about how various intracellular signalling processes are integrated and regulated in Chapter 13.

3.4.3 The functional domains of Src

To illustrate some of the principles of multidomain protein function, we will use as an example, the Src protein, a very well-characterized tyrosine kinase that you will meet again later in this course (Chapters 13 and 19). As described earlier, Src contains four domains: two kinase domains, which together comprise the catalytic component of this protein, and two distinct binding/regulatory domains. The binding domains are of the **SH2** and **SH3** types. The identification of domains in other proteins, homologous to those in Src, led to the 'Src homology' nomenclature. If we represent the amino acid sequence of Src in a linear form, the domains can be mapped as indicated in Figure 3.28.

Figure 3.28

Representation of the tyrosine kinase Src, showing the linear map of its domains. The N-terminus is fatty acylated. The locations of intramolecular interactions (described in the text) are indicated.

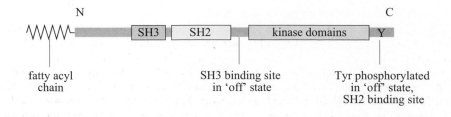

○ Note that the N-terminus of Src has a fatty acyl chain attached. Where do you think Src is located in the cell?

● Src is anchored to the cytosolic surface of the plasma membrane.

The general domain structure depicted in Figure 3.28 is common to all members of the Src family of tyrosine kinases. The conformation of the protein kinase fold of Src differs between 'on' (catalytically active) and 'off' (inactive) forms. The protein kinase domain is extremely well conserved, not only among tyrosine kinases, but also among the family of serine/threonine kinases. A marked similarity in the general three-dimensional structure of the kinase fold in its 'on' state in these enzymes is reflected in their common catalytic activity.

In the three-dimensional schematic representation of Src (Figure 3.29), the kinase domain can be seen to comprise two distinct lobes or subdomains. The smaller N-terminal lobe (N lobe) is composed of a five-stranded β sheet and one prominent α helix (called helix αC). The larger C lobe is predominantly helical. Figure 3.29b also shows the substrates for the kinase, namely ATP and a stretch of peptide sequence containing a tyrosine residue, in their appropriate binding sites. ATP binds in a deep cleft between the two lobes and the peptide binds across the front of the ATP binding pocket, close to the terminal (or gamma, γ) phosphate of the ATP. Close to the peptide substrate is a loop termed the 'activation loop'.

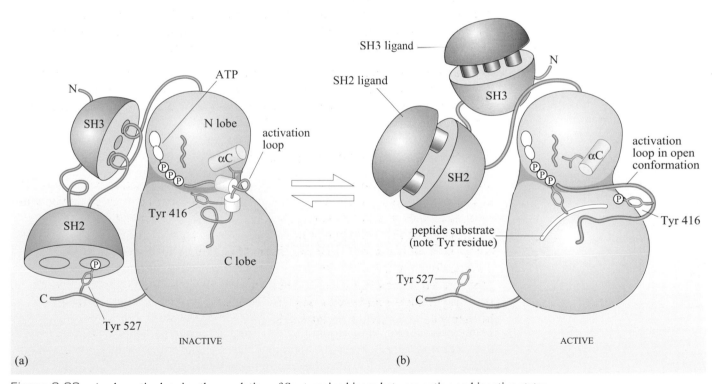

Figure 3.29   A schematic showing the regulation of Src tyrosine kinase between active and inactive states. (a) The inactive conformation is stabilized by intramolecular interactions between the SH2 domain and phosphorylated Tyr 527 in the C-terminal tail and between the SH3 domain and a specific sequence in the link between the SH2 domain and the kinase domain. (b) In the switch to the active conformation, these interactions are disrupted and the SH2 and SH3 domains dissociate and bind to other specific ligands. The inhibitory phosphate group on Tyr 527 is removed and Tyr 416 is phosphorylated. As a result, the activation loop adopts an open conformation and the peptide substrate can bind to the C lobe of the kinase domain. (Adapted from Huse and Kuriyan, 2002.)

How do the SH2 and SH3 domains regulate Src's kinase activity? The basis for the regulatory activity of these domains is their specificity for particular binding motifs (Table 3.5). In the inactive form of the enzyme, a tyrosine near the C-terminus (Tyr 527) is phosphorylated and is bound to the SH2 domain (Figure 3.29). This interaction positions the SH3 domain so that it binds to an internal proline-rich motif in the region linking SH2 to the kinase domains. These *intra*molecular interactions stabilize an inactive conformation of the kinase.

Src is activated when the SH2 and SH3 domains bind specific ligands. These ligands, components of a signalling cascade in which Src participates, bear the specific motifs recognized by the SH2 and SH3 domains and compete with the internal binding sites. Thus the SH2 domain binds to a ligand containing a phosphorylated tyrosine residue and the SH3 domain recognizes and binds to a proline-rich domain in another signalling protein. Binding of the SH2 and SH3 ligands disrupts intramolecular interactions and permits removal of the inhibitory phosphate from Tyr 527. With phosphorylation of a tyrosine residue in the activation loop (Tyr 416), this loop is stabilized in an open extended form that permits binding of the peptide substrate, and the enzyme is fully activated.

Summary of Section 3.4

1   Protein domains allow segregation of different functions in the same protein. They can have a binding function, a structural function or a catalytic function.

2   Binding domains mediate interactions between proteins of related function (such as those in a signalling cascade) and often are important in regulation of activity. Interactions via these binding domains are often dependent on the phosphorylation state of one of the binding partners. Examples of binding domains in signalling proteins include SH2 and SH3 domains.

3   The tyrosine kinase Src contains an SH2 and an SH3 domain. These domains regulate the kinase activity of Src, which is associated with two further domains of the protein. Activation of Src kinase activity requires removal of an inhibitory phosphate group from a tyrosine residue near the C-terminus and phosphorylation of another tyrosine residue in the activation loop. These events can occur only if intramolecular interactions are disrupted by binding of the SH2 and SH3 domains to other specific ligands.

3.5 Protein families and structural evolution

The availability of genomic sequence data from every major taxonomic group of organisms on Earth has allowed extensive comparisons to be made between their protein-coding regions, with over 800 000 protein sequences from these organisms being available for comparison in 2003. From these comparisons, it has become apparent that there is extensive homology between the amino acid sequences of many proteins, even between apparently distantly related organisms. In some proteins, this homology extends across the entire protein; in others, it lies within small regions called **conserved domains**.

The biochemical function of almost 80% of these conserved domains is known, e.g. the ATPase domain or the lipase domain. This means that for any particular protein, it is possible to predict aspects of its biochemical function solely by examining the domains that it contains. Sequence comparisons are therefore a powerful predictive tool and are performed routinely in molecular research.

For example, when the genomic DNA of an organism becomes newly available, comparative analysis with sequences from other organisms allows the function of most of the test organism's proteins to be predicted instantly. In the case of clinically important bacteria or viruses, this knowledge can allow rapid identification of drug or vaccine targets. Knowing the functional domains within a protein does not, of course, necessarily tell you what function that protein plays within a cell. For example, knowing that a protein is an ATPase does not tell us anything about what other proteins it interacts with in the cell or in which pathways it functions.

3.5.1 Amino acid sequence homologies and why they occur

Consider two genes encoding proteins that have 50% of their amino acid sequence in common.

○ How can this sequence homology be explained in terms of evolution?

● The most parsimonious explanation is that the similarities result from the fact that the two organisms share a common evolutionary past and that the genes encoding the proteins in each of the organisms arose from a common ancestral gene.

Through the process of natural selection, randomly occurring DNA mutations that alter amino acids within the protein and have a detrimental effect upon the organism are selected against, i.e. they are not transmitted to the next generation and are lost from the population. As a consequence of natural selection, differences can accumulate between the two proteins; some of these changes might enhance or modify function, some might have no effect, but critical amino acids will remain unaltered. Over many millions of years of evolution, this process results in proteins in which regions that are critical for function are highly conserved.

3.5.2 Conserved protein domains

By comparing the extensive protein databases, it is possible to identify many thousands of conserved domains. For example, within eukaryotes, over 600 domains have been identified with functions related to nuclear, extracellular and signalling proteins. The majority of conserved domains are evolutionarily ancient, with less than 10% being unique to vertebrates.

Figure 3.30 (overleaf) shows the amino acid sequence of the SH2 domains of several tyrosine kinases belonging to the so-called Src family. Src, described in the previous section, was the first tyrosine kinase to be discovered and has given its name to a family of nine homologous proteins. The SH2 domain is common to all these kinases and is highly conserved between species. This domain is found only within eukaryotic proteins and the number of SH2-containing proteins has increased in more recently evolved eukaryotes compared to more evolutionarily ancient species. Thus only one SH2-containing protein has been found in the yeast *Saccharomyces cerevisiae* and two in *Arabidopsis thaliana*, whereas *Caenorhabditis elegans* and *Drosophila melanogaster* have about 80 proteins with SH2 domains, and mammals have over 330.

In Figure 3.30, the sequences of the SH2 domain of four different Src family kinases, as well as homologous proteins in other species, have been aligned; that is, equivalent residues have been represented in the same vertical column with regions of sequence identity highlighted. Notice that the sequences for the Src SH2 domain from human, mouse and chicken are all identical (100% identity), whereas that of *Drosophila* has 55 residues out of the 108 in the sequence that are identical to those in human Src

Figure 3.30
Partial amino acid sequence alignment of the SH2 domains from four members of the Src family of tyrosine kinases: Src, Fyn, Lck and Lyn. For Src and Fyn, amino acid sequence data for several different species are included. For each protein, numbering is based on the most N-terminal amino acid in the polypeptide being numbered 1. Amino acid identities are highlighted in green.

Src	human	61	SIQAEEWYFGKITRRESERLLLNAENPRGTFLVRESETTKGAYCLSVSDFDNAK
	mouse	50	SIQAEEWYFGKITRRESERLLLNAENPRGTFLVRESETTKGAYCLSVSDFDNAK
	chick	62	SIQAEEWYFGKITRRESERLLLNPENPRGTFLVRESETTKGAYCLSVSDFDNAK
	Drosophila	156	SVNSEDWFFENVLRKEADKLLLAEENPRGTFLVRPSEHNPNGYSLSVKDWEDGR
Fyn	human	143	SIQAEEWYFGKLGRKDAERQLLSFGNPRGTFLIRESETTKGAYSLSIRDWDDMK
	mouse	143	SIQAEEWYFGKLGRKDAERQLLSFGNPRGTFLIRESQTTKGAYSLSIRDWDDMK
	chick	143	SIQAEEWYFGKLGRKDAERQLLSFGNPRGTFLIRESETTKGAYSLSIRDWDDMK
Lck	human	121	SLEPEPWFFKNLSRKDAERQLLAPGNTHGSFLIRESESTAGSFSLSVRDFDQNQ
Lyn	human	123	TLETEEWFFKDITRKDAERQLLAPGNSAGAFLIRESETLKGSFSLSVRDFDPVH
Src	human	115	GLNVKHYKIRKLDSGGFYITSRTQFNSLQQLVAYYSKHADGLCHRLTTVCPTSK
	mouse	104	GLNVKHYKIRKLDSGGFYITSRTQFNSLQQLVAYYSKHADGLCHRLTTVCPTSK
	chick	116	GLNVKHYKIRKLDSGGFYITSRTQFSSLQQLVAYYSKHADGLCHRLTNVCPTSK
	Drosophila	210	GYHVKHYRIKPLDNGGYYIATNQTFPSLQALVMAYSKNALGLCHILSRPCPKPQ
Fyn	human	197	GDHVKHYKIRKLDNGGYYITTRAQFETLQQLVQHYSERAAGLCCRLVVPC
	mouse	197	GDHVKHYKIRKLDNGGYYITTRAQFETLQQLVQHYSEKADGLCFNLTVV
	chick	197	GDHVKHYKIRKLDNGGYYITTRAQFETLQQLVQHYSEKADGLCFNLTVI
Lck	human	175	GEVVKHYKIRNLDNGGFYISPRITFPGLHELVRHYTNASDGLCTRLSRPCQTQK
Lyn	human	177	GDVIKHYKIRSLDNGGYYISPRITFPCISDMIKHYQKQADGLCRRLEKACISPK

(51% identity). A sequence identity level of 30% or more is generally indicative of homology between two proteins. In some cases, residues are conservatively 'substituted' in a homologous protein by others that have similar physical and chemical properties. Thus the structures that such proteins adopt may not differ greatly.

○ Tyrosine (Y) has a bulky aromatic ring in its side-chain and is uncharged at neutral pH. Which other amino acids might be conservatively substituted for tyrosine?

● Phenylalanine (F) or tryptophan (W) might replace tyrosine without significantly affecting the folding of the protein.

○ Consider the first 15 amino acids of the human and *Drosophila* Src SH2 domains in Figure 3.30. Try to identify some of those amino acid residues that are non-identical in the two sequences but that are similar in terms of their chemical properties and structure.

● `SIQAEEWYFGKITRR`
  ` ++   + +    +   +`
  `SVNSEDWFFENVLRK`

The '+' signs denote those amino acids that are similar but not identical.

In some cases, conservation between two proteins extends across the entire length of the protein, but in many cases, the regions of conservation are scattered throughout its length. This distribution results from domain shuffling, wherein segments of genes are duplicated, rearranged or swapped, as discussed in Section 3.2.3 and illustrated in Figure 3.16.

3.5.3 Predicting conformation from sequence

Given the amino acid sequence of a protein, it is possible to use computational methods to try to fit the sequence into folding patterns. This operation is called 'threading'. Different conformations can be ranked according to how well they accommodate the sequence; that is, the most stable conformation is ranked highest. Of course, this technique can only be used for those folds that have been definitively described by X-ray diffraction or NMR, and the structure of those proteins whose sequence does not conform to the restrictions of any known folding patterns must be determined experimentally.

Summary of Section 3.5

1   Proteins that serve similar functions often have similar amino acid sequences. The sequence of a protein can point to a particular function and can also be used to predict protein conformation.

2   Homologous proteins contain statistically significant (i.e. above random) similarities in their amino acid sequences.

3   The SH2 domain is an example of a domain that is highly conserved across different eukaryotes and is common to many different proteins.

3.6 Dynamic proteins

In some ways, proteins can be thought of as molecular machines, that through evolution have become highly specialized and efficient. Despite the somewhat static representations of proteins that you have met so far, proteins are in fact dynamic molecules. Not only are there internal movements, with conformational changes that are integral to protein function and regulation of function, but proteins, by virtue of their specific interactions with other cellular components, are essential to all the dynamic processes that constitute the life of a cell.

In this section, we are going to consider ways in which proteins can function in a responsive and interactive way, and we will try to relate such dynamic activity to protein structure. Given the vast number of different proteins, this discussion is far from exhaustive and only a few key well-characterized proteins have been chosen to illustrate the basic concepts.

3.6.1 All proteins bind other molecules

All proteins bind to other molecules (generically termed **ligands**). Ligands that can bind to proteins include:

- ions, e.g. Ca^{2+};
- small molecules, e.g. H_2O, O_2 and CO_2, glucose, ATP, GTP, NAD;
- macromolecules, i.e. proteins, lipids, polysaccharides, nucleic acids.

These interactions are specific and key to the protein's function and, of course, are critically dependent on the conformation of the protein. As we have seen with Src, protein conformation can be plastic; that is, proteins shift and adapt in response to interactions with specific ligands, thereby changing their activity and their capacity for further interactions.

Regardless of the nature of the ligand, the following general principles apply to the binding activity of proteins.

1   The interaction between a protein and a ligand is always **specific**; in other words, the protein discriminates between many different molecules and binds only one particular molecule or one of a number of very closely related (i.e. chemically and structurally similar) molecules.

2   Interactions are driven by the formation of non-covalent bonds, i.e. hydrogen bonds, ionic bonds, van der Waals forces and/or hydrophobic interactions (see Section 2.7 of Chapter 2).

3   Protein–ligand interactions range from weak and transient to strong and persistent, depending on the summative strength of the non-covalent bonds. Ligands that bind strongly tend to 'fit' the protein particularly well, like the correct piece of a jigsaw, thereby maximizing the number of non-covalent bonds that can form between the ligand and the amino acid residues of the protein.

4   The part of the protein that binds the ligand is called the **ligand binding site**. A protein may have binding sites for more than one ligand, though they usually are located in different parts of the protein.

5   Ligand binding sites are often clefts or 'pockets' at the protein surface and can be formed by amino acids from different parts of the polypeptide when it folds (Figure 3.31).

6   A measure of the strength of binding of a ligand to a protein is given by the equilibrium dissociation constant, (K_D) (Section 2.7.5).

Figure 3.31
Ligand binding sites, which are often formed in clefts or pockets on the protein surface, can be formed by amino acid residues contributed by different parts of the linear polypeptide sequence when it folds into a three-dimensional structure.

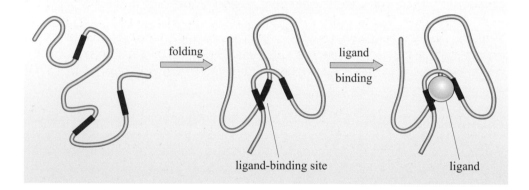

folding   ligand binding

ligand-binding site   ligand

3.6.2 Regulating protein conformation and activity

Allosteric regulation

In many proteins, the binding of a particular ligand at one site affects the conformation of a second remote binding site for another ligand on the same protein. This effect is called **allosteric regulation** and it is an important mechanism by which a protein's binding capacity and/or its activity are regulated. Thus the switch between two different protein conformations can be controlled by binding of a regulatory ligand.

○   What example of allosteric regulation have you already encountered in this chapter?

●   Binding of Src to a phosphorylated tyrosine residue on another protein, via the SH2 domain, affects the conformation of the Src kinase domain, switching it to an active conformation.

Allosteric regulation is a feature of most proteins, including enzymes, receptors and scaffold proteins, and you will come across many examples in this course.

In biosynthetic enzyme pathways, where a series of distinct enzymes catalyse individual reactions in the pathway, a downstream product often acts as an allosteric regulator of an enzyme further upstream, switching it to an inactive conformation. This type of allosteric regulation is termed **feedback inhibition** and it serves to control the level of activity of the pathway as a whole, switching off production when product levels have reached the required level. Allosteric regulation of enzyme activity can be either *positive* or *negative*, switching an enzyme on or off respectively.

Cooperative binding

A feature of some proteins comprising more than one subunit is that binding of a ligand to its binding site on one subunit, can increase the affinity of a neighbouring subunit for the same ligand, and hence enhance binding. The ligand-binding event on the first subunit is communicated, via conformational change, to the neighbouring subunit. This type of allosteric regulation is called **cooperative binding**.

Haemoglobin, as we have already discussed, is a tetramer consisting of two pairs of identical subunits (α and β) (Figure 3.20). Each subunit can bind an O_2 molecule via its associated haem (Figure 3.24) and haemoglobin demonstrates cooperative binding of this ligand. Thus, binding of O_2 by one subunit facilitates the binding of O_2 molecules by the other subunits of the tetramer. This characteristic makes haemoglobin a more efficient O_2 transporter than it would be if the O_2 binding sites were independent of one another. As a result, O_2 saturation of haemoglobin can be virtually complete in the lungs whilst, in the tissues, where the O_2 concentration is low, O_2 dissociates readily. The thermodynamics of cooperative binding of O_2 by haemoglobin will be discussed in Chapter 4, but at this point it is appropriate to consider the molecular basis for this effect.

The crystal structures of both the oxygenated form (oxy-Hb) and the deoxygenated form (deoxy-Hb) of haemoglobin have been determined (pdb files 1gzx and 1a3n respectively). Oxygenation of haemoglobin causes extensive changes in the both the tertiary and quaternary structure of the protein. The quaternary structure of deoxy-Hb is referred to as the **T state** (for *tense*), whilst that of oxy-Hb is known as the **R state** (for *relaxed*). The R state has a higher affinity for O_2 than does the T state. (Note that these terms are used to describe alternative structures of allosteric proteins in general, the T form being the one with the lower affinity for the ligand.) Individual globin subunits can adopt either the T or the R conformation and a change in the conformation of one subunit can affect the conformation of a neighbouring subunit, thereby altering its affinity for O_2. This is the basis for cooperative binding of O_2 by haemoglobin.

Max Perutz (1914–2002) proposed what is currently accepted as the molecular mechanism of haemoglobin oxygenation. Transition between the T and R states is triggered by stereochemical changes at the haem groups. In deoxy-Hb, the Fe^{2+} ion is about 0.6 Å (60 pm) out of the haem plane because of steric repulsion between the nearby histidine and the N atoms of the porphyrin ring. On binding of O_2 to the haem, on the opposite side from the His residue, the Fe^{2+} ion is pulled into the plane of the haem, dragging the His residue with it (Figure 3.32a). These movements, in turn, affect the orientation and position of neighbouring side-chains and as a result, the tertiary structure of the subunit switches to the R form.

Figure 3.32 (a) Binding of O_2 at the haem in haemoglobin causes the Fe^{2+} ion to move into the plane of the haem and causes conformational changes in the associated subunit; the oxygenated structure is shown in red and the deoxygenated structure is shown in blue. (b) Simplified schematic to show the relative rotation of the $\alpha\beta$ dimers that switches haemoglobin from the T state (blue) to the R state (red).

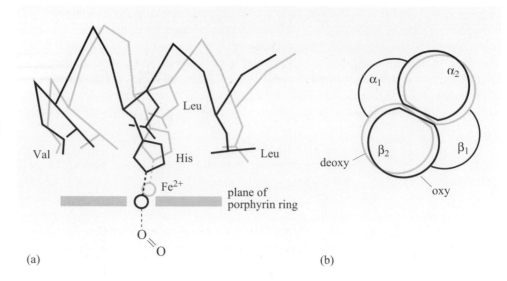

(a)

(b)

How does the change in conformation of one subunit affect the conformation of a neighbouring subunit? The answer lies in the interactions at the interface between the subunits. The α_1–β_1 and α_2–β_2 contacts are equivalent. These interactions are extensive and stable, so that each of these dimers moves as one. In contrast, the α_1–β_2 (and the equivalent α_2–β_1) contact is weak. When O_2 binds at one of the haems, the α_1–β_2 (and α_2–β_1) interaction is disrupted. As a result, one pair of $\alpha\beta$ subunits rotates relative to the other pair by 15° (Figure 3.32b). In this way, the conformational change caused by O_2 binding at one subunit is transmitted to ligand-free subunits. This conformational change effectively switches ligand-free subunits to the R state, increasing their affinity for O_2.

Phosphorylation of proteins as a means of regulating activity

Phosphorylation is an important mechanism for regulating the activity of many proteins, either switching on or switching off some activity of the protein.

○ What protein that we have already discussed is both positively and negatively regulated by phosphorylation?

● Src kinase activity is switched on by dephosphorylation of Tyr 527 and phosphorylation of Tyr 416. Dephosphorylation of Tyr 416 and phosphorylation of Tyr 527 together switch off the kinase activity.

In a reaction catalysed by a specific protein kinase, the terminal (γ) phosphate group on an ATP molecule is transferred to a hydroxyl group on an amino acid side-chain (Ser, Thr or Tyr) in the target protein (Figure 3.33). Removal of the phosphate group is catalysed by a phosphatase. The energy required to drive the cycle of phosphorylation and dephosphorylation derives from the hydrolysis of the ATP.

The cycle of phosphorylation and dephosphorylation can be very rapid, making the activity of the protein exquisitely sensitive to regulation in this way. Frequently, the kinases and phosphatases that catalyse these switches are themselves regulated, either by allosteric regulators or by phosphorylation (as in the case of Src kinase). This kind of cascade of activation and inactivation permits amplification and integration of upstream signals, as well as feedback regulation by downstream components.

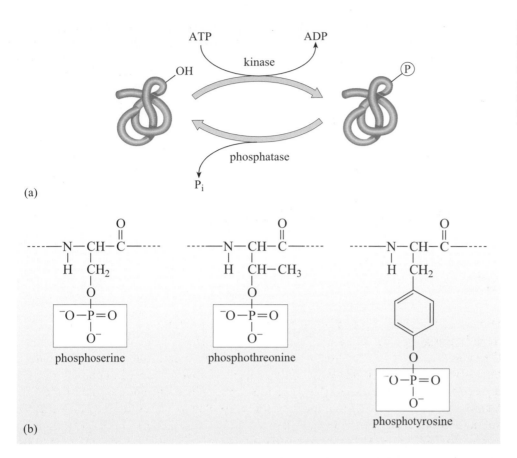

Figure 3.33
Protein phosphorylation.
(a) A phosphate group is transferred
from ATP to a hydroxyl group on the
protein by a kinase and can be
removed by a phosphatase.
(b) Phosphorylation can occur on Ser,
Thr or Tyr residues.

How does phosphorylation of a protein affect its activity? Addition of a phosphate group at a crucial residue can change the conformation of a protein or alter the interactions of the protein with substrates or other molecules. There are several ways in which phosphorylation-induced change can happen:

▶ The phosphate group may prevent binding of a substrate or ligand. Being strongly negatively charged, the phosphate may disrupt electrostatic interactions between a protein and its ligand. Alternatively, it may block ligand-binding by steric hindrance.

▶ Phosphorylation may cause a dramatic change in the conformation of the protein, as in the case of Src, where the activation loop changes to an open conformation, allowing the substrate to bind.

▶ The phosphorylated residue in the context of the protein may be recognized by another protein. Some adaptor proteins recognize specific phosphorylated motifs and 'recruit' the protein to a protein complex where it may be a substrate in a further reaction. For example, the '14–3–3 proteins' (named, for historical reasons, according to their chromatographic properties), which regulate certain protein kinases, recognize specific motifs containing phosphoserine residues.

◯ Which protein domains have you come across that recognize phosphorylated amino acid residues?

◼ SH2 and PTB domains bind to specific motifs containing phosphorylated tyrosine residues (Table 3.5).

There are very many different protein kinases in eukaryotic cells and many share a common structure for their kinase domain. Variations in amino acid sequence and higher-order structure account for their substrate specificity. Though less numerous than kinases, there are also many phosphatases in eukaryotic cells. Some phosphatases are highly substrate-specific, acting on only one or two phosphoproteins, but there are others that can act on a broad range of substrates. In the latter, regulatory domains serve to target the enzyme activity to particular substrates.

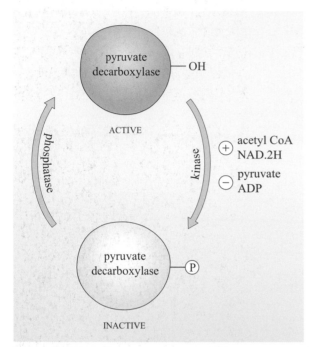

Figure 3.34   Regulation of pyruvate decarboxylase by phosphorylation. The phosphorylated enzyme is inactive. The kinase that phosphorylates pyruvate decarboxylase is positively regulated by acetyl CoA and NAD.2H and negatively regulated by pyruvate and ADP.

Regulation by phosphorylation is a particularly common mechanism in intracellular signalling; you will encounter many examples of this regulatory mechanism in Chapter 13 and indeed throughout this course. However, other proteins that are not signalling molecules are also regulated in the same way, notably some enzymes in metabolic pathways. An example is pyruvate dehydrogenase, which catalyses the oxidation of pyruvate, the end-product of glycolysis, to give acetyl CoA and CO_2. Acetyl CoA then enters the citric acid cycle. Pyruvate dehydrogenase is not actually a single enzyme but is an example of a multienzyme complex (see Section 3.7.4) and comprises three different enzymes. One of these enzymes, pyruvate decarboxylase, is inactivated by phosphorylation of a specific Ser residue. Dephosphorylation reactivates the enzyme. The kinase that catalyses the phosphorylation of pyruvate decarboxylase is subject to allosteric regulation by a number of small molecules, including acetyl CoA, pyruvate and ADP, as indicated in Figure 3.34.

Acetyl CoA is a positive allosteric regulator of pyruvate decarboxylase kinase which, in turn, phosphorylates and hence inactivates pyruvate carboxylase. In this way, acetyl CoA inhibits its own synthesis.

▢ Of what kind of regulation is this an example?

◼ Feedback inhibition.

G proteins

A large family of proteins, called **G proteins**, are regulated by binding of GTP. All known forms of life on Earth use G proteins to regulate protein synthesis and in eukaryotes there are ten families of G proteins which, between them, regulate many functions, from signal transduction to transport processes, cytoskeletal rearrangements and protein synthesis.

Generally, when they are bound to GTP, G proteins are in their active conformations and can bind to and stimulate effector proteins. Hydrolysis of the GTP is catalysed by the G protein itself; G proteins are therefore also known as a **GTPases**. On hydrolysis of GTP, the γ-phosphate is released and the GDP remains bound to the protein. In this GDP-bound form, the protein is inactive and cannot bind to effector proteins. Thus there are similarities in the regulation of G proteins with the regulation of proteins by direct phosphorylation.

In the same way that the phosphorylation state of some proteins is determined by the balance of kinase and phosphatase activities, the switch between GTP-bound and GDP-bound conformations of a G protein depends on the activity of other proteins, as well as the G protein's own GTPase activity. Proteins known as **GTPase activating proteins (GAPs)** enhance the GTPase activity of the G protein whilst **guanine nucleotide exchange factors (GEFs)** accelerate the dissociation of GDP from the G protein, allowing it to be replaced by GTP. Note that, in some cases, these regulatory functions may reside in intrinsic domains of the G protein itself. We will concentrate here on two of the main families of G protein: small G proteins, of which Ras is an example; and trimeric G proteins.

Small G proteins consist of a single domain of about 200 residues and require extrinsic GAPs to stimulate the hydrolysis of bound GTP. There are a number of different families of small G proteins. Ras is the prototypical small G protein and is involved in transduction of growth factor signals. Other small G proteins are involved in a variety of cellular processes, including intracellular transport, vesicle formation and targeting, cytoskeletal changes and cell polarization, regulation of cell growth, and assembly of the mitotic spindle.

The role of **Ras** in signalling from growth factor receptors will be considered in detail in Chapter 13. For now, we will focus on the structural aspects of this protein. Ras (M_r 21 000) is equivalent to the core GTP-binding domain common to all G proteins. It contains a six-stranded β sheet sandwiched between five α helices. Figure 3.35 shows the structure of Ras in both its GTP- and GDP-bound forms. The nucleotides bind in a shallow groove formed by loops at the surface of the protein and this binding requires Mg^{2+} ions.

Trimeric G proteins (Figure 3.36) have three subunits (α, β and γ). They transduce signals from a family of receptor proteins known as 7-helix transmembrane receptors, of which there are more than 1000. Many species express numerous different α, β and γ subunits and there is considerable diversity in the G proteins assembled from them. Gα subunits have M_r values in the range 39 000–45 000 and consist of two domains: a GTP binding domain similar to the single domain of small G proteins such as Ras, and a domain that further enhances binding of the GTP molecule. Both the Gα and the Gγ subunits are anchored to the intracellular surface of the plasma membrane. Gα is usually myristoylated whilst Gγ is prenylated (Figure 3.25). The Gβ and Gγ subunits bind to each other very tightly but bind reversibly to Gα. The association of Gα with Gβγ and the activity of these subunits depend on whether GTP or GDP is bound to Gα. The signalling activity of trimeric G proteins will be discussed in Chapter 13.

Other G proteins include certain proteins involved in the initiation and elongation stages of translation of mRNA. As well as binding GTP, these proteins bind amino-acyl tRNAs and deliver them to the ribosome. Hydrolysis of the GTP occurs when the appropriate amino acid is added to the peptide. Translation is discussed in detail in Chapter 11.

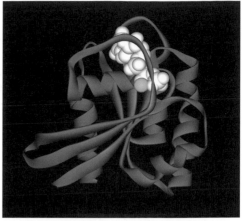

(a)

(b)

Figure 3.35   Ribbon models of the small G protein Ras with (a) GTP bound (pdb file 121p) and (b) GDP bound (pdb file 1q21). The nucleotides are shown in white in space-filling format. Notice the Mg^{2+} ion (green), which participates in binding of the nucleotide.

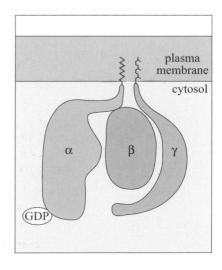

Figure 3.36   Simple schematic of a trimeric G protein (with GDP bound), shown associated with the plasma membrane.

3.6.3 Protein–protein interactions

You should by now be beginning to appreciate the importance of protein–protein interactions in different cellular processes. Indeed, such interactions are intrinsic to virtually every cellular process, e.g. DNA replication, transcription, translation, control of the cell cycle, signal transduction, secretory and metabolic processes.

There are three main types of protein–protein interaction, termed surface–string, helix–helix and surface–surface interactions (Figure 3.37).

Surface–surface interactions are the most common type of protein–protein contact. They require precise matching of complementary surfaces in the two proteins and tend to be relatively strong. The requirement for a good fit makes surface–surface interactions very specific.

In surface–string interactions, an extended loop of one protein makes contact with the surface of another protein. An example of this kind of interaction is that which occurs between a peptide containing a phosphotyrosine residue and the SH2 domain of Src and other related proteins. Another surface–string interaction takes place between the kinase fold of Src and part of the protein that it phosphorylates.

Helix–helix interactions involve α helices from two different proteins wrapping around each other to form a coiled-coil. Such an interaction occurs in a number of gene-regulatory proteins. Towards the end of this chapter, we will look at some of the techniques employed to study protein–protein interactions.

Figure 3.37
The three main types of protein–protein contact.

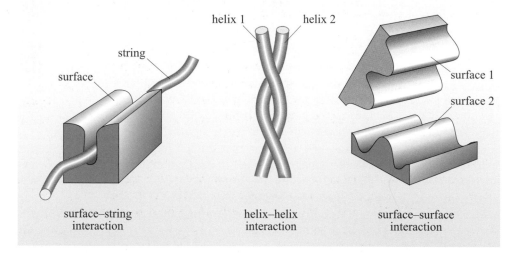

Summary of Section 3.6

1   Proteins are dynamic molecular machines. All proteins bind to other molecules, whether ions, small molecules or macromolecules, and these interactions are critical to the protein's function. The activity of proteins is regulated by changes in conformation.

2   In allosterically regulated proteins, binding of one ligand affects the conformation of a remote part of the protein, thereby regulating interaction with a second ligand. Cooperative binding is a type of allosteric regulation in which conformational changes are communicated between subunits (e.g. in O_2 binding in haemoglobin).

3   A common mechanism for regulating protein conformation and activity is through cycles of phosphorylation (by kinases) and dephosphorylation (by phosphatases).

4   G proteins are regulated by binding and hydrolysis of GTP. Generally, the GTP-bound form of the protein is active and the GDP-bound form is inactive. Many G proteins require other proteins to enhance their GTPase activity (GAPs) or to accelerate exchange of GDP for GTP (GEFs). Two of the largest families of G proteins are small G proteins (exemplified by Ras) and trimeric G proteins.

5   Trimeric G proteins contain α, β and γ subunits and the α subunit has the GTP binding site and GTPase activity. These G proteins transduce signals from 7-helix transmembrane receptors.

3.7 Catalytic proteins

Among those proteins of known function, the majority are enzymes. Enzymes act as catalysts, i.e. they increase the rates of reactions, making and breaking bonds, without themselves undergoing any permanent change. They are highly specific for particular reactions and are excellent examples of how a protein's function is entirely dependent on its structure.

First of all, a protein must bind its substrate (or substrates) in a specific fashion; it must then convert the substrate(s) into the product (or products) and finally release these. In the case of enzymes, the binding site for a substrate is also referred to as the **active site**, as an indication that the substrate undergoes chemical modification.

An enzyme-catalysed reaction can be represented as follows:

$$E + S \rightleftharpoons ES \rightleftharpoons ES^{\ddagger} \rightleftharpoons EP \rightleftharpoons E + P$$

where E is the enzyme, S is the substrate, P is the product, ES is the enzyme with substrate bound (enzyme–substrate complex) and EP is the enzyme with product bound (enzyme–product complex). $ES^{\ddagger}$ (called the **transition state**) is the highest-energy intermediate in the enzyme-catalysed reaction and is very unstable, due to the strained conformation of both the substrate and the enzyme in this complex.

The transition state in an enzyme-catalysed reaction has a lower energy than that for the same reaction in the absence of enzyme. Thus the enzyme reduces the energy barrier presented by the conversion of substrate to product and hence speeds up the reaction. In Chapter 4, you will learn more about the thermodynamics of enzyme-catalysed reactions. For the present, we will consider how the structure of an enzyme, and in particular the configuration of the amino acid residues at the active site, facilitate catalysis.

3.7.1 Catalytic mechanisms

In general terms, the following mechanisms operate at the active site of an enzyme to bring about the conversion of substrate to product:

1   Charged groups at the enzyme active site alter the distribution of electrons in the substrate. By affecting the electron distributions in key atoms in the substrate, the enzyme can destabilize existing bonds and favour the formation of new bonds. This principle is illustrated overleaf, using as an example the hydrolysis of an amide bond.

2   In binding the substrate, the enzyme forces it to change its conformation. This conformational change puts a strain on the substrate and drives it towards the transition state.

3   Many enzymes temporarily form a covalent bond between the substrate and an amino acid side-chain at the active site. This is termed **covalent catalysis**.

4   Where an enzyme catalyses a reaction between two substrates (reactants), these will bind at the active site such that they are in close proximity and in the appropriate orientation for the reaction to occur.

   ☐ Refer back to the description of Src tyrosine kinase activity (Section 3.4.3); note the orientation of the ATP and polypeptide substrates at the active site. How does the orientation of these reactants facilitate the phosphorylation of the polypeptide?

   ⬛ The ATP molecule is bound such that its chain of three phosphates points towards the target tyrosine residue of the polypeptide, thus facilitating the transfer of the terminal γ-phosphate of ATP to the tyrosine residue.

5   Many enzymes require metal ions for catalytic activity (see Section 3.3.2). These ions may serve to stabilize negative charges in the active site, mediate redox reactions or bind substrates. Catalysis that is driven through the stabilization of negative charges (by a metal ion or by a positively charged amino acid side-chain) is described as **electrophilic catalysis**.

Redistribution of electrons in the substrate

An electrophile is an atom, ion or molecule that has an affinity for electrons and can function as an electron acceptor. A nucleophile is an atom, ion or molecule that has an affinity for atomic nuclei and can function as an electron donor.

Consider the hydrolysis of an amide bond (e.g. a peptide bond) (Figure 3.38). This reaction requires that the N—C bond is broken and that new bonds are formed between an OH group and the C atom and between an H atom and the N atom, with the OH and H groups deriving from a water molecule (H_2O).

Many enzymes have charged groups at critical positions in their active sites, such that they can affect bonds in the bound substrate. An acidic atom or group, such as the N atom on histidine, has a partial positive charge at neutral pH and has a tendency to donate its proton (H^+) to other atoms. If the substrate binds so that the O atom of its carbonyl group is in close proximity to the acidic group, then the latter, with its net positive charge, tends to draw the electrons of the carbonyl double bond towards itself, giving the C of the carbonyl group a partial positive charge (Figure 3.39a). This C atom is now much more attractive to the electronegative O atom of the water molecule and the hydrolysis reaction illustrated in Figure 3.38 is accelerated. (Remember that water is a polar molecule with an electronegative region pointing away from the H atoms; see Chapter 2.) This kind of catalysis is called **general acid catalysis**.

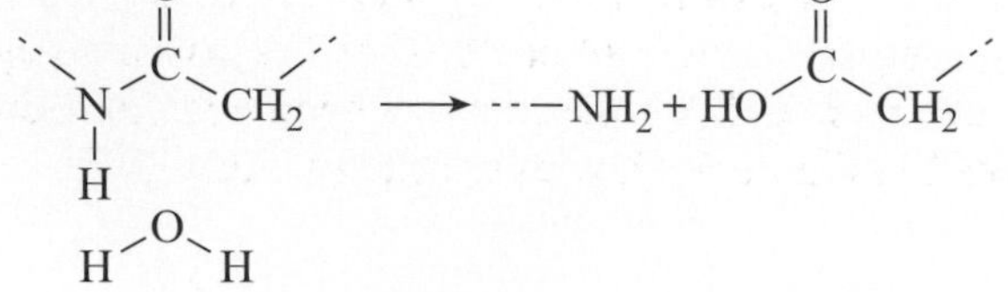

Figure 3.38
Hydrolysis of an amide bond.

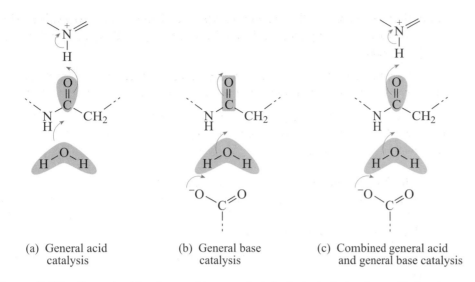

(a) General acid
   catalysis

(b) General base
   catalysis

(c) Combined general acid
   and general base catalysis

Figure 3.39   General acid and general base catalysis in the hydrolysis of an amide bond.

A basic group, such as the carboxylate group of aspartate and glutamate side-chains, positioned close to the water molecule, can similarly affect electron distribution. In this case, the negatively charged carboxylate group tends to push electrons in the water molecule towards the O atom, making this molecule more polar and more ready to donate electrons to the C atom of the amide bond (Figure 3.39b). This type of catalysis is **general base catalysis**. Enzymes can, in fact, use both general acid and general base catalysis simultaneously; thereby further accelerating the reaction (Figure 3.39c).

Enzymes are extremely efficient catalysts because they simultaneously use several catalytic mechanisms. We will now look more closely at two enzymes, lysozyme and carboxypeptidase A, to demonstrate how enzymes apply these mechanisms to great effect. These enzymes have been chosen because they have been studied extensively and their mechanisms are particularly well characterized. They also have very different modes of action.

3.7.2 Lysozyme

Lysozyme was the first enzyme for which the X-ray structure was determined at high resolution. This was achieved in 1965 by David Phillips, working at the Royal Institution in London. Phillips went on to propose a mechanism for lysozyme action that was based principally on structural data. The Phillips mechanism has since been borne out by experimental evidence, as we shall see later.

Lysozyme is found widely in the cells and secretions (including tears and saliva) of vertebrates, and hen egg white is particularly rich in this enzyme. Lysozyme catalyses the hydrolysis of glycosidic bonds that link *N*-acetylmuramic acid (NAM) and *N*-acetylglucosamine (NAG) in polysaccharides of bacterial cell walls. In doing so, it damages the integrity of the cell wall and thereby acts as a bacteriocidal agent. The NAM–NAG bond is represented in Figure 3.40, with the site of cleavage by lysozyme indicated.

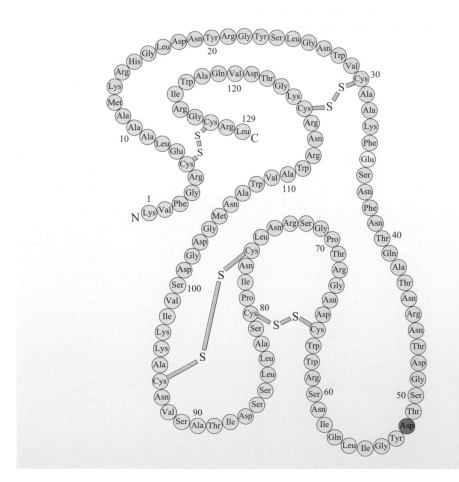

Figure 3.40   Part of the polysaccharide component of bacterial cell walls, showing the alternating *N*-acetylmuramic acid (NAM) and *N*-acetylglucosamine (NAG) residues. This polysaccharide is a substrate for lysozyme, which hydrolyses the glycosidic bond at the position indicated. (For clarity, and to permit a linear representation of the molecule, some of the bonds are shown in a zig-zag form.)

Lysozyme is a relatively small enzyme. Hen egg white lysozyme consists of a single polypeptide of 129 amino acids in length (Figure 3.41) with M_r 14 600. From X-ray diffraction data, we can see that there is a distinct cleft in the lysozyme structure (Figure 3.42). The active site is located in this cleft. In the amino acid sequence in Figure 3.41 and in the space-filling model of lysozyme in Figure 3.42, those residues that line the substrate binding pocket in the folded protein have been highlighted.

Figure 3.41   The amino acid sequence of hen egg white lysozyme, with the residues that line the substrate binding pocket highlighted in grey. Asp 52 and Glu 35, key residues in the active site, are highlighted in red and yellow respectively.

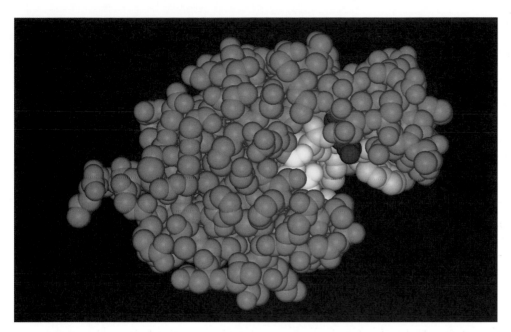

Figure 3.42
Figure 3.42
A space-filling model of hen egg white lysozyme in which key residues have been highlighted. Asp 52 is in red; Glu 35 is in yellow; some of the residues lining the substrate binding pocket are shown in grey.

The active site of lysozyme is a long groove that can accommodate six sugars of the polysaccharide chain at a time. On binding the polysaccharide, the enzyme hydrolyses one of the glycosidic bonds. If the six sugars in the stretch of polysaccharide are identified as A–F, the cleavage site is between D and E, as indicated in Figure 3.40. The two polysaccharide fragments are then released. Figure 3.43 depicts the stages of this reaction, which are also described in detail overleaf.

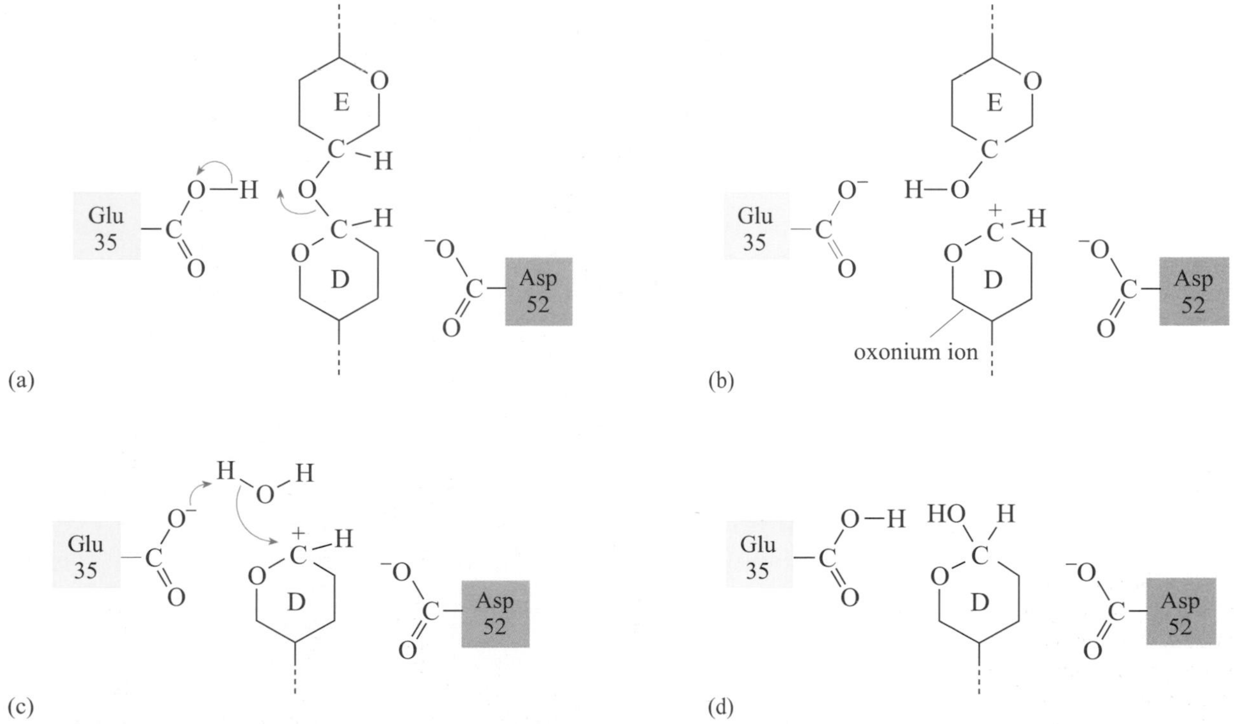

(a)

(b)

(c)

(d)

Figure 3.43   The catalytic mechanism of lysozyme. Note that only key residues involved in catalysis (Glu 35 and Asp 52) are shown. The stages are described in detail in the text. (Based on Phillips, 1966)

1 On binding to the enzyme, the substrate adopts a strained conformation. Residue D is distorted (not shown in the diagram) to accommodate a $-CH_2OH$ group that otherwise would make unfavourable contact with the enzyme. In this way, the enzyme forces the substrate to adopt a conformation approximating to that of the transition state.

2 Residue 35 of the enzyme is glutamic acid (Glu 35) with a proton that it readily transfers to the polar O atom of the glycosidic bond. In this way, the C—O bond in the substrate is cleaved (Figure 3.43a and b).

3 Residue D of the polysaccharide now has a net positive charge; this reaction intermediate is known as an *oxonium ion* (Figure 3.43b). The enzyme stabilizes this intermediate in two ways. Firstly, a nearby aspartate residue (Asp 52), which is in the negatively charged carboxylate form, interacts with the positive charge of the oxonium ion. Secondly, the distortion of residue D enables the positive charge to be shared between its C and O atom. (Note that this sharing of charge between atoms is termed *resonance* in the same way as the sharing of electrons between the atoms of the peptide group.) *Thus the oxonium ion intermediate is the transition state.* Normally, such an intermediate would be very unstable and reactive. Asp 52 helps to stabilize the oxonium ion, but it does not react with it. This is because, at 3 Å distance, the reactive groups are too far apart.

4 The enzyme now releases residue E with its attached polysaccharide, yielding a glycosyl-enzyme intermediate. The oxonium ion reacts with a water molecule from the solvent environment, extracting a hydroxyl group and re-protonating Glu 35 (Figure 3.43c and d).

5 The enzyme then releases residue D with its attached polysaccharide and the reaction is complete.

☐ The catalytic mechanism of lysozyme involves both general acid and general base catalysis. Which residues participate in these events?

◼ Glu 35 participates in general acid catalysis (donates a proton) and Asp 52 participates in general base catalysis (stabilizing the positive charge of the oxonium ion).

The Phillips mechanism for lysozyme catalysis, as outlined above, is supported by a number of experimental observations. In particular, the importance of Glu 35 and Asp 52 in the process has been confirmed by **site-directed mutagenesis (SDM)** experiments. SDM is a very powerful technique for examining the role of individual amino acid residues in a protein's function and will be discussed in some detail in Section 3.8.1. SDM involves the use of recombinant DNA technology to selectively replace the residue of interest with a different amino acid with critically different properties. The resulting protein can then be tested functionally, e.g. with respect to substrate binding or catalytic activity. When this technique was applied to lysozyme to replace Glu 35 with a glutamine residue (Gln), the resulting protein could still bind the substrate (albeit less strongly) but it had no catalytic activity. *Glu 35 is therefore essential for lysozyme's catalytic activity.* When Asp 52 was replaced with an asparagine (Asn) residue, the mutant protein had less than 5% of the catalytic activity of normal (wild-type) lysozyme, in spite of the fact that the mutant form actually had a twofold higher affinity for the substrate. It follows that *Asp 52 is essential for lysozyme's catalytic activity.* Experiments using chemical agents that covalently modified these residues, without significantly affecting the X-ray structure, similarly proved that they were essential for catalytic activity.

3.7.3 Carboxypeptidase A

Carboxypeptidase A is a protease that hydrolyses the C-terminal peptide bond in polypeptide chains. Whilst this enzyme demonstrates strict specificity with regard to the position of the amide bond (i.e. it must be C-terminal), it does not discriminate on the basis of the identity of the terminal residue; in fact, it will cleave off any residue with the exception of arginine (Arg), lysine (Lys) or proline (Pro). However, carboxypeptidase A is most efficient at removing terminal residues with aromatic or bulky aliphatic side-chains (Tyr, Trp, Phe, Leu, Ile).

The three-dimensional structure of carboxypeptidase A was elucidated by William Lipscomb at Harvard in 1967. It has a single polypeptide chain of 307 amino acid residues and an M_r of 34 500. It is a compact globular protein and is a metalloenzyme, having a tightly bound zinc ion that is essential for its activity. The zinc ion is in a pocket near the surface of the protein and is coordinated by a glutamate side-chain (Glu 72) and two histidine side-chains (His 69 and His 196). The substrate binds in the pocket, near to the zinc ion. Figure 3.44 shows a space-filling representation of carboxypeptidase A, with the zinc ion, Glu 72, His 69 and His 196 highlighted, and another representation, this time with a substrate bound. The substrate used to obtain this X-ray structure was glycyltyrosine (Figure 3.45), an analogue of the natural peptide substrate.

Carboxypeptidase A hydrolyses glycyltyrosine very slowly. Analogues of natural substrates, such as this molecule, that are processed very slowly by the enzyme, are often chosen for X-ray crystallographic studies of enzyme–substrate complexes. It is necessary to use substrate analogues because obtaining crystals for analysis can be a very lengthy process and the natural substrate would not remain bound to

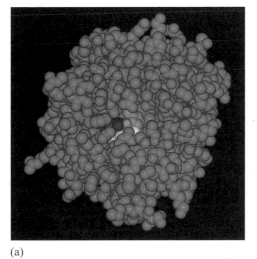

(a)

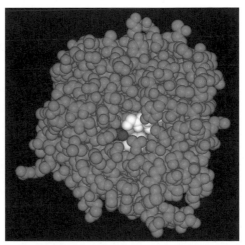

(b)

Figure 3.44 Space-filling representation of bovine carboxypeptidase A (a) without substrate bound (pdb file 2ctb) and (b) with substrate (glycyltyrosine, shown in white) bound (pdb file 3cpa). (c) A close-up view of the substrate binding site with the polypeptide backbone shown in ribbon format, coloured as in (b). The zinc ion is shown in pink and key residues involved in coordinating the zinc ion are highlighted in space-filling format as follows: Glu 72, red; His 69, yellow; His 196, orange.

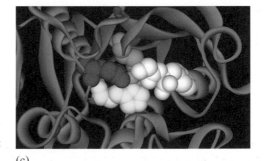

(c)

Figure 3.45
Binding of the substrate analogue glycyltyrosine in the active site of carboxypeptidase A. Only key residues involved in substrate binding and catalysis are shown. (Based on Lipscomb *et al.*, 1970)

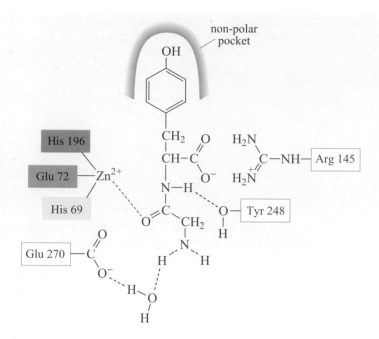

the enzyme for long enough to permit crystallization. From the crystal structures of the enzyme–substrate complex, the mode of binding of glycyltyrosine to the enzyme has been deduced and is depicted in Figure 3.45. The tyrosine side-chain of the substrate occupies a non-polar pocket, whilst its terminal carboxyl group interacts electrostatically with the positively charged side-chain of arginine 145 (Arg 145). The NH hydrogen of the peptide bond is hydrogen-bonded to the OH group of tyrosine 248 (Tyr 248) and the carbonyl oxygen atom of the peptide bond is coordinated to the zinc ion. The terminal amino group of glycyltyrosine hydrogen-bonds, via an intervening water molecule, to the side-chain of Glu 270.

○ How do you think the binding of the substrate analogue, glycyltyrosine, to the active site of carboxypeptidase A would differ from that of a polypeptide substrate?

● A polypeptide substrate would not have a terminal amino group in the active site, so would not form the interaction with Glu 270.

The interaction between Glu 270 and the glycyltyrosine molecule is thought to be responsible for the very slow rate of hydrolysis of this substrate analogue by the enzyme.

In binding substrate, the active site of carboxypeptidase A undergoes structural rearrangement to bring the groups that participate in catalysis into the correct orientation. This process is known as **induced fit**. The *induced fit model* of enzyme action was first proposed by Koshland. The side-chains of Arg 145 and Glu 270 both move 2 Å, water molecules are displaced from the non-polar pocket and, most striking of all, the phenolic hydroxyl group of Tyr 248 moves 12 Å when this residue swings into place for catalysis. This last movement is huge when you consider that, at its widest, the enzyme is only 50 Å across!

The movement of the hydroxyl group of Tyr 248 brings it from near the surface of the enzyme to the vicinity of the peptide bond to be hydrolysed. The different structural rearrangements effectively close the active-site pocket, excluding water and making the environment of the active site hydrophobic. Clearly, a peptide substrate could not access the active site if it was in this closed conformation. To permit substrate binding, carboxypeptidase A has to have a very different conformation in the unbound state than it does in the catalytically active state. Thus in undergoing these substantial rearrangements, induced by the substrate, it creates the correct environment for catalysis.

The mechanism of catalysis of the peptide bond by carboxypeptidase A is illustrated in Figure 3.46. The carbonyl group of the peptide bond is coordinated to the zinc ion, making the C=O bond more polarized than usual. This effect is enhanced by the non-polar environment of the zinc ion, which increases its effective charge. In this way, the zinc ion stabilizes the negative charge that develops on the O atom (electrophilic catalysis). This large dipole makes the C atom of the carbonyl group more vulnerable to nucleophilic attack, because it has a partial positive charge. The negatively charged Glu 270 removes a proton from a water molecule and the resulting OH$^-$ directly attacks the vulnerable carbonyl C atom (general base catalysis). Tyr 248 simultaneously donates a proton to the NH group of the peptide bond. In this way, the peptide bond is hydrolysed.

Carboxypeptidase B specifically removes C-terminal Arg or Lys residues from peptides. Whilst being very similar to carboxypeptidase A in terms of overall structure, carboxypeptidase B has a negatively charged aspartate (Asp) side-chain in an appropriate position to bind the positively charged side-chains of Arg and Lys.

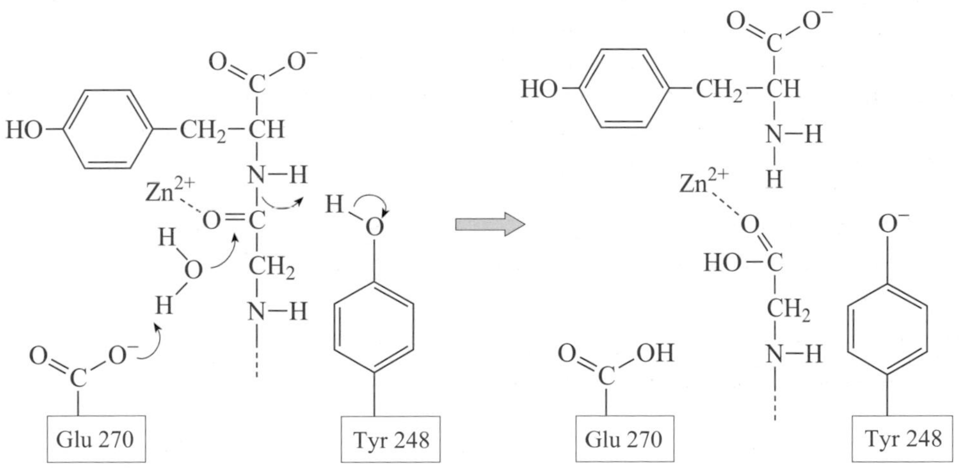

Figure 3.46
The catalytic mechanism of carboxypeptidase A. The stages are described in detail in the text.

3.7.4 Multienzyme complexes

In free solution, the rate of an enzyme-catalysed reaction depends on the concentration of the enzyme and the concentration of its substrate. For an enzyme operating at suboptimal concentrations, the reaction is said to be *diffusion-limited*, since it depends on the random collision of the enzyme and substrate. If we consider a metabolic pathway, the product of one reaction is the substrate for the next enzyme in the pathway. Direct transfer of a metabolite from one enzyme to another would avoid dilution of the metabolite in the bulk aqueous environment and would increase the rate of reaction.

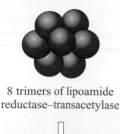

8 trimers of lipoamide
reductase–transacetylase

+6 dimers of dihydrolipoyl
dehydrogenase

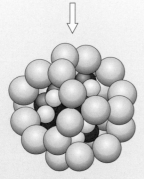

+12 dimers of pyruvate
decarboxylase

Figure 3.47
Pyruvate dehydrogenase is a
multienzyme complex comprising
multiples of three different enzymes:
eight of lipoamide reductase–
transacetylase (a trimer), six of
dihydrolipoyl dehydrogenase
(a dimer) and 12 of pyruvate
decarboxylase (a dimer), giving a total
of 60 polypeptide chains per complex.

In the cell, enzymes of a particular pathway are frequently organized spatially so that such *metabolic channelling* can occur. Some enzymes are associated with other enzymes involved in a particular pathway to form **multienzyme complexes**. For the enzymes in such complexes, the diffusion of the substrate is not rate-limiting. Pyruvate dehydrogenase (Figure 3.47) is a complex of three different enzymes that collectively catalyse the oxidation of pyruvate as described previously (Section 3.6.2). In fact, in eukaryotic cells, most enzymes do not diffuse freely in the cytosol but are effectively concentrated in particular parts of the cell along with other enzymes or proteins involved in related processes. Concentration of enzymes in this way can be achieved by specific protein–protein interactions.

Summary of Section 3.7

1   The majority of proteins of known function are enzymes. Enzymes are biological catalysts, increasing the rates of reactions. Enzymes are not permanently altered by catalysis of a reaction.

2   The transition state is an unstable intermediate enzyme–substrate complex in which the enzyme and the substrate are in highly strained conformations.

3   There are a number of different catalytic mechanisms employed by enzymes including general acid and general base catalysis, covalent catalysis and electrophilic catalysis.

4   General acid and general base catalysis involve charged groups at the active site of the enzyme that help make and break bonds by causing a redistribution of electrons in the bonds of the substrate.

5   Lysozyme hydrolyses glycosidic bonds in the polysaccharides of bacterial cell walls. It uses both general acid and general base catalysis.

6   Carboxypeptidase A hydrolyses C-terminal peptide bonds and uses both electrophilic and general base catalysis. In binding its substrate, carboxypeptidase A undergoes a dramatic structural rearrangement to create the required active site conformation for catalysis. This process is known as induced fit.

7   The efficiency of enzyme-catalysed reactions in the cell is increased by metabolic channelling in multienzyme complexes, in which the product of one reaction is passed to the next enzyme in a pathway. Since the metabolite does not diffuse into the general aqueous environment, it is effectively concentrated near the enzyme.

Molecular modelling 5

Go to the Study Skills file: *Molecular modelling 5*. This activity entails using ViewerLite™ to examine the structure of the enzymes lysozyme and carboxypeptidase A. You will highlight key residues in these proteins that are responsible for substrate binding and catalysis. This activity will help you to appreciate the spatial relationship of these residues in each of the enzymes. In the case of carboxypeptidase A, you will be able to compare the conformation of the enzyme in its unbound and substrate-bound states.

3.8 Studying protein function

From the different components of this course you will already be aware of some of the many experimental techniques employed to study protein structure, including X-ray diffraction, CD, NMR and SDS–PAGE. There are also many techniques that have been developed to study protein function, of which several are described in this section.

> SDS–PAGE and Western blotting (immunoblotting) techniques are widely used to analyse and characterize proteins. These techniques have been described in S204, Book 3 *The Core of Life,* Vol. I, Chapter 2, and their theory and applications are explored in some detail in *Experimental investigation 1.* You should attempt this activity, as directed, at the end of this chapter.

3.8.1 Site-directed mutagenesis

The application of site-directed mutagenesis (SDM) to the study of protein function has been illustrated with the enzyme lysozyme, as described previously. SDM is a very powerful technique in the study of protein function, allowing the experimenter to assess the importance of particular amino acid side-chains in a protein. It is most commonly used in the study of enzymes; however, it is also very useful in identifying key residues in protein–protein interactions. In this section, we will consider the methodology and design of SDM studies.

Provided that the gene encoding the protein of interest is available and there is a suitable system for expressing the gene, it is possible, using recombinant DNA technology, to produce a mutant protein in which a specific amino acid has been replaced with a different amino acid. To produce the desired mutant protein, it is necessary to change a single base in the gene encoding the protein of interest, such that the codon for the target amino acid is changed to that encoding the desired replacement amino acid.

> Molecular cloning techniques are widely used to manipulate DNA fragments. These techniques have been described in detail in S204, Book 4 *Microbes,* Section 6.4.

One of the principal methods that is used for SDM is based on a technique called *primer extension.* A typical site-directed mutagenesis procedure, using this method, is outlined in Figure 3.48. The coding sequence of the normal gene is first cloned into a plasmid vector that can exist as single-stranded DNA (ssDNA), but which, during replication in a host cell, goes through a double-stranded form (dsDNA). A short DNA oligonucleotide (10–20 nucleotides in length) is synthesized that is complementary to the region of the gene to be mutated, except for the single base change in the appropriate codon (X in Figure 3.48); for example, changing TTG, the codon for Gln, to TTC, the codon for Glu. The oligonucleotide is annealed to the ssDNA form of the cloned sequence and serves as a primer for DNA synthesis by DNA polymerase. After synthesis, the two ends of the new strand are joined using a DNA ligase enzyme and this double-stranded DNA (termed a heteroduplex)

Figure 3.48
Site-directed mutagenesis of a protein-coding region using primer extension. X is the substituted base.

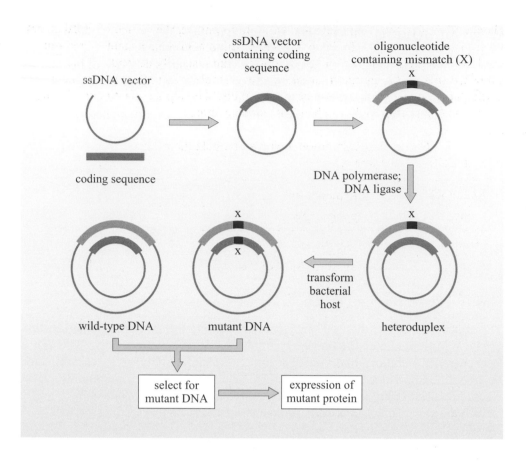

is used to transform host bacteria. The vector (with its insert) is replicated in the host and mutant clones can be selected on the basis of their ability to hybridize to the original oligonucleotide primer under suitable discriminating conditions. The mutant gene can be subcloned into an appropriate vector and expressed in large quantities in transformed cells. The resulting mutant protein can then be analysed with regard to its structure and function (e.g. catalytic activity) and comparisons made with the normal (wild-type) protein.

Given the number of amino acids in an average protein and the possibility of substituting each residue with a choice of 19 other amino acids, it is clear that SDM experiments require careful design. There are two main questions that should be considered in designing a strategy for SDM. Firstly, which amino acid should be mutated, and secondly, which amino acid should it be replaced with? It is also possible to produce mutant proteins in which two or even three residues have been mutated.

The selection of an amino acid for mutation is often based on detailed knowledge of the protein's three-dimensional structure. For example, from the X-ray structure of an enzyme with a bound substrate analogue, amino acids likely to be involved in binding the substrate or catalysing the reaction might be identified on the basis of their proximity to the substrate and their chemical properties. These residues are interesting targets for mutagenesis. Similarly, identification of highly conserved residues in comparisons of amino acid sequences of related proteins can indicate important roles for these in the protein and can form the basis for an informed choice of target residues for mutagenesis.

Having identified the amino acid that we want to mutate, the choice of replacement must then be considered. In Table 3.6, some amino acid replacements commonly used in SDM are listed. The choice of replacement generally depends on the supposed role of the residue in question. For example, to test the importance of a particular residue in an enzyme mechanism, it could be replaced with one of similar overall size but differing in its chemical characteristics.

Table 3.6 Some of the common amino acid replacements used in SDM experiments.

Amino acid	Replacement
Ala	Ser, Gly, Thr
Arg	Lys, His, Gln
Asn	Asp, Gln, Glu, Ser, His, Lys
Asp	Asn, Gln, Glu, His
Cys	Ser
His	Asn, Asp, Gln, Glu, Arg
Leu	Met, Ile, Val, Phe
Lys	Arg, Gln, Asn
Ser	Ala, Thr, Asn, Gly
Tyr	Phe, His, Trp
Trp	Phe, Tyr

○ Why do you think it would be advisable to use a residue of similar size for such a substitution?

● Matching the residue for size would minimize any steric effects that might alter the overall structure and thereby confound observation of the effect of changes to the chemistry of the residue.

For example, Glu could be replaced by Gln, which is similar in size and shape but lacks the negative charge. (This was one of the mutations used to determine the role of Glu 35 in the catalytic mechanism of lysozyme; see Section 3.7.2.) Substitution of a particular amino acid residue with a larger residue can result in steric interference and should be avoided. It is preferable to use residues that are smaller than the wild-type residue, as they tend not to disrupt the overall structure of the protein. Proline is commonly substituted for amino acids in parts of the protein that are thought to have key structural roles or to undergo some structural rearrangements as a part of normal functioning. The introduction of proline in such a position affects the geometry of the polypeptide backbone, usually causing a bend, and rendering it relatively inflexible.

3.8.2 Studying protein–protein interactions

The investigation of protein–protein interactions is a very important aspect of understanding proteins. Identifying binding partners can give insight into a protein's function. Many different methods and technologies have been developed to identify and characterize interactions between proteins, a few of which are described here.

Physical methods for demonstrating an interaction between proteins

To identify those unknown proteins in a complex mixture that interact with a particular protein of interest, **protein affinity chromatography** can be used (Figure 3.49a). This approach uses a 'bait' protein attached to a matrix. When this baited matrix material is then exposed to a mixture of proteins, only proteins that interact with the bait are 'pulled out' from the mixture. Typically, this mixture is actually an extract prepared from cells or tissue and it is passed through a chromatography column packed with inert beads that carry the bait. Proteins that interact with the bait protein are retained by the matrix and can be eluted (washed off) and then analysed. Elution may be achieved by changing the salt concentration or the pH or alternatively free bait protein could be used to displace the bound proteins. Protein microarrays (see Table 3.7, in next section) can be used as a high-throughput version of protein affinity chromatography.

○ What requirement might make protein affinity chromatography a difficult procedure to use in practice?

● The necessity for a purified preparation of the bait protein and selective coupling of this protein to the matrix makes this procedure technically demanding.

The same principle is used in **co-immunoprecipitation** (Figure 3.49b). This technique uses an antibody that specifically recognizes the bait protein. The antibody is incubated with, for example, cell extract and binds to the bait protein. Beads coated with a protein that binds to immunoglobulins are used to pull the antibody out of the mixture, functioning in the same way as the affinity matrix in protein affinity chromatography. The beads can be spun down in a centrifuge. Along with antibody, the bait protein and the proteins that interact with the bait are precipitated in a complex. Co-immunoprecipitation has a distinct advantage over cross-linking of proteins (described below) in that the proteins are not modified in any way. Preservation of the protein in its native state is an important consideration for further analysis of its function.

○ Co-immunoprecipitation is much more versatile and is used much more widely than is affinity chromatography. Why do you think this might be?

● Affinity chromatography requires a source of purified bait protein and selective attachment of this protein to the beads. Co-immunoprecipitation uses beads that capture all immunoglobulins and they can be used with any immunoglobulin.

Having effectively isolated binding partners for a particular protein, how can we identify or characterize them? In practice, characterization of a protein involves a number of different experimental approaches. One of the most convenient ways of learning something about the protein is to analyse it by SDS–polyacrylamide gel electrophoresis (SDS–PAGE). From SDS–PAGE it can be determined whether a protein of interest has more than one subunit and the M_r of the component subunits

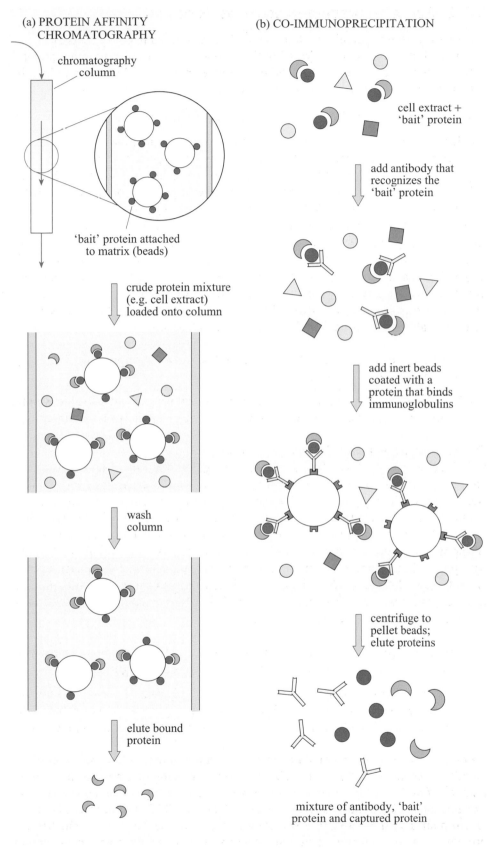

(a) PROTEIN AFFINITY CHROMATOGRAPHY

chromatography column

'bait' protein attached to matrix (beads)

crude protein mixture (e.g. cell extract) loaded onto column

wash column

elute bound protein

(b) CO-IMMUNOPRECIPITATION

cell extract + 'bait' protein

add antibody that recognizes the 'bait' protein

add inert beads coated with a protein that binds immunoglobulins

centrifuge to pellet beads; elute proteins

mixture of antibody, 'bait' protein and captured protein

Figure 3.49
Capture of interacting proteins using a bait protein in (a) protein affinity chromatography and (b) co-immunoprecipitation.

can be estimated. An accurate determination of the mass of the protein can be obtained from mass spectrometry. **Matrix-associated laser desorption ionization-time-of-flight spectrometry (MALDI-TOF)** determines the mass and charge of peptides derived from a protein of interest. It is possible to fragment individual peptides from a protein, breaking peptide bonds, and from the differences in the masses of the products, the sequence of the peptide can be deduced. Partial sequence information can then be used to search databases to identify a match or homologous proteins.

Apart from confirming that two proteins do in fact interact, it is important to characterize their interaction. Chemical **cross-linking** of interacting proteins uses reagents that react with specific amino acid side-chains to covalently link those parts of two proteins that are close together. The range over which cross-linking can occur is determined by the length of the cross-linking reagent. This technique can not only help determine if two proteins do interact, but can also give information on which parts of the two proteins participate in the interaction.

A particularly powerful method for studying protein–protein interactions is **surface plasmon resonance (SPR)**. In SPR, the bait protein is attached to a special 'biosensor chip' consisting of a very thin layer of metal on top of a glass prism (Figure 3.50). The bait is immobilized on a dextran polymer on the surface of the metal film and this surface is exposed to a flow of an aqueous solution (the mobile phase) containing a protein that is thought to interact with the bait.

A light beam is passed through the prism and is reflected off the metal film, but some of the light energy is transferred to 'packets' of electrons called *plasmons*, on the surface of the metal film. This effect reduces the intensity of the reflected light and is dependent on the precise angle of incidence of the light beam, defined as the resonance angle (θ in Figure 3.50). The resonance angle is in turn determined by the refractive index of the solution up to 300 nm away from the metal film on which the bait protein is immobilized. If the protein in the mobile phase binds to the bait protein, the local refractive index changes, leading to a change in resonance angle. All proteins have the same refractive index and there is a linear correlation between the change in resonance angle and the concentration of protein near the surface. Thus it is possible to determine changes in protein concentration at the surface that are due to protein–protein binding. The value of this method is that the kinetics of the binding interaction can be followed in real time by analysing the rate of change of the signal. The rate of change of the signal on addition of the potential binding partner to the mobile phase is an indication of the association kinetics for the two proteins, and washing the interacting protein off the bait allows similar analysis of dissociation kinetics. Apart from protein–protein interactions, SPR is used to study many other interactions including those between proteins and DNA, carbohydrates or small ligands.

Library-based methods for demonstrating an interaction between proteins

As well as the biochemical approaches to studying protein–protein interactions, there is a variety of qualitative methods for screening 'libraries' of cloned genes or gene fragments whose protein products might interact with a protein of interest. Such an approach has the advantage that the genes that encode those proteins that bind are available immediately for expression, facilitating subsequent analysis of the protein.

The refractive index of a material is a measure of the velocity of light through it.

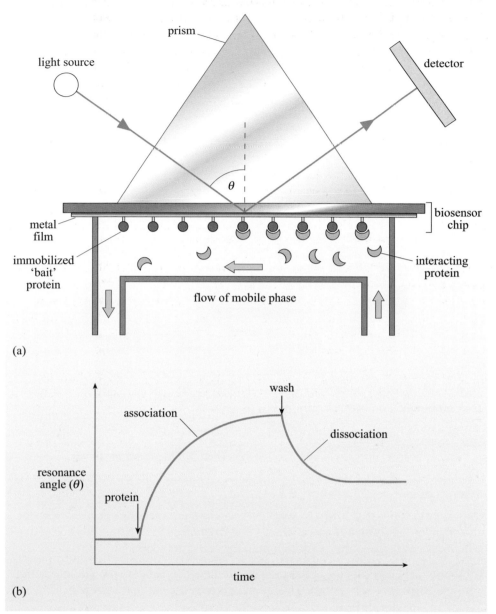

Figure 3.50
Surface plasmon resonance.
(a) When a protein in the mobile phase binds to the immobilized bait protein, there is a change in the refractive index at the surface of the metal film and a consequent change in the intensity of the reflected beam of light.
(b) These changes can be monitored (over a period of minutes) and interpreted in terms of the association and dissociation of the proteins.

The **two-hybrid system** uses transcriptional activity as a measure of protein–protein interaction, as illustrated in Figure 3.51. The 'read-out' from this system is expression of a so-called **reporter gene**, i.e. a gene whose expression is readily monitored (as, for example, enzyme activity, or fluorescence). The technique exploits the fact that the protein that activates transcription of the reporter gene consists of two domains: (1) the DNA binding domain, which targets the activator to specific genes, and (2) the activation domain, which contacts other components of the transcriptional machinery, enabling transcription to occur. Though normally these two domains would be part of the same polypeptide, transcription of the reporter gene can still occur if they are on different polypeptides but are brought

Figure 3.51
The two-hybrid system for demonstrating an interaction between proteins. The DNA-binding domain hybrid alone does not activate transcription (a) nor does the activation domain hybrid (b). However, interaction of proteins X and Y brings the activation domain close to the DNA-binding domain and transcription can occur (c).

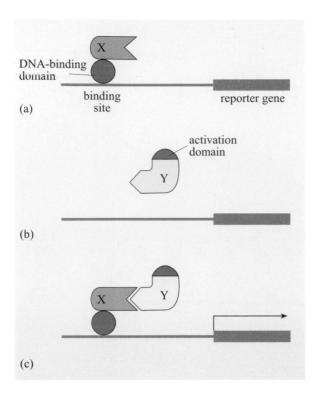

together physically. The two-hybrid system entails expression, using recombinant DNA techniques, of two hybrid proteins as follows:

1   The DNA binding domain is fused to the bait protein, X.

2   The activation domain is fused to the potential binding partner, Y.

If X and Y interact, the DNA binding domain and the activation domain are brought together such that transcription of the reporter gene can occur. The two-hybrid assay is commonly performed in yeast cells containing a reporter gene. The major advantage of this system is that it allows the screening of large libraries consisting of many genes fused to the DNA encoding the activation domain.

Another widely used library-based method for detecting protein–protein interactions is **phage display** (Figure 3.52). This approach uses a virus that infects *E. coli*, known as a **bacteriophage** (or 'phage'). Similarly to the two-hybrid system, recombinant DNA techniques are used to make a **gene construct** by fusing DNA encoding the proteins of interest with a gene encoding a protein that forms part of the coat of the phage. Expression of this construct produces a hybrid of the bacteriophage coat protein and the protein of interest. A coat protein is chosen for this manipulation so that the hybrid will be displayed on the surface of the mature engineered phage. Engineered phage derived from a library of such constructs can be screened for the ability to bind to a bait protein. Immobilized bait protein could be used in the same way as described for affinity chromatography (Figure 3.49a), to fish out any phage expressing interacting proteins. The recovered phage can then be used to infect *E. coli*. In this way, the phage can be replicated to increase its yield and facilitate subsequent isolation of the DNA encoding the interacting protein.

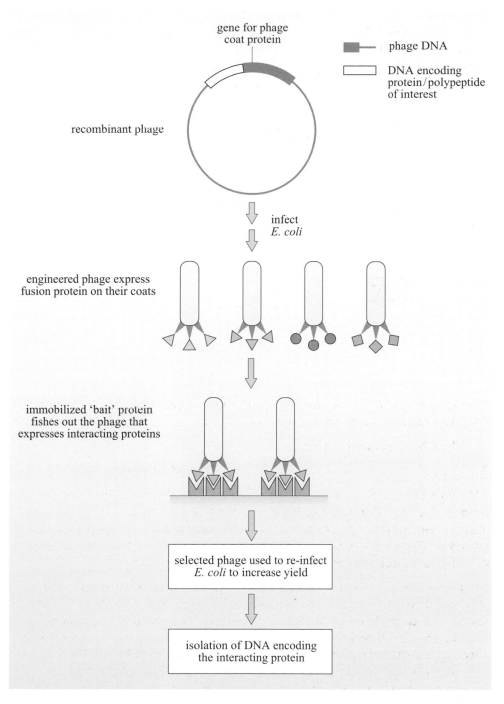

Figure 3.52
Phage display, a method for demonstrating an interaction between proteins. A gene construct is made containing DNA encoding the protein of interest fused to a phage gene encoding a coat protein. Expression of the recombinant phage DNA in *E. coli* produces engineered phage displaying a hybrid of the phage coat protein and the protein of interest. In a variation of protein affinity chromatography, immobilized bait protein can then be used to selectively fish out those phage expressing interacting proteins.

3.8.3 Proteomics

Traditionally, the study of the biochemistry or structure of a protein necessitated its purification to a high degree. The development of protocols for cloning, manipulation and expression of genes greatly facilitated this kind of study, as will be clear to you from the previous section. In recent years, a number of high-throughput techniques have, to an extent, obviated traditional approaches and permit simultaneous analysis of all the expressed proteins in a cell or organism, known as the **proteome**. The term **proteomics** has been coined to describe such studies.

Proteomics is founded on the technological achievements of genomics, the large-scale analysis of every gene in an organism, and encompasses all aspects of protein structure and function, including post-translational modifications and interactions, and comparisons not only between tissues in an organism but within a single cell under different conditions or at different stages in the life of the cell or organism.

Unlike the genome of an organism, which remains largely unchanged in the lifetime of the cell or organism, the proteome is highly dynamic. Thus, the proteome varies as expression of genes is switched on or off in response to stimuli and the level of expression of different genes is modulated, whilst post-translational modifications and protein interactions add further layers of complexity. As well as identifying and determining the physiological role of proteins, the proteomic approach can highlight changes that occur in pathological situations and can facilitate identification of targets for therapeutic intervention in disease.

Table 3.7 details some of the technologies and methodologies on which proteomics is based, some of which have been described in previous sections. By way of example, Figure 3.53 illustrates one type of experiment that is routinely performed to assess the biological effects of a treatment at the proteomic level, namely two-dimensional polyacrylamide gel electrophoresis (2-D PAGE) with mass spectrometry.

Figure 3.53   Comparative 2-D PAGE of extracts prepared from (a) control (untreated) and (b) treated cells. The first separation was performed by isoelectric focusing, which separates proteins according to their charge in a pH gradient. The lane containing the separated proteins was then cut from the gel and overlaid on another gel and proteins were further separated by SDS–PAGE (i.e. according to mass). A comparison of the two gels reveals some distinct differences, such as those highlighted in the enlarged regions. The proteins in these spots were eluted and analysed by MALDI-TOF. The experimental amino acid sequence data were then used to search a database for matching protein sequences. In this way, the identity of the proteins in the three positions indicated was determined. Two of the spots in gel (b) correspond to protein X. Thus there is evidently a change in the M_r of this protein in treated cells. This shift may result from post-translational modification. There is an increase in the level of protein Y in the treated cells compared to the untreated cells.

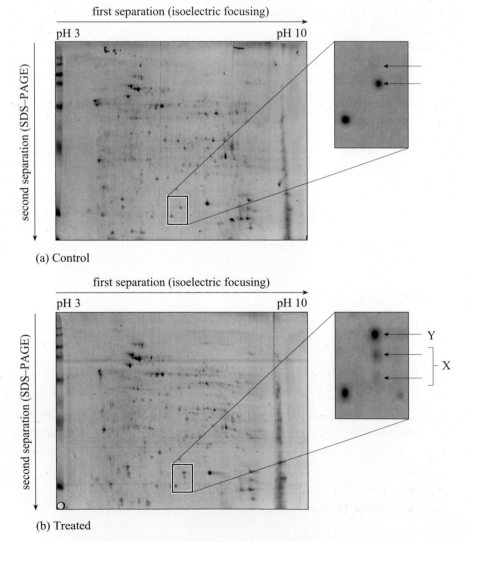

(a) Control

(b) Treated

Table 3.7 Methodologies used in proteomics.

Methodology	Description	Application
Two-dimensional polyacrylamide gel electrophoresis (2-D PAGE)	Proteins are separated in one dimension on the basis of their charge in a pH gradient (isoelectric focusing) and in the second dimension on the basis of their mass (Figure 3.53).	Separation of many thousands of proteins from each other; allows purification of individual proteins and their modified forms.
Mass spectrometry (e.g. MALDI-TOF)	A mass spectrometer separates molecular species according to their mass / charge ratio. Can be used on small quantities. For example, proteins eluted from 2-D gels and subjected to proteolysis can be analysed in this way. See also Section 3.8.2.	Accurate mass and sequence information for peptides to identify all proteins present in any sample. Allows comparisons between, for example, diseased and normal tissues. Analysis of post-translationally modified forms of proteins; e.g. comparisons between proteins after treatment with glycosylases or phosphatases, or after use of antibodies specific for modified forms.
Protein microarrays (*Note*: DNA microarrays, which are used to study nucleic acids, are described in Chapters 5 and 10.)	Up to 10 000 purified proteins can be immobilized on a glass slide under conditions that preserve the proteins' native conformations, allowing them to be 'probed' in a number of different ways. Binding is read and interpreted automatically. Interacting proteins can be eluted for analysis, e.g. by mass spectrometry.	To rapidly screen for protein–protein interactions using a fluorescently labelled protein. To rapidly screen for enzyme–substrate interactions, e.g. identifying target proteins for a particular kinase using radio-labelled phosphate. To examine binding of other ligands including nucleic acids, carbohydrates, receptors, antibodies or even components of whole cell extracts.
Interaction studies e.g. two-hybrid system and phage display	See Section 3.8.2.	These library-based methods allow large numbers of proteins to be screened for interactions.
Bioinformatics	A combination of mathematical, computer and statistical methods to analyse biological data.	Proteomics databases exist for an increasing number of model organisms. Such databases can assist in the identification of proteins and the prediction of their function. They are also used in drug design.

Summary of Section 3.8

1   Site-directed mutagenesis is an important technique for studying protein function. Using recombinant DNA technology, selected amino acids can be substituted with different residues to alter the structure and function of a protein. One widely used method employs primer extension. SDM studies can help identify residues that are critical for interactions or catalytic activity.

2   Protein–protein interactions can be studied in a number of different ways – using biochemical or physical methods or using library-based methods.

3   Physical methods include variations on 'fishing' approaches in which a bait protein is used to physically pull interacting proteins out of a mixture of proteins. Such methods include protein affinity chromatography and co-immunoprecipitation.

4   Chemical cross-linking of proteins can provide information on interacting residues, and surface plasmon resonance can be used to study the kinetics of binding interactions between proteins.

5   Library-based methods for studying protein–protein interactions rely on recombinant DNA technology and include the two-hybrid system and phage display. An advantage of these techniques is that the gene encoding the interacting protein is immediately available for further studies.

6   Proteomics is the study of all the proteins expressed in an organism or cell in terms of their function, structure, modifications and interactions, indeed all aspects of their biochemistry.

Experimental investigation 1

Go to the Study Skills file: *Experimental investigation 1*. This activity will familiarize you with the techniques and procedures of SDS–PAGE and Western blotting, which are widely used in the study of proteins. Based on your understanding of these principles, you will then devise, carry out and interpret a series of experiments in order to characterize a protein in terms of its subunit composition and M_r and to study its phosphorylation by kinases.

Learning outcomes for Chapter 3

When you have studied this chapter, you should be able to:

3.1   Define and use each of the terms printed in **bold** in the text.

3.2   Describe the different levels of protein structure and their interdependence.

3.3   Explain how steric limitations determine secondary structure in polypeptides.

3.4   Describe, using examples, the relationship between protein structure and function.

3.5   Understand the significance of domains in protein function and how they have arisen.

3.6   Describe modifications of proteins and explain how these can affect the localization, function or activity of the protein.

3.7   Give examples of how interaction of proteins with other molecules is critical to their function.

3.8   Describe experimental approaches to the study of protein–protein interactions.

3.9   Explain how site-directed mutagenesis can be used to study protein function.

3.10 Interpret and manipulate electronic three-dimensional models.

3.11 Devise simple experiments to analyse protein structure using SDS–PAGE and Western blotting techniques, and interpret the results of such experiments.

Questions for Chapter 3

Question 3.1

What is the relationship between secondary structures, supersecondary structures and protein folds?

Question 3.2

What information does a Ramachandran plot for an amino acid residue give us and how are such plots generated?

Question 3.3

Describe the domain structure of Src. How does the domain organization of a protein relate to its function?

Question 3.4

What are the different types of covalent modification of proteins?

Question 3.5

How does phosphorylation affect the function of some proteins?

Question 3.6

What advantages are there in the use of the two-hybrid system compared to biochemical approaches for identifying proteins that interact with a specific 'bait' protein of interest?

Question 3.7

In site-directed mutagenesis, the choice of the replacement amino acid, substituted for a particular residue, depends on the properties of the residue to be replaced. What considerations are made in choosing the replacement amino acid?

References

Huse, M. and Kuriyan, J. (2002) The conformational plasticity of protein kinases, *Cell*, **109**, pp. 275–282.

Lipscomb, W. N., Reeke, G. N. Jr, Hartsuck, J. A., Quiocho, F. A. and Bethge, P. H. (1970) The structure of carboxypeptidase A. 8. Atomic interpretation at 0.2 nm resolution, a new study of the complex of glycyl-L-tyrosine with CPA, and mechanistic deductions, *Philosophical Transactions of the Royal Society (Biological Sciences)*, **257**(813), pp. 177–214.

Ramachandran, G. N. and Sasisekharan, V. (1968) Conformation of polypeptides and proteins, *Advances in Protein Chemistry*, **23**, pp. 283–437.

Phillips, D. C. (1966) The three-dimensional structure of an enzyme molecule, *Scientific American*, **215**(5), pp. 75–80.

Further sources

Aloy, P. and Russell, R. B. (2002) The third dimension for protein interactions and complexes, *Trends in Biochemical Sciences*, **27**, pp. 633–638.

Bijlmakers M-J. and Marsh M. (2003) The on-off story of protein palmitoylation, *Trends in Cell Biology*, **13**, pp. 32–42.

Ouzounis, C. A., Coulson, R. M. R., Enright, A. J., Kunin, V. and Pereira-Leal, J. B. (2003) Classification schemes for protein structure and function, *Nature Reviews: Genetics*, **4**, pp. 508–519.

Phizicky, E. M., Bastiaens, P. I. H., Zhu, H., Snyder, M. and Fields, S. (2003) Protein analysis on a proteomic scale, *Nature*, **422**, pp. 208–215.

Phizicky, E. M. and Fields, S. (1995) Protein–protein interactions: methods for detection and analysis, *Microbiological Reviews*, **59**, pp. 94–123.

4 THERMODYNAMICS AND BIOENERGETICS

One of the first principles of biology is that all living organisms need energy to form and maintain the complex macromolecules and cells of which they are composed. Energy must be captured and converted into a form that can be stored and utilized by the organism. For example, the photosynthetic systems of green plants trap energy from sunlight and use this energy to convert carbon dioxide and water into glucose and oxygen. Solar energy is therefore effectively converted into chemical energy in the form of glucose. Glucose can be stored by the plant cell, mainly as starch, which is hydrolysed to release the stored chemical energy as required. Most importantly, for captured energy to be useful, the flow of energy in living things must be tightly controlled. There is a clear link between the metabolic pathways that transform energy within cells and the processes for which this energy is required. This chapter is concerned with these relationships and ultimately with the question of how life works.

Classical thermodynamics is a very formal science concerned with the transformation of energy in physical systems. Nevertheless, as all biological processes must conform to the laws of physics and chemistry, it is clear that the transformation of energy in biological systems must also be constrained by the principles of thermodynamics. Whilst the laws of thermodynamics in biological systems cannot give us any detailed descriptions of molecular structures or explanations of biological processes, they do set limits on the types of processes that can occur. Enzymes, as biological catalysts, increase the rates of specific reactions in the cell, but whether a reaction can take place at all and in which direction are questions of thermodynamics. Hence, ultimately, thermodynamics provides the criteria for judging the validity of any proposed metabolic reaction.

4.1 Thermodynamic systems

What is thermodynamics? Very briefly, **thermodynamics** is the study of energy and its transformations. This is an attractive definition for a biologist as it can encompass the whole of biology if read as 'the study of energy transformations within living systems'. Energy is one of those useful abstractions that are discussed in the way most people talk about 'the wind' as a flow of air without reference to its chemical composition or physical properties. Essentially, however, energy is the ability to bring about change, i.e. to do work. In thermodynamics, one considers the exchange of energy that takes place between a system and its environment, a system being the matter within a defined region. Although physicists consider a number of different types of system, all biological systems belong to just one group called 'open systems' – they exchange both matter and energy with their environment, as shown in Figure 4.1.

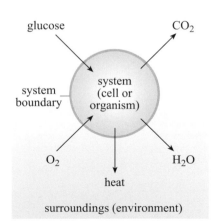

Figure 4.1 An example of an open system in which matter and energy are exchanged with the environment.

4.1.1 The laws of thermodynamics

All of thermodynamics is explained by two apparently simple laws, referred to as the first and second laws of thermodynamics. The first law of thermodynamics states that energy is neither created nor destroyed, although it may be converted from one form into another. The total energy stored within a system is called the **enthalpy** (symbol H), from the Greek meaning 'warming within'. Enthalpy depends on the pressure (P), volume (V) and heat energy (E) of the system – so we say that H is a *function* of P, V and E. Most biological systems do not change their pressure or volume significantly as reactions occur, so for biologists, changes in enthalpy are equivalent to changes in the heat energy. If we consider a molecule, its enthalpy, H, approximates to the sum of the energy of the individual bonds in that molecule. If the molecule undergoes a reaction, the difference in enthalpy of the reactants and products is a measure of the heat energy released or absorbed during the reaction and is given by ΔH. Reactions in which H decreases (i.e. ΔH is negative) release heat to the surroundings; that is, they are *exothermic*. Conversely, those reactions in which H increases (ΔH positive) are *endothermic*.

The second law of thermodynamics brings into play another quantity or thermodynamic function called **entropy (S)**, meaning literally 'a change within'. Entropy is a measure of the amount of disorder or randomness in a system. If we consider the Universe as a whole, then the second law states that if the overall change in S during a reaction is positive, i.e. $\Delta S > 0$, then the process or reaction will proceed spontaneously. With every reaction that occurs, the Universe as a whole becomes more disordered, i.e. its entropy increases. Processes that would entail a *decrease* in the entropy of the Universe simply do not occur. In other words, everything 'runs down'. In biology, application of the second law allows us to predict the *direction* of biochemical reactions.

When a system has reached maximum entropy it is said to be at equilibrium, and this position is maintained without energy input. Although the idea that thermodynamic equilibrium represents the state of maximum entropy seems logical, biological systems appear to run contrary to this principle. Indeed, the fact that living organisms do not exist in a state of equilibrium leads some people to believe that some supernatural force must be operating in organisms to prevent their decay. However, organisms *do* obey the laws of thermodynamics: for a biological system, such as a growing cell, the increasing level of order within the system ($\Delta S_{cell} < 0$) is more than offset by a greater increase in the level of disorder in the environment ($\Delta S_{env} > 0$). Thus if one considers the entropy balance as a whole

$$\Delta S_{cell} + \Delta S_{env} > 0 \tag{4.1}$$

It is perfectly possible therefore to have highly ordered living systems, at the expense of a more disordered environment.

From this reasoning, one can conclude that living systems are not in equilibrium, but rather, they are in a steady state that depends on the continuous input of energy. (You came across the term 'steady state' in Chapter 2, but in the specific context of a sequence of biochemical reactions.)

☐ In thermodynamic terms, what happens when the energy input to a cell is insufficient to maintain the highly ordered structure of that cell?

⬤ If the cell is becoming less ordered, then $\Delta S_{cell} > 0$. The living system is starting to degenerate.

In this chapter you will encounter many symbols and equations related to thermodynamics. These are summarized in Box 4.1.

The symbol Δ (delta) is used to denote the difference between two quantities. ΔS is the difference between the entropy of a system at the start of a process or reaction and that at the end.

◻ Since a system can only become ordered if its surroundings are disordered to an even greater extent, how is the order that is evident in an organism achieved?

◼ The increase in order in an organism is offset by 'disordering' (i.e. degrading) the nutrients it consumes from its surroundings.

Thus an organism derives not only energy, but also order or negative entropy, from the nutrients that it consumes.

Erwin Schrödinger, Austrian physicist and winner of the Nobel Prize for Physics in 1933, stated in his much respected booklet *What is Life?*:

> '…Every process, event, happening – call it what you will; in a word, everything that is going on in Nature means an increase of the entropy of the part of the world where it is going on. Thus a living organism continually increases its entropy – or, as you may say, produces positive entropy – and thus tends to approach the dangerous state of maximum entropy, which is death. It can only keep aloof from it, i.e. alive, by continually drawing from its environment negative entropy – which is something very positive as we shall immediately see. What an organism feeds upon is negative entropy. Or, to put it less paradoxically, the essential thing in metabolism is that the organism succeeds in freeing itself from all the entropy it cannot help producing while alive.'

4.1.2 Energy transfer in living systems

Living systems require a continual supply of energy to synthesize, organize and transport complex molecules within cells.

◻ What principle sources of energy are 'trapped' by living organisms?

◼ Light energy and energy from oxidation processes.

Organisms can be classified according to the energy source that they utilize. Plants, algae and photosynthetic bacteria can obtain energy by absorption of light. In these organisms (termed **phototrophs**), light energy is absorbed by pigments in photosynthetic reaction centres and used to excite electrons which are then used to reduce CO_2 and split H_2O. This process of chemical reduction permits the synthesis of organic molecules such as glucose. Thus the light energy absorbed by photosynthetic cells is effectively stored in the form of chemical bonds. All animals and fungi and many protoctists and bacteria are **chemotrophs**, which use the energy stored in chemical bonds, as an energy source. Energy is released from molecules (which may be organic or inorganic, depending on the organism) by oxidation, entailing the transfer of electrons to an acceptor (molecular oxygen in aerobic respiration).

In terms of the thermodynamics of a system, the energy that is available to do work is called 'free energy', known more correctly as the **Gibbs free energy (G)**, after Josiah Willard Gibbs, who defined this term in 1878. To the biologist, Gibbs free energy is perhaps the most useful thermodynamic function. It is important because, as you will see in the next section, it allows us to predict whether or not a change or reaction will occur spontaneously.

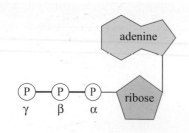

Figure 4.2
Simplified representation of an ATP molecule. The three phosphoryl groups are identified as α, β and γ as indicated. The two high-energy phosphoanhydride bonds are highlighted in red.

The oxidation of most organic compounds is thermodynamically favourable and yields energy that can be trapped in other compounds for use in energy-consuming processes. Trapping of the free energy derived from oxidation of organic compounds or from light (by photosynthesis) is achieved by using an energy carrier, ATP. This molecule occurs in all known living organisms and can be thought of as the principal energy currency of the cell, a free energy donor. This molecule supplies the free energy necessary to drive many cellular processes including biosynthesis of macromolecules, transport, movement and communication. ATP contains two so-called 'high-energy bonds', i.e. bonds whose hydrolysis results in a large negative change in free energy. The high-energy bonds in ATP are the phosphoanhydride bonds between the α and β phosphoryl groups and between the β and γ phosphoryl groups (Figure 4.2).

Catabolic processes, i.e. those that entail the breakdown of molecules, comprise many discrete steps, with small, manageable 'packets' of energy being released at each step. For example, glucose is oxidized to CO_2 and H_2O in a series of more than 20 reactions. The large amount of energy produced (2870 kJ mol^{-1} glucose) is partitioned between these reactions in such a way that the energy can be used for anabolic reactions that require less energy. The complete oxidation of a mole of glucose yields 36–38 moles of ATP, trapping just 1100–1160 kJ mol^{-1} glucose catabolized. In other words, the available energy for subsequent biological reactions is less than 50% of the potential; the rest is lost as heat.

Heat production should not, however, be considered as wastage of energy, because it influences the direction and speed of flow of metabolic pathways. The key reactions that control the direction of a metabolic pathway are the ones that are by their nature thermodynamically irreversible, i.e. their reversal requires energy input. The other reactions in a metabolic pathway may be reversible, but they are not critical for determining the overall direction of the pathway. Control of a metabolic pathway can only be exerted at those reactions where energy dissipation occurs. For example, shown in Table 4.1 are the energy changes for three reactions, all of which are steps in glycolysis. These reactions have large negative changes in free energy (see Section 4.2), i.e. the free energy of the products is much less than the free energy of the reactants. A large amount of energy is therefore released as heat at each of these steps. The enzymes that catalyse these reactions, namely hexokinase, phosphofructokinase and pyruvate kinase, are all sensitive to regulation by allosteric effectors and/or covalent modification and determine the rate of glycolytic flux.

Table 4.1   Standard free energy changes at pH 7.0 and 25 °C ($\Delta G°'$; defined in Section 4.2) for three reactions in glycolysis.

Reaction	Enzyme	Standard free energy change ($\Delta G°'$) / kJ mol^{-1}
ATP + glucose → ADP + glucose 6-phosphate	hexokinase	−16.7
ATP + glucose 6-phosphate → ADP + fructose 1,6-bisphosphate	phosphofructokinase	−14.2
ADP + phosphoenolpyruvate → ATP + pyruvate	pyruvate kinase	−31.4

By contrast, reactions in which energy is conserved do *not* determine the direction of flow of the pathway. In some cases, there is little energy difference between the substrates and the products, but in other cases a reaction in which much energy is generated is linked to a reaction or process that traps energy.

For a thermodynamically unfavourable reaction to take place, it needs to be linked or *coupled* to one that is favourable. The phenomenon of **coupling** is most important in biology. For example, the generation of a single molecule of ATP (from ADP and P_i) at the inner mitochondrial membrane requires the movement of three or four protons from the intermembrane space into the matrix of the mitochondrion. Movement of the protons is down a concentration gradient and is therefore thermodynamically favourable. A proton-pumping ATP synthase (F_0-F_1 ATP synthase) couples this proton movement to the thermodynamically unfavourable synthesis of ATP. Many enzymes and ion pumps act as molecular machines that couple one reaction to another, by storing chemical bond energy within their structure and transferring it to products as the reaction progresses (Figure 4.3).

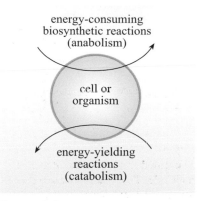

Figure 4.3
A simplified representation of reaction coupling. The energy required to drive the *energy-consuming* biosynthetic (i.e. anabolic) reactions is derived from a simultaneous *energy-producing* (catabolic) reaction.

○ In terms of entropy (*S*), what do you understand by the terms thermodynamically favourable and unfavourable reactions?

● $\Delta S > 0$ for a thermodynamically favourable reaction; $\Delta S < 0$ for a thermodynamically unfavourable reaction.

Summary of Section 4.1

1   Energy transfer in living systems is governed by the laws of thermodynamics. The high level of order seen in a cell is only possible because of the increased disorder produced in the surroundings as a result of metabolism.

2   The first law of thermodynamics states that energy is neither created nor destroyed; it is converted from one form into another.

3   The second law of thermodynamics states that for a process or reaction to occur spontaneously, the overall change in entropy must be positive, i.e. $\Delta S > 0$. From this law it follows that the flow of energy is directional and it is possible to predict the direction of reactions.

4   All biological systems are open systems, in which matter and energy are exchanged with the environment.

5   ATP is used to trap and deliver free energy and can be thought of as the universal currency of free energy in biological systems.

6   Thermodynamically unfavourable reactions are coupled to ones that are energetically favourable.

7   The control of a metabolic pathway can only be exerted where energy dissipation occurs.

Box 4.1	Thermodynamic parameters and their definitions

The table below summarizes the parameters and constants that are important in the study of thermodynamics.

Thermodynamic parameter	Symbol	Definition
enthalpy	H	Thermodynamic property: measure of total energy of a system
entropy	S	Thermodynamic property: measure of degree of disorder in a system
temperature	T	Absolute temperature in kelvin (K)
Gibbs free energy	G	Thermodynamic property of a system: measure of the free energy available to do work (at constant temperature and pressure). $$G = H - TS$$
change in enthalpy	ΔH	$\Delta H = \Delta G + T\Delta S$
change in entropy	ΔS	$\Delta S = (\Delta H - \Delta G)/T$
Gibbs free energy change	ΔG	The change in free energy for a system undergoing a transformation $$\Delta G = \Delta H - T\Delta S$$ For any reaction, the difference in Gibbs free energy between reactants and products is given by: $$\Delta G = \Delta G^\circ + RT \ln \frac{[\text{products}]}{[\text{reactants}]}$$ where ΔG° is the free energy change for the reaction under standard conditions (reactants and products each at a concentration of $1.0\,\text{mol}\,l^{-1}$, at a temperature of 298 K). $\Delta G^{\circ\prime}$ is the standard free energy change for a reaction at pH = 7. (For a reaction in which H^+ or H_2O are not among the reactants and products, $\Delta G^{\circ\prime} = \Delta G^\circ$.)
universal gas constant	R	Fundamental constant in physics, chemistry and biology; $8.314\,\text{J}\,\text{K}^{-1}\,\text{mol}^{-1}$
Faraday constant	F	Represents the electronic charge on 1 mole of electrons (named after Michael Faraday, who quantified the relationship between a chemical reaction and flow of electrons): $96.494\,\text{kJ}\,\text{V}^{-1}\,\text{mol}^{-1}$
Kelvin	K	The SI unit for absolute temperature (named after Lord Kelvin, the scientist who first defined the absolute scale of temperature). $273\,\text{K} = 0\,^\circ\text{C}$
Joule	J	The SI unit for energy (after the physicist James Joule).

4.2 Applying thermodynamics to biochemical reactions

In applying thermodynamics to biochemical reactions, we are interested in which reactions are thermodynamically favourable. If we know which reactions are thermodynamically favourable ($\Delta S > 0$), then we can predict which reactions will occur spontaneously and identify those reactions that must be coupled to other reactions.

As discussed in the previous section, and according to the second law of thermodynamics, for a reaction to occur spontaneously the overall entropy of the system and its surroundings must increase. However, it is not practicable to use this criterion to define spontaneous biochemical processes, because to do so would require measurement of not only the entropy change of the system of interest, but also that of the surroundings, i.e. the rest of the Universe! Instead we use the Gibbs free energy (G). Free energy is energy that is available to do work. The Gibbs free energy function is derived from a combination of the first and second laws of thermodynamics and, importantly, applies at *constant temperature and pressure*. For the biologist, this limitation does not represent a problem, since temperature and pressure vary little in biological systems.

The energy that is potentially available in a reactant is defined by the simple equation:

$$G = H - TS \tag{4.2}$$

The energy available in a biochemical system is related to the enthalpy and entropy of *all* of the reactants, and the absolute temperature (T). When we are considering a biochemical reaction, we are concerned with the change in free energy, ΔG, a quantity that has two components:

- ΔH, the change in enthalpy;
- ΔS, the change in entropy, multiplied by the absolute temperature T.

  The equation that relates these parameters is:

$$\Delta G = \Delta H - T\Delta S \tag{4.3}$$

○ Given that both ΔG and ΔH are expressed as the number of kilojoules per mole of reactant (kJ mol^{-1}), what is the SI unit for ΔS?

● ΔS is expressed in $\text{kJ mol}^{-1}\,\text{K}^{-1}$.

For a conversion comprising a series of biochemical reactions, the total change in free energy can be obtained by simply subtracting the sum of the values of G for the initial reactants from the sum of the values of G for the final products. Alternatively, addition of all the ΔG values for the individual reactions in the pathway gives the overall ΔG for the pathway. For many reactants, the value of G has been determined. Similarly, the values of ΔG for many reactions are well known, based on the enthalpy change, ΔH, for the formation or breakdown of many biological compounds, as measured by a technique called calorimetry.

ΔG serves as an 'accounting' device that allows us to determine the direction in which a reaction or process will go, or the amount of energy required to make it go, as follows:

$\Delta G < 0$:   The reaction is energetically favourable and can occur spontaneously.

$\Delta G > 0$:   The reaction is energetically unfavourable and an input of free energy is required to drive the reaction in this direction.

$\Delta G = 0$:   The system is at equilibrium and there is no net change.

It is important to realize that the value of ΔG for any reaction depends on the conditions, i.e. the concentrations of the reactants, the temperature and the pH. It is useful, though, to be able to express values of ΔG for different reactions under comparable conditions. For this purpose, **standard conditions** are defined as those where all the reactants and products are present at a concentration of $1\ mol\ l^{-1}$ and at a temperature of 298 K (25 °C). ΔG of the reaction under standard conditions is given a special designation called $\Delta G°$ (pronounced 'delta-jee-nought'); that is, $\Delta G°$ is the difference between the free energy of the reactants and the free energy of the products under standard conditions. The relationship between ΔG and $\Delta G°$ depends on the actual concentrations of the reactants and products, and a mathematical derivation shows the following:

$$\Delta G = \Delta G° + RT \ln \frac{[\text{products}]}{[\text{reactants}]}$$

ln is the natural logarithm, i.e. log to the base 2.718. $\ln x = 2.303 \log_{10} x$.

or

$$\Delta G = \Delta G° + 2.303\, RT \log_{10} \frac{[\text{products}]}{[\text{reactants}]} \tag{4.4}$$

where R is the universal gas constant ($8.314\ J\ K^{-1}\ mol^{-1}$), T is the absolute temperature (in kelvin, K), ln is the natural logarithm and [products] and [reactants] denote the molar concentrations of each of the products and each of the reactants respectively.

So if one knows $\Delta G°$, this relationship can be used to determine ΔG for different concentrations of reactants and conditions.

We can now take this one stage further. Recall from Chapter 2, Section 2.5.2, that the equilibrium constant of a reaction, K_{eq}, is determined by the concentrations of products and reactants when the reaction has reached equilibrium.

$$K_{eq} = \frac{[\text{products}]}{[\text{reactants}]} \tag{2.4}$$

As you can see from the discussion above, when a reaction is at equilibrium (i.e. $\Delta G = 0$), $\Delta G°$ is also determined by the concentrations of the products and reactants. Hence the reaction equilibrium constant, K_{eq}, and $\Delta G°$ are both ways of describing what the concentrations of reactants and products are in a system at equilibrium. Put simply, $\Delta G°$ of a biochemical reaction is a thermodynamic way of expressing its equilibrium constant.

$$\Delta G° = -RT \ln K_{eq} = -2.303\, RT \log_{10} K_{eq} \tag{4.5}$$

Despite its general utility for comparing reactions, $\Delta G°$ has serious limitations for biochemists, particularly when we consider water and hydrogen ions, which are both important reactants and/or products in many biochemical reactions.

○ The pH inside a cell is around 7 and the concentration of water in a cell is greater than 55 mol l⁻¹. How do these conditions differ from standard conditions?

● Under standard conditions, the concentration of all reactants are 1 mol l⁻¹. Thus calculations using standard conditions are inappropriate for 55 mol l⁻¹ water. Similarly, under standard conditions, the concentration of H^+ ions is 1 mol l⁻¹, which is highly acidic.

It is inappropriate, from a biochemist's viewpoint, to use standard conditions that are completely non-physiological. Consequently biochemists often use a further descriptive quantity called $\Delta G^{\circ\prime}$, which is the standard free energy change at pH 7.0 (i.e. all reactants and products at 1 mol l⁻¹ except for H^+ which is at 10^{-7} mol l⁻¹). $\Delta G^{\circ\prime}$ tends to be much more frequently used than either ΔG° or ΔG. Note that, for a reaction in which neither H^+ nor H_2O is among the reactants or products, $\Delta G^{\circ\prime}$ and ΔG° are equivalent.

It is important not to confuse ΔG and $\Delta G^{\circ\prime}$. Remember that we use ΔG, *not* $\Delta G^{\circ\prime}$, to establish whether a reaction proceeds spontaneously ($\Delta G < 0$). For any reaction, $\Delta G^{\circ\prime}$ is constant, representing the free energy change under defined standard conditions. However, ΔG for the same reaction is variable, and, depending on the concentrations of the reactants and products, may be greater than, less than or the same as $\Delta G^{\circ\prime}$.

To illustrate how the concentrations of reactants and products affect the free energy of reactions, let us consider the hydrolysis of ATP to ADP and P_i.

$$ATP \rightleftharpoons ADP + P_i$$

ΔG for the forward reaction (i.e. hydrolysis of ATP) is given by

$$\Delta G = \Delta G^{\circ\prime} + RT \ln \frac{[ADP][P_i]}{[ATP]} \qquad (4.6)$$

As the reaction proceeds, the concentration of ADP increases, and the value of ΔG for the reaction also increases (becomes less negative). If the concentration of ADP continues to increase, at some point ΔG will become zero.

○ What happens when $\Delta G = 0$?

● The reaction has reached an equilibrium where the rate of ATP breakdown equals its rate of synthesis.

In Figure 4.4, ΔG for the hydrolysis of ATP is plotted against the percentage of ATP hydrolysed at pH 7 and 25 °C. Note that with increasing hydrolysis of ATP, shown along the horizontal axis, the concentration of ATP decreases and the concentration of ADP increases. Under standard conditions, i.e. when ATP, ADP and P_i are all at 1 mol l⁻¹, $\Delta G = -30.5$ kJ mol⁻¹.

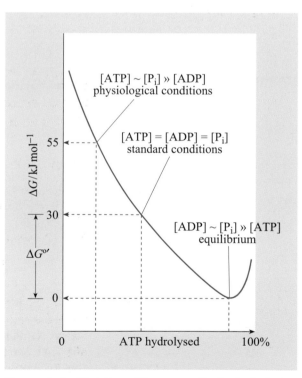

Figure 4.4   Variation of free energy for the hydrolysis of ATP with percentage of ATP hydrolysed. The relative concentrations of reactant (ATP) and products (ADP and P_i) corresponding to physiological conditions, standard conditions and equilibrium conditions are indicated. '~' indicates similar levels and '>>' indicates 'much greater than'.

○ What does this value of ΔG represent?

● Under these standard conditions $\Delta G = \Delta G^{\circ\prime}$.

However, in a cell, the concentration of ATP is normally much higher than that of ADP. In skeletal muscle cells, [ATP] can be as high as 10 times [ADP]. Under physiological conditions, therefore, the free energy of this reaction, is actually in the region of -46 to -55 kJ mol^{-1}, depending on the exact concentrations of ATP, ADP and P$_i$ (-55 kJ mol^{-1} in Figure 4.4). Thus hydrolysis of ATP under physiological conditions in a cell releases significantly more energy than hydrolysis of ATP under standard conditions.

You can see from this example that ΔG gives a measure of how far a reaction is away from equilibrium ($\Delta G = 0$). In living systems, many reactions are far from equilibrium, and we will consider this dynamic state in the next section.

Summary of Section 4.2

1   The change in Gibbs free energy (ΔG) is a useful accounting device that determines whether a reaction is thermodynamically favourable. The value of ΔG depends on the intrinsic nature of the reactants and products (their enthalpy and entropy), and their concentrations.

2   A reaction proceeds spontaneously (i.e. is thermodynamically favourable) if it has a negative free energy change ($\Delta G < 0$). Reactions with positive ΔG must be coupled to thermodynamically favourable chemical processes.

3   ΔG° is the free energy change for a reaction under standard conditions (all reactants and products at 1 mol l^{-1} and $T = 298$ K); however, when dealing with biological systems, the term $\Delta G^{\circ\prime}$, denoting the standard free energy change at pH 7, is used.

4   Equilibrium in a reaction is reached when $\Delta G = 0$.

4.3 Applying thermodynamics to dynamic biological systems

As already mentioned with respect to ATP hydrolysis, many of the key reactants within a cell are not at their equilibrium levels. Let us consider the case of ATP again.

○ From Figure 4.4, what can you say about the relative concentrations of ATP, ADP and P$_i$ at equilibrium ($\Delta G = 0$)?

● At equilibrium, the concentrations of ADP and P$_i$ are similar and are much greater than that of ATP.

Now take a look at Table 4.2, which shows the actual concentrations of the molecules in various cells.

Table 4.2 ATP, ADP and P_i concentrations in various cells (mmol l^{-1}).

	[ATP]	[ADP]	[P_i]
human erythrocyte (red blood cell)	2.25	0.25	1.65
human hepatocyte (liver cell)	3.38	1.32	4.80
rat brain	2.59	0.73	2.72
rat muscle	8.05	0.93	8.05
E. coli	7.90	1.04	7.90

The data are for the entire cell contents, although the cytosol and mitochondria have very different concentrations of ADP. For erythrocytes, the concentrations are those of the cytosol.

○ What can you say about the relative concentrations of ATP and ADP in the cells in Table 4.2? How do these values compare with equilibrium concentrations?

● In all cases, ATP concentration is higher than ADP concentration. The reverse is true at equilibrium.

The large negative ΔG value for the hydrolysis of ATP within a cell reflects the fact that cells keep their relative concentrations of ATP and ADP as much as a factor of 10^{10} away from the equilibrium values.

In most biochemical pathways, the product of one reaction becomes the substrate for subsequent reactions. So in a linear chain of reactions, the relative levels of the reactants and products depend on the rates of their generation and consumption, which are related to the activities, at any one time, of the enzymes catalysing these reactions. Further complexity occurs because many metabolites can be channelled through multiple pathways. For example, as shown in Figure 4.5, pyruvate is an intermediate in the pathways of amino acid (alanine) synthesis, lactate production, oxaloacetate synthesis and acetyl CoA and CO_2 production.

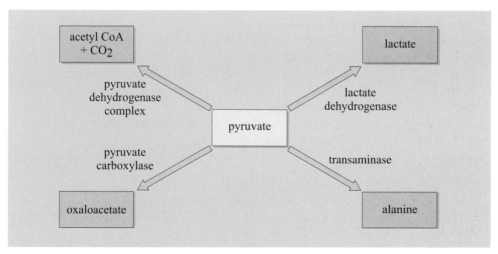

Figure 4.5 Four alternative pathways that utilize pyruvate.

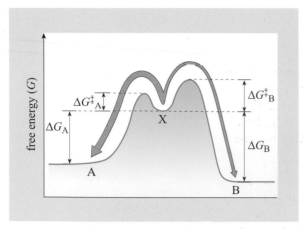

Figure 4.6   The relative rates of conversion of a substrate (X) into two products (A and B) depend on the activation energies of the reactions that produce A and B from their common substrate ($\Delta G^{\ddagger}_A$ and $\Delta G^{\ddagger}_B$ respectively) rather than the ΔG values of the two reactions.

The relative fluxes of metabolites through different pathways depend on the relative activities of enzymes, on the relative concentrations of reactants and on the conditions in the particular region of the cell. While thermodynamics can predict what is possible, it is the enzymes and the internal organization of the cell that determine what actually happens, by determining reaction rates and controlling the metabolic flux through different pathways (Figure 4.6). Thus a reaction with a negative ΔG can occur spontaneously but it may do so at such a slow rate as to be barely perceptible. The rate at which a reaction occurs depends on the Gibbs free energy of activation (symbolized by $\Delta G^{\ddagger}$) which is the difference between the free energy of the reactants and that of a high-energy intermediate known as the transition state (described in Chapter 3, Section 3.7). $\Delta G^{\ddagger}$ therefore represents the energy barrier that must be overcome for the reaction to occur. *It is $\Delta G^{\ddagger}$, not ΔG, that determines the rate at which the reaction occurs*. In Figure 4.6, X can be converted into either A or B. Both reactions have negative ΔG and therefore can occur spontaneously. However, conversion of X into B has a higher free energy of activation ($\Delta G^{\ddagger}_B$) than does conversion of X into A ($\Delta G^{\ddagger}_A$) and therefore occurs at a slower rate.

Perhaps the most significant advantage of the thermodynamic approach to biological systems is that it gives a uniform way to treat them all. In other words, any change can be described thermodynamically, whether it is the conversion of pyruvate to acetate and carbon dioxide, the dilution of a compound, the diffusion of a molecule down a concentration gradient, the transition from a liquid to a gas, or a complex sequence of biochemical reactions. For example, when several reactions take place sequentially in the cell, the free energy difference for the complete transformation depends only on the free energy difference between the initial reactants and the final products. Where more than one pathway exists, with different intermediates, the free energy difference for the overall transformation is independent of the reaction pathway (Figure 4.7). Whichever pathway is taken, ΔG tells us in which direction a change will occur. Beyond this, ΔG tells us very little.

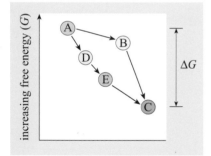

Figure 4.7
The overall free energy change when A is converted to C is independent of the pathway, i.e. ΔG is the same for the conversion A → B → C as it is for A → D → E → C.

Since energy changes associated with transformations are independent of path, ΔG tells us nothing about the mechanism of the reaction. Thermodynamics can examine the energy efficiency, conservation and coupling between various processes without requiring a detailed knowledge of the underlying mechanism. But once thermodynamics has told us that a reaction is possible, it is up to biologists to discover whether or not an organism makes use of that reaction, and if so, how.

Summary of Section 4.3

1   The relative rates of metabolic flux through different pathways depend on the specific activities of enzymes, the relative concentrations of reactants and the conditions in the particular region of the cell in which the process is occurring.

2   ΔG for a reaction does not influence the rate at which the reaction occurs. Rather, the rate of the reaction depends on the Gibbs free energy of activation ($\Delta G^{\ddagger}$).

3   The overall ΔG for a transformation is independent of the pathway, and hence the mechanism, of the transformation.

4.4 The second law of thermodynamics and the evolution of life

The physicist Erwin Schrödinger was often criticized by biologists for interpreting life by the laws of physics in an attempt to reconcile biology with chemistry and physics. He suggested that biologists should apply a thermodynamic perspective to the both the question of how life first arose, i.e. the production of 'order from disorder', and the study of living organisms, i.e. the generation of 'order from order'.

The emergence of life and its evolution from simple chemicals into complex organisms is very improbable from a thermodynamic point of view. Consider a scenario in which sunlight causes evaporation of water from a mountain pool. The energy of the sunlight may drive an unfavourable reaction between simple compounds in the pool, promoted by evaporation and concentration, leading to the formation of new compounds. However, these new compounds need to be chemically stable even after rehydration by rainfall. Moreover, they need to take part in successive energy-requiring processes until the chance emergence of compounds able to 'harvest' energy and self-replicate. In thermodynamic terms, the evolution of life moves through a series of increasingly unlikely states.

The fact that the order of living things did arise from disorder has led some to question whether cells contradict the second law of thermodynamics, since their growth and differentiation represent an increased synthesis of highly structured materials, and therefore a decrease in the randomness (entropy) of the system. However, as discussed previously, increasing order in one system or compartment (a pool, a cell, an organism) is acceptable if it is offset by increasing disorder in the rest of the Universe. Metabolism of high-energy components extracted from the environment to give lower-energy components within an organism is thermodynamically favourable and represents a flow of energy down a gradient. The free energy released in this process is used to drive otherwise unfavourable reactions and the local decrease in entropy in the system or compartment is permissible since that of the Universe as a whole increases. Growth and development, which are dependent upon metabolism, can therefore be viewed as resulting from the thermodynamic advantage of dissipating energy gradients. If we accept this view, then it represents a criterion for evaluating growth and development in living systems. It follows that ageing is associated with a decline in the organism's ability to dissipate energy gradients, ultimately leading to death, the state of 'maximum entropy', as described by Schrödinger (Section 4.1.1).

This chapter highlights the importance of compartments (e.g. a cell or an organism) in thermodynamics and explains why it is possible to have an increase in order, provided that the overall disorder of the Universe increases. Seen in this way, you can appreciate that the formation of primordial cells (discussed in Chapter 1), when viewed thermodynamically, was essential for the evolution of life – order can only increase in a defined compartment. It is therefore no coincidence that cells are universal components of living systems. From a thermodynamic perspective, life (locally ordered systems) can only develop within discrete compartments (cells), by increasing the disorder of the rest of the Universe, i.e. by metabolism.

Summary of Section 4.4

1   Life is a thermodynamically favourable process, since the order (decrease in entropy) created within discrete compartments is offset by increasing disorder in the environment.

2   Order inside living organisms arises as a result of metabolism.

4.5 Bioenergetics

Broadly speaking, **bioenergetics** is the study of energy transformations in living systems; in other words, it is the application of thermodynamics to living things. In practice, this means the processes by which ATP is generated and utilized in living organisms. The amount of ATP in a cell is sufficient to supply the free energy needs of the cell for only 1–2 minutes; consequently it must be continually regenerated. In fact, in some cells, such as brain cells, the ATP reserve is sufficient for only a few seconds. This accounts in part for the relative vulnerability of brain tissue in instances of temporary oxygen deprivation.

> In this section, we examine in some detail thermodynamic aspects of the generation and utilization of the proton/electrochemical gradient by membrane-bound protein complexes in the inner mitochondrial membrane. ATP generation by mitochondria was covered in S204, Book 3 *The Core of Life*, Vol. I, Section 5.3, which provides the background for this discussion.

4.5.1 Energy conservation and conversion in mitochondria

All animals, fungi and most bacteria and protoctists derive free energy from the oxidation of complex organic molecules. In aerobic respiration in these organisms, electrons are not transferred directly from the fuel molecules to O_2 but are transferred to special carriers, namely the coenzymes NAD and FAD. In eukaryote cells, the final steps in the utilization of carbohydrates and fatty acids occur in mitochondria, where energy released on oxidation of NAD.2H and FAD.2H (the reduced forms of NAD and FAD) is 'trapped' and used to synthesize ATP. In the presence of O_2, the mitochondria convert the reducing power of NAD.2H and FAD.2H into utilizable energy, in the form of ATP, by a process known as **oxidative phosphorylation**. This function has earned the mitochondrion the name 'powerhouse of the cell'.

Note that the reduced forms of NAD and FAD are represented as NAD.2H and FAD.2H respectively to emphasize the fact that both these coenzymes can provide two reducing equivalents (electrons) on oxidation. You may encounter these molecules as NADH and $FADH_2$ in other textbooks.

NAD.2H and FAD.2H are oxidized by the **electron transport chain (ETC)**, a system of electron carriers located in the inner membrane of mitochondria, with O_2 being the ultimate electron acceptor. During the transfer of electrons from NAD.2H and FAD.2H along the electron transport chain to O_2, the energy released is used to pump protons from the mitochondrial matrix across the inner mitochondrial membrane. This pumping of protons results in an electrochemical proton gradient across the membrane, such that the intermembrane space becomes more acidic than the matrix (a difference of 1.4 pH units). During the transport of two electrons from NAD.2H to O_2, approximately 10 protons are pumped across the membrane to establish the electrochemical gradient. The free energy stored in the electrochemical gradient is called the **proton motive force** and is used to drive the synthesis of ATP. This coupling of electron transfer along the electron transport chain to ATP synthesis by means of an electrochemical gradient is known as **chemiosmosis** and was described by Peter Mitchell in 1961. Mitchell was awarded the Nobel Prize in 1978 for his work in this area.

A knowledge of the spatial organization within a mitochondrion is important for understanding the bioenergetics of oxidative phosphorylation (Figure 4.8). A typical mitochondrion is 0.5–1 µm wide and 2–8 µm long, with an outer membrane and a folded inner membrane. The outer and inner membranes produce two separate compartments: the intermembrane space and the matrix enclosed by the inner membrane. Three-dimensional images show that the inner membrane involutions (cristae) have narrow and very long tubular connections, which lead to the possibility that gradients of ions, small molecules and macromolecules may occur both between and within mitochondrial compartments. From Figure 4.8 it is evident that the compartments are not of uniform size or distribution in the mitochondrion, and local differences may be reflected in the concentration of adenine nucleotides and the magnitude of pH gradients produced by chemiosmosis in different parts of the organelle.

Two principle types of reaction occur at the inner mitochondrial membrane.

1   Electrons are passed from NAD.2H or FAD.2H, via a series of electron carriers in the ETC (also known as the respiratory chain), to O_2. At three different points in the ETC (complexes I, III and IV) H^+ ions (protons) are pumped into the intermembrane space.

2   Protons flow back down the electrochemical gradient, into the mitochondrial matrix, via the F_0-F_1 ATP synthase, driving the synthesis of ATP.

The energy transfer in this system starts with oxidation of NAD.2H and FAD.2H and the release of some of the chemical energy stored in these reduced coenzymes. The electrons removed in these oxidation reactions are passed between the complexes of the electron transport chain and the energy associated with the electrons, released in discrete steps, is used to pump protons into the intermembrane space. In this way, the energy released by oxidation of NAD.2H and FAD.2H is converted into the potential energy of the electrochemical proton

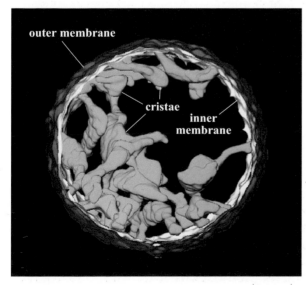

350nm

Figure 4.8
Electron micrograph of an isolated rat liver mitochondrion in cross-section, showing the outer membrane (coloured red) and the inner membrane (yellow) with its many elaborate involutions, the cristae, highlighted in green. The inner mitochondrial membrane is essential for coupling electron transport with ATP synthesis and is often referred to as a 'coupling membrane'. This membrane acts as an efficient and regulated energy-transducing unit, organizing electron transfer and the associated reactions leading to ATP synthesis.

gradient. The electrochemical potential is then reconverted into chemical bond energy by the F_0-F_1 ATP synthase. As explained below, the two processes are normally tightly coupled, so much of the energy is conserved in ATP.

Seen in thermodynamic terms, the increased order that occurs when protons are concentrated in the intermembrane space can only take place when driven by the electron movement in the oxidation–reduction (redox) gradient, using energy provided by the oxidation of NAD.2H or FAD.2H. In short, the decreased entropy of the protons is offset by the decreased enthalpy of NAD.2H or FAD.2H on oxidation. With the return of the protons to the mitochondrial matrix (down the electrochemical gradient), their entropy increases, which offsets the increase in enthalpy associated with the synthesis of ATP from ADP and P_i.

4.5.2 The mitochondrial electron transport chain and proton pumping

The mitochondrial electron transport chain (ETC) is a series of electron carriers, each having a higher affinity for electrons than the previous one. Thus in a sequence of linked redox reactions, electrons are passed from one electron carrier to the next in the series, represented in Figure 4.9a. The ETC contains four large protein complexes (numbered I to IV), arranged asymmetrically in the inner mitochondrial membrane. Each of the complexes consists of several protein components with prosthetic groups that act as electron carriers. Electrons are transferred from NAD.2H to complex I (also known as the NAD.2H dehydrogenase complex) and passed to a highly mobile carrier called ubiquinone (Q in Figure 4.9). Ubiquinone in turn passes electrons to complex III (also known as the cytochrome b/c_1 complex). Cytochrome c shuttles back and forth, delivering electrons from complex III to complex IV (the cytochrome oxidase complex) which ultimately uses the electrons to reduce O_2. Oxidation of FAD.2H is catalysed by complex II and the electrons are passed to ubiquinone, from whence they are transferred through the ETC in the same way as those removed from NAD.2H. Complexes I, III and IV pump protons into the intermembrane space.

In Figure 4.9b the components of the ETC are represented against an axis indicating their **redox potential** (in volts) which is a measure of their affinity for electrons. The oxidized and reduced forms of an electron carrier are collectively referred to as a redox couple and their redox potential is a measure of their affinity for electrons relative to that of a standard redox couple (defined as 0 V). The redox potentials for the components of the mitochondrial ETC indicated in Figure 4.9 are standard values ($E^{\circ\prime}$), i.e. those under standard conditions.

▢ What could you say about the redox potential of (a) a strong oxidizing agent and (b) a strong reducing agent?

◼ A strong oxidizing agent has a high (positive) redox potential. A strong reducing agent has a low (negative) redox potential.

The difference in the redox potential between different components of the ETC dictates the flow of electrons through the chain, from compounds with low redox potentials to those with higher redox potentials. Thus electrons are passed from either complex I or II (depending on whether they derive from oxidation of NAD.2H or FAD.2H) to complex III and then to complex IV.

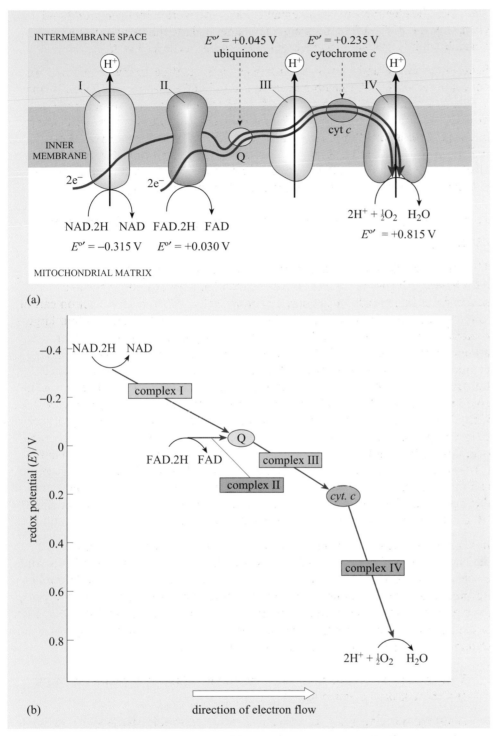

Figure 4.9   (a) Components of the electron transport chain depicted in situ in the inner mitochondrial membrane. The flow of electrons (e^-) is indicated. (b) Standard redox potentials ($E^{o\prime}$) at pH 7 of electron carriers in the mitochondrial electron transport chain. Note how large redox potential differences release enough energy to pump protons.

The standard free energy change ($\Delta G^{\circ\prime}$) associated with transfer of electrons from one component of the ETC to another is related to the difference in standard redox potential ($\Delta E^{\circ\prime}$) between the two electron carriers, according to Equation 4.6:

$$\Delta G^{\circ\prime} = -nF\Delta E^{\circ\prime} \qquad (4.7)$$

where n is the number of electrons transferred and F is the Faraday constant (see Box 4.1).

Let us consider the net redox reaction accomplished by the ETC, i.e. the transfer of two electrons from NAD.2H to O_2. The standard redox potentials for NAD.2H and O_2 are, respectively, -0.315 V and 0.815 V.

$$\text{NAD.2H} \rightleftharpoons \text{NAD} + 2H^+ + 2e^- \qquad E^{\circ\prime} = -0.315 \text{ V}$$

$$\tfrac{1}{2}O_2 + 2H^+ + 2e^- \rightleftharpoons H_2O \qquad E^{\circ\prime} = +0.815 \text{ V}$$

(e^- denotes an electron.)

◻ The overall reaction is:

$$\text{NAD.2H} + \tfrac{1}{2}O_2 \rightleftharpoons H_2O + \text{NAD}$$

What is the change in redox potential ($\Delta E^{\circ\prime}$) for this reaction?

◼ $\Delta E^{\circ\prime}$ for the transfer of two electrons from NAD.2H to O_2 is

$$(0.815 - (-0.315)) \text{ V} = 1.13 \text{ V}.$$

The free energy change for this reaction is then given by:

$$\Delta G^{\circ\prime} = -nF\,\Delta E^{\circ\prime} = -2 \times 96.494 \times 1.13 = -218 \text{ kJ mol}^{-1}$$

◻ How many moles of ATP could be synthesized if the free energy released from the reduction of O_2 by one mole of NAD.2H was used with 100% efficiency to drive ATP synthesis from ADP and P_i? (Hint: in Section 4.2 you learned that the standard free energy change ($\Delta G^{\circ\prime}$) for the hydrolysis of ATP to ADP and P_i is -30.5 kJ mol^{-1}.)

◼ The synthesis of ATP from ADP and P_i requires an input of 30.5 kJ mol^{-1}. Thus the free energy released on reduction of O_2 by one mole of NAD.2H would be sufficient to drive synthesis of

$$\frac{218 \text{ kJ}}{30.5 \text{ kJ mol}^{-1}} = 7.1 \text{ moles of ATP}$$

assuming 100% efficiency.

The ETC effectively allows the overall free energy change associated with the reduction of O_2 by NAD.2H (-218 kJ mol^{-1}) to be released in three steps, each of which drives the pumping of protons necessary to generate the proton motive force which ultimately drives ATP synthesis. As you might expect, oxidative phosphorylation is not 100% thermodynamically efficient. In fact, oxidation of one NAD.2H, with transfer of two electrons via the ETC, results in the synthesis of only three ATPs as a result of oxidative phosphorylation.

◻ What is the thermodynamic efficiency of oxidative phosphorylation under standard biochemical conditions?

■ $\Delta G^{\circ\prime}$ for synthesis of one mole of ATP under standard conditions is 30.5 kJ mol^{-1}, so the synthesis of three moles of ATP requires 91.5 kJ mol^{-1}. Oxidation of one mole of NAD.2H via the ETC releases 218 kJ mol^{-1} of free energy under standard conditions. Therefore the efficiency with which this free energy is utilized by oxidative phosphorylation under standard biochemical conditions is

$$\frac{91.5 \times 100}{218} = 42\%$$

Under physiological conditions in mitochondria, oxidative phosphorylation is actually thought to operate at close to 70% thermodynamic efficiency, and is thus much more efficient than calculations based on standard conditions might lead us to believe. The standard free energy changes for the redox reactions facilitated by each of complexes I to IV, are detailed in Table 4.3, along with the difference in redox potential between the components.

Table 4.3 Standard free energy changes and changes in redox potential (at pH 7) associated with transfer of two electrons between components of the mitochondrial electron transport chain.

Transfer of electrons	$\Delta G^{\circ\prime}$ / kJ mol^{-1}	$\Delta E^{\circ\prime}$ / V
NAD.2H to ubiquinone (complex I)	−69.5	0.360
FAD.2H to ubiquinone (complex II)	−2.9	0.015
ubiquinone to cytochrome c (complex III)	−36.7	0.190
cytochrome c to O_2 (complex IV)	−112.0	0.580

The changes in redox potential with transfer of two electrons through complexes I, III and IV in each case corresponds to sufficient free energy to drive the synthesis of an ATP molecule. As has been noted already, the synthesis of ATP is achieved by using this free energy to pump protons and generate a proton motive force across the inner mitochondrial membrane. The electrochemical proton gradient (proton motive force) across the inner mitochondrial membrane depends on both the membrane potential and the proton concentration gradient and is approximately 230 mV (see Figure 4.10). Approximately 22 kJ are required to pump one mole of protons up this gradient. Interestingly, it is thought that complexes I and III both pump two protons per electron, while complex IV pumps only one proton, despite the larger potential energy release by complex IV. Since two electrons are extracted from each NAD.2H, a total of 10 protons are pumped for each NAD.2H oxidized. Notice that the oxidation of FAD.2H by complex II does not release sufficient free energy to synthesize ATP and this complex serves only to introduce electrons from FAD.2H into the ETC. These electrons are then passed through complexes III and IV; hence only six protons are pumped into the intermembrane space as a result of oxidation of FAD.2H.

Coupling between electron transport and oxidative phosphorylation is very tight, and NAD.2H and FAD.2H are oxidized only if ADP is simultaneously phosphorylated to ATP. This tight coupling of the ETC to ATP synthesis can be demonstrated experimentally using uncouplers. An example of an uncoupling agent is 2,4-dinitrophenol (DNP), an acidic aromatic compound that can carry protons across the inner mitochondrial membrane, thereby dissipating the proton gradient. Addition of DNP to a respiring mitochondrial preparation effectively uncouples oxidation of NAD.2H from ATP synthesis. Electron transport from NAD.2H to O_2 via the ETC continues but, because there is no proton gradient, there is no synthesis of ATP (but much heat is produced).

4.5.3 Thermodynamics of ATP synthesis

As has already been mentioned, the synthesis of ATP by oxidative phosphorylation on the inner mitochondrial membrane is effected by the F_0-F_1 ATP synthase, which uses the free energy stored in the electrochemical proton gradient (the proton motive force) to synthesize ATP from ADP (Figure 4.10). Note that the F_0-F_1 ATP synthase can operate in either direction. In other words, it can either use the proton gradient to synthesize ATP or it can use ATP to generate a proton gradient. Many other ATP-dependent ion pumps also work in this way.

Figure 4.10
Under the influence of the proton motive force (pmf), which depends on the distribution of charge (membrane potential) and the proton concentration gradient (ΔpH), protons flow from the intermembrane space into the mitochondrial matrix via the F_0-F_1 ATP synthase. Passage of protons is coupled to ATP synthesis, and it is estimated that the transfer of three protons is required to synthesize one molecule of ATP.

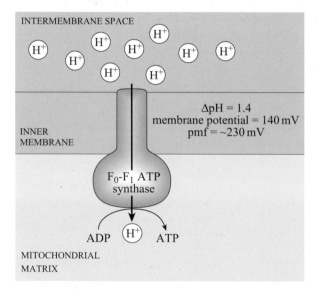

INTERMEMBRANE SPACE

$\Delta pH = 1.4$
membrane potential = 140 mV
pmf = ~230 mV

INNER MEMBRANE

F_0-F_1 ATP synthase

ADP H^+ ATP

MITOCHONDRIAL MATRIX

The exact number of protons required to synthesize one molecule of ATP is not known, but the return of protons to the mitochondrial matrix releases about 22 kJ mol^{-1} of free energy (i.e. the same as that required to pump them out of the matrix into the intermembrane space), provided the electrochemical gradient remains at 230 mV. Most estimates indicate that around three protons pass back into the matrix per molecule of ATP synthesized. Therefore movement of three moles of protons down the electrochemical gradient releases about 3 × 22 kJ, i.e. approximately 66 kJ of free energy.

○ What can you deduce about ΔG for the synthesis of one mole of ATP?

● ΔG must be less than 66 kJ mol^{-1}.

The electrochemical proton gradient, which couples electron transport to ATP synthesis, is the means by which ATP synthesis is regulated. Essentially, variation in the size of this gradient allows the ETC to sense changes in F_0-F_1 ATP synthase activity. A fluctuating ATP / ADP ratio is the main 'controller' of ATP synthesis.

As we saw in Section 4.2, ΔG depends on the concentrations of the reactants and products, ATP, ADP and P_i. For the synthesis of ATP from ADP and P_i, ΔG is given by Equation 4.8. (This equation is of the same form as Equation 4.6 for the hydrolysis of ATP, which you met in Section 4.2, but with products and reactants transposed.)

$$\Delta G = \Delta G^{\circ\prime} + RT \ln \frac{[\text{ADP}]}{[\text{ADP}][P_i]} \tag{4.8}$$

Suppose that the [ATP]/[ADP] ratio in the mitochondrial matrix falls as a result of a sudden increase in demand for ATP. It follows that $\Delta G_{\text{ATP synthesis}}$ is lowered and movement of protons down the electrochemical gradient via F_0-F_1 ATP synthase will result in increased ATP production. The increased flow of protons back into the mitochondrial matrix will dissipate the electrochemical proton gradient more rapidly, lowering the concentration of protons in the intermembrane space and decreasing the resistance to proton pumping (i.e. the free energy required to pump protons into the intermembrane space). Increased electron transport activity restores the proton gradient. This respiratory control mechanism restores the ATP/ADP ratio to the point where the energy for proton movement is balanced by the energy required to synthesize ATP; in other words, there is a dynamic equilibrium.

○   What principle does this control mechanism illustrate?

●   This is an example of the Le Chatelier principle, described in Chapter 2.

Respiratory control ensures that electrons only flow through the ETC when ATP is needed.

Any deviations from optimal efficiency of oxidative phosphorylation are largely overcome by thermodynamic 'buffering'. For example, the uncoupling protein UCP1, found in the mitochondria of brown adipose tissue, acts as a proton channel, which dissipates the proton gradient. This specialized adipose tissue therefore serves to generate heat (hence UCP1's alternative name, thermogenin). Physiological levels of ADP and ATP effectively block the flow of protons through the channel formed by UCP1, but this block can be counteracted by free fatty acids, the concentration of which is under hormonal control. Whilst in some organisms such a mechanism serves to generate heat, it can also regulate the degree of coupling. Partially uncoupling the ETC from ATP synthesis can help set the optimum efficiency of oxidative phosphorylation. Thus such controls provide adaptive advantages both to the organism and to the individual cell.

Summary of Section 4.5

1   The transfer of electrons from NAD.2H and FAD.2H via the electron transport chain is coupled to ATP synthesis in the mitochondria, by generation of an electrochemical proton gradient across the inner mitochondrial membrane. The free energy of electron transport is used to pump protons across the membrane into the intermembrane space, and with return of the protons to the matrix, the free energy released drives the synthesis of ATP.

2   The flow of electrons along the electron transport chain is dictated by the relative redox potentials of the ETC components. The difference in redox potential between successive components is in proportion to the free energy change associated with the electron transfer.

3   In thermodynamic terms, decreased entropy of the protons pumped into the intermembrane space is offset by decreased enthalpy of NAD.2H on oxidation; increased enthalpy of ATP (ATP synthesis) is offset by increased entropy of protons on their return to the mitochondrial matrix.

4   ATP production is tightly regulated to meet a cell's energy demands. The tight coupling of electron transport to ATP synthesis, by the proton motive force, is an important mechanism for regulating ATP synthesis.

4.6 The significance of the Gibbs free energy in biological systems

We have seen how the Gibbs free energy allows us to predict the direction of spontaneous change in biological systems and understand its significance in relation to equilibrium in reversible biochemical reactions. As discussed earlier, the ways in which cells utilize fuels or light energy to synthesize ATP conform to the laws of thermodynamics and the magnitude of the Gibbs free energy allows us to understand why these processes work. However, this thermodynamic function is invaluable not only for an understanding of bioenergetics and metabolism, but also for comprehending other biophysical phenomena such as osmosis, solvation of ions, transport and both inter- and intramolecular interactions. In this section, we will look briefly at some particular examples of intermolecular interactions, specifically enzyme–substrate, protein–protein and protein–DNA interactions, to illustrate why the Gibbs free energy is such a useful concept for the biologist.

4.6.1 Thermodynamic analysis of biomolecular interactions

Measurement of thermodynamic parameters can provide important information on the likelihood of molecular interactions, equilibrium points and the stability of complexes. But how can these thermodynamic parameters be quantified? Recent improvements in the sensitivity of laboratory instruments have made such measurements relatively easy. Calorimetric methods, in particular **isothermal titration calorimetry (ITC)**, which is outlined in Box 4.2, and **differential scanning calorimetry (DSC)** are used as analytical tools to obtain fundamental data about intermolecular and intramolecular forces.

Box 4.2	Studying the thermodynamics of molecular interactions using isothermal titration calorimetry (ITC)

ITC is a technique used to detect and investigate molecular interactions by measuring associated heat changes. It has been applied to the study of interactions between macromolecules, drug–protein interactions and macromolecule–solute interactions. The experimental system, shown in Figure 4.11, contains two cells, one holding a solution of one of the interacting molecules (sample cell) and the other holding solvent (reference cell). The reaction cells are maintained at the same temperature by a feedback control circuit. Ligand is injected into the sample cell in increasing (known) amounts and, if an interaction occurs between the ligand and the target molecule in the sample cell, the heat content changes. Heat changes due to the ligand–target interactions are measured as the amount of electrical power required by the feedback control circuit to heat the reference cell (for exothermic interactions) or the sample cell (for endothermic interactions). Titration of the ligand into the sample cell results in discrete pulses of feedback power, and from these measurements it is possible to determine the dependency of the heat change on the molar ratio of the interacting molecules (Figure 4.11b). From this relationship it is possible to determine the equilibrium dissociation constant (K_D), the stoichiometry of the interaction (i.e. the relative amounts of the two species that are involved in the interaction), and ΔH for the interaction. ΔG can then

be derived from K_D and ΔS can be calculated from $\Delta G = \Delta H - T\Delta S$. Figure 4.11b shows binding isotherms, i.e. plots of total heat change against molar ratio, from a hypothetical ITC experiment to study the interaction of protein X with proteins Y and Z. Addition of Y to X resulted in the production of heat energy, indicative of an exothermic interaction, whereas addition of Z to X had no effect on the heat content of the sample cell, indicating that there was no detectable interaction between X and Z.

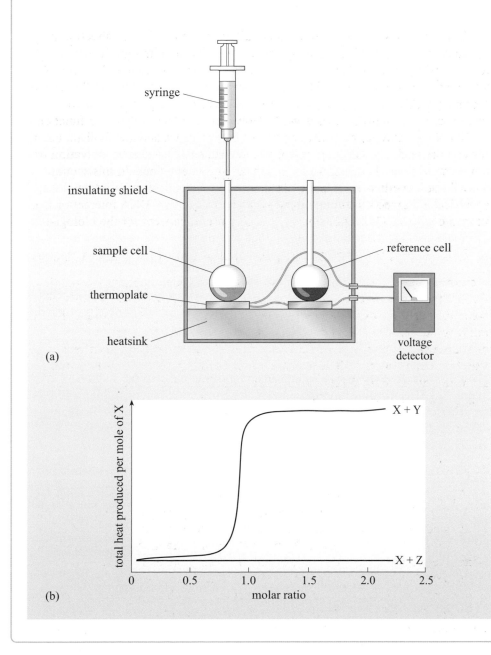

(a)

(b)

Figure 4.11
(a) Schematic drawing of an isothermal titration calorimeter. (b) Binding isotherms from an ITC experiment to study the interaction of protein X (the target) with protein Y or with protein Z. The molar ratio is the ratio of the number of moles of Y or Z to the number of moles of X in the sample cell. From the isotherm for X + Y, it is apparent that X binds Y with a 1 : 1 stoichiometry.

DSC is used to examine the decomposition of molecular complexes such as enzyme–substrate or receptor–ligand complexes at different temperatures. It essentially measures the amount of energy required to increase or decrease the temperature of the complex at a constant rate, i.e. the magnitude and direction of thermal transitions. From this information, it is possible to determine the activation energy and predict the stability of molecular complexes.

The DSC technique is particularly useful in the pharmaceutical industry, for example in studying drug delivery systems. The problems associated with the use of, for example, drugs that are rapidly metabolized on administration (e.g. peptides), can be overcome by complexing the drug with a carrier delivery system which protects it from degradation. A good delivery molecule should ideally be stable for a short time with no side-effects; it should bind tightly to the drug but be readily released when the drug reaches its target. The DSC method is the best method to study the stability of such delivery systems, and provides information on the association/dissociation behaviour of the drug–delivery system complex.

4.6.2 Enzyme–substrate interactions: thermodynamic considerations

Understanding the specific and reversible interactions that occur between enzymes and their substrates is central to an understanding of the mechanisms of enzyme action. These interactions are non-covalent and are identical in character to those that determine protein conformation.

○   What are the different interactions that determine protein conformation?

●   Hydrogen bonding, van der Waals, electrostatic and hydrophobic interactions.

As mentioned in Chapter 3, Section 3.7, where we considered catalytic mechanisms in terms of enzyme structure, an enzyme-catalysed reaction can be represented as follows:

$$E + S \rightleftharpoons ES \rightleftharpoons ES^{\ddagger} \rightleftharpoons EP \rightleftharpoons E + P$$

where E is the free enzyme, S is the substrate, ES is the enzyme–substrate complex, $ES^{\ddagger}$ is the transition state, EP is the enzyme–product complex and P is the product. Note that there is a dynamic equilibrium between free, substrate-bound and product-bound forms of the enzyme, which is sensitive to substrate concentration.

The driving force for an enzyme–substrate interaction is the overall lowering of the free energy of the system when reactants are converted into products. Enzymes are biological catalysts that can speed up reactions by a factor of as much as 10^{14}. Like any other catalyst, they increase the rate at which a reaction approaches equilibrium, by lowering the free energy of activation ($\Delta G^{\ddagger}$), i.e. the minimum energy input required to initiate a chemical reaction under given conditions (Figure 4.12). Effectively, the enzyme lowers the activation barrier by stabilizing the transition state. As stressed in Section 4.3, enzymes do not alter the overall energy change (ΔG), since this thermodynamic property is independent of the path of the reaction.

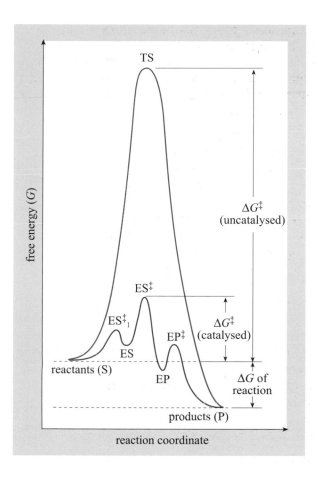

Figure 4.12
Energy profiles for catalysed
versus uncatalysed reactions. The
different species are as described in
the text. (Note that $ES^{\ddagger}_1$ and $EP^{\ddagger}$
are higher-energy intermediate
forms of ES and EP respectively,
which, for simplicity, have been
omitted from the generalized
representation of an enzyme-
catalysed reaction in the text.) The
overall energy difference between
reactants and products is the same
in catalysed and uncatalysed
reactions. The enzyme-catalysed
reaction proceeds at a faster rate
because the free energy of
activation ($\Delta G^{\ddagger}$) is lower than
for the uncatalysed reaction.
(TS = transition state for the
uncatalysed reaction.)

There are two principal mechanisms by which enzymes lower the free energy of activation:

By altering the electronic configuration of the reactants

Chemical reactions often involve alterations in electronic configurations of the reactant molecules, phenomena described in Chapter 3 (Section 3.7.1). For example, reactant molecules may have groups with strong repulsive forces that must be brought together. The enzymes may act to provide the place for some of the electrons of one reactant to be 'buried', so that the repulsion is reduced, thereby enhancing the reaction. In this case, the energy of activation is reduced by the ability of the enzyme to provide a 'sink' for electrons and a surface upon which the reaction can occur.

By change of entropy

Another method of enzyme action is through an increase in the entropy of activation, $\Delta S^{\ddagger}$. An increase in $\Delta S^{\ddagger}$ would seem unlikely, since enzyme catalysis involves binding of *two* molecules (enzyme and substrate) to give a *single* species (enzyme–substrate complex). However, the *overall* $\Delta S^{\ddagger}$ may increase through a change in the conformation of the enzyme itself during catalysis. Conformational change could, for example, increase the entropy of water molecules that may have been ordered by the substrate or by the active-site pocket of the enzyme. If the increase in the entropy of the water molecules outweighs the decrease in entropy associated with two molecules becoming one complex, then $\Delta G^{\ddagger}$ is reduced and the reaction rate is increased.

4.6.3 Thermodynamics of subunit association and oxygen binding in haemoglobin

Haemoglobins arc a useful model system for experimental analysis of protein–ligand and protein–protein interactions, including assembly of subunits. In the red blood cells of vertebrates, haemoglobin plays a fundamental role in the transfer of oxygen from the lungs to all other organs and cells in the body. Oxygen is loaded onto haemoglobin in the lungs, where the partial pressure of oxygen is high, and unloaded in the other tissues of the body, where the partial pressure of oxygen is low. Vertebrate haemoglobin is a tetramer, $\alpha_2\beta_2$, and each subunit can bind one O_2 ligand molecule (see Section 3.6.2). Under physiological conditions, the $\alpha_2\beta_2$ tetramer is the most stable combination of the individual subunits; that is, the $\alpha_2\beta_2$ tetramer has the lowest free energy compared with all other possible combinations of these subunits. The free energy of dissociation, i.e. the amount of work that must be done to dissociate haemoglobin tetramers, depends on the primary structure of the protein.

There are nearly 500 known naturally-occurring human variant haemoglobins of which around 95% arise from the substitution of a single amino acid in one or other of the subunits. These mutations result in a diverse range of physiological effects, and the study of these variants has shed light on the structure–function relationship of proteins. The haemoglobin variant that gives rise to sickle cell anaemia in homozygous individuals (HbS) has a hydrophobic valine residue in place of a hydrophilic glutamate residue (Glu 6), which is presented on the surface of the folded β subunit (Figure 4.13). HbS molecules aggregate into long rigid fibres, causing the abnormal shape of red blood cells typical of sickle cell anaemia.

Figure 4.13
Molecular model showing the tetrameric structure of normal adult haemoglobin. The individual polypeptide chains are shown as different-coloured ribbons (α subunits, yellow and blue; β subunits, cyan and green) and the haem group (red) is shown in ball-and-stick representation. Glu 6 on the β subunits is indicated in pink. Substitution with a Val at this position (the HbS mutation) causes the protein to aggregate. The position of the 'Kansas' mutation (Asn 102 on the β subunits) is indicated in white. Note how this mutation lies in the pocket containing the oxygen-carrying haem group. The substituted residue in the 'Georgia' mutation is Pro 95 on the α subunits (indicated in orange). This residue is located at the contact between the two α subunits.

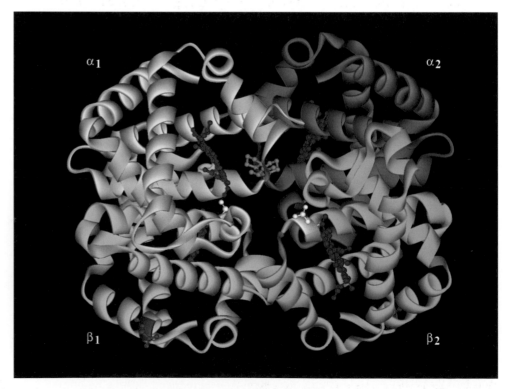

⚪ Why might substitution of a surface glutamate residue by a valine residue cause aggregation of the protein?

⚫ Presentation of a hydrophobic valine residue on the surface of the protein in an aqueous environment would not be energetically favourable. Aggregation would be favoured if the valine residue was buried as a result.

Many variant haemoglobins have a reduced stability of the quaternary structure. This instability can be quantified in terms of the free energy difference between tetrameric ($\alpha_2\beta_2$) and dimeric ($\alpha\beta$) states as shown in Table 4.4.

Table 4.4 ΔG for dissociation of one mole of $\alpha_2\beta_2$ tetramer into two moles of $\alpha\beta$ dimers for normal and two variant haemoglobins.

Type of haemoglobin	Amino acid substitution in mutant globin chain	ΔG of dissociation / kJ mol^{-1} Hb
normal adult		34–46
Hb mutant (Kansas)	β subunit: Asn replaced by Thr in position 102	21
Hb mutant (Georgia)	α subunit: Pro replaced by Leu in position 95	15

⚪ Based upon the ΔG values for dissociation of the tetramers in Table 4.4, what can you say about the stability of the two variant haemoglobins?

⚫ Both mutants have a less positive free energy change for dissociation of the tetramer and are therefore *less* stable than the normal tetramer. The Georgia variant is less stable than the Kansas variant.

In Chapter 3, we discussed the structural changes that occur on oxygenation of haemoglobin. What follows is a brief revision of the mechanism of cooperative binding in haemoglobin. In the T state, haemoglobin has a lower affinity for O_2 than it does in the R state and the binding of O_2 to individual globin subunits causes a conformational change in the subunit which results in a switch of the tetramer as a whole from the T to the R state. This switch increases the affinity for O_2 of the unliganded subunits. Similarly, dissociation of O_2 from individual subunits causes a switch from the R state to the T state, which more readily discharges its remaining ligand. From a thermodynamic point of view, this switch between the T and R states can be explained by considering the free energy of the two states at different degrees of ligand binding (Figure 4.14). The relative stabilities of the T and R states vary depending on the number of O_2 binding sites (up to four) that are occupied. In the absence of O_2 ligand, the T state is more stable than the R state, having a lower free energy. When all four O_2 binding sites are occupied, the R state has a lower free energy than the T state and is thermodynamically favoured.

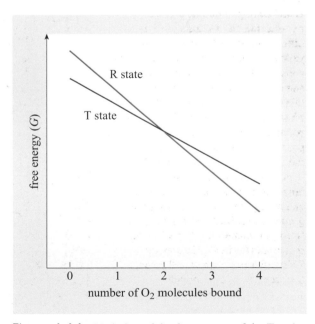

Figure 4.14   Variation of the free energy of the T and R states of haemoglobin with O_2 binding.

4.6.4 Protein–DNA interactions

Thermodynamic analysis of the binding of specific DNA sequences to proteins is of considerable interest for biologists because of the crucial role of transcription factors and other proteins as regulators of cellular activities. Recognition of a specific DNA sequence by proteins can involve non-polar interactions and direct or indirect hydrogen bonding with the DNA bases, sugars (deoxyribose units) and phosphate groups of the DNA backbone. These interactions will be discussed further in Chapter 5.

○ Can you name the various DNA binding domains present in proteins?

● These domains include leucine zipper, zinc finger and helix–turn–helix (Chapter 3, Section 3.2.3).

The different site-specific protein–DNA complexes vary greatly in their structural and thermodynamic properties. As in the case of protein–protein interactions, a better understanding of the energetic 'engineering' principles of protein–DNA binding might lead to more rational design of therapeutic drugs.

The free energy change associated with binding of the protein to its target DNA is given by $\Delta G° = \Delta H° - T\Delta S°$. The enthalpic and entropic contributions to the free energy of DNA binding for a number of different site-specific DNA binding proteins of diverse biological functions show that DNA binding proteins utilize different thermodynamic strategies, as illustrated in Figure 4.15. Notice that, despite the wide range in values for $\Delta H°$ and $-T\Delta S°$, the values for $\Delta G°$ lie within a very narrow range. For example, in the case of GCN4, a favourable enthalpic contribution (i.e. a large negative ΔH) drives an unfavourable entropic contribution ($-T\Delta S° > 0$), whereas with TATA binding protein (TBP) it is the other way around.

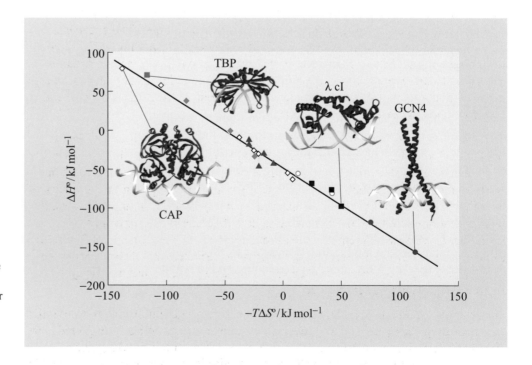

Figure 4.15
Diverse thermodynamic strategies for site-specific protein–DNA interactions. The enthalpic ($\Delta H°$) and entropic ($-T\Delta S°$) contributions to the free energy of binding at 298 K. Data points corresponding to the values for four of the protein–DNA interactions are indicated with structural representations.

The narrow range of ΔG for the binding of these proteins to their target DNA can be explained if we consider their function. Thus if the protein is to perform a site-specific biological function, it must bind tightly to its DNA recognition site. Critically, however, the binding affinity must allow for reversibility. What is striking in the set of data presented in Figure 4.15 is how functional requirements correlate with the use of thermodynamic strategy: the variations of ΔH and ΔS will almost cancel each other out, and give correspondingly small variations in values of ΔG between different DNA binding proteins. Ironically, the entropy / enthalpy compensation is rather frustrating for drug designers since it leaves them with ΔG as the only parameter that really matters for the function of the system.

4.6.5 A thermodynamic approach to drug design

The association of a ligand with its target molecule typically involves changes in the intramolecular and intermolecular interactions. The changes in bonding interactions that occur upon ligand binding are reflected in the binding enthalpy and entropy, which in turn determine the free energy of ligand association.

Improvements in instrumentation and experimental methodology such as ITC (described in Box 4.2) permit the direct measurement of the enthalpic and entropic contributions to ligand binding affinity. Such measurements provide information about tightening or loosening of interactions, including folding or unfolding of the structure and effects resulting from the binding or release of solvent molecules to or from the interacting molecules. Thus, determination of enthalpy and entropy parameters by ITC can provide a clearer understanding of the important attributes of binding, which is of utmost importance for drug designers interested in the interaction of potential drugs with target molecules (proteins or nucleic acids). Such studies can be used to predict which potential drug could be used to mimic or inhibit a physiological ligand.

The optimization of compounds as viable drug candidates usually involves optimization of their binding affinity towards the selected target. The binding affinity is determined by the change in Gibbs free energy of binding, ΔG, which is in turn determined by the changes in enthalpy, ΔH, and entropy, ΔS, on binding, according to the relationship $\Delta G = \Delta H - T\Delta S$. This equation clearly shows that many combinations of ΔH and ΔS values can give rise to the same ΔG value and therefore elicit the same binding affinity.

However, importantly for drug designers, there is a significant difference in the 'behaviour' of drugs that bind to the same target molecule with a similar value for ΔG but different values for ΔS or ΔH. Many drug molecules are hydrophobic and conformationally constrained, so cannot easily adapt to changes in the geometry of the binding site. Such ligands are described as *entropically dominated*. To design ligands that *are* able to adapt to a changing target geometry (described as *enthalpically dominated*) requires the introduction of certain elements of flexibility, or the relaxation of the conformational constraints. Since enthalpically dominated ligands have larger conformational entropy, to optimize their binding affinity a smaller binding enthalpy is required.

For example, in recent years DNA has become increasingly important as a potential target for drug therapies. Indeed, several anti-cancer and antibiotic compounds are aimed at interfering with the template function of DNA, either blocking gene transcription or inhibiting DNA replication. The aim is to develop sequence-specific drugs with high DNA binding affinity. Such drugs should have enough conformational entropy (i.e. be sufficiently enthalpically dominated) to allow them to fit into the three-dimensional structure of the DNA in a flexible fashion whilst having a binding enthalpy small enough to ensure sequence-specific binding.

Despite its evident potential, the thermodynamic approach to drug development is still at an early stage in terms of general acceptance and widespread use by the pharmaceutical industry. The main reason for this is that, for many important molecules involved in development of different diseases, there is still not enough data on the structural details of binding sites (i.e. atomic resolution). Accumulation of detailed knowledge of this kind will allow for the design of drugs with high binding affinity. Furthermore, though in principle thermodynamic measurements of drug–target interactions, such as described here, can be used to screen new drugs, in practice this application is limited by the development of the technology necessary to correlate thermodynamic data with structural details.

Summary of Section 4.6

1   Thermodynamics can be applied to many biological systems, and can tell us much about the interactions between biological molecules as well as the feasibility of biochemical pathways.

2   Enzymes control the pathway and kinetic flux of biochemical reactions, by affecting the activation energy of different reactions, but they do not affect whether a reaction is thermodynamically favourable.

3   Measurement of thermodynamic parameters can provide useful information on the binding of potential drugs to target molecules.

Learning outcomes for Chapter 4

When you have studied this chapter, you should be able to:

4.1 Define and use each of the terms printed in **bold** in the text.

4.2 Outline the laws of thermodynamics and why they are relevant to biology.

4.3 Describe how the laws of thermodynamics place limitations on the biochemical transformations that may occur and relate these limitations to the requirements for the coupling of reactions.

4.4 Apply thermodynamic considerations to the processes of ATP generation in mitochondria, including the electron transport chain, the production of the proton motive force and the generation of ATP, and how these processes are coupled to each other.

4.5 Identify thermodynamic functions, their meaning and the SI units in which they are expressed.

4.6 Explain how changes in the concentrations of reactants or products will affect ΔG for a reaction.

4.7 Give examples of the ways in which thermodynamics can help us to understand interactions between biological molecules.

Questions for Chapter 4

Question 4.1

When one mole of glucose is completely oxidized at 25 °C, to CO_2 and H_2O, 2870 kJ of free energy is released. What is ΔG for this reaction?

Question 4.2

Explain, using thermodynamic arguments, why the production of one molecule of ATP requires the passage of at least three protons across the F_0-F_1 ATP synthase on the inner mitochondrial membrane.

Question 4.3

Using Equation 4.6 (reproduced below), calculate the value of ΔG for ATP breakdown in a human erythrocyte at 298 K.

$$\Delta G = \Delta G^{\circ\prime} + RT \ln \frac{[ADP][P_i]}{[ATP]} \qquad (4.6)$$

The concentrations of reactants and products within a human erythrocyte are as follows: ATP, 2.25 mmol l^{-1}; ADP, 0.25 mmol l^{-1}; P_i 1.65 mmol l^{-1} and $\Delta G^{\circ\prime}$ for ATP hydrolysis is −30.5 kJ mol^{-1}. (The universal gas constant, $R = 8.314 \times 10^{-3}$ kJ mol^{-1} K^{-1}.)

Question 4.4

If there is a fall in demand for ATP within a muscle cell, what effect will this have on the proton motive force and the value of ΔG for mitochondrial ATP synthesis?

Question 4.5

Suppose that a mutation in a protein X reduces this protein's affinity for protein Y. How will the mutation affect ΔG for the binding of Y to X?

References

Devlin, T. M. (2002) *Textbook of Biochemistry with Clinical Correlates* (5th edn), Wiley-Liss.

Harris, D. A. (1995) *Bioenergetics at a Glance*, Blackwell Science Ltd.

Haynie, D. T. (2001) *Biological Thermodynamics*, Cambridge University Press.

Further sources

Haynie, D. T. (2001) *Biological Thermodynamics*, Cambridge University Press.

Schrödinger, E. (1945, reprinted 1992) *What is Life?*, Cambridge University Press.

5 NUCLEIC ACIDS AND CHROMATIN

5.1 Introduction: the biological role of nucleic acids

Some of the earliest observations of macromolecules within living cells were of nucleic acids in the form of chromosomes. These long dark-staining objects, which became visible in the nucleus of cells at specific stages of cell division, were large enough to be detected using primitive light microscopes. Giant **polytene** chromosomes, found in certain cells such as the salivary gland cells of *Drosophila* (see Figure 5.1a), contain many thousands of copies of each chromosomal DNA aligned in register alongside each other and hence were readily observed by early microscopists. From such early observations came the term 'nucleic acid', referring to the nuclear location of these structures. When the thread-like nucleic acids were isolated from cells and analysed biochemically, they were found to be composed of three relatively simple components: sugar, phosphate and base. For many years, this chemical composition, which is relatively simple compared to that of proteins, led to nucleic acids being overlooked as candidate genetic macromolecules. Of course, we now know much more about the structure, function and variety of nucleic acids, even down to the order of every base along the DNA and RNA chains of complex genomes such as are found in mammals and plants; and the central importance of nucleic acids in all living organisms cannot be overestimated.

In autumn 2003, completed genome sequences were available for 18 Archaebacteria, 140 Eubacteria, 1364 viruses and 20 eukaryotes, including four plants.

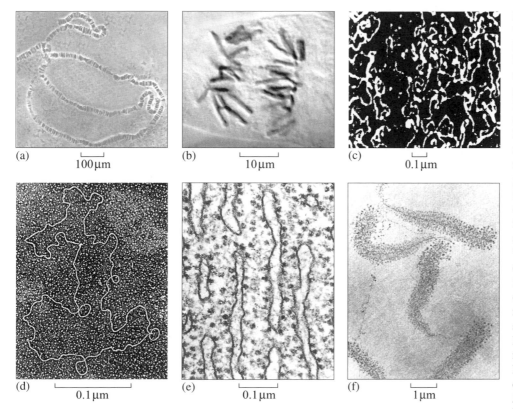

(a) 100 µm

(b) 10 µm

(c) 0.1 µm

(d) 0.1 µm

(e) 0.1 µm

(f) 1 µm

Figure 5.1
Views of nucleic acids in the cell. Early observations were made using light microscopes, e.g. of polytene chromosomes in *Drosophila* salivary gland cells (a), and of chromosomes in plant cells (b). More recent developments allow us to visualize DNA directly, using the atomic force microscope (AFM) (c), or the electron microscope (EM) (d). The AFM produces a molecular view of a surface indirectly, by measuring deflections caused by atomic-level weak attractive forces between a carbon-tipped probe as it passes across the sample surface. Whilst AFM does not require any chemical modification of the DNA, in EM the macromolecular structure of nucleic acids is labelled with heavy metals to reveal a high level of structural detail. Major cellular RNA-containing components, such as ribosomes, can also be seen using the EM (e). Under normal microscopy conditions, mRNA can be seen on *Drosophila* chromosomes at sites of high gene transcription (f).

5.1.1 Nucleic acids: genetic, functional and structural roles in the cell

The first role that one immediately thinks about for nucleic acids is that of an inherited genetic material, principally in the form of DNA. In some cases, the inherited genetic material is RNA instead of DNA. For example, almost 60% of all characterized viruses have RNA genomes and these are more common in plant viruses than in animal viruses. There is considerable variation in the amount of genetic material present within organisms (Table 5.1). RNA genomes tend to be smaller than DNA genomes, ranging between 10 and 30 kilobases (kb) in size (but rarely larger), compared to over several hundreds of kilobases for DNA viruses. The most likely reason for this limitation in the size of RNA genomes is that RNA replication is considerably more prone to errors than is DNA replication (over one million times more so) and therefore the hazard of lethal mutations occurring in RNA is much higher.

○ What advantage might a high error rate in replication of its genome confer on a virus?

● Within any population of a virus, the high rate of replication error will create considerable genetic variation due to the misincorporation of individual bases. Variation arising from such mutations will contribute to the overall evolution of the virus within a host.

You will encounter several cases where we discuss absolute masses of macromolecules within the cell, such as in 'pg'. The relationship between the units you will encounter in the course and 1 gram (1 g) is as follows:
1 μg (microgram) = 10^{-6} g;
1 ng (nanogram) = 10^{-9} g;
1 pg (picogram) = 10^{-12} g.

If we examine the contents of the cell, we will see that the nucleic acids that comprise an organism's inherited genome (usually DNA) are commonly the minority nucleic acid within a cell. For example, nucleic acids represent approximately 12% by mass of a typical bacterial cell, compared to 16% for protein; but only 15% of this nucleic acid component (i.e. less than 2% of the cell mass) is chromosomal DNA; the rest is RNA of various types. Similarly, if you consider a typical human cell, the genome of 6.2×10^9 base pairs (bp) in each diploid cell equates to around 6 pg of DNA, whereas the same cell contains 20–30 pg of RNA, depending upon the level of its transcriptional activity. The bulk of this RNA (80%) comprises ribosomal RNAs (rRNAs), which make up the translation machinery, approximately 15% are small functional RNAs, such as transfer RNAs (tRNAs), and the remaining 5% is messenger RNA (mRNA).

Other sources of nucleic acids within the cell are mitochondria and, in plant cells, chloroplasts. These organelles contain their own DNA genomes and RNA transcribed from them. The contribution of mitochondria or chloroplasts to the total nucleic acid content of any one cell depends upon their number, which can vary considerably depending upon the cell's metabolic activity. In mammalian cells, a mitochondrion can contain 10 000 copies of the 16 kb mitochondrial genome (mtDNA) and in some cells mitochondrial DNA can represent as much as 0.1% of the cellular DNA.

Many bacteria and some fungi, in addition to their genomic DNA, carry naturally occurring circular DNAs called **plasmids**, which are easily exchanged between individual cells within a population. Many antibiotic-resistance genes are carried on plasmids, a feature that is now exploited for genetic manipulation techniques where plasmid DNA is manipulated *in vitro* and re-introduced into cells.

Table 5.1   The genome content and size of various organisms.

Organism*	Genome size in number of base pairs (DNA) or nucleotides (RNA)**
Rhinovirus 1A	RNA: 7200 nt
Coronavirus	RNA: 29 751 nt
HIV	RNA: 9700 nt
SV40	5240
Adenovirus 2	35 900
Epstein–Barr virus (EBV)	1.7×10^5
Escherichia coli	4.7×10^6
Saccharomyces cerevisiae (a budding yeast)	1.25×10^7
Trypanosoma brucei (a protoctist)***	1.27×10^7
Schizosaccharomyces pombe (a fission yeast)	1.4×10^7
Dictyostelium discoideum (a slime mould)	5.4×10^7
Caenorhabditis elegans (a nematode worm)	9.7×10^7
Arabidopsis thaliana (wall cress)	1.0×10^8
Drosophila melanogaster (fruit-fly)	1.7×10^8
Fugu rubripes (puffer fish)	3.6×10^8
Danio rerio (zebra fish)	1.7×10^9
Mus musculus (house mouse)	2.7×10^9
Homo sapiens (human)	3.1×10^9
Rattus norvegicus (brown rat)	3.1×10^9
Xenopus laevis (African clawed toad)	3.1×10^9
Zea mays (maize)	3.9×10^9
Nicotiana tobacum (tobacco)	4.8×10^9

* Viruses are not considered to be free-living organisms. Those listed here are included for purposes of comparison.

** Genome sizes (other than those of viruses and *E. coli*) are the haploid genome size.

*** Estimate only: the nuclear genome also contains numerous mini-chromosomes with varying ploidy.

5.1.2 Nucleic acids and the flow of genetic information

The 'flow' of information from an organism's genome to the synthesis of its encoded proteins is referred to as the **central dogma** and emphasizes the crucial roles that nucleic acids play within the cell (Figure 5.2). The synthesis of proteins (translation) is directed by the base order in mRNA, copied directly from that in the DNA of the genes by transcription. Translation involves RNAs in the form of the ribosome and tRNAs. More detailed examinations of the specific functions performed by nucleic acids in these processes will be covered in later chapters in the course. In this chapter we will be focusing on the relationship between the molecular components of nucleic acids, the structures they form in the cell and how they interact with proteins. We will also examine the approaches used to analyse these structures and discuss how the unique properties of nucleic acids have been exploited as molecular tools.

In those organisms that have large genomes, there is a balance between the necessary compaction of large amounts of genetic material within the confines of the cell and enabling sufficient access to this material for the operation of the cell's maintenance and expression systems. Evolutionarily, this balance has been successfully achieved in the eukaryotes through the emergence of the **histones**.

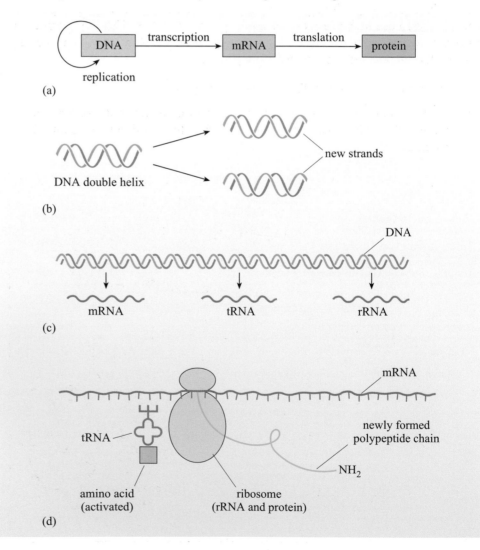

Figure 5.2
The roles of nucleic acids in the cell.
(a) The central dogma describes the flow of genetic information in the cell.
(b) Replication of DNA.
(c) Transcription of DNA to give mRNA, tRNAs and rRNAs.
(d) Translation of mRNA in protein synthesis involves rRNAs in the ribosome and tRNAs.

These proteins are complexed with DNA as **chromatin**, and it is in this form that eukaryotic DNA is packaged in the nucleus. We will complete this chapter by discussing histones and their roles in both genome packaging and expression.

5.2 The molecular structure of nucleic acids

We now know the detail of the order of individual bases, i.e. the genome sequence, of many of the organisms listed in Table 5.1. You saw in Chapter 3 how information from this genome sequence has allowed the identification of conserved protein domains, many examples of which will be discussed throughout this course. Here we will focus on the structures of nucleic acids within the cell, and we will start this discussion by outlining some of the general principles that apply to all nucleic acid structures.

5.2.1 The primary structure of nucleic acids

Nucleic acids found in the cell have primary structures that arise from the directional polymerization of single nucleotide units, described in Chapter 2 (Section 2.3.5). The links between each nucleotide are formed by esterification reactions between the sugar's C5′ hydroxyl group and the α-phosphate of an incoming nucleoside triphosphate (NTP) to form a phosphoester linkage, which is shown in Figure 5.3. The sugar is ribose in the case of RNA, deoxyribose in DNA. This polymerization process leaves a free hydroxyl on the incoming nucleotide (on the 3′ C of the sugar) to serve for the next reaction in chain elongation.

◯ What provides the energy for this reaction to proceed?

⬤ Each NTP molecule carries two phosphoanhydride bonds in its triphosphate unit, one of which provides the energy to drive this reaction (see Chapter 2, Section 2.3.5).

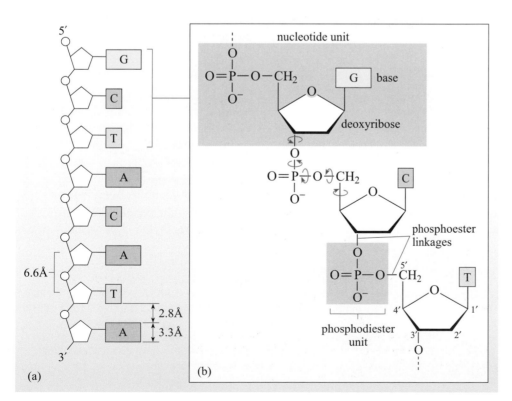

(a)　(b)

Figure 5.3
A schematic representation of a nucleic acid backbone. (a) A side view showing the spacing between the bases. (b) Backbone structure (DNA in this case), highlighting the nucleotide units and the phosphoester linkages. Bases are represented by their initial letter, as described in Chapter 2. Note that rotation is possible around five bonds in the sugar–phosphate backbone.

The resultant phosphodiester–sugar backbone consists of what are commonly called 5′–3′ (pronounced 'five-prime to three-prime') linkages, where the prime refers to the carbon atoms of the sugar unit, as shown in Figure 5.3b. Thus the 5′ C of one sugar is linked, via a phosphate group (called a phosphodiester group in this context) , to the 3′ C of the next sugar. The bases are joined to the sugar via their N1 position in the case of the pyrimidines (thymine, cytosine or uracil) or their N9 position in the case of the purines (adenine and guanine) Figure 5.4a.

The molecular natures of the nucleic components, the sugar, the phosphate and the base, exert a major influence over both the structures and functions of the macromolecular nucleic acids that comprise them.

☐ From your studies in Chapter 2, what properties of the three nucleotide components (phosphate, sugar, base), can you predict from their molecular structures?

◼ The phosphates and sugars carry polarized bonds, so are hydrophilic in nature. In contrast, the bases, which are primarily rich in carbon–carbon and carbon–hydrogen linkages, have fewer polarized bonds and are more hydrophobic.

☐ From this knowledge of nucleotide chemistry, what would you predict about the higher-order structure of a polynucleotide chain in the physiological conditions found within a cell? (Hint: think of how proteins behave.)

◼ Such structures would most likely carry the bases buried within the inside, allowing hydrophobic interactions between them, and with the hydrophilic sugar–phosphate backbone on the outside.

Nucleic acids adopt a level of structure analogous to that of protein secondary structure, and just as the chemical properties of the constituent amino acid residues affect the conformation of a protein, so the chemical properties of nucleotides affect nucleic acid secondary structure. We will discuss how the secondary structure of nucleic acids depends on the chemistry of the constituent nucleotides, later in this chapter.

Once incorporated into nucleic acids, the five common bases can also be modified by specific enzymes. Some examples of modified bases are shown in Figure 5.4b and c. These modifications provide additional structural components of nucleic acids and, to a certain extent, provide variety comparable with that found in proteins and polysaccharides. Modified nucleotides serve as recognition features on nucleic acid chains – particularly DNA – for the binding of other macromolecules. The only modification commonly found within DNA is that of methylation, and methylated bases are observed in many organisms. For example, many bacteria contain methylated adenine, which serves to distinguish the genomic DNA from viral non-methylated DNA. We will see how bacterial methylation plays a key role in

Figure 5.4   The structures of the individual components of nucleic acids.
(a) The five common bases and the sugar components in nucleic acids: deoxyribose in DNA and ribose in RNA. Bases are joined to the sugar via N1 (pyrimidine) and N9 (purine). In some cases, bases in nucleic acids are covalently modified post-transcriptionally. The addition of a methyl group (highlighted here in purple) is a common modification. Some of the modified nucleosides found in (b) RNA and (c) DNA are shown here: 5-methylcytidine is often found in eukaryote DNA, while N^6-methyladenosine is present in many bacterial DNAs.

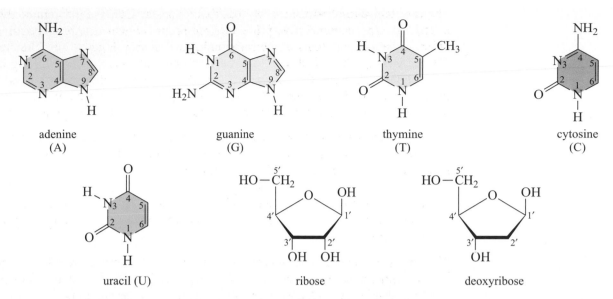

adenine
(A)

guanine
(G)

thymine
(T)

cytosine
(C)

uracil (U)

ribose

deoxyribose

(a) Base and sugar components of DNA and RNA

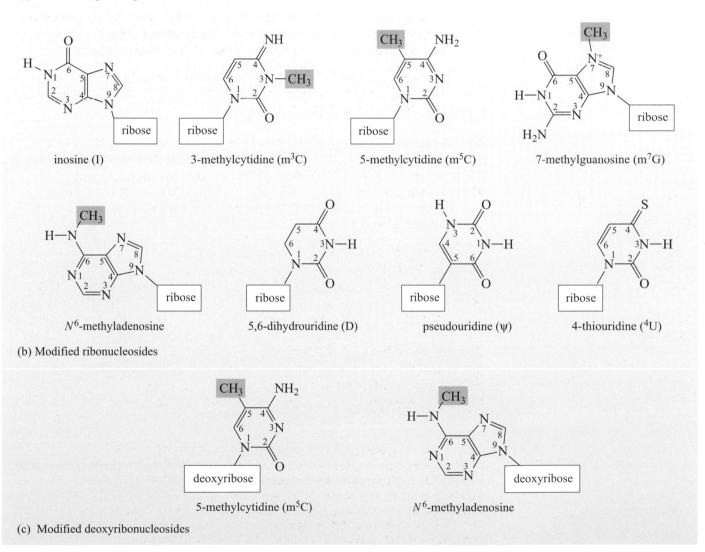

inosine (I)

3-methylcytidine (m³C)

5-methylcytidine (m⁵C)

7-methylguanosine (m⁷G)

N^6-methyladenosine

5,6-dihydrouridine (D)

pseudouridine (ψ)

4-thiouridine (⁴U)

(b) Modified ribonucleosides

5-methylcytidine (m⁵C)

N^6-methyladenosine

(c) Modified deoxyribonucleosides

replication and repair in Chapter 9. In many eukaryotes, the methylation of cytosine is associated with alterations in transcriptional competence, a subject we will discuss further in Chapter 10. Post-transcriptional modification of RNA nucleotides is particularly common. We will examine the extensive use of modified RNA nucleotides within tRNAs in Section 5.4 and discuss the mechanism by which these modificarions occur, in Chapter 10.

5.2.2 General features of higher-order nucleic acid structure

Polynucleotide chains are intrinsically flexible molecules and have the potential to form many different higher-order structures. Their flexibility derives from rotation around bonds in the sugar–phosphate backbone (Figure 5.3b). *In vivo*, the structures that form are obviously determined by both the proteins that synthesize the nucleic acid chains (polymerases) and the ancillary proteins that bind to and modify them. We will discuss these aspects of structure later in this chapter. What drives the formation of these structures are the properties of the component nucleotides and the interactions between them in the form of **base pairing** and **base stacking**.

Base pairing

Nucleic acid folding patterns are dominated by base pairing, which results from the formation of hydrogen bonds between pairs of nucleotides. In nucleic acids, as in proteins, the highly directional nature of this hydrogen bonding is the key to secondary structure.

◯   What is the basis for this directionality?

⬤   Hydrogen bonds are highly directional because the interacting atoms (e.g. O—H--N) must lie in an approximately straight line for strong bonding (see Chapter 2, Section 2.7.3).

The hydrogen bonding between complementary base pairs in a duplex (double-stranded) molecule is shown in Figure 5.5a. Note that the cytosine–guanine (C–G) coupling incorporates three hydrogen bonds and is therefore stronger than the adenine–thymine (A–T) coupling, with only two hydrogen bonds. Similarly, in RNA, the A–U base pair has two hydrogen bonds. As a general rule, nucleic acid chains tend to fold so as to maximize base pairing. This folding produces two common secondary structures found *in vivo*, the double helix (or duplex) in DNA, and the hairpin in RNA. The base pairing just described lends itself to long stretches of regular, hydrogen-bond-stabilized nucleic acid folding patterns, comparable to the secondary structures of proteins. It was by appreciating the significance of these G–C and A–T base pairs that Watson and Crick were able to come up with their model of the DNA double helix, in their famous *Nature* paper of 1953, from which the term **Watson–Crick pairing** arose.

You will be studying the history of the discovery of the structure of DNA and examining the original research publications from Watson and Crick in an activity at the end of this section.

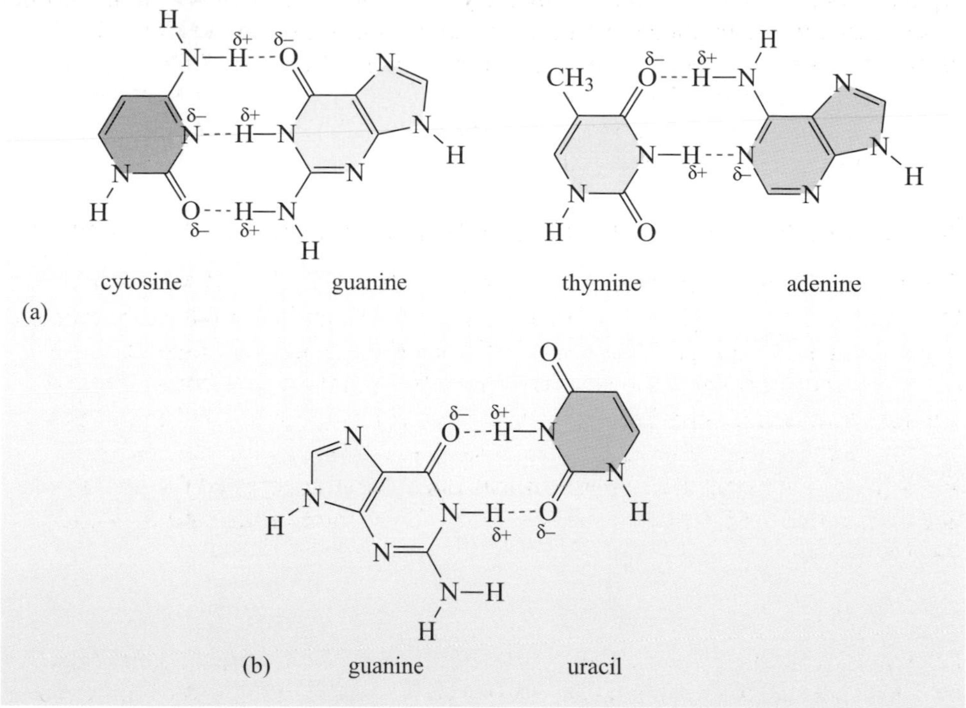

Figure 5.5
Hydrogen bonding between nucleotides. (a) The normal base-pairing between A and T and between G and C is shown, with the polar nature of the participating groups indicated. (b) Pairing between G and U, which is found in codon–anticodon third base interactions in the ribosome.

X-ray diffraction of nucleic acids has revealed several examples of base pairing that do not conform to the G–C / A–T pairing described by Watson and Crick. One example, to be described in a later section, is the G–G pair found in telomeric DNA. This non-Watson–Crick base pairing produces a characteristic three-dimensional shape that stabilizes specialized nucleic acid structures and is recognized by nucleic acid binding proteins. Poorly matched base pairs (for example, A–C and G–T), in which the hydrogen-bonded atoms are imperfectly aligned, also insert extra flexibility at specific sites in RNA chains. Another example of a common 'mispair' is G–U, shown in Figure 5.5b. G–U pairing is found in the codon–anticodon interaction in the ribosome, a subject we will discuss in more detail in Chapter 11.

Base stacking

Although the base pairing brought about by hydrogen bonding is responsible for the *specificity* of the base interactions, much of the stability of a duplex nucleic acid is due to interactions that result from base stacking. If you look back at Figure 5.3a, you will notice that, when seen from a side view, our schematic representation of a polynucleotide has a 'gap' between each base. Remember that the surfaces of the bases have few polarized bonds; consequently, base surfaces are hydrophobic. As a result, the most energetically favoured conformation is attained by reducing exposure of the base surfaces to the aqueous environment, which is achieved by the bases moving closer together. In this conformation, the backbone is 'tilted' by an angle of 30° from horizontal, as shown in Figure 5.6a–c. Tilting the backbone in this way brings the planar rings of adjacent base pairs to a position where they lie vertically one above the other, an arrangement that maximizes hydrophobic interactions and in addition, maximizes van der Waals attractive forces between them. To give you an idea of how strong these interactions are along a stretch of DNA, the free energy values for base stacking for various adjacent bases are shown in Table 5.2. We will see later how base stacking plays a central role in the structure of the DNA double helix.

Figure 5.6
Base stacking reduces exposure of the hydrophobic bases to the aqueous environment. (a) Simple 'strands' diagram of the DNA duplex with the base pairing shown. (b) Pictogram in which each base pair is shown as a single block spanning the duplex and the sugar–phosphate backbones are represented by solid lines. (c) Pictogram showing how stacking results in the bases interacting and twisting, such that the backbone angle is 30°. This twisting produces the helical structure. (d) The intercalation of ethidium bromide, a hydrophobic molecule, between the bases in a nucleic acid duplex (right) results in a chain that is lengthened. (The intercalated ethidium bromide molecules are represented here as orange bars.)

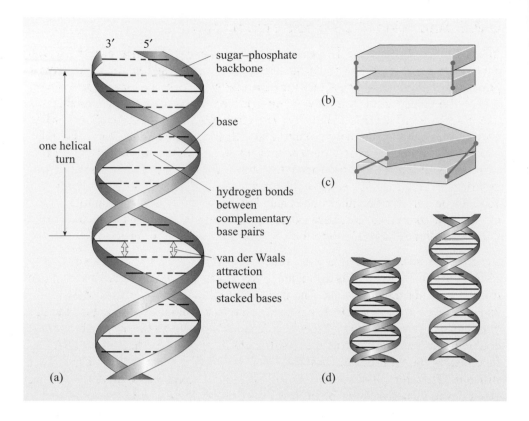

Table 5.2 Base stacking energies for various adjacent base pairs.

Dinucleotide pair (5′–3′) – (3′–5′)	Stacking energy per stacked pair / kJ mol^{-1}
(GC)–(GC)	−61.0
(AC)–(GT)	−44.0
(TC)–(GA)	−41.0
(CG)–(CG)	−41.3
(GG)–(CC)	−34.6
(AT)–(AT)	−27.5
(TG)–(CA)	−27.5
(AG)–(CT)	−27.1
(AA)–(TT)	−22.5
(TA)–(TA)	−16.0

ethidium bromide

The hydrophobicity of the bases in duplex DNA is exploited to allow its easy visualization with a chemical called ethidium bromide. Ethidium bromide (see margin) is a hydrophobic molecule that, in an aqueous environment, **intercalates** between stacked bases of DNA as shown in Figure 5.6d. This has the effect of partially unstacking the bases and lengthening the helix. To the advantage of molecular biologists, this intercalation alters the fluorescent properties of ethidium bromide, allowing us to visualize its interaction with DNA using UV light at 260 nm.

5.2.3 Analysing nucleic acid structures

In studying nucleic acid structures, many different experimental approaches can be adopted. In many cases, nucleic acid structures are examined *in vitro*, under non-physiological conditions, such as after denaturation or chemical synthesis. Nucleic acids within a cell are formed under very specific conditions and the structures that they adopt are influenced not only by the nature of their synthesis (by DNA or RNA polymerases), but by ancillary proteins that influence their folding. Nevertheless, there are a number of techniques that are routinely used to analyse nucleic acids *in vitro*, many of which you will encounter later in the course. These techniques are described in Box 5.1. For example, electrophoresis not only gives us information about the length of a polynucleotide chain but it also provides some limited information about its shape, because the speed with which a polynucleotide moves through a gel matrix is related to the degree of compaction of the molecule.

Despite the success of resolving the structure of DNA by X-ray diffraction in the 1950s, the application of this technique to RNA was initially limited. There are two main reasons for this limitation. The first is that cells contain mixtures of RNA molecules and RNA is relatively unstable. Therefore, unlike for DNA, it is virtually impossible to purify individual species of RNA. Secondly, unlike DNA, for which a double-helical secondary structure is sufficient for most of its functions, RNA function, as you will see later in the course, is critically dependent upon its tertiary structure. Therefore, like proteins, each RNA species must be isolated in sufficient quantities in its native form for successful crystallization and analysis. Only relatively recently have X-ray diffraction studies made inroads into revealing the structures of RNA molecules, as we will see later in this chapter and in Chapter 11, where we discuss the structure of ribosomal RNAs in relation to translation.

Box 5.1   Analysis of nucleic acids by electrophoresis and hybridization

Nucleic acids can be separated according to size by gel electrophoresis, most commonly performed using a horizontal gel (Figure 5.7a). This is in contrast to the vertical gel electrophoresis set-up, which you encountered in *Experimental investigation 1* (in Chapter 3) and which is generally used for analysis of proteins.

The size of DNA molecules is usually expressed in terms of the number of base pairs. The phosphate backbone, containing one phosphate per nucleotide, gives the molecules a uniform negative charge per base pair. The secondary structure of DNA is such that these negatively charged phosphates lie on the outside of the molecule, meaning that, unlike proteins, no denaturation or pretreatment with SDS is required. Thus the degree of migration in the gel is directly related to the length of the DNA chain.

DNA electrophoresis is usually performed using an agarose (polymerized galactose) gel matrix for molecules larger than 500 bp, and the size of the molecule is determined by comparison with a calibration set of DNA fragments, as shown in Figure 5.7b. DNA fragments smaller than 500 bp are usually studied using a polyacrylamide gel matrix, which has a smaller pore size and so allows greater length discrimination of small DNA molecules. After electrophoresis, DNA is detected by 'staining' with ethidium bromide, the dye that intercalates between stacked bases (Figure 5.6d) and in doing so becomes fluorescent when exposed to UV irradiation.

RNA can also be examined by electrophoresis, but due to the physical characteristics of RNA molecules there are two important differences compared with DNA electrophoresis. The first is that RNA must be pretreated to disrupt any internal base pairing; that is, its secondary structure is effectively destroyed. This pretreatment is necessary because the extensive base pairing in RNA molecules means that they have very diverse conformations, which can affect the relative mobility of the molecules. RNA samples are therefore

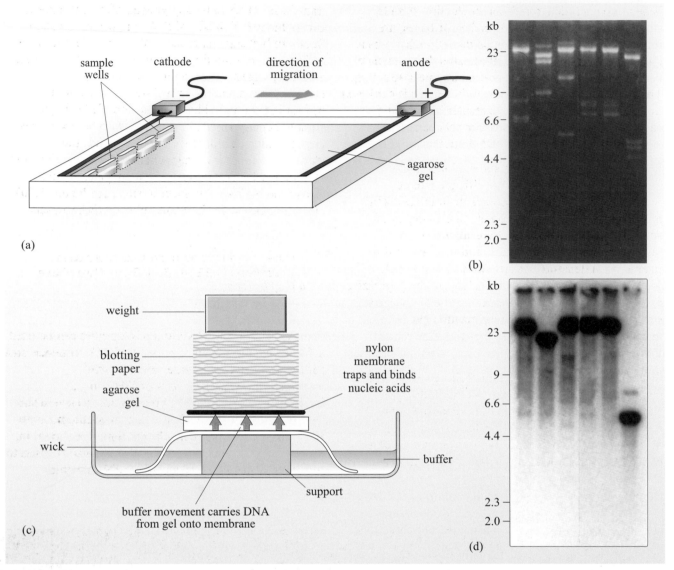

Figure 5.7 (a) Electrophoresis of nucleic acids. (b) An agarose gel loaded with six digested DNAs and stained with ethidium bromide. The scale on the left corresponds to DNA size markers. (c) Transfer of nucleic acids to a nylon membrane by capillary action. (d) Southern blot of the agarose gel in (b) hybridized with a radio-labelled DNA probe. (The positions of the size markers are indicated.)

pretreated by heating or by the addition of agents such as formamide, which disrupts the hydrogen bonds and denatures the RNA. The second important difference between electrophoresis of DNA and that of RNA is that the latter must be performed under conditions that buffer against alkalinity, since RNA is vulnerable to hydrolysis in alkaline conditions.

Measuring the mobility of nucleic acids through gels allows their size to be estimated, but a second technique, called hybridization, further extends the utility of electrophoresis. Nucleic acids in solution or attached to solid-phase matrices can be dissociated into single strands by denaturing at 100 °C. In the case of DNA, denaturation can also be achieved by treatment with alkali.

○ Why does heat or alkali treatment lead to the denaturation of duplex DNA?

■ Heat provides energy to the system so that base pairing, favoured at lower temperatures, is disrupted. Alkali leads to the deprotonation of individual atoms in bases leading to loss of polarity and, as a consequence, loss of hydrogen bonding.

When two such denatured polynucleotide strands, containing complementary stretches of bases, are mixed together under conditions that allow base–base hydrogen bonding to occur, these stretches associate with each other in a process called **strand annealing**. This property of two polynucleotide strands is exploited in many techniques used in molecular biology and is called **hybridization**. It can occur between DNA–DNA, RNA–RNA and RNA–DNA strands.

Hybridization has become a standard laboratory analytical tool for detecting specific nucleotide sequences in intact chromosomes or in nucleic acid mixtures fixed to a solid support. Short lengths of single-stranded DNA or RNA are labelled with radioactive or fluorescent tags, and then allowed to interact with denatured target strands. The labelled nucleic acid, also known as a *probe*, will then hybridize to any section of the target that has complementary stretches of bases and this hybridization can be visualized after detection of the radioactive or fluorescent tag.

One application of hybridization techniques is in the analysis of nucleic acids after electrophoresis, as shown in Figure 5.7c and d. After electrophoresis, nucleic acid molecules are transferred onto solid membranes, usually by capillary action in a process called blotting. Blotting of nucleic acids is analogous to the transfer of proteins from a polyacrylamide gel (*Experimental investigation 1*), though in the latter, transfer is achieved by applying an electrical current across the gel. Transfer of DNA molecules is called Southern blotting and transfer of RNA molecules is called Northern blotting. A complex mixture of nucleic acids, separated according to their length by electrophoresis, can be transferred to a membrane by blotting and individual chains identified using a complementary labelled nucleic acid probe. Examples of applications of these techniques include the identification of DNA fragments generated by digestion of genomic DNA with restriction enzymes (which cleave the backbone at specific sites; see Figure 5.7d) or of mRNA species in whole cellular RNA extracts.

Southern and Northern blotting techniques are described in S204, Book 3 *The Core of Life*, Vol. II, Box 9.1.

In a similar manner, DNA and RNA probes can be used to indicate the position of a specific DNA sequence on a chromosome in a technique called **in situ hybridization (ISH)**. Results of ISH using a fluorescently labelled DNA probe (fluorescence in situ hybridization, FISH) against a human X chromosome and a *Drosophila* polytene chromosome are shown in, respectively, Figure 5.8a and b. ISH can also be used to detect the distribution of specific mRNAs within tissues.

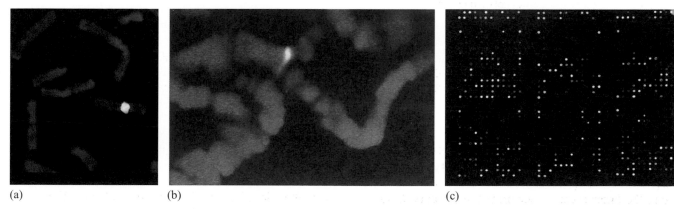

(a)   (b)   (c)

Figure 5.8 Application of hybridization techniques. (a) Fluorescence in situ hybridization (FISH) using a probe to identify the X chromosome centromere (yellow signal) on human metaphase chromosomes (stained red with propidium iodide). (b) FISH of *Drosophila* polytene chromosomes using a specific probe to identify a single gene. (c) A section of a microarray containing individual spots of *Drosophila* coding DNA. The slide was hybridized first with RNA taken from one-week-old *Drosophila* that had been treated with a specific drug, and then with control RNA from untreated *Drosophila*. The resulting signals were analysed and differences between the two samples presented in this image. The slide contains 1400 genes, most of which are unaffected by the drug. Green spots correspond to genes that have increased levels of expression and yellow spots represent decreased expression.

Hybridization of complementary nucleic acid strands has also been exploited in the recent development of gene chips or microarrays. In these investigations, single-stranded DNA molecules are attached to a solid support (a membrane or a glass slide) and labelled DNA or RNA is used to probe the array, as shown in Figure 5.8c. Image analysis software can be used to quantify how much hybridization occurs. By using many thousands of target DNAs, such as copies of genes or markers along a chromosome, this approach can be used to analyse hybridization to many targets simultaneously. One major application of this technique is to use a gene chip that carries target DNAs for every gene within an organism. After hybridization with fluorescently labelled whole-cell mRNA, the expression of each individual gene can be quantified. This technique can be exploited to detect differences between different cell or tissue types, different developmental stages or to compare physiological and disease states.

Summary of Section 5.2

1   Nucleic acids are intrinsically highly flexible molecules.

2   The chemical properties of nucleic acid components are primary determinants in structure formation.

3   The formation of nucleic acid structures is driven by base pairing and stacking interactions between the hydrophobic bases. In DNA, these interactions drive the formation of the double helix, whose structure is maintained under torsional stress by twisting. RNA secondary structure is driven by maximal base-pairing rules.

4   The five common bases found in nucleic acids can be modified after synthesis.

5   Base pairing is exploited in the laboratory in many techniques that utilize strand annealing (hybridization) between a labelled nucleic acid and a target polynucleotide.

5.3 Structural aspects of DNA

Having outlined the general principles of nucleic acid structures, we will now focus on how these principles influence the formation of specific structures found in DNA.

5.3.1 The helical structure of DNA

The helical structure of DNA arises because of the specific interactions between bases and the non-specific hydrophobic effects described earlier. Its structure is also determined through its active synthesis; that is, duplex DNA is synthesized by specialist polymerases upon a template strand. Within the helix, the two complementary DNA chains form what is called an **antiparallel helix**, where strands have opposite 5′ to 3′ polarity.

We outlined earlier the general principle of base pairing. Now we will go into more detail about why these base pairs arise within a duplex DNA. The specificity of Watson–Crick base pairing results from both the hydrogen-bonding factors we described earlier and steric restrictions imposed by the two deoxyribose–phosphate backbones. If we consider the steric restrictions first, we can start by asking how much 'room' there is between the two backbones and which bases will fit within this space to make suitable pairs.

First, the 'gap' across the helix between each of the deoxyribose–base glycosidic bonds is approximately 10.8 Å and a purine–pyrimidine base pair fits perfectly within this space, whereas two pyrimidine bases would be too far away from each other to allow hydrogen bonding. Thus spatial considerations limit each base pair to being between a purine and a pyrimidine. Note that mispairings, such as that between two purines, do occur during replication, but such mispairings distort the helix and are readily detected and corrected. Apart from the spatial considerations, specific requirements apply for the formation of hydrogen bonds between the bases in helical DNA, and the final positions of the hydrogen atoms within each base pair will be influenced by the positions of the bases after stacking interactions have occurred. Consequently, each base pair has a well defined position.

○ Look back at Figure 5.5a and try to visualize pairing between A and C bases. Describe the result.

● There is no potential for hydrogen bonding between these bases.

Similarly, there is only potential for formation of a single hydrogen bond between G and T bases.

To satisfy steric restrictions of base pairing and to maximize the hydrophobic interactions between successive base pairs, the two polynucleotide chains in DNA are coiled around a common axis. In the structure of DNA proposed by Crick and Watson in 1953, known as **B-DNA**, adjacent bases are separated by 3.4 Å along the helix axis and the helix rotates 36° between each base.

○ How many base pairs are present within one helical turn of B-DNA?

● Since the helix turns by 36° for each base, it will take 10 base pairs to rotate through one helical turn (360°).

The structure of the B-DNA helix is shown in Figure 5.9a. In this figure, the bases extend horizontally across the helical plane, and as described earlier, base stacking results in the backbone spiralling around at an angle of approximately 30°. If you take a closer look at the sugar–phosphate backbone in B-DNA, you can see that it spirals around the core. In the case of B-DNA, the helix is described as being 'right-handed', because if you look at the helix end-on, the 5′–3′ strand corkscrews away from you in a right-handed or clockwise spiral.

As can also be seen from Figure 5.9a, B-DNA has two obvious 'grooves' in its structure; the larger is known as the **major groove**, the narrower as the **minor groove**. These grooves result from the geometry of the sugar–base structure and base-pair interaction, as shown in Figure 5.9b. Within the major groove, a large portion of the base is exposed and it will perhaps not surprise you to learn that this is where most protein–DNA interactions occur that depend upon the specific recognition of individual bases within the DNA. Such interactions depend upon the formation of hydrogen bonds between amino acid side-chains in the protein and atoms in the bases that are not involved in base pairing; these atoms are identified in Figure 5.9c. You will see later in this chapter how the accessibility of bases within the major groove permits protein–DNA interactions without interfering with base pairing.

Figure 5.9

(a) The structure of B-DNA in space-filling format (left) and with the DNA helix represented as tubes (right), with the major and minor grooves indicated. (b) The major and minor grooves arise from the geometry of the deoxyribose–base unit across the helix, which has distinct edges, with the angle on one side being > 180° and the angle on the other side being < 180°. (c) Binding sites in the major groove. Several atoms on the purine and pyrimidine bases (those highlighted by yellow arrows) are available for hydrogen bonding with specific amino acid side-chains in DNA binding proteins. (dR = deoxyribose)

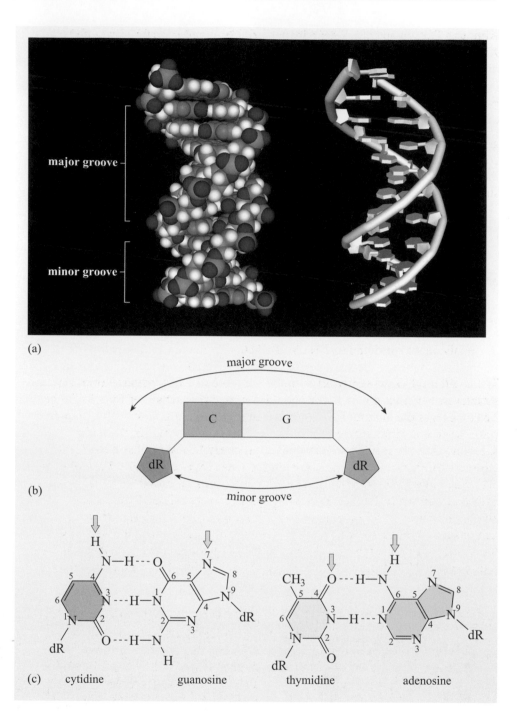

(a)

(b)

(c)   cytidine   guanosine   thymidine   adenosine

○ Look back at the structure of the modified nucleoside 5-methylcytidine in Figure 5.4b. What will be the position of the methyl group in a B-form helix?

● The methyl group of 5-methylcytidine will project into the major groove.

The position of the methyl group on 5-methylcytidine in DNA is significant. Projecting into the major groove as it does, this group can potentially interfere with protein–DNA interactions. We will see the importance of this interference when we consider the influence of DNA cytidine methylation in the regulation of transcription, where the methyl group can directly interfere with the binding of transcription factors.

Although Watson and Crick described the right-handed helical B form of DNA, X-ray diffraction studies have identified other forms of DNA structure. These different structures are dependent upon crystallization conditions or base composition and two forms, **A-DNA** and **Z-DNA**, are shown for comparison in Figure 5.10.

Like B-DNA, A-DNA is a right-handed helix. In A-DNA, the major and minor grooves are of similar dimensions and there are 11 base pairs per helical turn compared with 10 in B-DNA. In Z-DNA, which has 12 base pairs per helical turn, the sugar–phosphate backbone forms a 'zig-zag' conformation, after which this structure is named.

○ Examine the structure of Z-DNA shown in Figure 5.10 in more detail. Compared with the A and B forms, can you describe the nature of the 'handedness' of the helix and its grooves?

● You will notice that, when compared to the A and B forms, Z-DNA is left-handed; that is, the backbone spirals the opposite way round the helical axis from that seen in the A and B forms. Due to the kinking of the backbone, the nucleotides themselves bulge out more, leaving only one groove which is equivalent to the minor groove in B-DNA.

These different DNA secondary structures have been demonstrated from crystal structures, but what do we know about the structure of DNA *in vivo*, in the cell? The B form is the lowest-energy state for the DNA duplex. In its native duplex state, when not denatured for transcription, replication or repair, the helical secondary structure of DNA in the cell is generally believed to be the B form. However, there is a degree of fluidity in the structure adopted by DNA within an active cell, and other secondary structures such as A- and Z-DNA could exist. Z-DNA is known to form *in vitro* within particular stretches of DNA with alternating purines and pyrimidines, such as with $5'-(GC)_n-3'$. It is difficult to demonstrate the occurrence of Z-DNA *in vivo*, as it is believed to form only transiently within genomic DNA, though it is thought to occur in association with transcription. Note that the A-form duplex is predominantly found in double-

A-DNA

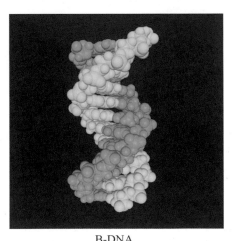

B-DNA

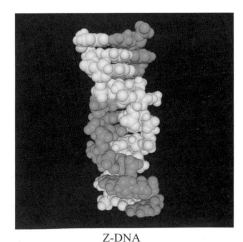

Z-DNA

Figure 5.10   Three secondary structures of DNA (A, B and Z), shown in space filling format, with each strand separately coloured. In each case, a stretch of DNA 12 base pairs in length is shown.

stranded RNA, which cannot form the B-helix structure due to steric conflict involving the 2′ hydroxyl groups of the ribose component. Furthermore, hybrid duplexes, consisting of one strand each of RNA and DNA, are also thought to adopt an A-form structure. Such hybrids must occur in the transcription of RNA from a DNA template.

It should be noted that DNA is capable of adopting other higher-order structures, particularly *in vitro*, and we will now discuss some of these structures that may have biological roles to play. In the cell, DNA is, of course, found complexed with a variety of cellular proteins, many of which contribute to higher-order structures where the basic helix is folded into more condensed states. DNA can loop around itself and around proteins specific for this role. A number of different conformations and structures adopted by this versatile molecule have been identified and characterized, many of which have a particular purpose within the cell.

5.3.2 Higher-order DNA structures: DNA twisting and torsional effects

As discussed earlier, the helical nature of DNA results for the most part from the properties of the bases, their interactions and the geometry of the helix itself. There is, however, another important contributor to the structure of DNA that is found within the cell. The DNA helix is actually under a torsional stress due to what is called **DNA twisting**, which arises when the two strands of the helix are twisted around the axis, as shown in Figure 5.11a.

The polynucleotide backbone is, of course, constrained by rigid bond lengths and angles and it can be twisted to only a limited extent. The torsional stress that this twisting introduces into the DNA helix acts as an internal 'store' of free energy which serves to drive the formation of various alternative conformational states that have higher energy requirements for their formation, including the cruciforms (Figure 5.11c) and Z-DNA.

Figure 5.11
(a) The DNA duplex can be twisted by rotation around its axis, either anticlockwise (positive twist) or clockwise (negative twist). The torsional stress of twisting results in the adoption of (b) supercoiled structures such as a supercoiled circular plasmid molecule or a solenoidal structure, or (c) cruciforms at inverted repeats.

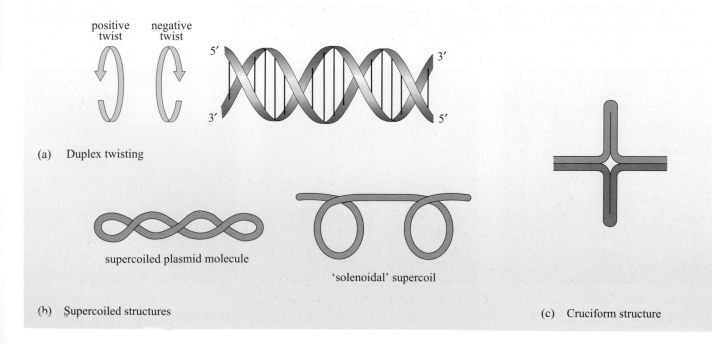

(a)   Duplex twisting

supercoiled plasmid molecule

'solenoidal' supercoil

(b)   Supercoiled structures

(c)   Cruciform structure

◯   As a way of visualizing the energy that this twisting of the helix can introduce into the molecule, imagine twisting a rubber band a few times. What happens when you let go of one end?

◼   The band spontaneously untwists, using the energy you put into it by twisting, and rotates a number of times about its own axis.

In its natural state within the cell, DNA does not behave like a twisted rubber band, as it does not have 'free' ends. The movement and conformation of the duplex DNA molecule *in vivo* is constrained by non-covalent interactions with proteins or, in the case of bacterial chromosomes and plasmid DNAs, direct covalent joining to form a continuous circle.

Twisting of DNA can occur in both directions, by rotation clockwise or anticlockwise around the axis of the helix. *In vivo*, B-DNA is negatively twisted; that is, the strands are rotated clockwise (Figure 5.11a).

With twisting of the DNA, parts of the helix deviate from the B form, adopting alternative conformations in an attempt to minimize the torsional strain. Such conformations, called DNA **supercoils**, can be either an intertwined (i.e. supercoiled) helix or a solenoidal structure, as shown in Figure 5.11b. *In vivo*, these structures are stabilized by interactions with protein components of the chromosome and we will discuss how this is achieved shortly. Depending upon the twist being introduced into the DNA chain, the supercoils can be either positive or negative.

◯   What type of supercoiling will exist in B-DNA *in vivo*?

◼   As B-DNA *in vivo* is negatively twisted, it will have negative supercoils.

In *E. coli*, the torsional stress is continually maintained by an enzyme called **DNA gyrase**, which introduces negative twists into the chromosome, resulting in it being negatively supercoiled. DNA gyrase belongs to a class of DNA processing enzymes called **topoisomerases**, which we will discuss in more detail shortly. This enzyme effectively converts the chemical energy released on hydrolysis of ATP into torsional energy in a negatively supercoiled DNA chain. As a result of DNA twisting, the Gibbs free energy content of supercoiled DNA is high. This free energy is available for various biological processes.

◯   The opening up of the DNA helix to allow for DNA replication, repair or transcription is an energy-demanding process. Why is this so?

◼   In order to denature duplex DNA, energy is required to overcome the base-pairing and base-stacking energies.

Negatively supercoiled DNA presents a considerably lower energy barrier for such unpairing than does non-twisted DNA, whereas positively supercoiled DNA presents a higher energy barrier. The most likely reason for the maintenance of a genome under negative supercoiling stress is that it allows the dynamic opening of the helix for transcription, replication and repair to be energetically more favourable than for non-supercoiled DNA. It is interesting to note that certain extremophile bacteria, which live at temperatures high enough to spontaneously overcome the energy barrier for denaturation of negatively supercoiled B-DNA, instead have positively supercoiled genomic DNA.

Torsional energy can be taken up by alternative DNA conformations

The energy introduced into DNA by twisting has great potential as a regulatory mechanism, since the free energy can be stored in a variety of different high-energy conformations along the chain.

☐ This fluidity of DNA structure can be demonstrated by considering an experiment with a circular eubacterial plasmid DNA molecule that has three naturally occurring negative supercoils introduced by DNA gyrase. What would you predict would happen if a short DNA fragment of sequence $5'-(GC)_n-3'$ is introduced into such a plasmid? (Hint: look back to Section 5.3.1 to remind yourself of the particular structural propensity of this sequence.)

▇ Remembering that this particular sequence of alternating purine and pyrimidine bases allows the DNA helix to adopt a Z-form helical structure, you would predict that the increased free energy introduced into the plasmid by DNA gyrase, instead of driving the formation of supercoils, could result in the formation of Z-DNA helix in the stretch of DNA carrying the GC-rich insert.

Transitions from B-DNA to alternative structures such as Z-DNA are, of course, energy-consuming because they require the unwinding of the helix, followed by rewinding in the opposite direction. The formation of a single 12 bp turn of Z-DNA requires an energy input equivalent to that required to form two negative supercoils. Whilst the formation of such Z-DNA regions *in vivo* is still uncertain, there are many examples of short DNA sequences, containing alternating purines and pyrimidines, that could form such structures. For example, the human genome contains over 45 000 stretches of $(CA)_n$.

Another DNA sequence that can form a novel conformation can occur at what are termed **inverted repeats**, stretches of DNA sequences that have internal complementarity. These sequences can fold up on themselves in the shape of a cross, forming a structure known as a **cruciform** (Figure 5.11c). Formation of a cruciform structure requires unpairing of the existing B-DNA helix, followed by re-pairing into two hairpins, one in each strand, and can serve to release local torsional stresses induced by twisting. Thus the free energy required for twisting is used to drive the unpairing and unstacking of the existing B-DNA, allowing the cruciform structure to be produced.

The fluidity of torsional stress along the DNA chain

The fluid changes in conformation and free energy of the DNA helix are influenced by many processes including the binding of proteins, some of which may have a regulatory function. Thus binding of a protein in one position along a DNA chain could result in alterations in the topology of the DNA, and hence changes in free energy availability, both locally and at some distance from the binding site. Changes in torsional energy may serve as an indicator of the state of the surrounding helix. For example, a decrease in torsional energy could indicate a break in a DNA chain, since the broken chain would be free to untwist and torsional stress would be released. Changes in torsional energy could therefore aid detection of such DNA damage.

When the DNA helix must be 'opened', by unpairing of its constituent bases, to allow access of replication or transcription machinery, the local untwisting of the helix must be accommodated by increased positive twisting of the flanking DNA helix. If we consider transcription, the RNA polymerase molecule is fixed as the helix is

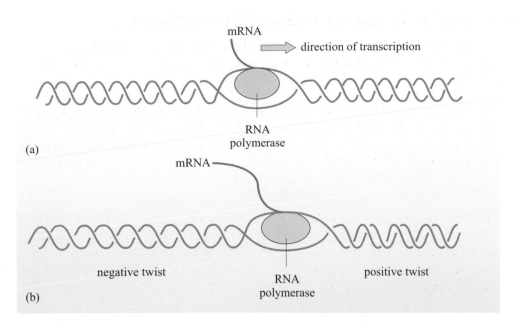

mRNA

direction of transcription

RNA
polymerase

(a)

mRNA

negative twist

RNA
polymerase

positive twist

(b)

Figure 5.12
(a) Transcription is believed to entail twisting of the DNA whilst the RNA polymerase molecule is fixed.
(b) As a result, alterations in twisting and supercoiling due to progressive unpairing of the DNA helix result in alterations in supercoiling ahead of, and behind, the RNA polymerase.

progressively unwound to allow the enzyme access. As a result, positive DNA twisting increases ahead of the transcription machinery, increasing the level of positive supercoiling, as shown in Figure 5.12. Positive supercoiling presents a considerably higher energy barrier to strand separation, a process that has to occur in order for transcription to continue. At the same time, the region behind the transcription machinery relaxes to accommodate the unwound region, effectively undergoing negative twisting and forming negative supercoils. Such torsional differences highlight the effect of the structure of DNA on its processing. Management of the altered torsional stresses that result from the processing of DNA occurs through the action of specific enzymes, the topoisomerases, which we will now discuss.

DNA topoisomerases

Topoisomerases create temporary strand breaks in DNA, thereby allowing the DNA to 'swivel' around the helical axis and releasing torsional strain within the area before resealing the break. With the cellular DNA in a supercoiled state, topoisomerases play a critical role in regulating both how tightly packed DNA is within the cell and the dynamic state of torsional energies during DNA processing. There are two classes of this enzyme: topoisomerase I (topo I) functions by breaking just one strand of the DNA, whilst the action of topoisomerase II (topo II) results in a double-strand break. DNA gyrase is a prokaryotic type II topoisomerase that utilizes ATP to introduce twist in the bacterial chromosome.

☐ What effect will topoisomerase action have on supercoiling?

⬤ DNA twisting results in alterations to supercoiling within the helix. Thus untwisting as a result of topoisomerase action modifies the degree of supercoiling in DNA.

Whilst both type I and type II topoisomerases cause regional relaxation or increased DNA supercoiling, topo II also has other functions. Since topo II breaks both strands of the DNA, simultaneous passage of both strands through a break in the duplex chain is possible. Thus topo II has the ability to knot and unknot DNA as well as to **catenate** (interlink) and decatenate circular double-stranded DNA, as shown in Figure 5.13.

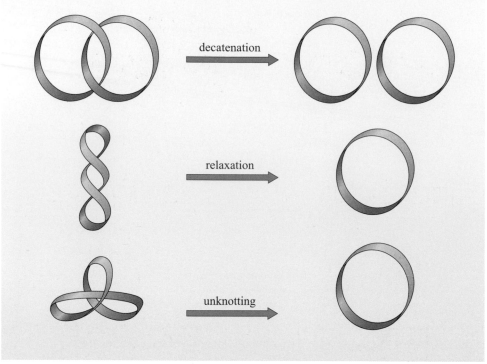

Figure 5.13   The functions of topoisomerase II in decatenating, relaxing and unknotting DNA.

○ Why is this activity essential during replication of the circular bacterial chromosome?

● After replication of the circular chromosome, the two daughter chains will be interlinked and will require separation before cell division can occur.

Topoisomerases are often highly expressed in rapidly proliferating cells and have been found to be present at very high levels in cervical, breast, colon and lung cancer cells.

○ Why do you think high levels of topoisomerase would be advantageous to cancer cells? (Hint: think back to changes to the DNA helix that could occur during replication, similar to those in transcription in Figure 5.12.)

● Rapidly growing and dividing cells, such as cancer cells, have a high level of replication and transcription. High topoisomerase activity would facilitate this DNA processing.

It is perhaps not surprising, therefore, that topoisomerases are targets for some cancer chemotherapy agents. Several derivatives of the drug camptothecin, which is a powerful topo I inhibitor, have been found to be effective against some human colon and ovarian cancers. Several topo II inhibitors have also been used successfully, a topic we shall discuss in Chapter 19. As already mentioned, topo II breaks the deoxyribose–phosphate backbone of both strands of the DNA, allowing passage of an unbroken stretch of double helix through the gap. The mechanism of action of topo II is outlined in Figure 5.14. Topo II inhibitors exert their effect in one of two ways: so-called *catalytic inhibitors* stabilize the topological complex (step 3, Figure 5.14), thereby preventing initial DNA cleavage; while *cleavage agents* inhibit topo II activity by preventing the already cleaved complex (step 5, Figure 5.14) from re-ligation.

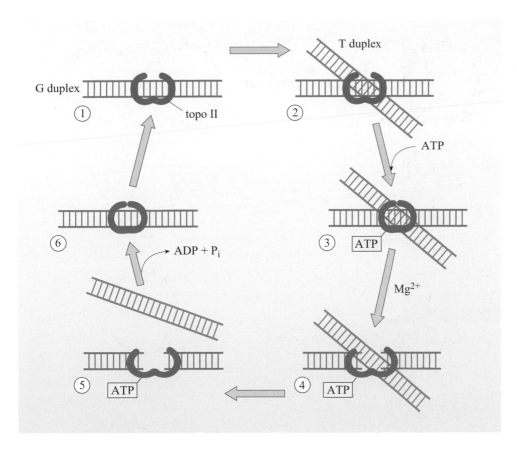

Figure 5.14
The mechanism of topoisomerase II action. Step 1: Topo II binds non-covalently to the gate (G) duplex (so called because it opens like a gate). Step 2: The G duplex–topo II complex binds at the crossover region with the transported (T) duplex (so called because this duplex will pass through the G duplex). Step 3: ATP binds and promotes formation of the topological complex. Step 4: Mg^{2+}-dependent cleavage of the G duplex. Step 5: The T duplex passes through the gap formed in the G duplex. Step 6: The G duplex is re-ligated and the bound ATP is hydrolysed. The enzyme is now free to enter another catalytic cycle.

5.3.3 Other structures in DNA

We will finish our discussion of DNA structure by examining two cases of unusual structures that can arise.

Triplex structures

An unusual form of three-stranded structure, called **triplex DNA**, can arise *in vitro* when a single-stranded region of DNA pairs with a paired duplex DNA helix through additional hydrogen bonding between the bases of all *three* strands.

○ Based upon your knowledge of the structure of helical DNA, where would you predict that a short DNA strand would 'sit' within this structure for such an interaction to occur?

● Within the major groove, where several potential hydrogen bonding sites are available, as shown in Figure 5.9c.

The formation of these hydrogen bonds arises because of what are termed **Hoogsteen bonds**, which form between bases in the incoming single-stranded DNA and the already paired bases in the duplex, as shown in Figure 5.15. The various combinations of bonds, C–G·C, T–A·T, T–A·A and C–G·G (where the dash denotes Watson–Crick base pairing and the dot denotes Hoogsteen pairing), have varying degrees of stability, with bonds between the purines being most stable. Whilst many *in vitro* studies have examined the possible structures of these triplex DNAs, their role *in vivo* remains unclear. Their significance lies in the

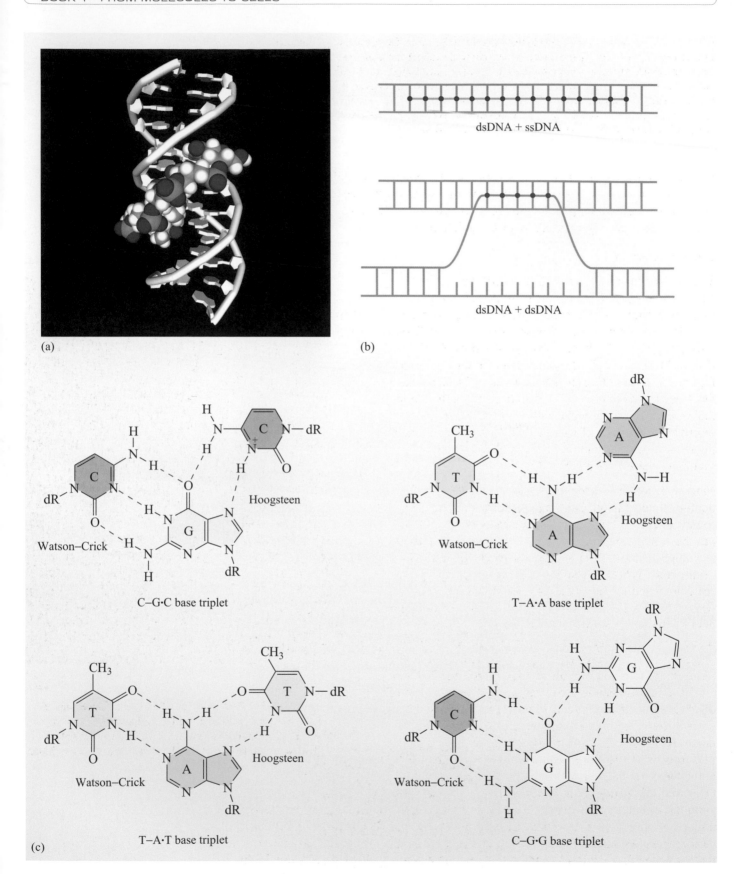

(a)

(b)

dsDNA + ssDNA

dsDNA + dsDNA

(c)

C–G·C base triplet

T–A·A base triplet

T–A·T base triplet

C–G·G base triplet

Watson–Crick

Hoogsteen

Figure 5.15 Triplex DNA and Hoogsteen pairs. (a) Triplex DNA secondary structure formed between a 14 base-pair helical duplex (shown as tubes) and a six-base single-stranded DNA (space-filling) lying within the major groove (pdb file 1bwg). (b) Possible interactions between duplex DNA and either single-stranded DNA or a second duplex DNA. (c) Molecular details of the Hoogsteen bonds to the Watson–Crick base pairs, resulting in four base triplet combinations (dR = deoxyribose). Notice that the formation of the C–G·C triplet requires a protonation of the cytosine base in the single-stranded DNA.

observation that triplex structures *in vitro* have been shown to inhibit transcription. Thus formation of these structures *in vivo*, for example between a duplex region and single-stranded DNAs or between two duplex regions (as shown in Figure 5.15b), could play a role in gene regulation.

Quadruplex structures

The ends of linear chromosomes are protected from potential damage by special elements called **telomeres**. In many organisms, telomeres consist of long stretches of DNA that contain many thousands of copies of G-rich repeat sequences. They are easily detected by FISH (Box 5.1), as shown in the case of human telomeres in Figure 5.16. We will discuss the specialized role of these DNA sequences in telomere replication in Chapter 9 and their role in cell senescence and tumorigenesis will be discussed in Chapters 14 and 19. Our attention here is on the unusual DNA structure believed to be formed by a section of these G-rich DNA elements.

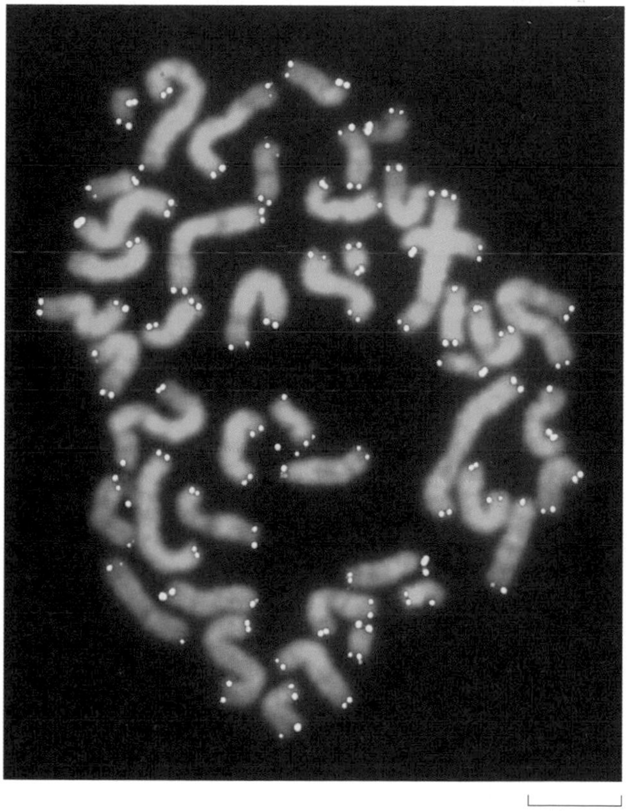

Most of a stretch of telomeric DNA is in the form of a double-stranded helix, but the terminal repeats are usually found as single-stranded DNA. *In vitro*, telomeric DNA has the ability to spontaneously undergo an intramolecular rearrangement and form a higher-ordered DNA called **quadruplex DNA**, as shown in Figure 5.17. This type of structure is termed an *intramolecular* quadruplex as it is formed from a single strand of DNA, the structure being held by the formation of Hoogsteen bonds between a tetrad of four guanine bases in a square planar formation (Figure 5.17a) and also referred to as a G4 quadruplex. Several different conformations have been identified in *in vitro* studies, as shown in Figure 5.17b. The existence of quadruplex DNA *in vivo* has been inferred because many proteins have been identified that can bind selectively to quadruplex DNA. These binding proteins include DNA helicases, which have a role in the uncoiling of the DNA helix during replication and repair. Besides the telomeres, the eukaryotic genome possesses other regions that have the potential to fold into quadruplex structures, including the promoter and regulatory regions of many genes. G4 quadruplex structures have also been described in various mRNAs within mammalian cells, these forming characteristic structures that are recognized by RNA binding proteins. An example is shown in Figure 5.17c.

10 μm

Figure 5.16 FISH detection of telomeres in metaphase human chromosomes (obtained from a lymphocyte), using a telomeric DNA probe. In this image, the telomeres light up yellow, whereas the rest of the chromosome is shown in blue.

Figure 5.17

(a) A quadruplex DNA is predicted to form in the single-stranded G-rich regions of eukaryotic telomeres due to Hoogsteen interactions between four guanines. (b) Three possible secondary structures for quadruplex DNA. (c) An example of a G4 quadruplex structure found in mRNAs. This structure is recognized by an RNA binding protein known as FMRP, which binds to hundreds of mRNAs in the mouse brain.

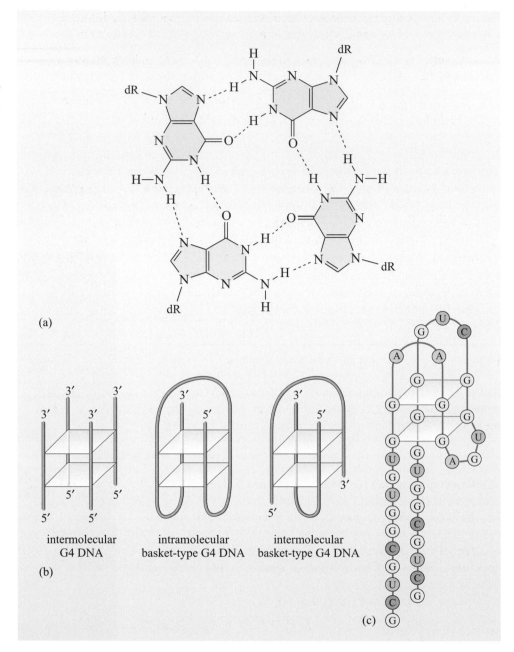

(a)

(b)

intermolecular
G4 DNA

intramolecular
basket-type G4 DNA

intermolecular
basket-type G4 DNA

(c)

Summary of Section 5.3

1   Watson–Crick base pairing arises due to hydrogen bonding between A and T and G and C and spatial limitations within the hydrophobic core of the helix.

2   DNA commonly folds into the B-form helix; other forms such as Z-DNA form *in vitro*. A-form helices are formed primarily by duplex RNA.

3   The twisting of DNA around its helical axis results in torsional stresses that promote the formation of high-energy alternative conformations such as supercoils.

4   DNA chains accommodate changes in DNA twist through alterations in their supercoiling.

5   Naturally occurring B-DNA is negatively twisted, a state that facilitates strand separating activities of DNA metabolism.

6   Enzymes called DNA topoisomerases are responsible for managing torsional stress in DNA.

7   Unusual DNA structures can form due to Hoogsteen bond formation between bases and are believed to occur in quadruplex and triplex DNAs.

Reading scientific literature 1

Go to the Study Skills file: *Reading scientific literature 1*. In this activity, you will be introduced to the different types of published scientific research paper and receive guidance on how to read and extract information effectively from such papers. The activity entails reading three papers concerned with the discovery of the structure of DNA.

5.4 RNA structure and function

5.4.1 The varied structures of RNA

RNA is a versatile cellular molecule with the ability to adopt a number of complex structural conformations. Although RNA is often thought of as a single-stranded molecule it is actually highly structured.

☐ Why does RNA adopt a higher-order structure?

◼ Remembering that the bases in nucleic acids are hydrophobic, base interactions that minimize exposure of the bases to water will drive RNA secondary structure formation, just as they do with DNA.

In effect, this means folding to maximize base pairing, since hydrophobic interactions arise from stacking of bases aligned by complementary hydrogen bonding.

☐ What type of helix is formed by duplex RNA?

◼ A-form helices are formed by duplex RNAs (Section 5.3.1).

The level of structural complexity in RNAs is much greater than that in DNA and many RNAs have a defined tertiary structure analogous to that observed in proteins. As we discussed earlier, it has been more difficult to study RNA structures than DNA structures by X-ray diffraction. However, for many RNAs, secondary structures can be predicted from theoretical folding patterns based upon RNA base sequence and by assuming maximal base pairing. By comparing similar predicted structures from different organisms (which will have slightly different base sequences), the most likely structure can often be determined. An example of this approach is the original 'evidence' for the cloverleaf structure of tRNA shown in Figure 5.18, which was derived by predicting the secondary structure of many different tRNAs. Only later were these interactions and the basic structure of tRNA confirmed by X-ray diffraction.

However, many RNA molecules are much larger than the small tRNA molecules, making it more difficult to choose between the many alternative theoretical conformations that could potentially form. Some RNAs may adopt different folding patterns under different circumstances, and thus modify their biological activity. Even so, although RNA structure prediction has its limits, some general structural motifs are apparent. It is clear that larger RNA molecules can be visualized as separate domains, each with a complex folding pattern made up of hairpin loops where the polyribonucleotide chain folds back on itself to allow base pairing between nearby lengths of RNA with complementary base sequences. Just as in proteins, each domain can be considered as an independently folded unit and the arrangement of these domains relative to each other defines the tertiary structure of the RNA. The stem of each hairpin loop is often a near-complementary base-paired region and, if long enough, the stem twists into a double helix, increasing stability by promoting base stacking. Two other features are important in the biological role of these hairpin loops. The unpaired bases in the tip of the loop, and those in the occasional nucleotide bulge along the stem, are susceptible to nuclease enzymes that recognize only single-stranded RNA (the so-called **single-strand nucleases**). Unpaired bases could also provide important opportunities for base pairing to other nucleic acid molecules and for recognition by specific proteins.

○ How might single-strand nucleases be used to confirm predicted RNA structures?

● If a folded RNA is treated with a ribonuclease specific for single-stranded molecules, the products of the reaction can be analysed, thereby confirming unpaired regions within the structure or revealing the accessibility of these regions within a tertiary structure.

We will discuss the structure of the ribosomal RNAs as determined by X-ray diffraction in more detail in Chapter 11 when we look at their role in protein synthesis, but for now we will focus on the structure of the tRNA molecule.

5.4.2 The structure of tRNA

Transfer RNAs are small and compact molecules. Comparisons of the base sequences of many tRNAs led to the predicted four-leaf clover structure shown in Figure 5.18a, which follows the rule of maximizing base-pairing interactions. This structure was largely confirmed by analysis with single-strand nucleases.

Two of the four main arms of the tRNA molecule are named according to their function, i.e. binding to the mRNA trinucleotide that encodes a specific amino acid (**anticodon arm**), or to the specific amino acid itself (**acceptor arm**). The **dihydrouridine** and **TψC arms** are named from the unusual bases that always appear in these locations (see Figure 5.4b for the structures of some of these bases). When the tertiary structure of the tRNA was determined by X-ray diffraction, it became clear that the cloverleaf structure is, in fact, folded into an L-shaped molecule in three dimensions, shown in Figure 5.17b. This three-dimensional structure is formed through several tertiary-structure-stabilizing interactions, as represented in Figure 5.17c, which include hydrogen bonds in base triples (three nearby bases linked through hydrogen bonding). A base triple may stabilize tertiary interactions between widely separated parts of a polynucleotide

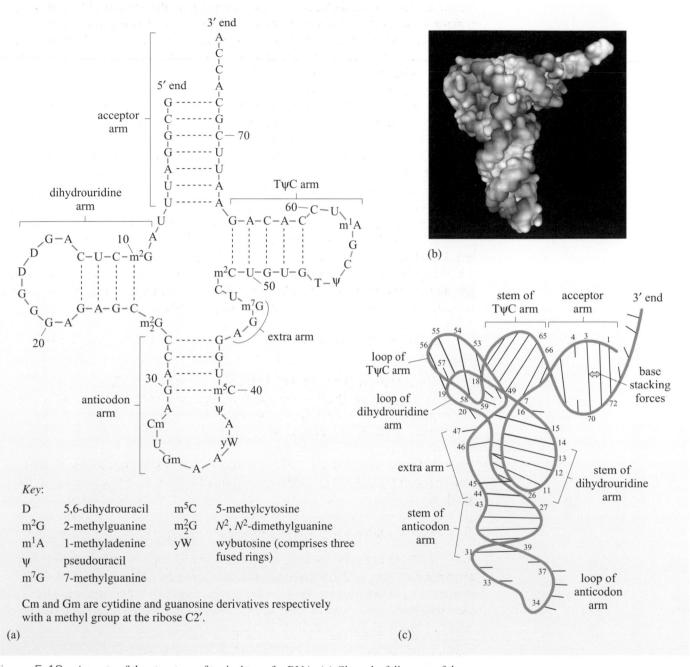

Key:

D	5,6-dihydrouracil	m^5C	5-methylcytosine
m^2G	2-methylguanine	m_2^2G	N^2, N^2-dimethylguanine
m^1A	1-methyladenine	yW	wybutosine (comprises three fused rings)
ψ	pseudouracil		
m^7G	7-methylguanine		

Cm and Gm are cytidine and guanosine derivatives respectively with a methyl group at the ribose C2′.

(a)   (c)

Figure 5.18 Aspects of the structure of typical transfer RNA. (a) Cloverleaf diagram of the secondary structure of tRNA as predicted from the sequence, according to the rule of maximizing base pairing. Note how base pairing produces four arms and a small extra arm. The dihydrouridine and TψC arms are so named because of their characteristic modified bases. The anticodon arm contains bases 34 to 36, which are complementary to the mRNA codon, and the acceptor arm is the site of amino acid attachment, a reaction catalysed by a tRNA synthase specific for both the amino acid and the tRNA. (b) Tertiary structure of a typical tRNA shown in surface view. The charged ribose–phosphate backbone (shaded red) can be traced (pdb file 1ehz). (c) Diagram illustrating tRNA tertiary structure. The ribose–phosphate backbone is shown as a heavy continuous orange line. The longer black lines represent hydrogen bonds in double-helical regions; short black lines represent single bases in unpaired regions. Red lines represent hydrogen bonds stabilizing the tertiary structure.

chain, just as non-covalent interactions between amino acid residues stabilize tertiary structure in proteins. Extensive methylation of tRNA confers resistance to cellular nucleases, and tRNA molecules tend to be longer-lived than mRNAs.

5.4.3 Hairpin formation and micro-RNAs

A class of small RNA molecules called **micro-RNAs** (miRNAs) has been identified in recent years. The roles of these small RNAs are only just beginning to be understood, but many are expressed only at specific developmental stages. Indeed, the first observations of miRNAs were made in *C. elegans* because of their mutant developmental phenotypes. The genes that encode these miRNAs are called *mir* genes (pronounced 'meer') and have now been identified within the genomes of various animals and plants. Many of the genes are evolutionarily conserved for sections of their sequence and all are inverted repeat sequences.

○ What can you predict about the structure of the mRNA synthesized from *mir* genes, assuming the rules of maximum base pairing?

● As the *mir* genes are inverted repeats, the mRNA will also contain an inverted repeat. The most likely structure to form will be a hairpin, as this will provide maximum pairing of the bases.

The hairpin structures are believed to be a critical part of miRNA function, as they are found in a divergent range of organisms. Shown in Figure 5.19 are miRNAs encoded by a gene called *mir-1*. The predicted structures of the hairpins of the *mir-1* miRNAs from *C. elegans*, *D. melanogaster* and human reveal that each is capable of forming into a hairpin chain. In most cases, the stem of the hairpin contains several mismatched bases, although the majority are perfectly matched.

MiRNA molecules are processed by a protein complex containing a ribonuclease called **dicer**, to produce small RNA chains that are between 21 and 25 nucleotides in length. Highlighted within each hairpin in Figure 5.19a is the small 21-nucleotide product RNA that is produced from each of these precursor miRNAs. Note that the base sequence of this 21-nucleotide RNA is identical between these three organisms.

These small RNAs derived from miRNAs by the action of dicer appear to exert their cellular effect through base-pairing interactions with other target nucleic acids; presumably the specificity of base pairing serves a role in the recognition of these targets. Most is known about their influence on the stability or translation of target mRNAs that contain a complementary sequence of bases (to be discussed further in Chapters 10 and 11). MiRNAs have also been implicated in alterations in chromatin structure. *Mir* genes are believed to be numerous in most eukaryotic genomes; for example, it is estimated that the human genome contains 250 *mir* genes.

5.4.4 Ribozymes

Several types of RNA have been shown to have catalytic activity directed towards strand cleavage. They were originally observed in the case of 'self-splicing' introns, i.e. segments of the immature non-protein-coding mRNA that remove themselves during the formation of mature RNA, as shown in Figure 5.20a. The term **ribozyme** has been coined to describe all such catalytic RNA molecules.

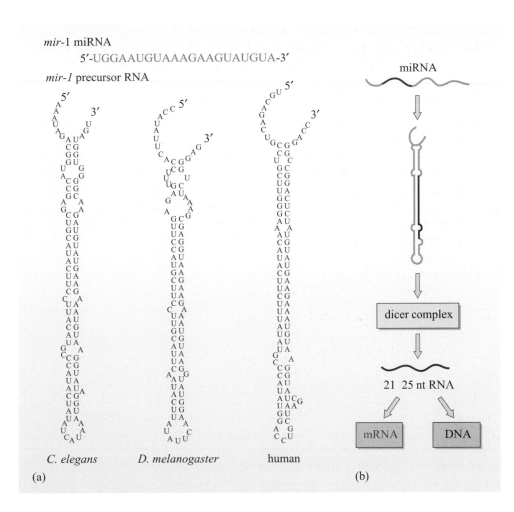

mir-1 miRNA

5'-UGGAAUGUAAAGAAGUAUGUA-3'

mir-1 precursor RNA

C. elegans   D. melanogaster   human

(a)

miRNA

dicer complex

21 25 nt RNA

mRNA   DNA

(b)

Figure 5.19

(a) MiRNAs form hairpin-like structures as shown here for the *mir-1* miRNAs. (b) MiRNAs such as *mir-1* miRNA are acted upon by the dicer complex, which processes the folded hairpin miRNA into a short (21–25 nt) RNA strand. Such miRNAs are involved in various cellular processes that target mRNA stability and translation and DNA modification. (Based on data from Moss and Poethig, 2002)

Some ribozymes are, as described above, self-splicing, i.e. they catalyse cleavage and resealing of their own nucleotide chain, whereas others catalyse these reactions on separate RNA molecules. The activity of a ribozyme, like that of any macromolecule, depends crucially upon its conformation, and we have already described in the previous section the hairpin loops, alternative folding patterns, and tertiary structure-stabilizing devices found in RNA molecules. The catalytic domain of a ribozyme can break and re-form phosphodiester bonds between nucleotides, lowering the activation energy for these reactions just as in protein-catalysed reactions.

Engineered ribozymes that are capable of cleaving specific RNA chains within cells are now used extensively as research tools, as shown in Figure 5.20b. In this case, a hammerhead ribozyme (so called because of the shape of the predicted RNA structure) has been engineered onto a carrier RNA chain that contains a stretch of sequence complementary to a target mRNA. When base pairing occurs, the catalytic ribozyme core is brought into close proximity to the target mRNA and cleaves it. Such cleavage results in degradation of the mRNA by cellular ribonucleases. It is hoped that such molecules could be used therapeutically to target unwanted gene expression such as by retroviruses (e.g. HIV) or mutated genes. Box 5.2 describes two further important applications of nucleic acids as targeting agents for therapeutic or experimental purposes.

Figure 5.20
Ribozymes. (a) Action of a self-splicing ribozyme, removing an intron by self-catalysing the splicing reaction. (Exons are nucleic acid sequences that code for protein; introns are the intervening, non-coding sequences.) A reaction between the C2′ hydroxyl group of ribose in nucleotide A and a target nucleotide in the upstream exon I leads to the breaking of a 5′–3′ phosphoester bond at the end of this exon. One of the cut ends is joined to the ribose C2′ in nucleotide A, closing the intron circle. A reaction between the other cut end and nucleotide A severs the intron tail, leaving the ends of the two exons to be sealed together. (b) A so-called 'hammerhead' ribozyme engineered for use in direct cleavage of a target mRNA chain. Note how homology between the ribozyme and its target drives this interaction. In this case, cleavage is directed downstream from the translation initiation (start) codon, ensuring that the mRNA is not translated.

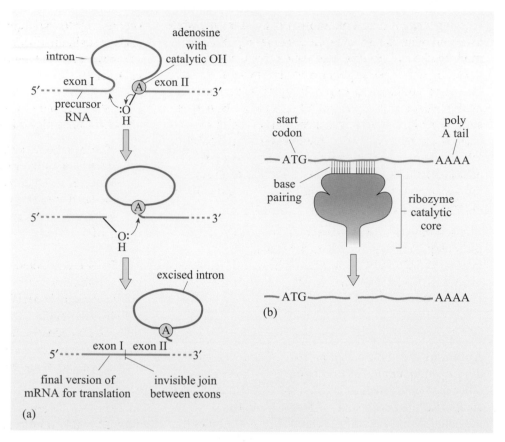

(a)

Box 5.2   The use of nucleic acids as targeting agents

We have already described how catalytic functions such as backbone cleavage found in ribozymes can be harnessed to target destruction of specific RNAs and how hybridization techniques are used to identify nucleic acids. In this section, we will examine two other applications of nucleic acids that depend upon their ability to base-pair and to form a wide range of secondary structures, namely antisense regulation of gene expression and the use of aptamers as structure-specific reagents.

Antisense regulation of gene expression

The term **antisense** refers to the use of a nucleic acid that is complementary to the coding (i.e. 'sense') base sequence of a target gene. When nucleic acids that are antisense in nature are introduced into cells, they can hybridize to the complementary 'sense' mRNA through normal Watson–Crick base pairing. Synthetic antisense DNA chains as short as 15–17 nucleotides in length have been used to block specific gene expression by

either physically blocking translation of the target mRNA or causing its degradation. The latter mechanism relies on induction of the ribonuclease RNAase H, which specifically cleaves the RNA–DNA duplex region, thereby triggering further degradation of the now damaged mRNA.

☐ What properties of the target mRNA might inhibit this process?

⬤ For this process to be successful, the target region must be available for base pairing with the incoming DNA chain. The RNA secondary structure may prevent the antisense DNA from hybridizing.

In practice, to ensure success, antisense sequences are tested against several different target sequences in the mRNA. Antisense sequences (oligonucleotides) have been designed that can specifically inhibit a single gene transcript and can even inhibit an allele or an mRNA carrying a specific combination of spliced exons, while avoiding other members of the same family. Various modifications of the oligonucleotides have been made that counteract their rapid degradation by cellular nucleases. Antisense therapeutic agents have been made that successfully target HIV, hepatitis B, herpes simplex and papillomavirus infections as well as various cancers. As well as using exogenous antisense DNA oligonucleotides, which have only transient effects, continuous expression of antisense RNAs can be achieved by introducing transgenes into whole organisms and cell lines.

You may note a similarity between antisense technology and aspects of the properties of intrinsic MiRNAs. We will discuss how small RNAs can be exploited as regulators of gene expression in Chapter 10.

Aptamers

Aptamers are nucleic acid molecules that have been developed to mimic the selective and tight binding of other molecules such as antibodies. In order to identify an aptamer that is capable of binding to a target molecule, a process called Selex (systematic evolution of ligands by exponential enrichment) is utilized. The strategy relies upon a combination of a selective binding assay and amplification by PCR. A 'library' of short single-stranded DNA oligonucleotides is synthesized *in vitro*, representing every combination of A, C, G and T at each position in the starting material. It is assumed that within this mixture, at least one oligonucleotide chain will be capable of binding specifically to the required target, such as a protein surface, using hydrogen bonding and van der Waals attractive forces along the nucleic acid chain and backbone.

☐   What feature of a single-stranded nucleic acid chain underlies this approach?

◼   The backbone carries five bonds around which there is potential rotation. In single-stranded molecules, rotation about these bonds is relatively easy and the library of short DNA molecules synthesized *in vitro* will assume many different conformations.

The DNA oligonucleotide library is mixed with the target, unbound chains are removed and then those that have bound specifically are eluted using agents that disrupt bonding. The eluted DNAs are amplified by PCR and subsequent selection rounds performed if required; thus those oligonucleotides (aptamers) that bind to the target are enriched.

There are a number of advantages in the use of aptamers for targeting specific molecules. Aptamers isolated in this way frequently display high association rates with their targets, with similar affinities to those of monoclonal antibodies. Their small molecular mass means that they can circulate easily throughout the body and, as nucleic acids, they are relatively easy to synthesize and are relatively stable. Finally, aptamers can carry therapeutic agents, radioisotopes and other imaging agents, providing potentially powerful tools for research and therapeutic purposes.

Summary of Section 5.4

1   RNA chains play fundamentally important roles within the cell, including genetic information transfer (mRNA), components of the translation machinery (rRNA in ribosomes and tRNAs) and as regulatory small RNAs.

2   The tertiary structure of RNA is determined by interactions that maximize base pairing. Despite instability and isolation problems, the tertiary structures of several major cellular RNAs are known.

3   Transfer RNA structure is highly specialized for its role in translation.

4   Hairpin RNAs called MiRNAs are present in many eukaryotes and are processed by a cellular ribonuclease called dicer to yield short 21–25-nucleotide RNAs, which exert effects upon mRNA stability, translation and DNA.

5   A class of strand-cleaving ribozyme RNAs exist as intron-splicing molecules. They have been exploited as therapeutic and experimental tools to target mRNAs in cells.

6   Short oligonucleotide chains can act as antisense regulators of mRNA levels.

7   The potential for single-stranded nucleic acids to adopt many different structural conformations has been exploited to develop aptamers that demonstrate selective high-affinity binding to target molecules.

5.5 DNA damage

The integrity of DNA as a genetic material is of paramount importance to an organism, and a multitude of proteins exist that serve to prevent or reverse damage to the DNA. However, like all biological macromolecules, DNA decomposes spontaneously. The reasons for the ease of decomposition of DNA are intimately linked to the chemical structures of the constituent bases and phosphodiester-linked sugars. The limited stability of DNA may be integral to the molecular basis of evolution. If DNA were extremely stable and its replication perfect, the sequence of bases within a gene would be passed on to each succeeding generation with no alterations. But small chemical changes to DNA that result in alterations to genes do occur, resulting in the variations in protein structure and function that underlie evolution. In this section, we will briefly examine the features of DNA that make it susceptible to damaging agents from both cellular activities and the environment.

5.5.1 The chemical stability of DNA

There are two main features of DNA that make it susceptible to damage. The first is the linkage between the deoxyribose C1′ atom and the base (Figure 5.3b), a bond that is highly susceptible to hydrolysis. The other feature of DNA that contributes to its chemical instability is the presence of a large number of oxygen and nitrogen atoms in the bases. We have seen earlier how the polarization of bonds within the bases contributes to the availability of hydrogen-bonding sites, but it also means that bases are prone to attack from other chemicals. It is not only in DNA that bases are susceptible, but also in the cellular pool of DNA precursor molecules, i.e. free deoxyribonucleotide triphosphates (dNTPs), that are utilized for DNA synthesis.

The frequent and relentless assault on the chemical integrity of DNA in the cellular environment would, at first sight, appear to compromise its central function as the vehicle of genetic information. It is for this reason that there exists a complex set of DNA repair enzymes, which very effectively, in most cases, reverses the chemical damage. We will discuss these enzymes in more detail in Chapter 9. Here we will provide an overview of the types of DNA damage that occur and how certain agents can have mutational effects. The chemical events involved are outlined in Table 5.3 and each is described in the following sections. Many of the pathways involved in their repair will be discussed in Chapter 9.

Table 5.3 Types of DNA damage and the chemical events involved.

(a) Depuration

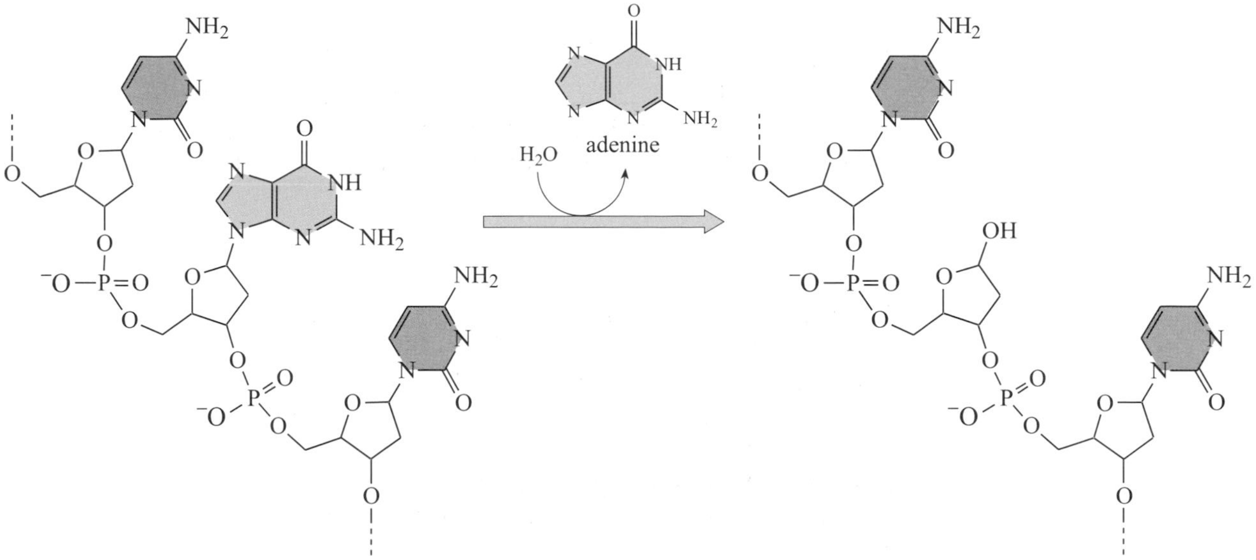

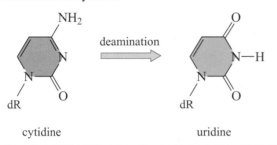

(b) Deamination of cytidine

cytidine → deamination → uridine

(c) Deamination of 5-methylcytidine

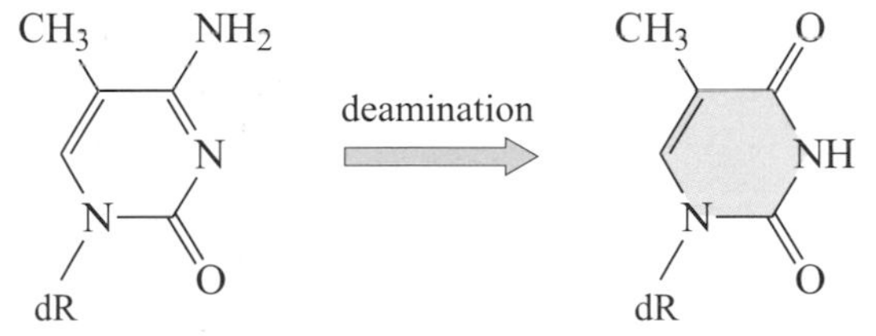

5-methylcytidine → deamination → thymidine

(d) Thymidine dimer formation as a result of UVB light exposure

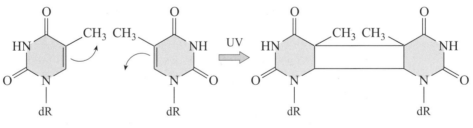

thymidine   thymidine   →UV→   thymidine dimer

(e) Alkylation-sensitive atoms in guanosine*

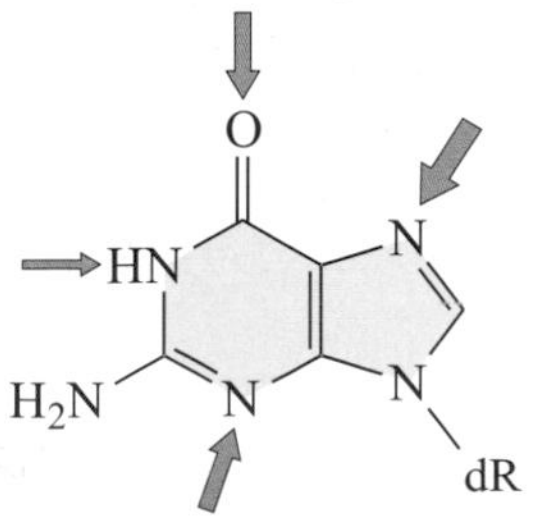

guanosine

(f) O^6-methylguanosine

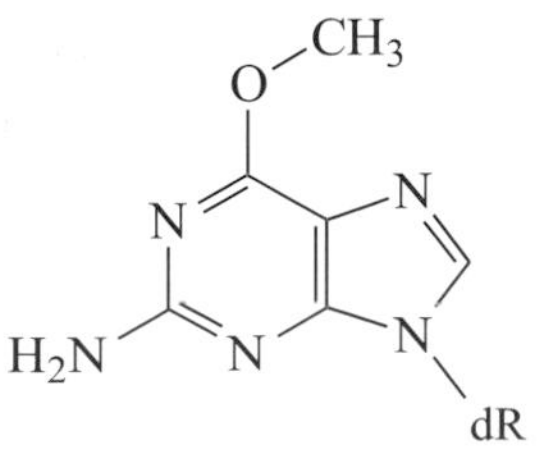

O^6-methylguanosine

* The thickness of the arrows corresponds to the relative sensitivity to alkylation.

The loss of a DNA base causes an abasic site

Hydrolysis of the deoxyribose C1′–base linkage results in the complete loss of a purine or pyrimidine base, resulting in what is called an **abasic site**, an event with obvious genetic consequences. This hydrolysis reaction is much more likely to occur at purine bases, resulting in **depurination** of the DNA (Table 5.3a). Loss of DNA bases occurs only slowly at normal physiological pH and temperatures, but the large number of bases in the genome of a cell (6.2×10^9 in the case of human cells) means that many thousands of individual events occur each day in every cell. This hydrolysis is also the reason why the DNA within dead tissues gradually loses its integrity, limiting our ability to analyse and manipulate DNA from preserved tissues.

The deamination of DNA

If you look back to Figure 5.4a, you will notice that cytosine carries an $-NH_2$ group. This group is liable to undergo what is called a deamination reaction, resulting in the formation of a carbonyl group. What you might notice is that deamination of cytidine generates the nucleoside uridine (Table 5.3b). Since uridine is commonly found in RNA, its presence in DNA is easily detected by the cell, and the damage is repaired. In contrast, deamination of 5-methylcytidine results in the formation of thymidine (Table 5.3c). Deamination occurs much more readily to 5-methylcytidine than to cytidine. The thymidine that results from deamination of 5-methylcytidine is not detected by the cell as DNA damage and is likely to remain and lead to mutation. Such deamination events are common sources of mutation on the human X chromosome, since this chromosome is subject to inactivation through extensive cytidine methylation (X-inactivation, see Section 5.7.2). As a consequence, many C → T mutations occur. Such mutations give rise to X-linked diseases such as haemophilia, which is caused by mutations in the factor IX gene.

Ultraviolet irradiation

The nucleic acid bases absorb electromagnetic radiation in the ultraviolet (UV) region of the spectrum. The major photoproducts in DNA, generated upon exposure to UVB light, are structures called pyrimidine dimers which are formed from two adjacent pyrimidine bases, as shown in Table 5.3d. The formation of such dimers introduces a substantial amount of strain into the structure of DNA. This damage is detected and the dimer repaired by specialist repair machinery, However, if pyrimidine dimers are left unrepaired, they can block replication.

Reactive oxygen species

The metabolism that occurs in every cell and is associated with the basic requirements of physiology inevitably leads to the production of reactive intermediates, many of which are capable of reacting with DNA or free dNTPs, which could subsequently be incorporated during synthesis. One particular group of such molecules are called reactive oxygen species (ROS). The essential feature of ROS is the presence of an unpaired electron on an oxygen atom in the molecule, which enables the ROS to react with DNA and lead to either strand breakage or the generation of modified bases such as 8-oxyguanine. The occurrence of a strand break is potentially lethal to a cell, and we will discuss the repair of such breaks in Chapter 9. Specific DNA repair pathways exist to remove 8-oxoguanosine triphosphate from the cellular dNTP pool and to remove 8-oxyguanine bases from DNA strands.

Alkylating agents

There are many different chemicals that directly chemically modify DNA. The methyl group ($-CH_3$) can be added to DNA at various sites, two of which we will discuss further. There are several alkylation-sensitive sites in guanosine (identified in Table 5.3e). For example, methylation at the 7-position of the guanine base (Figure 5.4b) results in increased susceptibility of the deoxyribose–base bond to hydrolysis; 7-methyldeoxyguanosine is hydrolysed over 100 times more rapidly than is deoxyguanosine.

○ What is the consequence of this hydrolysis reaction?

● The result will be an abasic site; in this case, loss of the guanine base.

Methylation at the O6 position of guanosine results in the formation of a modified nucleoside (O^6-methylguanosine), shown in Table 5.3f. Unlike 7-methyldeoxyguanosine, 6-methyldeoxyguanosine is chemically stable. When this modification occurs, the normal G–C base pairing is disrupted by the presence of the methyl group at one of the hydrogen-bonding positions. (Look back to Figure 5.5a to confirm that this is so.) O^6-methylguanine actually forms a more stable base-pair with thymine that it does with cytosine. If this modification occurs during DNA replication, mispairing with thymine can occur and, on subsequent replication steps, an A is placed opposite the T. Thus a G–C → A–T mutation occurs. There exists a unique repair enzyme for O^6-methylguanosine, called O^6-methylguanosine methyltransferase, which acts as a suicide protein, removing the methyl group but inactivating itself irreversibly.

'Bulky' agents

So far we have only considered damage caused by 'small' groups such as methyl groups. There is, however, a class of so-called 'bulky' DNA-damaging agents that have been widely studied. Many polyaromatic hydrocarbons (PAH) induce skin cancer in experimental systems and one such molecule benzo(a)pyrene, BaP), is found in tobacco smoke. BaP itself is an extremely stable and unreactive molecule, but it is metabolized within the cell to a highly reactive derivative that forms characteristic DNA modifications at the C2 amino group of guanine. The C2 amino group is normally 'buried' within the inner core of the DNA double helix, but the BaP metabolite is small enough to fit into the minor groove of DNA. Here it reacts with the guanine and intercalates between the stacked bases, thereby distorting the helix (Figure 5.21).

Summary of Section 5.5

1 The stability of DNA makes it suitable as a store of genetic information.

2 The susceptibility of DNA to chemical damage allows mutations to arise.

3 DNA damage can occur due to chemical interactions with reactive molecular species or irradiation. If not repaired, such damage results in base loss or mutations due to mispairing in replication.

4 Most DNA damage is detected and repaired by the cell.

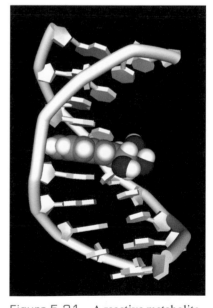

Figure 5.21   A reactive metabolite of BaP (space-filling) reacts with nine base-pair helical duplex DNA (tubes) through the minor groove, resulting in its intercalation and helix distortion. (Based upon pdb file 1dxa)

217

5.6 Protein–nucleic acid interactions

The biological functions of both DNA and RNA are dependent on complex, and sometimes transient, three-dimensional nucleoprotein structures. It is in such structures that the enzymatic manipulation of DNA in the essential biological processes such as DNA replication, transcription and recombination occur, and it is important to understand the interactions that drive these processes. Whether it is the activity of enzymes associated with DNA, such as DNA topoisomerases, or the packaging of DNA on the histone proteins in the nucleosome, or DNA transcription with all its associated proteins such as RNA polymerase and transcription factors, the interactions of nucleic acids with proteins are particularly important to the cell. The type of interaction between proteins and DNA ranges from highly site-specific to completely non-specific. In this section, we will outline the principles of how these two types of interactions occur.

5.6.1 Non-covalent bonding in site-specific binding

The affinity of a protein for DNA is determined in thermodynamic terms by the free energies of the individual components compared to the free energy of the DNA–protein complex. In Chapter 4 you saw that DNA binding proteins, which contain different binding motifs, demonstrate a wide range of thermodynamic strategies (Section 4.6.4, Figure 4.15).

The affinity of a site-specific DNA binding protein for its specific DNA sequence is generally of the order of 10^4–10^7 times greater than its affinity for non-specific sequences. Stable protein–DNA interactions arise from the combination of non-covalent interactions that we have seen in other macromolecules: hydrogen bonding, electrostatic interactions, hydrophobic interactions and van der Waals forces. These interactions can occur between protein side-chain groups and either the DNA deoxyribose–phosphate backbone or the bases. There are many types of proteins that interact with DNA, both specifically and non-specifically. Below we will briefly consider examples of how each of these types of interaction occurs, to illustrate the principles involved.

5.6.2 The recognition of specific DNA sequences by proteins

Transcription factors act by binding to specific DNA regions, dependent upon the recognition of particular sequences of bases, usually through direct interactions in the major groove. They are known to use certain motifs for DNA binding and many contain the helix–turn–helix (HTH) or zinc finger motifs that were described in Chapter 3 (Section 3.2.3, Table 3.3). We will now discuss the molecular properties of these two protein motifs that confer DNA binding ability on the proteins that contain them.

The classical HTH motif consists of two α-helical segments connected by a turn in the peptide chain that allows the helices to cross over each other (see Table 3.3). One of the helices serves to position the second *recognition* helix into the major groove of DNA, wherein specific hydrogen-bond formation occurs with the bases exposed in the groove. An example of this interaction is shown in Figure 5.22a and b for the Ultrabithorax (Ubx) homeodomain protein, a member of a family of proteins that play a critical role in *Drosophila* development. In this case, the protein utilizes two supporting helices to direct the recognition domain, comprising a third

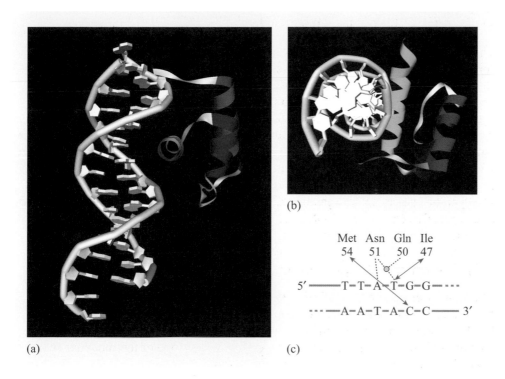

Figure 5.22
(a) and (b) Interaction between *Drosophila* Ubx protein and DNA showing the positioning of a recognition helix (cyan) in the major groove, supported by two other helices (red and pink), in side and top-down views (based on pdb file 1b8i). Only one of the DNA binding domains is shown. (c) Recognition between the protein and bases is mediated through both hydrogen bonding (red dashed lines) and hydrophobic interactions (blue double-headed arrows). In the case of Asn 51 and Gln 50 of Ubx, hydrogen bonding to the thymine involves a water molecule (shown here as a blue circle).

helix, into the major groove. The two views of this interaction show how the recognition domain is positioned within the major groove. The interactions between the Ubx recognition domain and DNA are mediated by hydrogen bonds and non-polar interactions, as shown in Figure 5.22c.

The zinc finger motif consists of a protein domain within which either a pair of cysteines and a pair of histidines (Cys–His) or two pairs of cysteines (Cys–Cys) act together to coordinate a zinc ion (Figure 5.23a). The stretch of polypeptide in between these pairs of amino acids loops out and folds into a finger-shaped configuration. Much of the specificity of binding within the major groove resides in several amino acid residues in each finger, each finger recognizing a three-base 'target' sequence in the DNA. An example of this interaction is shown in Figure 5.23b, where the mouse Zif 268 protein is shown interacting with a DNA helix. This protein carries three Cys–His fingers which can be seen lying within the major groove.

Within each finger, three specific amino acids, Arg, Glu and Arg, are responsible for the specificity of the recognition site – in this case, three figures interact with three sequential DNA triplets of 3'-GCG-5', as shown in Figure 5.23c.

Extensive studies have been undertaken to determine a code that links specific amino acids to specific target triplets so that the DNA target sequences for any zinc finger-containing protein can be identified more easily. This would prove useful, as zinc finger-containing proteins are extremely common. For example, the *Drosophila* genome encodes 230 such proteins with an average of three fingers per protein and the human genome encodes almost 600 zinc finger-containing proteins with an average of eight fingers per protein.

☐ What technique, that you have already come across, could be used to generate zinc finger proteins and/or target DNAs to investigate the specific interaction?

Figure 5.23
(a) Zinc finger domains coordinate a single zinc ion and are either Cys–His (as here) or Cys–Cys types.
(b) Molecular model view of the binding of the mouse Zif 268 protein to DNA: three zinc fingers (cyan) lie within the major groove of the helix; the zinc atoms are shown in yellow (based on pdb file 1aay).
(c) Specific recognition of a target DNA by Zif 268 is a result of interactions between three amino acids and a triplet recognition sequence for each zinc finger (based upon data presented in Bulyk *et al.*, 2001).

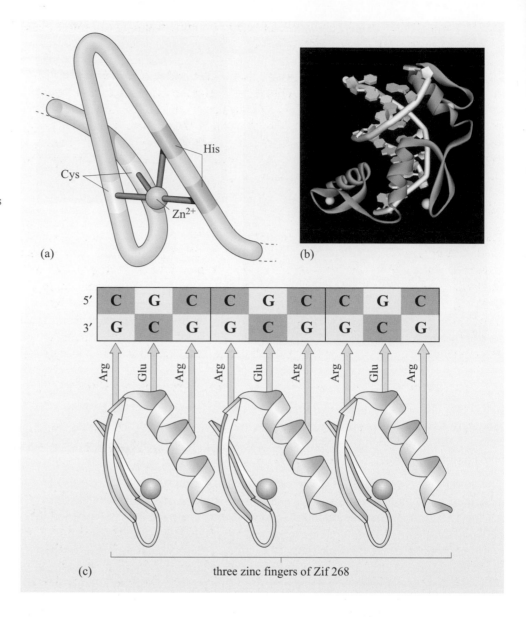

■ Genetic engineering techniques such as site-directed mutagenesis (Chapter 3, Section 3.8.1) could be used to create both novel zinc fingers and target DNAs for such studies.

There are now computer programs that can apply DNA recognition rules for contacts between amino acid side-chains in a recognition domain and DNA bases in the major groove, to analyse transcription factor families, including the helix–turn–helix and the zinc finger proteins. Whilst these programs cannot predict the binding sites for engineered proteins, they can be used to create a generalized framework on the basis of which mutagenesis experiments can be designed. A direct examination of the strength of binding between an engineered protein and its target DNA is then assessed experimentally.

○ From your studies in Chapter 4, what techniques could be used to determine the strength of interaction (binding) between an engineered protein and its target DNA?

⬤   Isothermal titration calorimetry (ITC), and differential scanning calorimetry (DSC) are two such techniques (Section 4.6.1).

In both zinc finger- and HTH-containing proteins, specific protein domains are utilized to increase the non-covalent bonding opportunities and hence the affinity and specificity of the protein–DNA interaction. You should notice, however, that the protein–DNA interface is not restricted to these domains, but that much of the rest of the DNA binding protein is in close proximity to the DNA chains. Interactions between these parts of the protein and the DNA, though non-specific, contribute to the overall binding affinity of the protein.

5.6.3 Non-specific DNA–protein interactions

As we saw above, most sequence-specific DNA binding proteins recognize and bind to their target DNA sequence with a high affinity by utilizing structural domains that make sequence-specific contacts with the DNA bases in the major groove. These contacts utilize extensive non-covalent bonding and hydrophobic interactions. In contrast, non-specific protein–DNA interactions occur with much lower affinity. The reason for this low binding affinity is that most non-sequence-specific interactions between protein and DNA involve only weak interactions, primarily electrostatic in nature, between the protein and the negatively charged DNA backbone.

▢   What proteins, that you have already encountered, must interact with DNA in this manner?

⬤   Your examples could include DNA topoisomerases, DNA polymerase and RNA polymerase, all of which must interact very closely with DNA. You will encounter many similar proteins throughout the course.

The major feature of proteins that interact with DNA in a non-sequence-specific manner is that they contain surfaces or structures that carry positively charged amino acid side-chains. Various common protein structures provide a framework for placement of these basic amino acids in positions that are complementary to the arrangement of phosphates, either *along* the DNA backbone or *across* the minor and major grooves. These protein structures include α helices and antiparallel β strands that can interact electrostatically with the major or minor groove phosphates, which are approximately 7 Å apart along the phosphate–deoxyribose backbone. In the case of α helices, the positioning of basic residues on the external faces of the helix could influence DNA-binding preferences and the recognition of either a particular local structure or the global configuration of the DNA. An example of a common motif is the SPKK motif ([Ser/Thr]–Pro–[Lys/Arg]–[Lys/Arg]), which is found in a variety of proteins that bind to the minor groove of DNA.

5.6.4 Conformational changes upon protein–DNA interactions

During binding, both the protein and the DNA can alter their conformation. In the case of proteins, this conformational change can involve small changes in side-chain location, but can also involve local refolding. These changes upon binding of specific DNA sequences serve to facilitate the interaction and also to enhance the binding of other proteins, such as when dimerization of two proteins occurs at a single recognition site. Changes such as these can be the basis of cooperative binding effects between proteins, where binding of one protein can enhance the binding of another.

Changes in DNA conformation also occur upon protein binding. Common conformational changes are bending of the DNA backbone or local untwisting of the helix. An example of this alteration to a short stretch of DNA helix is given in Figure 5.24, which shows the binding of a protein called TATA binding protein (TBP) to its recognition site (a sequence of eight base pairs containing the sequence TATA) in a eukaryotic gene promoter. Note how this short DNA duplex is almost bent back on itself. TBP is an evolutionarily highly conserved protein and binding of its specific recognition sequence occurs through interactions with DNA in the minor groove.

○ Why does the binding of TBP to the minor groove appear to present a paradox?

● As a sequence-specific binding protein, TBP needs to be able to detect the bases that are 'shielded' within the minor groove of B-DNA. As discussed extensively above, most DNA recognition interactions occur in the major groove where bases are exposed (see Figure 5.9b).

To achieve interactions with the bases, upon binding to DNA, TBP inserts the side-chains of two hydrophobic phenylalanine residues between the bases in the minor groove, thereby disrupting base stacking – in a similar way to an intercalating agent – and causing the helix to untwist at the site of interaction.

○ What effect would this untwisting have upon the space between adjacent base pairs and the turn per base pair? (You may want to refresh your memory of normal B-DNA structure, covered in Section 5.3.1.)

● It reduces the turn for each base pair and widens the spacing between bases.

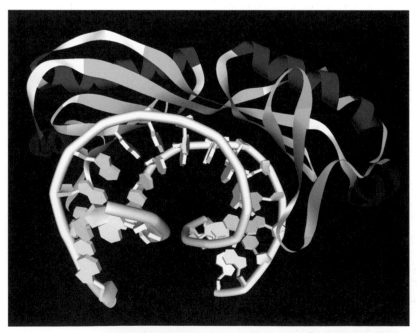

Figure 5.24   The binding of TBP to its target DNA sequence results in conformational changes in DNA; the DNA backbone is represented as tubes (based on pdb file 1cdw).

Binding of TBP to its target DNA sequence actually decreases the turn in the DNA helix from 36° to 21° and bases are stretched apart to 5.5 Å separation, compared to 3.4 Å in B-DNA. The width of the minor groove effectively doubles, whilst at the same time it becomes shallower, bringing TBP into contact with the bases. Binding specificity is achieved through numerous hydrophobic interactions between TBP amino acid side-chains and atoms in the eight base-pairs that constitute the recognition site. Thus, by inducing an alteration in DNA conformation, specificity of interaction is achieved.

The effect of TBP binding is a bending and kinking of the helix backbone, shown in Figure 5.24. As a result, areas of the DNA chain are brought into closer proximity to each other. We will discuss further the function of TBP and the role that this DNA bending plays when we deal with transcription in Chapter 10.

Summary of Section 5.6

1   Sequence-specific protein–DNA interactions are achieved through the formation of non-covalent bonds between amino acid side-chains in the protein and bases in the major groove of the DNA.

2   Non-sequence-specific protein–DNA interactions are achieved primarily through electrostatic interactions between positively charged amino acid side-chains and the negatively charged DNA backbone.

3   Protein and DNA conformation can be altered after binding, which can enhance further binding of proteins through cooperativity, or cause structural alterations to the DNA helix.

5.7 DNA packaging and chromatin

Until now, we have discussed DNA primarily as a double helix, but in its natural state within the cell it is found packaged as a complex mixture with many different proteins and other components. You have already seen examples of proteins with specific roles to play, such as topoisomerases and the proteins with various DNA binding domains, but in this section we will turn our attention to the proteins that serve to pack and organize the DNA into what we call chromatin.

The packaging of the long DNA chains in chromatin essentially plays three critical roles within the cell.

1   *Protection.* The intrinsic chemical properties of DNA and its reactions with reactive agents generated within the cell or from exposure to the environment make it extremely vulnerable to both chemical and physical damage, as you saw in Section 5.5. This DNA damage could be deleterious or even lethal to the cell, through the loss or mutation of genetic information encoded by the ordered base pairs. Whilst several specialist DNA repair systems exist to repair much of this damage (to be discussed in Chapter 9), part of the front-line protection against damage is provided by packaging chromosomal DNA into chromatin. The packaging components, which are found in great abundance within the cell, serve to protect the chemically vulnerable sites in the DNA backbone and bases, as well as shielding the long strands of DNA from physical forces that could cause it to break.

2   *Compaction.* If you glance back to Table 5.1, you can see that the amounts of DNA that cells contain are large. Packaging serves to compact the extremely long strands of DNA into a size that will fit within the living cell. In the case of the *E. coli* bacterial chromosome, this compaction is over 1000-fold, condensing the single 4.6 Mb (4 600 000 bp) chromosome, with an extended length of 1 mm, into a structure between 0.5 and 1 μm in length. Even greater compaction is required in eukaryotic cells. For example, an average human chromosome, with a naked DNA length of over 10 cm, is compacted down over 10 000-fold to less then 10 μm. In order to compact and package DNA to such levels, the DNA helix itself also undergoes changes, with the ATP-dependent formation of supercoils through the action of specialist enzymes such as DNA topoisomerases (discussed in Section 5.3.2).

3   *DNA metabolism.* The DNA within both prokaryotic and eukaryotic cells is, of course, the storage facility for the cell's genetic information and chromosomes serve as platforms for key cell processes and systems. These include transcription, which must occur within the context of chromatin, and DNA storage and segregation, in which specialist chromatin components play central roles. DNA metabolism is itself a dynamic process and chromatin plays central roles in processes such as transcription; so it is not surprising that chromatin components themselves are very dynamic, changing with the cell cycle and, in multicellular organisms, differing between cell lineages.

In this section, we will focus on the components of chromatin of prokaryotic and eukaryotic cells and how these contribute to the three roles outlined above. The various roles of chromatin components and their contribution to the chromosomal environment in gene transcription, DNA replication and repair will be discussed in greater detail in subsequent chapters.

5.7.1 The eubacterial chromosome

Some of the diverse roles of chromatin components can be illustrated by examining the *E. coli* chromosome. Like most prokaryotes, *E. coli* has a single chromosome consisting of a single double-stranded circular DNA molecule. There is no nucleus present, but the *E. coli* DNA is within a discrete entity in the cytoplasm called the **nucleoid.** The nucleoid contains a multitude of proteins and is in close proximity to the ribosomes, where translation occurs. In addition to proteins, small, highly positively charged compounds called polyamines are present.

◯   Based upon what you have learnt about the structure of the DNA double helix, what function do you think polyamines play in packaging DNA?

◼   The highly positively charged polyamines serve to bind to and counteract the negative charges of the phosphates in the DNA helical backbone, thus aiding compaction by eliminating repulsive forces.

These polyamines include **spermine** and **spermidine**, whose structures are shown in Figure 5.25. They play key roles in assisting with DNA packaging and illustrate a central principle that applies to all DNA packaging systems: in order to compact long DNA strands, the intramolecular repulsive forces must be overcome.

$$\overset{+}{H_3N}-(CH_2)_3-\overset{+}{NH_2}-(CH_2)_4-\overset{+}{NH_2}-(CH_2)_3-\overset{+}{NH_3}$$
spermine

$$\overset{+}{H_3N}-(CH_2)_4-\overset{+}{NH_2}-(CH_2)_3-\overset{+}{NH_3}$$
spermidine

Figure 5.25
Spermine and spermidine are two highly positively charged small molecules present in *E. coli* that facilitate DNA packaging by helping to counteract the repulsive forces between stretches of the negatively charged DNA backbone.

In addition to polyamines, over 20 proteins are found as structural components of *E. coli* chromatin. They have diverse functions, but we will discuss several that are important in the process of chromosome packaging. The eubacterial chromosome is highly dynamic, with virtually continuous transcription and/or replication. As such, the many proteins found associated with DNA in these organisms are intimately involved in this metabolism, in contrast to the primarily more structural role played by such proteins in eukaryotic cells.

Mitochondria and chloroplasts contain their own genetic material in the form of circular or linear DNA strands that encode various proteins essential for the organelle's function and maintenance. Both these organelles are considered, in evolutionary terms, to have origins in ancient symbiotic relationships with Eubacteria, as discussed in Chapter 1. Support for this view is found in the structure of the chromosomes within these organelles. The DNA in both mitochondria and chloroplasts is packaged with proteins that are related to those found in many Eubacteria.

DNA supercoiling and protein binding in the E. coli *chromosome*

As discussed earlier, the DNA of the *E. coli* chromosome is highly negatively supercoiled due to the action of the DNA gyrase enzyme (Section 5.3.2). This negative supercoiling serves to assist in compaction of the DNA, with the repulsive forces of the sugar–phosphate backbones being counteracted by polyamines. Many of the proteins that are major components of the chromosome play roles in both its packaging and in the metabolic processes that take place on the DNA. These proteins are often called the 'histone-like' proteins, not because of any sequence similarity to the eukaryotic histone proteins, but because, like the histones, they are small, basic (and therefore positively charged) DNA-binding proteins. Three such proteins, called HU, H-NS and IHF, are shown in Figure 5.26. We will describe briefly their roles in DNA packaging in *E. coli*.

The HU, H-NS and IHF proteins all function as dimers. The HU and H-NS proteins both interact with chromosomal DNA non-specifically and serve to stabilize negative supercoils in the DNA. Whilst they do not bind DNA in a sequence-specific manner, both these proteins show some preference for binding DNA that has a 'bendable' structure. The HU protein is one of the most common proteins on the *E. coli* chromosome and it plays a central role in stabilizing the compacted chromosome structure. An *E. coli* contains approximately 20 000 molecules of the H-NS protein, which binds approximately once every 300–400 bp along the chromosome. HU and H-NS help compact the DNA strand, but each also plays supporting roles in replication and transcription by establishing or maintaining appropriate structural and torsional environments for these processes.

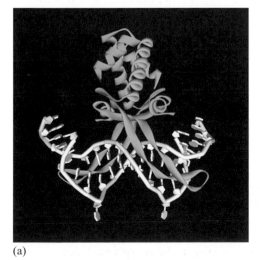
(a)

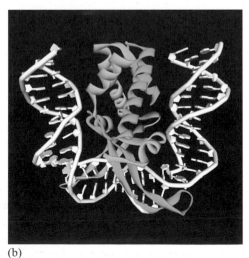
(b)

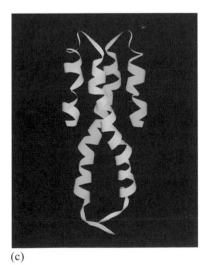
(c)

Figure 5.26   (a) The HU protein dimer complexed with DNA (pdb file 1p51). (b) Binding of an *E. coli* IHF dimer to DNA induces a 180° turn (pdb file 1ihf). (c) Structure of the N-terminal domain of *E. coli* H-NS dimer (pdb file 1lr1). All structures show protein secondary structures and tubular DNA.

The IHF dimer binds DNA such that two central α helices cross at the core of the structure, as shown in Figure 5.26b. Note how the two separate subunits cross over and two 'fingers' extend around the DNA strand into the minor groove. Binding of IHF induces almost a 180° bend in the DNA over a 40 bp region – one of the largest DNA bends induced by any DNA binding protein identified to date. Rather like TBP, IHF utilizes two hydrophobic residues (in this case, prolines), which are located on the tips of these fingers, to intercalate between bases. In forming hydrophobic bonds with the bases, the proline residues disrupt the base stacking of the DNA. Numerous positively charged residues that contribute to the bending process lie along the body of the protein. Bends in DNA such as those introduced by HU, H-NS and IHF assist in chromosome compaction.

The DPS protein compacts the eubacterial chromosome during stress

When an *E. coli* cell enters into stationary phase, transcription and cell division cease completely. In such cells, the normal chromatin components, such as those described above, are replaced by a negatively charged protein called DPS. The interaction between DPS and DNA appears to be a specialized bacterial adaptation to survive starvation. In normal conditions of growth, the DNA within the bacterial cell is distributed evenly throughout the entire cytoplasm. In stationary cells, however, the DNA undergoes a dramatic change in its properties. Rather than being distributed evenly, it becomes localized as a tightly packaged, almost crystal-like structure associated with the DPS protein. This DNA, when examined *in vitro*, is protected from both enzymatic digestion by DNAases and from oxidative damage by hydrogen peroxide.

◯ What is apparently contradictory in the interaction between the negatively charged DPS protein and DNA?

◼ As discussed earlier, DNA carries a negatively charged backbone and yet it interacts with the negatively charged DPS protein.

The transition to this highly protected and condensed state is believed to be signalled by a reduction in the environmental concentration of divalent cations (e.g. Mg^{2+}), which the bacterium uses as an indicator of the availability of nutrients. At a critical cation concentration, the remaining cations within the cell are thought to form cationic bridges between the DPS protein and the DNA helix. Importantly, no energy expenditure is required to form or maintain the DPS–cation–DNA complex within the cell. In times of decreased nutrient availability and limited energy supply, the purely chemical nature of this transition provides obvious advantages. This DNA structure persists until environmental conditions alter, leading to reversal of the tight packaging.

Similar strategies are adopted in other organisms, including plant seeds and spores, in which the cell cannot use energy-dependent repair processes to protect its genetic material. Under extreme conditions, such tight protein–DNA interactions serve to protect genomic DNA from damage.

5.7.2 The eukaryotic chromosome

Whilst the bulk of eukaryotic DNA is packaged by proteins different from those in the eubacterial chromosome, the principles of bending DNA and neutralizing the negative charges in its backbone are shared. Eukaryotic cells have considerably larger genomes than do prokaryotes (in most cases over 1000 times the size of the *E. coli* genome – see Table 5.1) and the DNA is found in the form of long linear chromosomes which are partitioned from the rest of the cell, within the nucleus.

Several degrees of DNA packaging and compaction are found within the eukaryotic nucleus, primarily reflecting the transcriptional and structural status of the DNA. The extent of DNA packaging also varies according to the stage of the cell cycle. For example, immediately prior to cell division, the DNA is particularly compacted and forms highly condensed structures suitable for physical separation at mitosis. The different degrees of packaging will be discussed later, but for now we will focus on the major protein components of eukaryotic chromatin, the histones.

The histone proteins

The genes for the histone proteins are very highly conserved across eukaryotes, reflecting their importance in DNA packaging. The histone family consists of five groups of proteins, histones H1, H2A, H2B, H3 and H4. An examination of their amino acid content gives us clues as to how the histones fulfil their role in DNA packaging. Rather like the polyamines in bacteria, these proteins are highly positively charged, with up to 20% of their amino acids being lysine or arginine, the charged side-chains serving to counteract the negative charges of the phosphate groups on the double helix backbone.

Further analyses of the genes for the histones H2A, H2B, H3 and H4 reveal that they have highly similar sequences, suggesting that this gene family arose from a single common ancestral gene, most likely through gene duplication. An example of how highly conserved these genes are is seen in the amino acid sequence of histone H4, which differs by only two amino acids over 102 residues between such evolutionarily distant species as the pea and the cow. Histones H2A, H2B, H3 and H4 are collectively known as the 'core' histones and all share a common structural motif called the **histone fold**, comprising three α helices connected by two loops (Figure 5.27). This histone fold provides the basic unit of DNA packaging in eukaryotic cells.

Outside of the region of the histone fold, the N-terminus of the histone forms a 'tail' comprising between 20 and 40 amino acids and having no defined secondary structure. The histone tails are very rich in lysine residues. These positively charged residues serve as targets for various secondary modifications such as methylation or acetylation which can neutralize their charge. Such modifications play a key role in the regulation of chromatin structure and will be discussed in more detail shortly.

The histone fold and formation of the nucleosome

We have seen how in the eubacterial chromosome, bending DNA serves to facilitate its compaction. A similar process occurs in eukaryotic cells in that DNA is bent and wrapped around a protein unit. In this case, the core unit is a protein–DNA complex termed a **nucleosome**. The nucleosome comprises the core histone proteins H2A, H2B, H3 and H4 arranged in a structure known as the **core histone octamer**, with an associated length of DNA. In order to understand how the nucleosome is assembled, we first need to study the structure of the individual histones that it contains.

Each histone protein folds to give the histone fold motif as shown in Figure 5.27. This folding involves the two small α helices (domains I and III) crossing over the central α helix (domain II). Note that the N-terminal 'tail' is not part of this fold but

Figure 5.27

Structure of the histone fold and assembly of the core histone octamer from component histone proteins. The symbols in the N-terminal region represent key lysine and serine residues that are subject to modification.

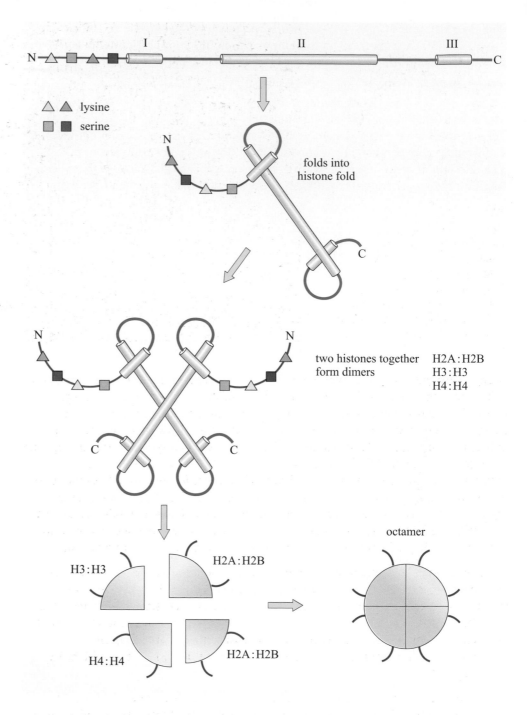

extends freely. The next stage is the dimerization of two of these folded histones through the crossing-over of the two central helices (domains II). Dimerization occurs between two molecules of H3 or H4, but histones H2A and H2B form H2A : H2B heterodimers. Finally, one each of H3 : H3 and H4 : H4 and two H2A : H2B dimers come together to form the core histone octamer. This structure resembles a small cylinder with the eight N-terminal tails protruding freely from it.

Between 146 and 180 bp of DNA can be wrapped in two turns around the histone octamer unit to form the nucleosome, the structure of which is shown in Figure 5.28. The DNA wraps around the histone octamer rather like a thread

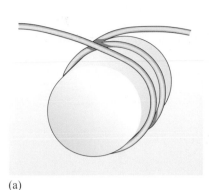

(a)

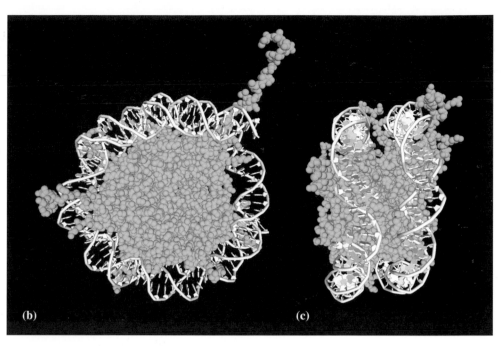

(b)   (c)

Figure 5.28   Structure of the nucleosome. (a) Pictorial representation showing DNA wrapped twice around the nucleosome core. Space-filling molecular views: (b) end on and (c) from the side of the nucleosome, with tubular DNA (pdb file 1aoi)

wrapped around a spool. Contact between the two components (DNA and protein) is between the DNA backbone and the surface of the octamer edges. The many interactions between the negatively charged DNA backbone and the positively charged histone proteins serve to stabilize the structure. Note that the interaction between the histone proteins and the DNA is not sequence-specific; thus the histone octamer is able to bind DNA of any sequence. As the DNA wraps around the octamer, torsional stress is introduced into it such that for every nucleosome, two left-handed superhelical turns are introduced into the DNA. If you look back at Figure 5.11b, you can see that one conformation adopted by supercoiled DNA is a solenoid. The DNA wrapped around an octamer adopts just such a conformation. Thus supercoiling of DNA is accommodated or maintained by the nucleosomes.

Along each long DNA chain within the eukaryotic nucleus it is estimated that, at any one time, over 80% of the DNA is packaged within nucleosomes. Between the nucleosomes are small lengths of 'linker' DNA. The location of a nucleosome along any particular stretch of duplex DNA, such as relative to regulatory elements in a gene's promoter, is called **translational positioning**. This positioning determines whether any segment of DNA lies within a nucleosome or within the linker region.

When isolated chromatin is partially denatured and examined under the EM, it is seen to have a 'beads on a string' structure known as the **10 nm fibre**, being about 10 nm thick (Figure 5.29a and b). The DNA that is wrapped around the histone octamer is inaccessible to many chemicals and enzymes, fulfilling a primary objective of DNA packaging. This protection of DNA can be exploited as a means of determining which part of any one region of DNA is or isn't associated with the octamer. If chromatin is isolated from a eukaryotic nucleus and treated with a nuclease that cleaves the DNA double helix, the DNA helix will be cleaved where it is unprotected, i.e. in the 'linker' regions. An analysis of the DNA isolated from this preparation using agarose gel electrophoresis reveals a ladder of nucleosomal fragments (Figure 5.29c).

Figure 5.29
Nucleosomal DNA analysis.
(a) Pictorial representation showing nucleosomes along a DNA strand (top) being treated with a nuclease that cleaves between nucleosomes (red arrows) to generate DNA chains carrying one, two or three nucleosomes.
(b) Electron micrograph of partially denatured nucleosomal DNA showing the typical 'beads on a string' appearance.
(c) Partial digestion of nucleosomal DNA linker regions with a micrococcal nuclease gives a mixture of fragments containing different numbers of nucleosomes, as in (a). The DNA from two chromatin samples treated in this way is shown, analysed by gel electrophoresis, revealing a ladder of fragments that correspond to different lengths of DNA. The fragments in successive bands differ in length by a stretch of DNA equivalent to one nucleosome repeat length (146 bp). Shown for comparison is the result of micrococcal nuclease digestion of naked DNA: a smear of fragments due to random cleavage.

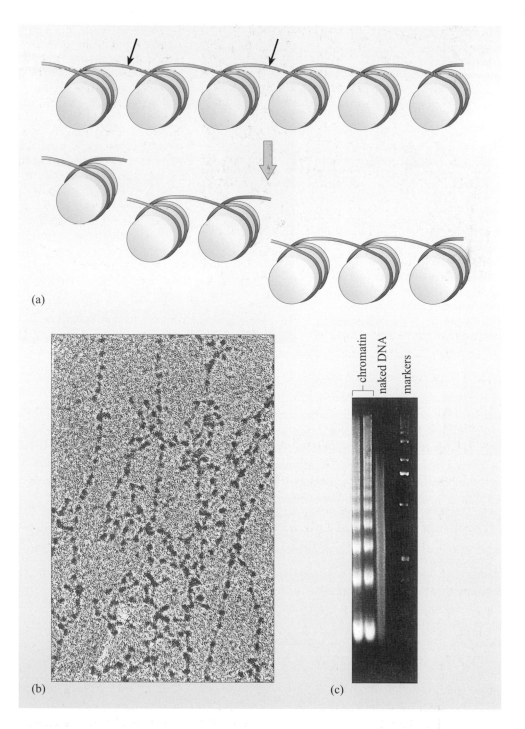

The precise position of the octamer core along any one DNA strand can also influence which 'face' of the helix is exposed on the surface of the nucleosome. Recall that helical B-form DNA has minor and major grooves and that most sequence-specific DNA interactions with proteins occur in the major groove where the bases are 'accessible' for recognition. The positioning of the nucleosome relative to the rotation of the DNA helix is called **rotational positioning**. If the position of the helix on the octamer is such that the bases of a particular region are facing into the core unit, the recognition site will not be accessible (Figure 5.30).

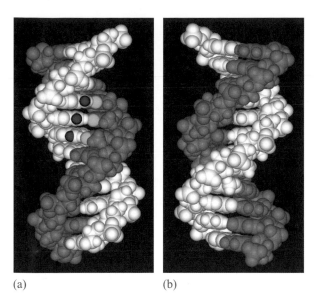

(a) (b)

Figure 5.30
Rotational positioning of DNA helix on the nucleosomal surface. The relative rotation of the DNA helix upon the surface of the nucleosome results in the major groove lying (a) face-out or (b) face-in. The DNA is shown as space filling, with strands coloured white and grey. Highlighted are the critical atoms within the adenine (C6 amino hydrogen, cyan) and thymine (C4 oxygen, blue) bases of the 5′-AAA/TTT recognition sequence with which proteins binding to this target site within the major groove would interact (see Figure 5.9c).

○ Consider the Zif 268 protein (Figure 5.23). What would the effect be if the 9 bp recognition sequence was positioned as in Figure 5.30b?

● The protein could not bind, as the major groove is inaccessible.

Thus the position of the nucleosome and rotation of the DNA upon it can influence accessibility of the DNA to proteins. Note that this is also the case for proteins that bind in the minor groove, such as TBP. The positioning of a nucleosome is dependent upon many factors including the presence of proteins bound to DNA, which serve to direct which face is accessible. Only very small rotations in DNA helix (5–6 base pairs) relative to the nucleosome core are required to shield or expose sites in the major groove. This provides an obvious point at which regulation can occur. We will discuss the assembly and positioning of nucleosomes upon DNA further in relation to DNA replication in Chapter 9 and transcription in Chapter 10.

Nucleosomal DNA packaging into a 30 nm fibre: the role of histone H1

When chromatin is isolated from the nucleus and examined under the electron microscope, it can be seen as a **30 nm fibre**. This fibre is formed through the action of the histone H1 on the nucleosomal DNA in the 10 nm fibre. In contrast to the other histone proteins, H1 does not contain the histone fold motif.

Compaction of the 10 nm fibre to give the 30 nm fibre is achieved by interaction of the H1 protein with both the linker DNA and the histone octamers, as shown in Figure 5.31. The H1 protein is rich in lysine residues, which are able to neutralize the negatively charged backbone. The C-terminal tail of H1, which interacts with the linker DNA regions between the nucleosomes, is critical in this respect. The lysine-rich N-terminal tails of the octamer histone proteins also make a major contribution to neutralizing the negative charge of the DNA backbone and facilitating compaction. As well as compacting the DNA, the pulling together of nucleosomes in this way shields both the exposed linker DNA regions and the exposed DNA faces on nucleosomal DNA. Thus H1-mediated compaction serves to further regulate access to DNA.

Figure 5.31
(a) Compaction of nucleosomal
DNA into 30 nm fibres through
interaction with histone H1.
(b) A schematic representation of
the structure of a histone H1 protein
molecule wrapped into the linker
DNA and nucleosomal DNA.

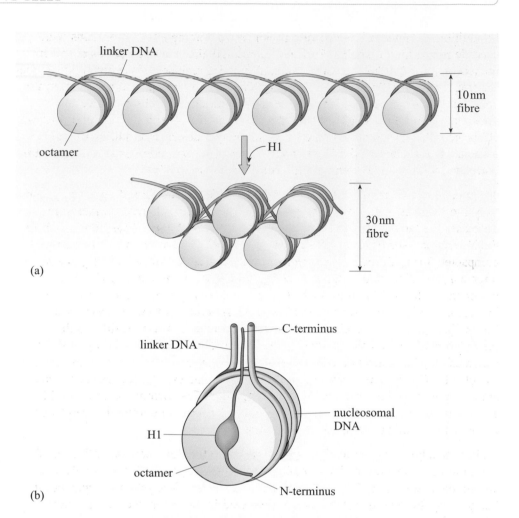

The genes encoding H1 histones are evolutionarily less well conserved than those
that encode the core histones, but similar lysine-rich, positively charged proteins are
found in organisms as diverse as fungi and protoctists, indicating that the role of
the 'linker' histone is well conserved. There are also many variant forms of H1 and
in several cases it is replaced by specialist proteins or other molecules. One example
of packaging being assisted by another molecule is the formation of highly
compacted chromatin in sperm where a variant H1 combines with positively
charged molecules called **protamines** to package DNA.

Core histone tail modification regulates DNA compaction

☐   What effect would neutralizing the positive charges on the octamer N-terminal
     tails have upon the compaction of DNA by H1?

◼   As the overall charge contribution from the octamer tails will be decreased, you
     would predict that compaction would be decreased.

As discussed earlier, the degree of compaction mediated by H1 is heavily influenced
by the charge status of the N-terminal tails of the octamer proteins, as these assist
in neutralizing repulsive forces. Covalent modification of these histone tails can
affect their net charge and thus their ability to mediate compaction of the DNA.

In addition, octamer tail modifications can create binding sites for proteins with specific recognition domains. Such proteins could alter the interactions between nucleosomes and influence compaction. The lysine residues of the core histone tails are frequently modified through the addition of methyl groups and acetyl groups or combinations of these. Similarly, the serine residues can also be modified by phosphorylation. Figure 5.32a shows four sites on the N-terminal region of histone H3 protein that are commonly modified. In many cases, such modifications are associated with transcriptional potential such as gene activation or silencing, or are correlated with cellular events such as mitosis (Figure 5.32b).

The most common modification of core histones is the addition of an acetyl group to lysine residues, which effectively removes the positive charge and therefore decreases the tails' ability to interact with the DNA backbone. Thus regions where the N-terminal tails of histones are extensively acetylated are less able to form compacted 30 nm fibres. In such regions, the DNA is described as being in a more open conformation, and is more accessible to transcription factors and DNA polymerases. Modification of the histone protein tails by acetylation is regulated by a family of **histone acetyltransferases (HAT)** and **histone deacetylases (HDAC)**. A family of proteins containing **SET domains** is responsible for the methylation of amino acid residues in the histone N-terminal tails. Many of these enzymes play key roles in the regulation of gene expression, as we will discuss in Chapter 10. Certain chemicals are known to inhibit histone deacetylase action and are commonly used to examine chromatin function. One example is trichostatin A. Treatment of cells with this drug results in the alteration of chromatin acetylation levels, with resulting alterations in gene expression.

As has already been described, it is possible to analyse how compact a region of chromatin is by examining its accessibility or sensitivity to nucleases. Analysis of chromatin sensitivity to DNAase I can be used to identify regulatory sequences in the genome. In regions of the genome protected in more compacted chromatin, DNAase I cannot access the DNA to cleave it. Regions where the chromatin fibre is less compacted have exposed stretches of DNA which are accessible to the

Figure 5.32
(a) Locations of residues in the N-terminal region of histone H3 that are subject to modification.
(b) Examples of specific modifications in the histone H3 N-terminal tail region associated with various cellular events.

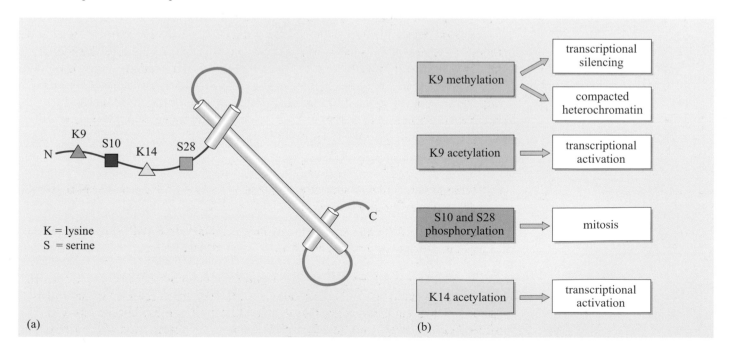

(a)

K9
S10
K14
S28
N

C

K = lysine
S = serine

(b)

K9 methylation	transcriptional silencing
	compacted heterochromatin
K9 acetylation	transcriptional activation
S10 and S28 phosphorylation	mitosis
K14 acetylation	transcriptional activation

DNAase I enzyme, so cleavage occurs. Analysis of chromatin susceptibility to DNAase I can be combined with restriction analysis and a Southern blot to reveal areas around genes that are accessible and hence most likely to be important sequences in gene regulation, as shown in Figure 5.33.

In addition to variations in the compactness of chromatin across a gene, the level of histone tail acetylation can also show very specific patterns, as illustrated in Figure 5.34. This figure shows the pattern of both DNAase I hypersensitivity and acetylation of H3 at lysine residue 9 (abbreviated as H3-K9-Ac) across the chicken

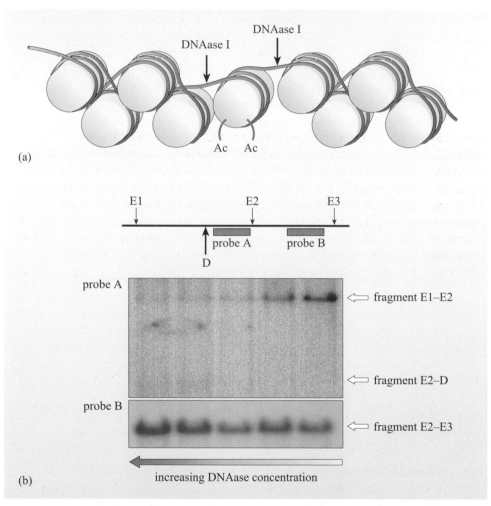

Figure 5.33   DNAase I hypersensitivity of chromatin. (a) Acetylation of the core histone tails causes the affected part of the chromatin structure to open up, making the DNA hypersensitive to cleavage by DNAase I. (b) Example of a DNAase hypersensitivity assay in the human FMR1 gene promoter region. Here, chromatin isolated from the nuclei of white blood cells was incubated with increasing amounts of DNAase I for 10 minutes, after which the DNA was separated from the chromatin proteins and treated with the restriction enzyme *Eco* RI (E = site of *Eco* RI cleavage). This DNA was then resolved by agarose gel electrophoresis, the fragments transferred by Southern blot to a membrane, and the fragment containing the FMR1 promoter detected using a specific hybridization probe (A). Treatment with increasing amounts of DNAase I causes the *Eco* RI fragment E1–E2, detected by probe A, to be cleaved at a single site (red arrow). Cleavage at this site reduces the intensity of the E1–E2 fragment and generates a smaller fragment (E2–D) (very pale). Hybridization of the same filter with probe B on the adjacent *Eco* RI fragment (E2–E3) serves as a control. This site of DNAase I hypersensitivity corresponds to the transcription start site of the FMR1 gene.

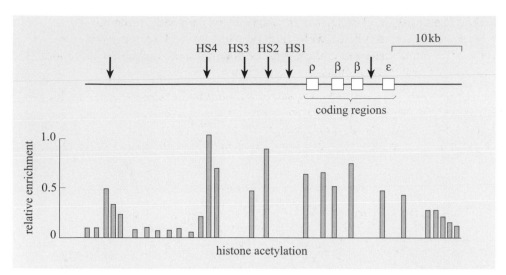

Figure 5.34
Chromatin analysis across the chicken β-globin gene cluster, which comprises four genes: adult (two β) and developmental (ρ and ε). Top: map of the locus indicating six DNAase I hypersensitive sites (red arrows), shown in relation to the coding regions of the β-globin genes; four of these hypersensitive sites (HS1–4) are known to be important in gene regulation. Bottom: the distribution of H3-K9-Ac across the locus as detected by chromatin immunoprecipitation (ChIp).

β-globin locus. At the top is a map of the genomic region, with the sites of hypersensitivity to DNAase I identified by arrows and the position of the β-globin gene cluster transcription units highlighted. Hypersensitivity sites HS1–4 play critical roles in gene regulation. The lower part of the figure shows the level of H3-K9 acetylation across this same region, assayed using a technique called **chromatin immunoprecipitation (ChIp)**, which is described in Box 5.3. This example uses an antibody that recognizes the H3-K9 modification. As you can see, the level of acetylation of the H3 N-terminal tail at lysine 9 changes dramatically across the region, being virtually absent over much of the locus, but reaching high levels in discrete positions, several of which correspond to HS sites (such as HS4 and HS2).

Box 5.3   Chromatin immunoprecipitation

Chromatin immunoprecipitation (abbreviated to ChIp) is a sensitive and common technique for analysing which proteins or specific protein modifications are associated with a region of DNA *in vivo*. (Note that this is the same principle as that of co-immunoprecipitation, encountered in Chapter 3, Section 3.8.2.)

Consider the region of DNA shown in Figure 5.35a. The DNA is wrapped into nucleosomes and two specific regions contain acetylated H3 N-terminal tails. Chromatin is isolated and cleaved at the linker regions to yield single nucleosomes and small DNA fragments. Nucleosomes carrying H3-K9-Ac are precipitated from this mixture using an antibody that specifically recognizes the acetylated H3. The precipitated nucleosomes are purified and the DNA extracted from them. PCR is then used to assay for the presence or absence of particular markers sequences – A, B, C and D in the example in Figure 5.35b. As a positive control, purified DNA is used without any immunoprecipitation. In this example, markers B and D are detected in the immunoprecipitated DNA, indicating that these regions of the chromosome were originally associated with nucleosomes containing H3-Ac. Using this approach it is possible to screen large regions of chromosomes *in vivo* for specific histone protein modifications.

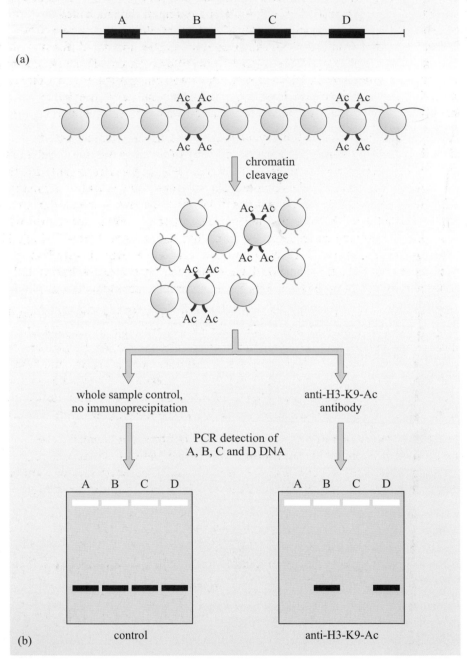

Figure 5.35 ChIp analysis of histone modification in chromatin. (a) A map of a hypothetical stretch of DNA containing four marker sequences, A–D. (b) A stretch of DNA spanning the markers A–D shown complexed with nucleosomes. When subjected to treatment that cleaves the DNA at linker regions, single nucleosomes are generated. An antibody against H3 acetylated at lysine 9 (anti-H3-K9-Ac) is used to precipitate nucleosomes that contain acetylated H3 (right). The DNA is purified from the protein and the presence or absence of marker DNA for the four loci is assessed by PCR. Positive testing for markers B and D indicates that these regions of DNA were originally associated with nucleosomes containing H3-Ac. As a control, this procedure is performed with no immunoprecipitation (left).

Histone tail methylation also varies across eukaryote genomes. Which residue is modified can have a profound effect on the processing of the associated nucleosomal DNA, as the examples below illustrate. Modification at one residue may facilitate expression of a gene, whilst similar modification of a different residue in the same histone tail may result in transcriptional inactivation. These effects may be attributed to alterations in the stability of the chromatin structure, either directly, by affecting the net charge associated with the histone tails, or indirectly, by recruiting specific regulatory proteins to the affected stretch of chromatin.

An extreme case of histone tail methylation in chromatin can be seen with the mammalian X chromosome. In females, one copy of the chromosome is subject to X-inactivation. This chromosome is highly compacted and transcriptionally silent (i.e. inactive). An analysis of the complete chromosome complement of a female cell (shown in Figure 5.36) shows that, in contrast to the rest of the chromosomes, most of the inactivated X chromosome (indicated by the arrow) is not stained when probed with an antibody that recognizes H3 methylated at lysine 4 (H3-K4-Me). The only region of the inactivated X chromosome that is labelled with this antibody is a very small region at the tip of one of the chromosome arms, a region known to be the only portion of this chromosome that is highly transcriptionally active.

Methylation of lysine 9 in histone H3 has a very different effect on transcriptional activity in the fission yeast *S. pombe*. Figure 5.37 illustrates the results of a ChIp analysis of the centromere from one chromosome of *S. pombe*. At the top is a map of the centromere and adjacent upstream and downstream regions and below are the levels of histone H3 methylated at the lysine 9 residue (abbreviated as H3-K9-Me). The pattern of H3-K9-Me modification shows a very clear association with the region around the centromere which is transcriptionally inactive.

As these examples illustrate, whilst the basic unit of chromatin structure, the histone octamer, remains the same across most of the DNA in the eukaryotic genome, the histone tails serve as a platform for many modifications. The pattern of these modifications in relation to their effects is known as the **histone code**.

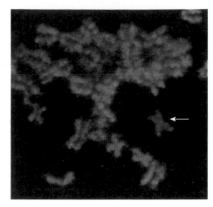

Figure 5.36
Detection of lysine 4 methylation of H3 (H3-K4-Me) in chromosomes (blue) in a female human cell in metaphase using a fluorescently labelled antibody that specifically recognizes H3-K4-Me. Note that staining (red) is absent from the majority of the transcriptionally silent, inactivated X chromosome (indicated by arrow).

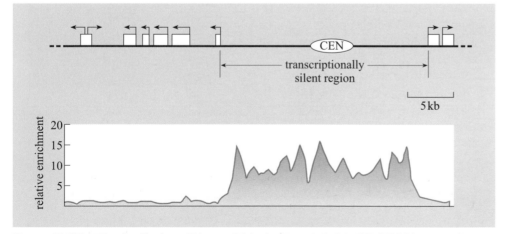

Figure 5.37 The distribution of histone H3 lysine 9 methylation (H3-K9-Me) across the *S. pombe* centromere and adjacent upstream and downstream regions, detected by ChIp analysis. The transcriptionally silent region spanning the centromere is shown. Outside this region, actively transcribed genes are indicated (boxes and arrows).

The modifications of the histone tails discussed here are only a few of the many that are found within the eukaryotic cell. Research to decipher the code in different organisms is still under way. What we can say is that the modifications serve as a signalling system that promotes further interactions and activity from other proteins. For example, many transcriptional activators exert their effect through the local acetylation of histone tails, which in turn establishes a local environment in which transcription can occur.

There are situations where core histone proteins are replaced by specialized components. For example, histone 2AX is found incorporated adjacent to DNA breaks and plays a role in their repair, and a histone H2A variant called macroH2A is associated with the inactivated mammalian X chromosome and is involved in maintaining transcriptional silencing. These histones will be discussed in more detail in Chapters 9 and 10.

Box 5.4   The archaeal chromosome and eukaryote evolution

Archaea lack a nuclear membrane and hence are classified as prokaryotes. However, these organisms exhibit many features in common with eukaryotic cells. Recent studies on Archaea have identified the presence of proteins that, when dimerized, contain structures very similar to the histone fold seen in all eukaryotes. However, unlike their eukaryotic counterparts, these proteins contain no 'tails' (Figure 5.38a).

The dimers are able to wrap the chromosomal DNA into nucleosome-like particles (Figure 5.38b). The core elements of these structures appear to be dimers of a histone-like protein, HMf, with 80 bp of DNA wrapped around a core dimer. The interface with the DNA is dominated by lysine and arginine residues, which serve to counteract the negative charges on the sugar–phosphate DNA backbone.

The exact evolutionary relationship between Archaea and eukaryotes is uncertain, but these and other data suggest that they could share several common features indicative of a common ancestor. The development of a DNA compaction system such as one based on proteins carrying a histone fold structure may have solved the problem of balancing DNA compaction whilst still allowing access to the information stored within the DNA as a transcription template. Interestingly, many of the features of transcription in Archaea are similar to those in eukaryotes, such as the conservation of a TATA box, TBP and sequence similarity between RNA polymerases.

(a)

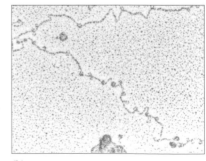

(b)

Figure 5.38   (a) The structure of the archaeal HMf dimer (cyan and green) highlighting secondary structure (pdb file 1bfm). (b) Nucleosome-like particles from *M. thermoautotrophicum*, a member of the Archaea.

Summary of Section 5.7

1   Packaging of DNA serves to protect against damage, to compact the DNA helix into a suitable size within the cell, and to act as both a platform for and an intrinsic part of the structural and regulatory machinery involved in DNA metabolism.

2   DNA compaction in prokaryotes achieved through a combination of supercoiling and interactions with proteins that aid DNA bending.

3   Compaction of the eubacterial chromosome is facilitated by positively charged polyamines, which neutralize repulsive forces between neighbouring regions of the negatively charged DNA backbone, and by small, positively charged DNA binding proteins, which bend the DNA.

4   Eukaryotic DNA is condensed through interactions with histone proteins to form nucleosomes, structures that introduce negative supercoils into the helix and play critical roles in DNA metabolism.

5   Four core histones, each containing a characteristic histone fold structure, form an octamer made from two H3, two H4 and two heterodimers of H2A/B. DNA wraps twice around this core to form the nucleosome. Histone H1 serves to compact this structure further, through interactions with linker DNA.

6   The tails of histone proteins can be modified by methylation, acetylation and phosphorylation, modifications that can alter specific interactions with other proteins and affect the ability to pack nucleosomes together into more compact structures.

7   The DNA within the eukaryotic nucleus is packaged into a series of different structures, from nucleosomes to higher-order fibres. The degree of compaction is influenced by the degree of histone octamer acetylation and this compaction is also intimately related to the regulation of processes that occur within the chromatin milieu. Regions that are transcriptionally silent are highly compacted and specific histone modifications occur within these regions.

8   Chromatin compactness and histone modification can be analysed using nucleases and immunoprecipitation assays.

5.8 Chromosomal organization in the eukaryotic nucleus

The average human cell has around two metres of DNA within its nucleus. In the interphase nucleus, in which transcription and replication are going on, this DNA is packaged into nucleosomes that are variably compacted, through association with H1, into larger 30 nm fibres. In fact, the average nucleus most likely contains DNA with a continuum of chromatin configurations, ranging from highly open 10 nm fibres, through to 30 nm fibres and fibres that are even more tightly packed together, called **chromonema fibres** (Figure 5.39). The formation of these even larger fibres is probably facilitated by both the H1 linker histone and the tails of the core histones.

Figure 5.39
Pictorial representation of levels of DNA compaction in chromatin in the eukaryotic nucleus.

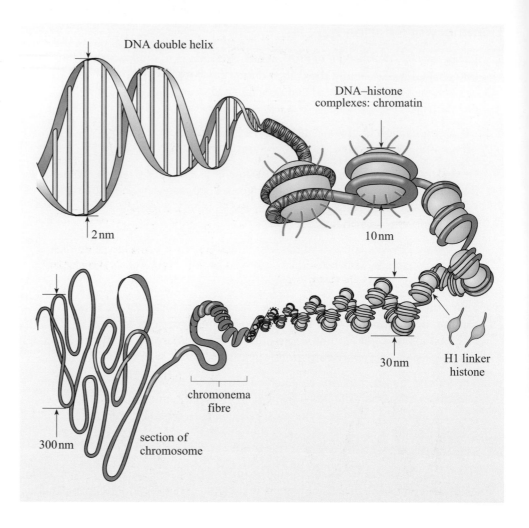

The nucleus is a dynamic site of activity and during each round of the cell cycle the entire genome must be duplicated and reassembled into chromatin. In addition to copying of the DNA, the cell must also ensure that the newly synthesized DNA is assembled in a chromatin structure that reproduces that of the original parent strands. We will consider how this is achieved in Chapter 9, when we discuss DNA replication in more detail.

Having examined the structure of the DNA fibres themselves, we will now briefly examine the higher-order structures that the DNA is packed into within the nucleus, how these structures further compact the DNA and their role in gene regulation.

5.8.1 Chromosome scaffolds

Most of the chromosomal DNA chains within the interphase nucleus are believed to be held on a scaffold or backbone structure made from various proteins, with loops of between 20 and 200 kb extruding from attachment sites. This chromosome structure is shown schematically in Figure 5.40. The scaffold, as well as permitting further compaction, serves to bring the DNA together in organized regions. There are many different protein components of these scaffolds, amongst them DNA topoisomerases.

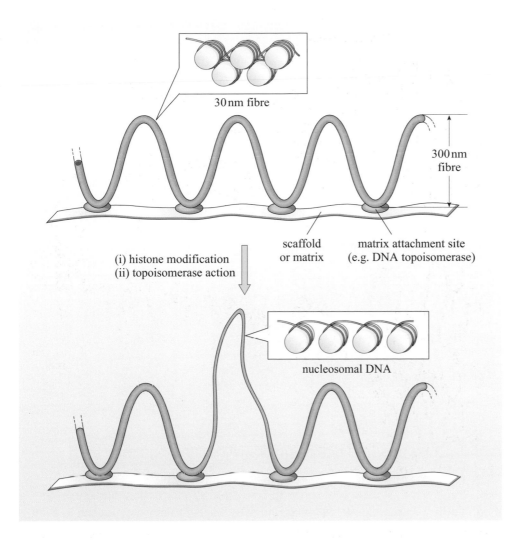

Figure 5.40
Loops of 30 nm chromatin fibre
held on a scaffold in the eukaryotic
nucleus. Loops can undergo
decondensation, as a result of
histone modification and/or
topoisomerase action, when access
is required by the cell (lower part
of figure).

How might DNA topoisomerases be involved in regulating the chromatin structure in loops?

DNA topoisomerases cut the DNA backbone and allow the strands to rotate around the helical axis, resulting in the addition or removal of DNA twists. The action of this enzyme could therefore result in relaxation or compaction of individual loops through the introduction or removal of supercoils.

Compaction is also influenced by the status of the histone tail modifications. As an example, remember that the addition of an acetyl group to lysine residues effectively removes their positive charge, reducing the ability of the histone tails to interact with the DNA backbone and thereby hindering compaction. Thus histone modification and topoisomerase activity can regulate the activity of genes in a looped region and thus regulate genes across longer stretches of DNA. These regions of chromatin are referred to as **domains**. An additional important implication of this scaffolding arrangement is that the action of topoisomerases and enzymes that modify chromatin could alter the compaction of individual loops without affecting neighbouring domains, as shown in Figure 5.40.

Finally, if you now look back at Figure 5.12, you can also see why transcriptionally active regions flanked by attachment sites need topoisomerase activity to release the torsional stresses that build up ahead of the transcription complex.

In most cases, visualizing such scaffold and loop structures with the light microscope is impossible, due to the limited resolution and the diffuse nature of the DNA. However, it is possible, even at the light microscope level, to see such arrangements in the so-called **lampbrush chromosomes** in the developing amphibian oocyte (egg cell). The DNA in these cells is highly transcriptionally active as the oocyte is synthesizing large stores of protein. If you look at the example in Figure 5.41, you can see large loops extending out from a scaffold-like structure. We will return to consider these arrangements in later chapters, when we discuss transcriptional regulation.

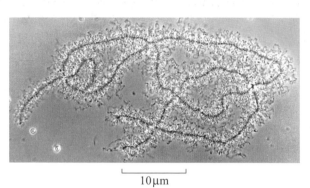

10 µm

Figure 5.41
Lampbrush chromosomes from the amphibian oocyte.

5.8.2 Chromosome distribution within the nucleus

DNA from any one particular chromosome is a single chain, many millions of bases long, and this chain is attached to a scaffold structure. It is not surprising then, that if we examine the interphase nucleus, each chromosome is seen to fill a localized area. This localized distribution of individual chromosomes is illustrated in Figure 5.42 with an examination of human chromosomes within the interphase nucleus. In these examples, special DNA probes have been used to detect the location of the entire chromosome by FISH (Box 5.1). This technique is known as **chromosome painting**. In Figure 5.42a, several different chromosomes are visualized using fluorescently tagged DNA from the whole chromosome as probes. As you can see, each chromosome is located within a defined area.

In order to explore a single human chromosome in more detail, a particular combination of DNA probes for different stretches along a single chromosome has been used, each probe being labelled with a different fluorophore (Figure 5.42b). In this way, the relative position of subsections of the chromosome can be determined. In the example in Figure 5.42b, DNA probes corresponding to different areas of human chromosome 5 have been used. As you can see, each copy of chromosome 5 is present within a very restricted area. Note also that the order of the colours on chromosome 5 in the interphase nucleus is the same as that on the mitotic chromosome shown alongside.

A further aspect of chromosomal localization is that some areas of individual chromosomes appear to be associated with specific areas of the nucleus in accordance with their transcriptional activity. For example, telomeres and many genes that are transcriptionally silent are often located in the **nuclear periphery**,

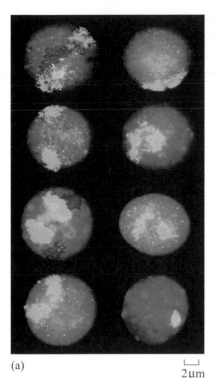

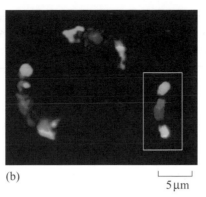

(b)

5 μm

Figure 5.42   Organization of DNA and localization of chromosomes in the human male interphase nucleus. (a) FISH using whole chromosome 'paints' for various chromosomes. All the nuclei are counterstained blue and chromosomes are stained red or green (from Boyle *et al.*, 2001). Different pairs of chromosomes are stained in each image. In the bottom right image, the single Y chromosome is stained. (b) FISH using specific probes for discrete regions of chromosome 5 to detect the linear organization of both chromosomes in the diploid interphase nucleus. A mitotic (metaphase) chromosome is indicated alongside (lower right, boxed). Notice that the pattern of colours in the chromosomes is the same in both interphase and metaphase.

(a)

2 μm

or edge of the nucleus. Genes that are highly transcribed, such as those involved in ribosomal RNA synthesis, are located in the **nucleolus**, a spherical body within the nucleus.

5.8.3 The organization of the mitotic chromosome

In order to prepare the chromosome for mitosis, a process in which DNA molecules become physically separated, an additional stage of compaction occurs to reach the highest level. The processes involved in this final stage of compaction are not clearly understood, but can be represented diagrammatically as in Figure 5.43. The process probably involves the coiling together of scaffolds into the higher-order structure.

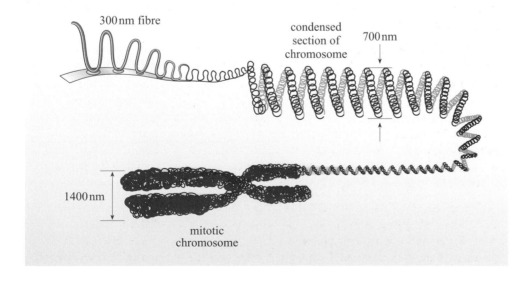

Figure 5.43
Compaction of chromatin scaffolds in the metaphase chromosome.

The H1 histone undergoes modification via phosphorylation, which appears to facilitate this further compaction. This additional level of compaction may represent a protective process to prevent physical shearing of the DNA chain within individual chromosomes during mitosis.

Summary of Section 5.8

1   Eukaryotic DNA is compacted through a hierarchical series of events, from nucleosomes to 10 nm and 30 nm fibres, then through further stages to the chromomena fibres, which are attached to scaffolds to form loops. In preparation for mitosis, these fibres are further compacted to prevent physical damage.

2   Chromosomes within the interphase nucleus occupy defined regions.

3   DNA within the eukaryotic interphase nucleus is in a dynamic and variable state. Scaffolds to which the DNA fibres are attached serve both structural roles in further compaction and as delineators of gene domains.

Learning outcomes for Chapter 5

When you have studied this chapter, you should be able to:

5.1 Define and use each of the terms printed in **bold** in the text.

5.2 Understand the properties of nucleotides, how they contribute to secondary and tertiary structures of nucleic acids at the molecular level, and how torsional states are maintained in cellular DNA.

5.3 Understand the different composition and roles of nucleic acids in the cell and their interactions with each other and with agents that cause DNA damage.

5.4 Describe the use of nucleic acids as tools in molecular research, including ribozymes, aptamers, antisense and hybridization tools.

5.5 Understand the function of DNA packaging within the cell and use examples to illustrate how packaging is achieved in various organisms.

5.6 Describe in detail the protein components of the nucleosome and key modifications to nucleosome components, and understand the interactions between the DNA double helix and the nucleosome.

5.7 Understand the various chromatin states within the interphase nucleus – their degrees of compaction and the hierarchy of chromatin assembly.

Questions for Chapter 5

Question 5.1

What effect does ethidium bromide intercalation have on supercoiled DNA?

Question 5.2

Imagine that you have recently isolated from a gene library a segment of human DNA that corresponds to a coding region. How could you investigate in the laboratory the chromosomal location of this gene and the sites of its expression?

Question 5.3

What three roles does DNA packaging fulfil within the cell?

Question 5.4

Why does the deacetylation of histone tails allow closer packing of nucleosomes?

Question 5.5

What effect does the wrapping of DNA around the histone octamer in the nucleosome have upon the DNA?

Question 5.6

Describe the major modifications that occur to core nucleosomal proteins. How do these modifications exert their effects?

References

Boyle, S., Gilchrist, S., Bridger, J. M., Mahy, N. L., Ellis, J. A. and Bickmore, W. A. (2001) The spatial organization of human chromosomes within the nuclei of normal and emerin-mutant cells, *Human Molecular Genetics*, **10**(3), pp. 211–219.

Bulyk, M. L., Huang, X., Choo, Y. and Church, G. M.. (2001) Exploring the DNA-binding specificities of zinc fingers with DNA micro-arrays, *Proceedings of the National Academy of Sciences* (USA), **98**(13), pp. 7158–7163.

Pereira, S. L., Grayling, R. A., Lurz, R. and Reeve, J. N. (1997) Archael nucleosomes, *Proceedings of the National Academy of Sciences* (USA), **94**, pp. 12633–12637.

Moss, E. G. and Poethig, R. S. (2002) MicroRNAs: something new under the sun, *Current Biology*, **12**, R688–R690.

Further source

Shaner, S. L (2001); Protein–DNA complexes: non-specific, *Encyclopedia of Life Sciences*, Nature Publishing Group. (online)

6 MEMBRANES

6.1 Introduction

In Chapter 1, we considered the significance, in evolutionary terms, of the cellular nature of living organisms and the advantages of compartmentalization afforded by membranes. In this chapter, we are going to examine the chemical and physical properties of biological membranes and begin to relate these properties to the function of membranes in the cell.

Every cell has membranes. The boundary of a cell is defined by the **plasma membrane**, which encloses the cell contents. Crucially, whilst separating the living contents from the non-living, the plasma membrane permits selective exchange between the two environments. Eukaryotic cells also contain intracellular membranes that define different inner compartments (organelles) with different functions. Figure 6.1a is an electron micrograph of a liver preparation showing the plasma membrane of a liver cell and the membranes that bound the intracellular organelles. At high power under the electron microscope, membranes can be seen to have a trilaminar (i.e. three-layered) appearance, often described as 'railroad tracks' (Figure 6.1c).

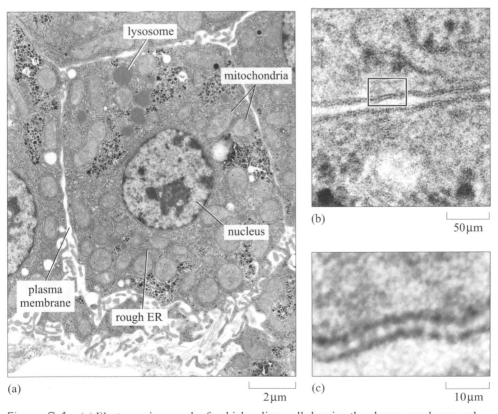

Figure 6.1   (a) Electron micrograph of a chicken liver cell showing the plasma membrane and membranes that define the intracellular organelles and compartments. (b) Electron micrograph showing two closely apposed membrane, which at higher magnification (c) can be seen to have a 'railroad track' appearance.

Throughout this course, you will encounter many examples of membrane function in different cellular processes. In general terms, biological membranes perform a number of important roles, as outlined below.

1   *A physical and chemical barrier*: keeping the contents of the cell together and providing a flexible yet mechanically stable barrier between the cell and its surrounding environment; separating different aqueous 'compartments' or organelles inside the cell. Compartmentalization of processes and components permits optimization of conditions and minimizes interference. Membranes serve as permeability barriers, controlling the movement of substances (nutrients, waste products, ions) into and out of the cell and its organelles, thereby regulating the composition of the fluid within each cellular compartment. There are a number of different mechanisms that *selectively* transport substances from one side of the membrane to another in a regulated fashion.

2   *Communication* between the cell and the extracellular environment or neighbouring cells. As the interface of the cell with its surrounding environment, the plasma membrane is crucial to the detection of extracellular signals, whether chemical or electrical. Specific receptors or channels located in the plasma membrane relay these signals to the inside of the cell. (The molecular mechanisms involved in this communication will be discussed in Chapter 13.) Note that communication also operates in the opposite direction, from inside the cell to the cell's environment, and similarly relies upon the membrane as a relay device.

3   *Recognition*. Interactions between cells are typically specified by particular components of their plasma membranes, e.g. adhesion molecules and integrins (discussed in Chapter 16). The presence or absence of certain molecules in the plasma membrane allows cells to recognize one another and respond as appropriate. Cell differentiation, the process by which the shape, properties and function of a cell are determined by the genes that it expresses, requires specific cell–cell recognition (to be discussed in Chapter 17).

4   *Energy conversion*. Specialized membranes, with appropriate molecular components, can convert light energy (as in photosynthetic membranes) or chemical energy (e.g. by oxidative phosphorylation on the inner mitochondrial membrane) into more usable forms (e.g. ATP). Such energy conversions are typically based on the generation of an ion gradient across the membrane, which is established by specialized membrane components. Ion gradients can also be used to produce electrical signals, as in neurons or muscle cells.

5   *A platform* for cellular processes. In many intracellular signalling pathways, the plasma membrane serves as a platform for bringing together key components (see Chapter 13). Enzymes in a metabolic pathway, arranged in or on a membrane (as opposed to free in solution), can form a kind of production line in which components of the pathway are effectively concentrated, greatly enhancing the efficiency of the metabolic process.

☐   What example have you already come across of a series of pathway components arranged in a membrane?

◼   The electron transport chain in the inner mitochondrial membrane (Chapter 4).

6.1.1 Membrane composition

Biochemical analysis of membranes shows that they have lipid, protein and carbohydrate components. Molecular composition varies greatly between different biological membranes. Table 6.1 details the relative content, by mass, of the lipid, protein and carbohydrate components in a variety of different biological membranes, including the plasma membrane of different cells and the membranes of some intracellular organelles.

Table 6.1 Protein, lipid and carbohydrate content (approximate percentage by mass) and protein to lipid ratio of biological membranes. (Adapted from Becker *et al.*, 2000)

Membrane	Protein / %	Lipid / %	Carbohydrate / %	Protein / lipid ratio
human erythrocyte plasma membrane	49	43	8	1.14
mammalian liver cell plasma membrane	54	36	10	1.50
endoplasmic reticulum	63	27	10	2.33
Golgi apparatus	64	26	10	2.46
nuclear envelope	66	32	2	2.06
mitochondrial outer membrane	55	45	0	1.22
mitochondrial inner membrane	78	22	0	3.54
chloroplast lamella	70	30	0	2.33
myelin sheath surrounding nerve axons	18	79	3	0.23

The composition of biological membranes is directly related to their physical properties and function. Apart from the relative proportions of lipid, protein and carbohydrate, the specific molecular composition (i.e. which proteins and which lipids) can vary considerably in biological membranes. Such diversity is particularly true of the protein component, which reflects the specialized function of cells and organelles, and is often subject to change during the lifetime of the cell, depending on regulatory processes.

Myelin is a specialized membrane structure that surrounds nerve axons. As you can see from Table 6.1, myelin has a very distinctive composition with a very low protein / lipid ratio (0.23) compared to other membranes. The high lipid content of myelin enables this sheath-like structure to act effectively as electrical insulation for the nerve cells and to facilitate rapid propagation of the action potential along the nerve axon.

☐ Compare the protein / lipid ratio of the inner and outer mitochondrial membranes. What do you think accounts for the difference in the composition of these membranes?

⬤ The inner mitochondrial membrane has a much higher protein / lipid ratio than does the outer membrane. This difference can be attributed to the high proportions of proteins in the inner membrane that participate in electron transport and oxidative phosphorylation.

○ Looking at the carbohydrate content of the membranes in Table 6.1, what do you note about the endoplasmic reticulum and Golgi apparatus and how do you explain this?

■ The membranes of the endoplasmic reticulum and the Golgi apparatus both have a carbohydrate content of 10%, which is comparable to that of plasma membranes but much higher than that of other intracellular membranes. The high carbohydrate content of ER and Golgi reflects the fact that glycosylation of membrane proteins occurs in these organelles (see Chapter 3).

6.1.2 The fluid-mosaic model of membrane structure

In 1972 Jonathan Singer and Gareth Nicolson proposed a model of membrane structure, termed the **fluid-mosaic model**, which accounted for the then current experimental observations of cell membranes. According to this model, illustrated in Figure 6.2, the basic structure of the membrane is a fluid lipid bilayer with membrane proteins that are either discontinuously embedded in this bilayer or attached to it. These proteins are described as, respectively, *integral* or *peripheral*. Key to this model is the idea that the lipids and proteins of the membrane are highly mobile in the plane of the membrane. In plasma membranes, many lipids and proteins have carbohydrate groups covalently attached and presented at the extracellular surface, accounting for the carbohydrate content detailed in Table 6.1. The carbohydrate groups form what is known as the **glycocalyx**, a tangled layer of carbohydrate chains on the outside of the cell, which has an important role in recognition and adhesion.

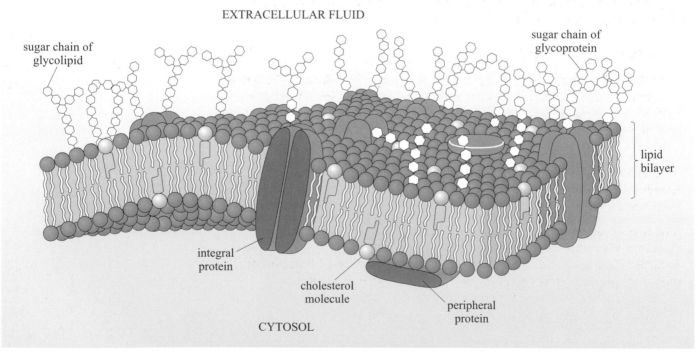

Figure 6.2   The fluid-mosaic model of membrane structure, as described by Singer and Nicolson (1972). A fluid lipid bilayer gives the membrane its structure and membrane proteins move around in the plane of the lipid bilayer. At the extracellular surface, some of the lipids and proteins have carbohydrate groups covalently attached.

Though still valid as an explanation of basic membrane structure, the fluid-mosaic model has been refined in a number of ways since it was proposed. Importantly, we now know that membranes are not always wholly fluid, but often contain patches of lipid in a solid-like state, referred to as **lipid rafts**. We will discuss the evidence for lipid rafts and their implications for membrane function later in this chapter. Other important developments in our understanding of membrane structure and function have come from the study of the three-dimensional structures of membrane proteins.

Membranes are dynamic structures. As well as the lateral movement of lipid and protein components in the fluid-mosaic membrane, lipids can 'flip' between the two lipid layers (termed **leaflets**). Membranes are also dynamic in terms of the lifetime of a cell. Some receptors in the plasma membrane can be internalized by the cell, along with some of the lipid bilayer, as a means of regulating their activity. Receptor internalization is often in response to ligand binding, and the receptor may be recycled to the membrane or degraded. Regulation of the level of expression, localization or activity of plasma membrane proteins is an important means of regulating a cell's response to extracellular signals and its interactions with other cells or with the extracellular matrix. Furthermore, regulation of the lipid composition of cell membranes can affect the activity of membrane proteins by influencing membrane fluidity and the distribution of proteins within the membrane.

To appreciate the physical properties and structure–function relationship of membranes, we need to understand the chemistry of their molecular components. The physical properties of membranes – impermeability to polar solutes, fluidity, flexibility and mechanical resistance – can be attributed to the lipid bilayer, so we will begin by looking at the different types of lipids that are found in biological membranes and the bilayer organization that they adopt.

Summary of Section 6.1

1   All cells have membranes and the plasma membrane defines the cell. Biological membranes have a number of important functions: as a barrier between the cell and the environment; separating compartments within a cell; as an interface with the surrounding environment; recognition; as a means of generating gradients for energy conversions; as a platform for cellular processes.

2   Membranes contain lipid, protein and carbohydrate components and the relative amounts of these constituents vary depending on the function of the membranes.

3   The fluid-mosaic model of membrane structure, proposed by Singer and Nicolson, describes the cell membrane as a fluid lipid bilayer in which proteins are embedded and can move around in the plane of the bilayer. Since it was first proposed, this model has been refined in a number of ways.

6.2 Lipids

The term 'lipid' describes many varied organic compounds characterized by their solubility in organic solvents (such as chloroform and methanol) and very poor solubility in water. Biological lipids include fats, oils, waxes and sterols.

Lipids are the 'fluid' part of the fluid-mosaic model proposed by Singer and Nicolson. Biological membranes contain an enormous number of different types of lipid; for example, the erythrocyte (red blood cell) plasma membrane contains about 100 different varieties. However, analysis of membrane lipids shows that most of them belong to one of three main classes: **glycerophospholipids**, **sphingolipids** and **sterols**. These molecules have a very important property in common: they are all amphipathic. That is, they have both a hydrophilic and a hydrophobic portion. In view of the relative dimensions of these parts of the lipid molecules, they are commonly described as, respectively, the *head* and the *tail* of the lipid. In glycerophospholipids and sphingolipids, the 'tail' consists of two long hydrocarbon chains; hence these lipids are frequently represented as indicated in Figure 6.3a. In Figure 6.3b, the major types of membrane lipid are represented schematically to highlight their amphipathic nature. Note that sphingolipids are classified as sphingophospholipids or sphingoglycolipids, according to the nature of the polar head group.

Figure 6.3
(a) A stylized schematic emphasizing the 'head and tail' structure of glycerophospholipids and sphingolipids. (b) Schematic representations of the major types of membrane lipid. All the membrane lipids are amphipathic, having both a hydrophilic and a hydrophobic component.

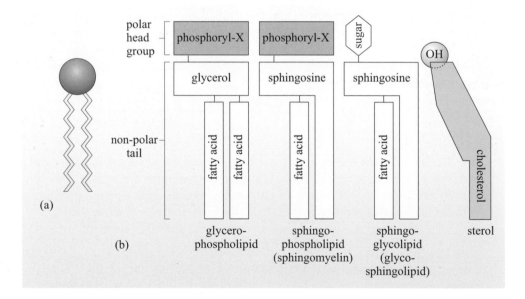

In an aqueous environment, how would you expect amphipathic lipid molecules to behave?

Their hydrophobic tails would associate with each other to exclude water, whilst the hydrophilic heads would point out into the aqueous environment.

Lipids can seem very complex at first glance, but on closer study, glycerophospholipids and sphingolipids can be seen to consist of a number of key generic building blocks (Box 6.1). Of these, **fatty acids** are particularly important in relation to the properties of the lipid. Fatty acids and the main groups of membrane lipid are described below.

Box 6.1 Building blocks of glycerophospholipids and sphingolipids

Glycerophospholipids and sphingolipids consist of a number of building blocks, as shown here. (The structures of common polar head groups are represented in Table 6.2.)

The building blocks for glycerophospholipids and sphingolipids

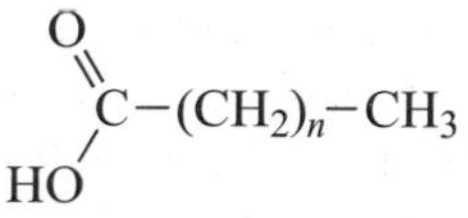

$$\underset{HO}{\overset{O}{\parallel}}{C}-(CH_2)_n-CH_3 \quad \text{saturated fatty acid}$$

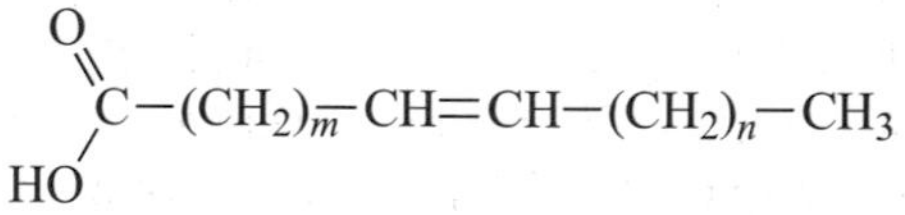

$$\underset{HO}{\overset{O}{\parallel}}{C}-(CH_2)_{\overline{m}}-CH=CH-(CH_2)_n-CH_3 \quad \text{unsaturated fatty acid}$$

glycerol

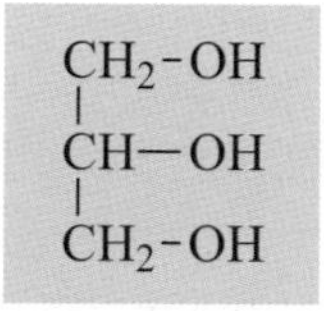

$$\begin{array}{c} CH_2\text{-}OH \\ | \\ CH\text{-}OH \\ | \\ CH_2\text{-}OH \end{array}$$

sphingosine

$$\begin{array}{c} HO-CH-CH=CH-(CH_2)_{12}-CH_3 \\ | \\ CH-\overset{+}{N}H_3 \\ | \\ HO-CH_2 \end{array}$$

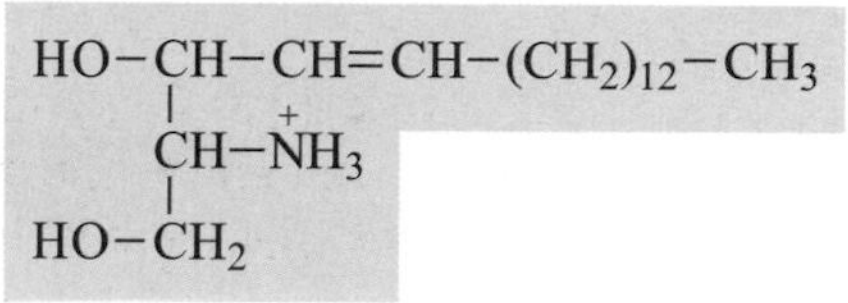

phosphoryl-X head group

$$X-O-\overset{O}{\underset{O^-}{\overset{\parallel}{P}}}-O^-$$

monosaccharide or oligosaccharide head group

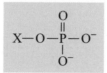

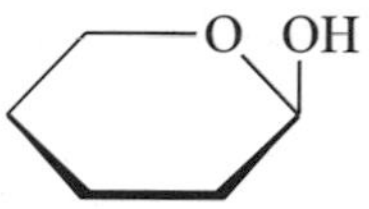

Glycerophospholipids

$$\begin{array}{c} CH_2-O-\overset{O}{\overset{\parallel}{C}}-R^1 \\ | \quad O \\ CH-O-\overset{\parallel}{C}-R^2 \\ | \\ X-O-\overset{O^-}{\underset{O}{\overset{|}{P}}}-O-CH_2 \end{array}$$

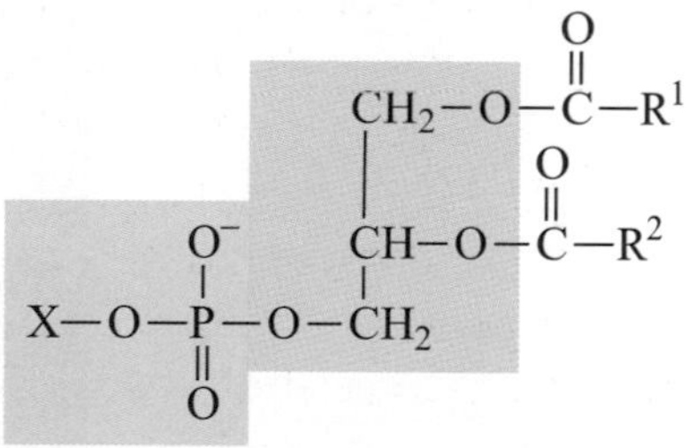

$R^1 = C_{16}$ or C_{18} saturated fatty acid

$R^2 = C_{16}$ or C_{20} unsaturated fatty acid

X = polar alcohol

Sphingolipids

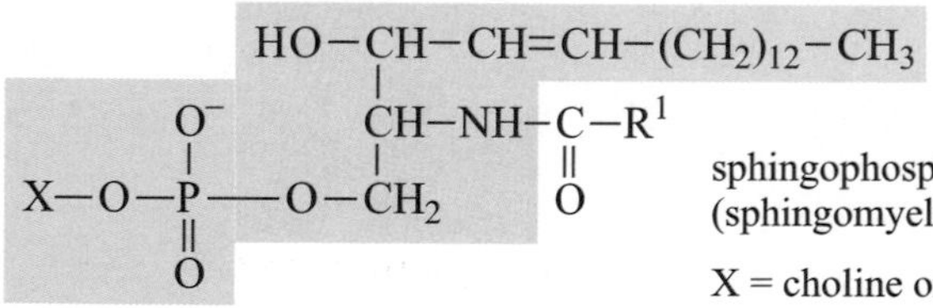

$$\begin{array}{c} HO-CH-CH=CH-(CH_2)_{12}-CH_3 \\ | \\ CH-NH-\overset{}{C}-R^1 \\ | \quad\quad \parallel \\ X-O-\overset{O^-}{\underset{O}{\overset{|}{P}}}-O-CH_2 \quad O \end{array}$$

sphingophospholipid (sphingomyelin)

X = choline or ethanolamine

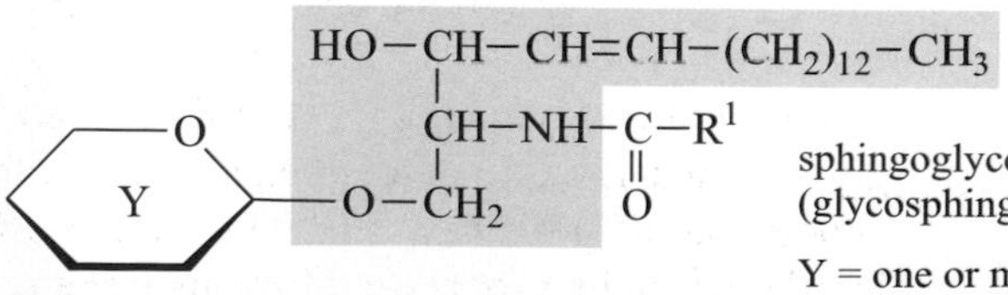

$$\begin{array}{c} HO-CH-CH=CH-(CH_2)_{12}-CH_3 \\ | \\ CH-NH-C-R^1 \\ | \quad\quad \parallel \\ O-CH_2 \quad O \end{array}$$

sphingoglycolipid (glycosphingolipid)

Y = one or more sugar residues

6.2.1 Fatty acids

As you learned in Chapter 2, fatty acids are carboxylic acids with long hydrocarbon chains. They are rarely found free in biological systems, but usually occur in an esterified form, i.e. joined via an ester linkage to an alcohol (refer to Table 2.3 in Chapter 2 to refresh your memory of these functional groups). Fatty acids are part of all membrane lipids, with the exception of the sterols.

Due to the mechanism by which they are synthesized (by stepwise addition of acetyl groups), most fatty acids have an even number of carbon atoms. In animals and higher plants, the most abundant fatty acid residues are those containing 16 and 18 carbon atoms, referred to as C_{16} and C_{18} fatty acids respectively. From Chapter 2 you will know that hydrocarbon chains can be unsaturated, i.e. they can contain double bonds. In fact, over half the fatty acid residues of animal and plant lipids are unsaturated or polyunsaturated (containing two or more double bonds). The degree of unsaturation of fatty acids critically determines their physical properties. In turn, the properties of the lipids that contain the fatty acids, and of the cell membranes that contain these lipids, are also determined by the degree of unsaturation of the fatty acid component. We shall explore the basis of this effect in a subsequent section.

Figure 6.4 depicts the structural formulae of the common C_{16} and C_{18} fatty acids in animals and higher plants. The double bonds in oleic acid and linoleic acid are represented in Figure 6.4 in the *cis* configuration (see Chapter 2, Section 2.2.3),

Figure 6.4
Structural formulae and space-filling models of the common C_{16} and C_{18} fatty acids in animals and higher plants. The commonly used names of the fatty acids are indicated, as well as the systematic nomenclature. For example, the fatty acid commonly known as oleic acid has 18 C atoms and a single double bond between carbons 9 and 10 (the carboxyl C atom being C1). The number of C atoms and double bonds is represented in shorthand by '18:1', whilst the systematic name, 9-octadecanoic acid, further identifies the location of the double bond.

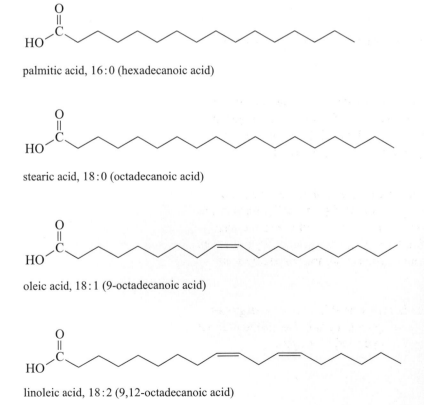

palmitic acid, 16:0 (hexadecanoic acid)

stearic acid, 18:0 (octadecanoic acid)

oleic acid, 18:1 (9-octadecanoic acid)

linoleic acid, 18:2 (9,12-octadecanoic acid)

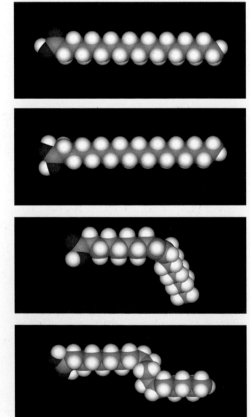

which is the most common configuration of unsaturated fatty acids. The *cis* configuration introduces a rigid 30° bend in the otherwise flexible fatty acid chain. As we shall see, this property of unsaturated fatty acids has important consequences for the arrangement of lipids in membranes. Note that, by convention, fatty acids are described in terms of their carbon atom content and the number of double bonds that they contain, as indicated in Figure 6.4. As well as their common names, there is a systematic nomenclature for fatty acids that identifies both carbon atom content and the number and location of any double bonds.

Note that fatty acids, as well as being part of many membrane lipids, are also incorporated into **triacylglycerols**. In these molecules, three fatty acids are esterified to glycerol, one at each of the hydroxyl groups (see margin and Figure 6.5). Triacylglycerols are rarely found in membranes; their main function is as an important energy reservoir in adipose tissue. Fats, being less oxidized than carbohydrates or proteins (as evidenced by their relatively very high C : O ratio), yield much more energy on oxidation.

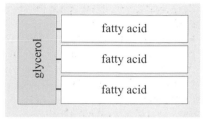

Generalized structure of a triacylglycerol.

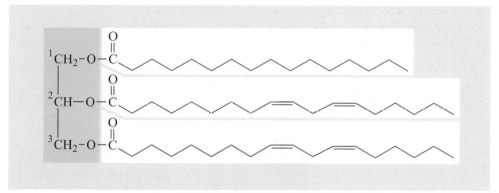

Figure 6.5   The structural formula of the triacylglycerol 1-palmitoyl-2,3-linoleoyl-glycerol. Note that triacylglycerols are non-polar molecules.

○ Triacylglycerols are non-polar molecules. (Look at Figure 6.5 and confirm that this is so.) In contrast, the carbohydrate glycogen, which is also an important energy storage compound, is polar (see Box 2.5). How might these properties affect the efficiency of energy storage by these two compounds under physiological conditions?

● Triacylglycerols, being non-polar, do not complex water but are stored in an unsolvated form. In contrast, glycogen is highly solvated (it actually binds twice its mass in water molecules!). Since the water does not contribute to the energy yield on oxidation of the glycogen, the efficiency of energy storage by glycogen, in terms of energy yield per unit mass, would be less than that expected from anhydrous (water-free) glycogen.

In fact, the oxidation of hydrated glycogen yields only one-third of the energy per unit mass derived from the oxidation of anhydrous glycogen, and fats provide about six times the metabolic energy of an equal mass of hydrated glycogen.

6.2.2 Glycerophospholipids

Glycerophospholipids are the most abundant lipid component of biological membranes. They consist of a central glycerol to which two fatty acids are attached, via ester linkages (as for triacylglycerols). The fatty acids are linked to the glycerol at positions 1 and 2, and position 3 is occupied by a phosphoryl-containing group (hence glycero*phospho*lipids). The fatty acid that occupies position 1 of the glycerol residue is typically C_{16} or C_{18} and saturated, whilst that occupying position 2 is usually C_{16} or C_{20} and unsaturated.

In the generalized glycerophospholipid structure, depicted in Box 6.1 and repeated here in the margin, X denotes a variable group. Among those glycerophospholipids that are most commonly found in cell membranes, X is derived from polar alcohols (i.e. OH-containing molecules), such as those indicated in Table 6.2. The nomenclature for phospholipids, detailed in Table 6.2, indicates the nature of the variable X group. Thus, for example, a phospholipid containing a phosphocholine group is a phosphatidylcholine and that containing a phosphoserine group is a phosphatidylserine. Note that the phosphoryl group carries a negative charge and, in some cases, the variable X group is also charged or polar. The space-filling model of a glycerophospholipid (actually a phosphatidylcholine) is depicted in Figure 6.6. Note that one of the fatty acyl chains is saturated and one is unsaturated.

Generalized structure of a glycerophospholipid.

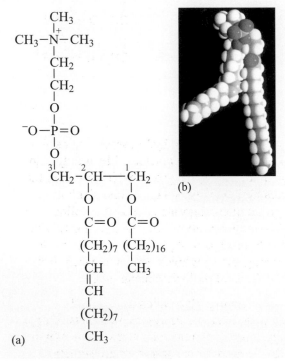

(a)   (b)

Figure 6.6   (a) Structural formula and (b) space-filling model of 1-stearoyl-2-oleoyl-3-phosphatidylcholine, a glycerophospholipid.

Table 6.2 Glycerophospholipids are classified according to the nature of the 'X' group in the generalized structural formula.

Name of X—OH	Formula of —X	Name of glycerophospholipid
water	—H	phosphatidic acid
ethanolamine	$-CH_2CH_2\overset{+}{N}H_3$	phosphatidylethanolamine
choline	$-CH_2CH_2\overset{+}{N}(CH_3)_3$	phosphatidylcholine (lecithin)
serine	$-CH_2CH(\overset{+}{N}H_3)COO^-$	phosphatidylserine
inositol	(inositol ring structure)	phosphatidylinositol
glycerol	$-CH_2CH(OH)CH_2OH$	phosphatidylglycerol
phosphatidylglycerol	(diphosphatidylglycerol structure)	diphosphatidylglycerol (cardiolipin)

6.2.3 Sphingolipids

Like glycerophospholipids, sphingolipids contain two hydrocarbon chains and have a polar head group. One hydrocarbon chain is contributed by a fatty acid component and the second belongs to a sphingosine group, which replaces the glycerol unit of glycerophospholipids. Sphingosine is a C_{18} amino alcohol. Attached to the terminal hydroxyl group of sphingosine is phosphocholine or phosphoethanolamine (giving a **sphingophospholipid**) or sugar groups (giving a **sphingoglycolipid**) (Box 6.1). The term **phospholipid** is often used to refer to both glycerophospholipids and sphingophospholipids, which between them comprise the major proportion of the lipids of biological membranes.

There is considerable variety among the sphingoglycolipids (also called glycosphingolipids). In the simplest structures, the head group consists of only one sugar residue. However, there are many different sphingoglycolipids (more than 60) that contain an oligosaccharide head group, and these are sometimes referred to as **gangliosides.** Principally found in cell surface membranes, the carbohydrate head groups of gangliosides extend out from the membrane surface and participate in cell–cell recognition. The head group can also act as a receptor for glycoprotein hormones secreted by the pituitary gland. Gangliosides represent a sizable proportion (6%) of brain lipids.

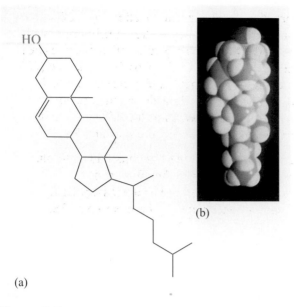

(a)

(b)

6.2.4 Cholesterol

Cholesterol is a major component of plasma membranes in animal cells but is less abundant in intracellular membranes. It is also the most abundant steroid in animals and is required as a precursor in the synthesis of steroid hormones. Such steroid hormones are crucial to the regulation of a large variety of physiological functions, including carbohydrate metabolism and sexual development. The structure of cholesterol is illustrated in Figure 6.7. This lipid contains a short aliphatic hydrocarbon chain linked to four fused rings, with a weakly polar hydroxyl group. The presence of the hydroxyl group and hydrocarbon chain on the basic steroid ring structure mean that cholesterol is classified as a sterol. Importantly, in terms of its effects on membrane fluidity, the ring portion of cholesterol is rigid whereas the short hydrocarbon tail is relatively flexible.

Figure 6.7 Structure of cholesterol. (a) Structural formula (the weakly polar hydroxyl group is shown in blue). (b) Space-filling model.

Box 6.2 Analysing membrane lipids

The solubility of lipids in organic solvents is exploited to separate these compounds from other biological material. Following extraction with organic solvent, a number of different chromatographic techniques can be used to fractionate lipids (i.e. separate them according to a particular physical property). Such techniques include thin-layer chromatography (TLC).

In TLC, lipids are resolved (separated) on the basis of their relative affinities for a hydrophilic stationary phase and a hydrophobic mobile phase (Figure 6.8). The stationary phase is usually a thin layer of silica gel (silicic acid) on a glass or metal plate onto which a sample of the lipid extract is spotted (at the origin). The organic solvent used to extract the lipids is allowed to evaporate and the edge of the plate is dipped into the mobile phase, which is usually a mixture of appropriate solvents (e.g. chloroform, methanol and water). The mobile phase moves up the plate by capillary action and as it passes the origin it carries the lipids with it. The lipids travel at different rates according to their polarity.

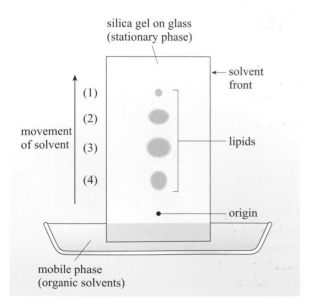

Figure 6.8 Analysis of membrane lipids by thin-layer chromatography (TLC). The lipid extract is spotted onto the edge of the TLC plate (stationary phase) and the plate is dipped into a solvent mixture (mobile phase). Non-polar lipids move quickly up the plate whilst polar lipids move more slowly.

Non-polar lipids have little affinity for the hydrophilic stationary phase and therefore move quickly up the plate with the solvent. More polar lipids, such as glycerophospholipids, move less quickly as they have a greater affinity for the stationary phase. When the solvent front has nearly reached the top of the plate, the plate is removed from the reservoir containing the mobile phase and dried. The lipids can be visualized using a chemically reactive spray. Running purified lipid preparations as standards can help identify the lipids in the mixture being analysed. By extracting lipid spots with, for example, chloroform, the lipid can be recovered for further analysis using more sophisticated chromatographic techniques.

◯ Figure 6.8 shows the fractionation, by TLC, of lipids from erythrocyte plasma membrane with spots attributable to phosphatidylethanolamine (PE), phosphatidylcholine (PC), phosphatidylserine (PS) and cholesterol. Spots 2 and 3 correspond to PE and PC respectively. Considering their relative polarities, identify which of the other two spots corresponds to each of cholesterol and PS.

⬤ Polar lipids move more slowly than do non-polar or weakly polar lipids. Therefore, spot 1 corresponds to cholesterol as the least polar lipid and spot 4 corresponds to the more polar PS.

Summary of Section 6.2

1   Most membrane lipids belong to one of three main classes: glycerophospholipids, sphingolipids or sterols. Glycerophospholipids are the most abundant lipid in biological membranes. All membrane lipids are amphipathic, having both hydrophilic and hydrophobic portions.

2   Glycerophospholipids and sphingolipids are built from key generic building blocks including fatty acids. Fatty acids are carboxylic acids with long hydrocarbon chains that can be saturated or unsaturated. Carbon–carbon double bonds in fatty acids are usually in the *cis* configuration, giving the hydrocarbon chain a 30° kink.

3   Glycerophospholipids have two fatty acids, which form the hydrophobic 'tail' of the molecule. The hydrophilic 'head' consists of a phosphoryl-containing group.

4   Sphingolipids contain two hydrocarbon chains, one derived from a fatty acid and one from sphingosine, and a polar head group. When the head group is a sugar, the lipid is known as a sphingoglycolipid or glycosphingolipid.

5   Cholesterol is a sterol and is a major component of plasma membranes in animal cells. It has a weakly polar hydroxyl group linked to four fused rings that form a rigid structure, and a more flexible short hydrocarbon chain.

6   Thin-layer chromatography can be used to analyse the lipid composition of membranes.

6.3 The lipid bilayer

Purified amphipathic membrane lipids spontaneously form different aggregates in aqueous solvents. The hydrophobic part of the molecule cannot form favourable interactions with water molecules, but will associate with other hydrophobic molecules. Thus the amphipathic lipids aggregate such that their hydrophobic tails are buried and excluded from the water molecules and their hydrophilic tails are exposed to the aqueous environment. With their two hydrocarbon tails, glycerophospholipids and sphingolipids have a more or less cylindrical shape. The steric requirements for packing of these lipids means that they tend to form bilayers in aqueous solutions (Figure 6.9a). These bilayers are similar in thickness to the lipid bilayer of biological membranes, i.e. approximately 5 nm thick.

Energetically speaking, the main driving force behind the formation of a lipid bilayer is hydrophobic interaction between the fatty acyl chains of lipid molecules. Close packing of the hydrophobic tails is favoured by van der Waals interactions between the acyl chains; the bilayer is further stabilized by hydrogen bonding and electrostatic interactions between the polar head groups and water molecules. In the bilayer represented in Figure 6.9a, the exposure of the hydrophobic tails of the lipids at the free edges to the aqueous environment is energetically unfavourable. To avoid such free edges, the bilayer spontaneously closes in on itself to form a continuous layer, thereby separating an enclosed compartment from the aqueous environment (Figure 6.9b). Note that lipids with a *single* fatty acyl chain will tend to form spherical aggregates called **micelles**, as this arrangement maximizes the hydrophobic interactions between the chains whilst excluding water from the hydrophobic core (Figure 6.9c).

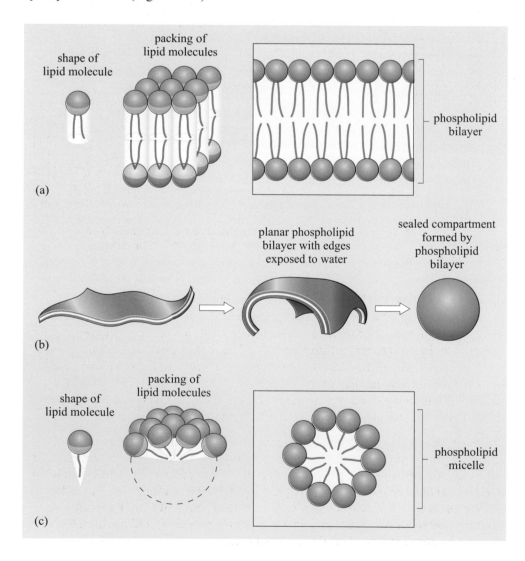

Figure 6.9
Packing of amphipathic lipids in an aqueous environment.
(a) Glycerophospholipids and sphingolipids have a roughly cylindrical shape and pack in bilayers.
(b) A bilayer will spontaneously close in on itself, forming a sealed compartment. (c) Micelles are spherical aggregates formed by lipids with single fatty acyl chains.

The physical properties of natural cell membranes can be closely modelled using artificial lipid bilayers. Mechanical agitation of a suspension of phospholipids in water results in the formation of multilamellar vesicles (MLVs). These onion-like vesicles are from 1–10 µm in diameter and have many bilayers separated from each other by water (Figure 6.10). If a suspension of MLVs is further agitated, this time using ultrasonic vibrations (a process called sonication), these structures become rearranged to form **liposomes**, which consist of single lipid bilayers forming closed spherical water-filled vesicles of 20–30 nm diameter. Larger liposomes of 100 nm in diameter can be produced by extrusion, under high pressure, of MLVs through a porous membrane (Figure 6.10).

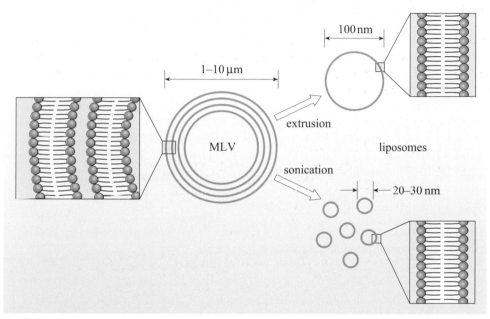

Figure 6.10   Artificial membranes can be prepared from purified lipid preparations. Mixing a suspension of phospholipids in water results in the formation of multilamellar vesicles (MLVs), which can be used to produce liposomes.

Liposomes are quite stable and can be isolated and manipulated using dialysis, chromatography or centrifugation techniques, and it is possible to manipulate the internal and external environments independently. This technology has been exploited to devise systems for drug delivery. Liposomes can fuse with the plasma membranes of cells. If they can be specifically targeted towards particular cells, they can be a convenient way of delivering drugs to where they are needed. By packaging, for example, an anti-cancer drug in liposomes, it is possible to greatly reduce toxic side-effects and improve the efficacy of the drug.

Liposomes made from synthetic lipids or natural lipids that have been extracted from biological sources have been studied extensively as model cell membranes, in particular with regard to the physical properties of the membrane and the behaviour of individual lipid molecules within a lipid bilayer. Planar artificial bilayers, called **black membranes**, can also be produced. These are formed across a small hole in a partition between two aqueous compartments (Figure 6.11) and are used to measure the permeability of artificial membranes.

Figure 6.11
A black membrane is an artificial membrane consisting of a planar lipid bilayer. The bilayer forms across a hole in a partition between two aqueous compartments.

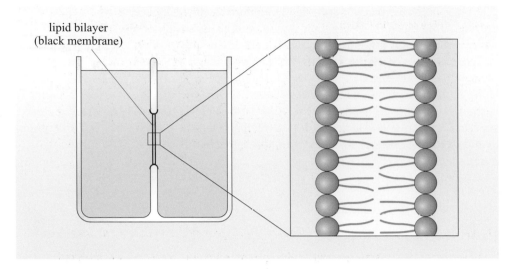

lipid bilayer
(black membrane)

From studies using artificial membranes derived from different phospholipids, it is clear that the thickness of the membranes is determined primarily by the length of the fatty acyl chains in the constituent lipids. The stability of the lipid bilayer also varies with the length of the fatty acyl chains in the lipids. In real biological membranes, which are 5–6 nm thick, depending on source, the fatty acyl chains are of optimal length for stability of the bilayer.

6.3.1 Fluidity of the lipid bilayer

The efficient functioning of membrane proteins in transport processes, signalling events, and intercellular communication is critically dependent on the fluidity of the membrane; consequently, this property is subject to precise regulation. Most organisms can regulate membrane fluidity, principally by regulating the lipid composition. There are a number of different factors that determine membrane fluidity. These factors can be studied conveniently using synthetic lipid bilayers such as those described above.

Bilayer fluidity varies with temperature

In a synthetic lipid bilayer in its fluid state, the fatty acyl chains are highly mobile, with rotation about the carbon–carbon single bonds. In this state, the lipid molecules as a whole are highly mobile in the plane of the bilayer. Being ordered in one direction (across the membrane) but not in others (i.e. in the plane of the membrane), this fluid bilayer is described as a **liquid crystal**. Below a characteristic melting temperature or **transition temperature (T_m)**, the lipid bilayer loses its fluidity and undergoes a transition to a gel-like solid phase. In the **gel state**, the fatty acyl chains are fully extended, with the C—C backbone forming a regular zig-zag in one plane. In this conformation, the fatty acyl chains pack tightly together in a hexagonal array (Figure 6.12). In the gel state, lateral diffusion of the lipids is very much slower than that in the liquid-crystal state (a difference of the order of 100-fold). The change from the disordered liquid crystal state to the ordered gel state results in a change in the X-ray diffraction pattern for the bilayer.

In a real biological membrane in the gel state, lateral movement of proteins is reduced and many membrane functions are compromised. Thus to function properly, biological membranes must be maintained in the fluid liquid-crystal state, i.e. at a temperature higher than their transition temperature.

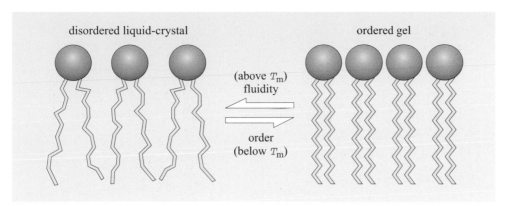

Figure 6.12
At temperatures above the transition temperature, the lipid bilayer is disordered in the plane of the membrane and the fatty acyl chains are highly mobile. This state is described as liquid-crystal. Decreasing the temperature below the transition temperature causes a transition to the gel state in which the fatty acyl chains are fully extended and tightly packed.

Bilayer fluidity varies with chain length and degree of fatty acid saturation

It is true of most substances that melting temperature increases with molecular mass and this is the case for individual fatty acids. Thus the melting temperatures of fatty acids increase with their chain length. The degree of saturation of a fatty acid also affects its melting temperature. Saturated fatty acids are highly flexible molecules, with relatively free rotation around the C—C bonds. However, steric interference between neighbouring methylene groups ($-CH_2-$) is minimized when the fatty acid adopts the fully extended conformation. Due to the rigid bend in the hydrocarbon chain caused by *cis* double bonds, unsaturated fatty acyl chains are unable to pack in the tight orderly fashion of saturated fatty acyl chains (Figure 6.13). The tight packing of saturated fatty acyl chains optimizes their van der Waals interactions. The disruption of these interactions caused by the bending of the fatty acyl chains means that less energy is needed to overcome them. The melting temperature (T_m) of unsaturated fatty acids is therefore reduced compared to that of saturated fatty acids of the same length and fatty acid melting temperatures decrease with increasing degree of unsaturation. To summarize, T_m of fatty acids:

↑ with ↑ chain length

↓ with ↑ unsaturation

Melting temperatures of saturated fatty acids range from 32–76 °C for chain lengths of 10–20 carbon atoms (Figure 6.14a). The effect of the degree of unsaturation is even more dramatic (Figure 6.14b).

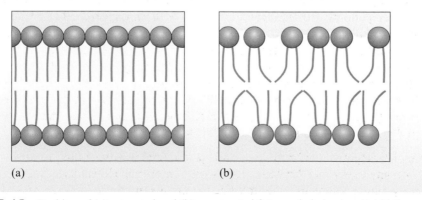

(a)   (b)

Figure 6.13 Packing of (a) saturated and (b) unsaturated fatty acyl chains in a lipid bilayer.

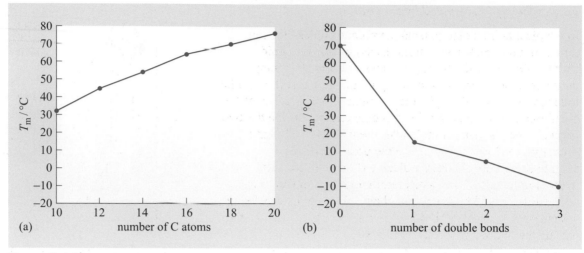

Figure 6.14   (a) The effect of chain length on the T_m of fatty acids (saturated). (b) The effect of degree of unsaturation on the T_m of fatty acids (C_{18}).

○ Bearing in mind the relative importance of degree of unsaturation and chain length in determining the melting temperature of fatty acids (Figure 6.14), put the fatty acids whose structures are shown in Figure 6.4 in order of increasing T_m.

● Linoleic acid; oleic acid; palmitic acid; stearic acid.

The melting temperature of the phospholipids varies with the length and degree of unsaturation of their fatty acyl chains in the same way as for the free fatty acids. Table 6.3 gives the melting temperature (T_m) for some phosphatidylcholine glycerophospholipids. The fatty acid components are identified by the number of carbon atoms and the number of double bonds that they contain.

Membrane lipids commonly contain one saturated and one unsaturated fatty acid. This helps to ensure that membranes are in the fluid state at physiological temperatures.

Table 6.3 T_m values of some phosphatidylcholine glycerophospholipids. (Data from Silvius, 1982)

Glycerophospholipid	Fatty acids*	T_m / °C
dimyristoyl-phosphatidylcholine	14 : 0, 14 : 0	23
dipalmitoyl-phosphatidylcholine	16 : 0, 16 : 0	42
distearoyl-phosphatidylcholine	18 : 0, 18 : 0	54
1-palmitoyl-2-oleoyl-phosphatidylcholine	16 : 0, 18 : 1	−5
dioleoyl-phosphatidylcholine	18 : 1, 18 : 1	−20

* The first number is the number of C atoms; the second number is the number of double bonds (Section 6.2.1).

Bilayer fluidity is regulated by cholesterol

In a typical animal cell, plasma membrane cholesterol can represent up to 50% (on a molar basis) of the total lipid content. On its own, cholesterol does not form bilayers; rather, it is incorporated into phospholipid bilayers. It is similar in length to a C_{16} fatty acid and is found in both leaflets of the membrane; however, a single molecule can not bridge the two leaflets. The cholesterol molecule orients itself such that its polar hydroxyl group is close to the polar head of a neighbouring phospholipid molecule (Figure 6.15). The hydrophobic part of the cholesterol molecules interacts with adjacent fatty acyl hydrocarbon chains. The rigid steroid ring system of the cholesterol molecule restricts the motion of the part of the hydrocarbon chains closest to the head group, rather like a splint. By restricting phospholipid mobility, cholesterol effectively reduces the membrane fluidity at higher temperatures. However, cholesterol also disrupts close packing of the hydrocarbon chains of the phospholipids, lowering the transition temperature of the membrane and reducing the likelihood of liquid-crystal to gel transition on cooling. *Thus cholesterol decreases membrane fluidity at high temperatures and increases it at low temperatures.* High levels of cholesterol effectively prevent formation of the gel phase. In such cases, the membrane has highly ordered extended phospholipids but these are not closely packed, due to the presence of cholesterol molecules. This state is called a **liquid-ordered** phase and is evident in lipid rafts (see Section 6.5).

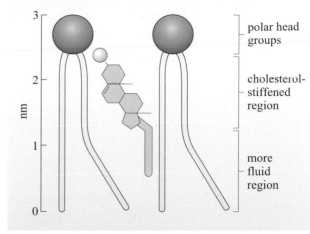

Figure 6.15   Cholesterol packs between phospholipid molecules and restricts movement of the fatty acyl tails.

Bilayer fluidity is regulated by the phospholipid head groups

Phospholipids with smaller head groups allow closer packing of the fatty acyl chains and therefore have the effect of increasing the melting temperature. Thus phosphatidylethanolamines have a higher T_m than phosphatidylcholines containing the same fatty acyl components (Table 6.4). Compare the head groups in Table 6.2 to confirm the difference in size of ethanolamine and choline.

Table 6.4 T_m values of some glycerophospholipids. Note the effect of different head groups on T_m. (Data from Silvius, 1982)

Glycerophospholipid	Fatty acids	T_m / °C
dipalmitoyl-phosphatidylcholine	16 : 0, 16 : 0	42
dipalmitoyl-phosphatidylethanolamine	16 : 0, 16 : 0	63
1-palmitoyl-2-oleoyl-phosphatidylcholine	16 : 0, 18 : 1	−5
1-palmitoyl-2-oleoyl-phosphatidylethanolamine	16 : 0, 18 : 1	20

Most organisms can regulate the fluidity of their membranes

Most organisms are able to regulate membrane fluidity. They do so primarily by changing their lipid composition, i.e. the degree of unsaturation of the fatty acids, the cholesterol content and the phospholipid head groups. For example, the ratio of unsaturated to saturated fatty acids in *E. coli* membranes increases from 0.4 at 40 °C to 2.9 when the temperature drops to 10 °C.

○ Though the fluidity of a lipid bilayer could be increased (i.e. T_m decreased) by reducing the proportion of long-chain, saturated fatty acids and increasing the proportion of shorter-chain, saturated fatty acids, in practice most organisms do not regulate membrane fluidity in this way. Why might this be?

● Shorter, saturated fatty acids will have a lower T_m, but the lipid bilayer that they form will be thinner than that formed by longer, saturated fatty acids. Thus regulation of membrane fluidity in this way would have the disadvantage of altering the overall membrane structure.

○ What type of phospholipids would you expect to be increased in the plasma membrane of arctic fish in winter?

● The proportion of unsaturated phospholipids in the cell membrane would be increased as a higher proportion of low-T_m phospholipids would be required to maintain membrane fluidity at low temperatures.

6.3.2 Movement of lipids within the bilayer

Consistent with the fluid-mosaic model, both lipids and proteins demonstrate relatively free **lateral diffusion** in membranes (i.e. they can move in the plane of the membrane). A lipid can traverse a distance of 2 μm in one second in a membrane, covering the length of an erythrocyte plasma membrane in 3–5 seconds. In fact, a lipid will not travel in a membrane in straight lines, as this statistic might imply. On the contrary, the lateral diffusion of lipids is random and erratic; hence rate is often expressed in units of area covered per second. In these terms, the lateral diffusion rate of a lipid is approximately 10^{-8} cm^2 s^{-1}. Lipids, and some proteins, are also free to rotate around their long axis. This type of movement is termed **rotational diffusion**. The fatty acid chains of membrane lipids are also highly mobile. In the fluid liquid-crystalline phase, there is rotation about the C—C bonds in these chains.

While membrane proteins *never* flip from one leaflet to the other, lipids can 'flip-flop' between the two leaflets of the bilayer, a type of movement called **transverse diffusion**.

○ Transverse diffusion of lipids occurs much less often than lateral diffusion. Why do you think this might be?

● Flip-flop requires the passage of the polar head group of the lipid through the hydrophobic interior of the bilayer, which is energetically unfavourable.

Indeed, the half-life ($t_{1/2}$) for transverse diffusion of phosphatidylcholines is of the order of days. Flip-flop of some phospholipids can be induced by a transmembrane pH gradient.

Mechanisms do exist, however, to remodel membranes and redistribute the lipid components. This process is particularly important when new membrane lipids are synthesized and introduced into established membranes. In eukaryotic cells, phospholipids are synthesized in the cytosolic leaflet of the endoplasmic reticulum (ER) membrane. **Scramblase** is a membrane-bound enzyme that catalyses the flip-flop of phospholipids in the ER membrane and has the effect of equilibrating the different phospholipids between the cytosolic leaflet and the leaflet in contact with the ER lumen (the lumenal leaflet) (Figure 6.16a). Vesicles, bound by newly synthesized membrane, bud off from the ER and move through the cytosol to fuse

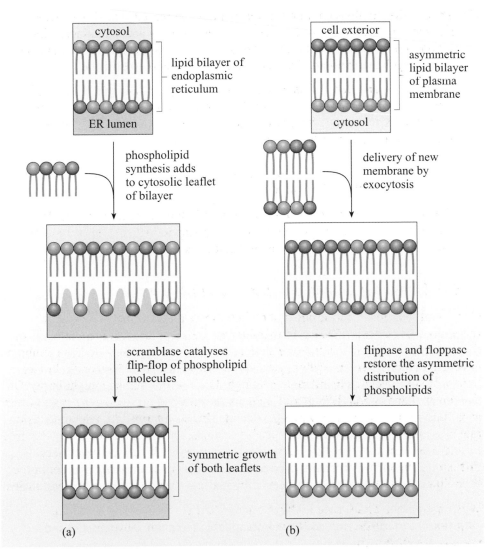

Figure 6.16
Phospholipid translocators catalyse flip-flop of phospholipids.
(a) Scramblase randomly distributes newly synthesized phospholipids between the two leaflets of the endoplasmic reticulum and is not specific for particular phospholipids.
(b) Delivery of new membrane disrupts the asymmetric distribution of lipids in the plasma membrane. Flippases catalyse the flip-flop of specific phospholipids from the extracellular leaflet to the cytosolic leaflet of the plasma membrane. Floppases catalyse the transport of specific phospholipids in the opposite direction. Working together, these enzymes restore the asymmetric distribution of the lipids of the plasma membrane.

with the plasma membrane and other intracellular membranes. In this way, the membranes of the cell are modelled and maintained with addition of newly synthesized lipids.

Plasma membranes have a characteristic asymmetric distribution of phospholipids (see Section 6.3.3). When newly synthesized membrane from the endoplasmic reticulum fuses with the plasma membrane by exocytosis, this distribution of phospholipids is disrupted. Enzymes called **flippases** and **floppases** are responsible for restoring and maintaining the asymmetric distribution of lipids in the plasma membrane. Flippases specifically catalyse the flip-flop of phospholipids that contain free amino groups (phosphatidylserine and phosphatidylethanolamine) from the extracellular to the cytosolic leaflet, whilst floppases transport specific lipids (including phosphatidylcholine) in the opposite direction (Figure 6.16b). Bidirectional scramblases are also found in the plasma membrane. Scramblases and flippases are collectively known as **phospholipid translocators**.

A further important element of lipid mobility is the exchange of lipids between membranes, though this process, like transverse diffusion, is slow. Cholesterol, having only a weakly polar group, can diffuse passively between the two leaflets of a membrane and also between two juxtaposed membranes. The half-life ($t_{1/2}$) for diffusion of cholesterol between membranes is of the order of 2–4 hours, whereas that of phospholipids is of the order of days. There are, however, **phospholipid exchange proteins** that can transfer specific phospholipids across the aqueous gap between two membranes.

6.3.3 Lipids are distributed asymmetrically in membranes

We have already mentioned the asymmetric distribution of lipids in the plasma membrane. In fact, this asymmetry is a feature of many biological membranes and extends not only to the type of lipid, but also to the degree of unsaturation of fatty acids in the phospholipid component. The distribution of lipids relates to their particular function. Thus glycosylated lipids (as with glycosylated proteins) are almost exclusively found in the extracellular leaflet of the plasma membrane. Here the carbohydrate groups extend into the extracellular environment, where they participate in signalling and recognition. In contrast, phosphatidylethanolamine, phosphatidylinositol and phosphatidylserine, lipids that participate in the transmission of signals from the plasma membrane to the interior of the cell, predominate in the cytosolic leaflet.

The asymmetric distribution of lipids can be demonstrated experimentally by using enzymes called phospholipases, which hydrolyse phospholipids, removing a single fatty acyl chain (e.g. phospholipase A$_2$, PLA$_2$, which removes the fatty acyl chain attached at the C2 of glycerol). Since phospholipases cannot cross the plasma membrane, only those phospholipids that are in the outer leaflet are susceptible when intact cells are treated with the enzyme. Following such treatment, the lipids can be extracted and analysed by TLC.

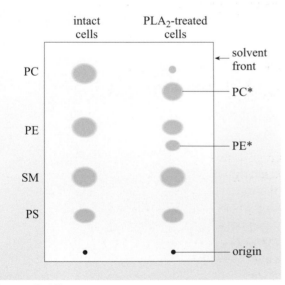

Figure 6.17   Analysis of the distribution of phospholipids in erythrocyte plasma membrane. TLC is used to compare the lipid composition of membranes prepared from untreated intact cells or cells that have been treated with PLA$_2$. Key: PC, phosphatidylcholine; PE, phosphatidylethanolamine; SM, sphingomyelin (sphingophospholipid); PS, phosphatidylserine. The products of hydrolysis of lipids by PLA$_2$ are denoted by *.

○ Would you predict that phospholipids that have had a fatty acyl chain removed by phospholipase treatment would travel faster or slower in TLC than the intact phospholipid?

● Removal of the hydrophobic fatty acyl chain will increase the affinity of the lipid for the (hydrophilic) stationary phase; thus it will travel more slowly and be retarded relative to the corresponding intact phospholipid.

Figure 6.17 illustrates the results from such an experiment. Note that the treatment of these cells with PLA$_2$ results in the appearance of two new spots on the chromatogram, corresponding to the products of hydrolysis of phosphatidylcholine and phosphatidylethanolamine (indicated as PC* and PE* respectively).

○ Compare the ratio of PC : PC* and PE : PE* in the extract from treated cells. What can you say about the distribution of these phospholipids between the inner and outer leaflet?

● There is more PC in the outer leaflet than in the inner leaflet and the reverse is true for PE.

○ Is there any phosphatidylserine (PS) in the outer leaflet of the plasma membrane?

● Assuming that the phospholipase is active against PS, as it is against PC and PE, the lack of any product from the hydrolysis of PS suggests that this lipid is absent from the outer leaflet of the membrane.

Notice that sphingomyelin is not a substrate for PLA$_2$. This is because the coupling of the fatty acyl group to sphingosine is via an amide linkage, not an ester linkage as in fatty-acylated glycerol. Thus, though sphingomyelin is structurally very similar to glycerophospholipids, its chemistry is very different.

In Figure 6.18, the proportions of the different types of phospholipid in the erythrocyte plasma membrane and their distribution between the inner and outer leaflets are represented as percentages of the total phospholipid content.

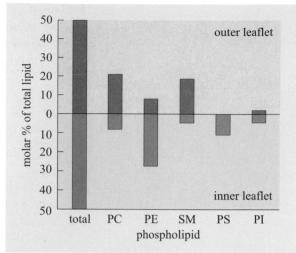

Figure 6.18   Asymmetrical distribution of lipids in the erythrocyte plasma membrane. The distribution of different lipids between the inner and outer leaflets is represented as a molar percentage of the total lipid content of the membrane. Key: PC, phosphatidylcholine; PE, phosphatidylethanolamine; SM, sphingomyelin (sphingophospholipid); PS, phosphatidylserine; PI, phosphatidylinositol. (Data from Rothman and Lenard, 1977)

6.3.4 Membrane permeability

Membranes are semipermeable barriers, i.e. they are permeable to some molecules and impermeable to others. They are highly permeable to hydrophobic molecules or small uncharged molecules such as water, but are impermeable to charged molecules, as the hydrophobic interior of the bilayer forms an effective barrier to the diffusion of these solutes. There is, however, a degree of permeability of lipid bilayers to polar molecules, depending on their size and polarity and, in biological membranes, the movement of substances across a membrane can be assisted by carrier proteins or channel proteins.

The many and varied transport mechanisms that operate across cell membranes to regulate the composition of the cytosol and other cell compartments will not be discussed here. These mechanisms have been covered in S204, Book 3 *The Core of Life*, Vol. I.

The simplest way in which a solute can cross a membrane is by diffusion. Passive diffusion, (i.e. diffusion that does not require energy), proceeds spontaneously down a concentration gradient until an equilibrium is reached in which the concentration of the solute is the same on both sides of the membrane. A measure of the ability of a solute to diffuse across a membrane is given by its permeability coefficient (P), which has units of metres per second (m s^{-1}) and parallels the solubility of that solute in organic solvents. Table 6.5 gives the permeability coefficient for a number of different solutes and an indication of the time taken to reach equilibrium across an artificial membrane by passive diffusion.

Table 6.5 The permeability coefficient (P) and the time taken to reach equilibrium across an artificial membrane (lipid bilayer) for a number of different solutes.

Molecule or ion	$P\,/\,\mathrm{m\ s^{-1}}$	Timescale for equilibrium to be reached
water	5×10^{-5}	milliseconds
glycerol urea	3×10^{-8}	seconds
tryptophan glucose	1×10^{-9} 5×10^{-10}	minutes to hours
Cl⁻ K⁺ Na⁺	8×10^{-13} 5×10^{-14} 1×10^{-14}	days to weeks

From Chapter 2, you should recall that, in aqueous solution, charged and polar molecules are surrounded by a shell of water molecules, known as the hydration shell. For charged and polar molecules to cross a membrane, they must shed this hydration shell before they can dissolve in the hydrophobic core of the lipid bilayer. Having crossed the hydrophobic interior, these molecules can then be rehydrated by water. The very low P values for charged and polar solutes reflect the energy barrier presented by the dehydration step. These sorts of measurements can be made using the black membranes described earlier in this section. In real biological membranes, the barrier to diffusion of many charged and polar molecules is overcome by having transport systems that effectively reduce the energy required for transmembrane diffusion.

The permeability of the plasma membrane to different substances is of critical importance to the pharmacologist interested in how drugs can penetrate cells and tissues. As mentioned above, the permeability coefficient of a compound is related to its solubility in organic solvent or lipid. Figure 6.19 illustrates the relationship between the lipid solubility of a compound and the rate at which it is taken up by (penetrates) brain tissue. Note that, for substances administered intravenously, to enter the brain they must first penetrate the plasma membranes of the endothelial cells lining the brain capillaries.

○ From Figure 6.19, the uptake rates of D-glucose, L-leucine and L-dopa (blue dots) are higher than would be predicted from their lipid solubilities. What could explain this difference between the observed and expected uptake rates of these compounds?

● The uptake of these compounds does not depend solely on their passive diffusion through lipid bilayers, but is facilitated by specific carriers in the plasma membrane of the endothelial cells lining the brain capillaries.

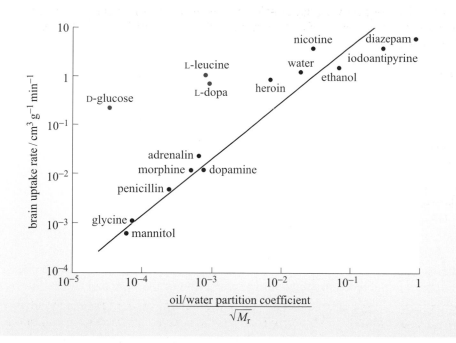

Figure 6.19
Plots of brain uptake rate versus lipid solubility for various compounds. Note the linear relationship between the two variables for those compounds that are indicated by red dots. The brain uptake rate is expressed as blood clearance rate ($cm^3 min^{-1}$; equivalent to the permeability coefficient multiplied by the surface area over which absorption of the compound can take place) per gram of brain tissue. Hence this variable has units of $cm^3 g^{-1} min^{-1}$. Lipid solubility is given by the oil / water partition coefficient (i.e. a measure of how readily the compound dissolves in oil compared to water) adjusted for differences in molecular mass.

Summary of Section 6.3

1   Purified amphipathic membrane lipids spontaneously form a lipid bilayer in aqueous solvents. Formation of the bilayer is driven by hydrophobic interactions between the fatty acyl chains of lipid molecules, and by hydrogen bonding and electrostatic interactions between the polar head groups and water molecules.

2   The physical properties of natural cell membranes can be modelled by artificial lipid bilayers such as liposomes and black membranes.

3   Bilayer fluidity is affected by temperature, the chain length and degree of saturation of the lipid fatty acid chains, the cholesterol content and the size of the phospholipid head groups.

4   In a lipid bilayer in its fluid (liquid-crystal) state, the fatty acyl chains are highly mobile, with rotation about the C—C bonds, and there is rapid lateral movement of lipid molecules in the bilayer. The transition temperature (T_m) of a lipid bilayer is the temperature below which it loses its fluidity and changes to a gel state. In the gel state, the fatty acyl chains are fully extended and tightly packed and lateral diffusion of the lipids is very slow.

5   The melting temperature of fatty acids increases with increasing chain length and decreases with increasing degree of unsaturation.

6   Cholesterol decreases membrane fluidity at high temperatures and increases it at low temperatures.

7   Phospholipids with smaller head groups allow closer packing of the fatty acyl chains and therefore increase the transition temperature of the bilayer.

8   Whilst lateral and rotational diffusion of lipids occurs quite freely, transverse diffusion or flip-flop of lipids is rare, as it requires the passage of the polar head group of the lipid through the hydrophobic interior of the bilayer. Phospholipid translocators such as scramblases, flippases and floppases catalyse flip-flop of lipids between leaflets in a membrane.

9   Lipids are distributed asymmetrically in membranes.

10   The rate of diffusion of a compound across a lipid bilayer parallels its solubility in organic solvents.

6.4 Membrane proteins

We will turn now to the protein component of membranes. The variety of membrane proteins and their importance in cellular function is evidenced by the fact that 30% of the proteins encoded by the human genome are membrane proteins. It is the proteins that perform the specific functions of the membrane, as opposed to the more structural and physical role of the lipid bilayer.

The diversity of membrane proteins is reflected in the variety of functions that they serve:

▸ Transport of specific molecules and ions into or out of the cell or organelle.

▸ Receptors for chemical signals from outside the cell or organelle (to be discussed in Chapter 13).

▸ Structural links between the cytoskeleton and the extracellular matrix.

▸ Intercellular recognition and adhesion: direct connections between neighbouring cells in a tissue are made via complex protein assemblies (to be discussed in Chapter 16).

▸ Catalysis: the membranes of organelles are characterized by distinctive enzyme components.

In Chapter 11 you will learn about how newly synthesized membrane proteins become associated with the lipid bilayer. For now we will concentrate on the structural aspects of different types of membrane proteins.

6.4.1 Integral and peripheral membrane proteins

The manner in which a protein associates with a membrane depends on its structure. Broadly speaking, membrane-associated proteins can be divided into two main groups, **integral** and **peripheral**. The distinction between these two groups is made on the basis of how readily, and under what conditions, they can be extracted from the lipid bilayer. This property depends on the nature of their association with the bilayer – specifically, whether they interact with the hydrophobic interior of the membrane and/or the hydrophilic exterior (Figure 6.20).

Integral membrane proteins are tightly bound to membranes by hydrophobic interactions with the non-polar tails of the lipids, whilst polar portions of the protein either associate with the polar head groups of the lipids (via hydrogen bonding and ionic interactions) or are buried deep in the protein. Thus, like lipids, integral membrane proteins are amphipathic, having hydrophobic surfaces where they embed in the membrane and hydrophilic surfaces where they are exposed to the aqueous environment. Integral proteins can associate with the lipid bilayer in a

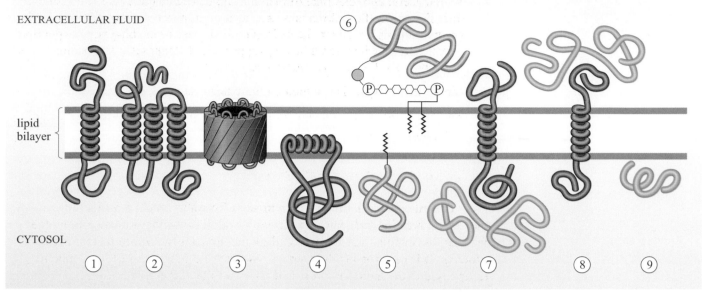

Figure 6.20 Membrane proteins can be categorized according to their association with the lipid bilayer. Transmembrane proteins span the lipid bilayer (1–3) and can traverse the membrane once only (single-pass) or more than once (multipass). The membrane-spanning portions of these proteins can have α-helical or β sheet structures as described in the text. Other membrane proteins are associated with the membrane on one side only. These proteins may be embedded in the lipid bilayer (4) or anchored in the bilayer by means of a lipid linkage, as in fatty-acylated or prenylated proteins (5) or GPI-anchored proteins (6). Peripheral proteins are associated with the membrane, either indirectly via non-covalent interactions with other membrane proteins (7, 8) or directly via interactions with the hydrophilic head groups of the lipids (9).

number of different ways, illustrated in Figure 6.20. Some, called **transmembrane proteins**, span the lipid bilayer. Others are embedded or anchored at only one surface of the membrane. Separation of integral proteins from the membrane requires treatment with agents such as organic solvents or detergents, which disrupt the bilayer. If detergents or organic solvents are removed following extraction, integral membrane proteins will tend to aggregate and precipitate as a consequence of interactions between their hydrophobic regions.

Peripheral proteins have no well-defined hydrophobic surface and associate with the membrane via hydrogen bonds and electrostatic interactions with the lipid head groups or with other membrane proteins. Peripheral proteins are relatively easy to dissociate from membranes. High concentrations of salts, a change in pH, or the presence of agents that can complex with and sequester calcium ions (*chelation agents*) can be sufficient to cause dissociation of peripheral proteins from the membrane and, unlike detergents and organic solvents, these treatments do not disrupt the lipid bilayer.

6.4.2 Studying membrane protein structure

There are particular problems associated with the study of integral membrane proteins. Whilst purified peripheral proteins behave as water-soluble globular proteins in aqueous solution, it is difficult to purify integral membrane proteins without significantly affecting their conformation and activity. Membrane proteins are insoluble in aqueous solutions, and organic solvents cause them to denature, making them very difficult to crystallize for X-ray diffraction studies. Thus structural and biochemical data on membrane proteins are very limited compared with those on water-soluble proteins. Indeed, only 30 unique structures of membrane proteins have been solved, compared with 3000 unique crystal structures of soluble proteins.

Nonetheless, progress is being made in the analysis of the structure and function of membrane proteins. Peripheral proteins and cytosolic or extracellular domains of integral membrane proteins, obtained by enzymatic cleavage from isolated membranes or by cloning in microbes, behave like soluble globular proteins and lend themselves to structural analysis. A number of techniques have also been developed to allow membrane proteins to be studied in situ in lipid bilayers. At high concentrations of the protein, it is possible to form two-dimensional crystals in a bilayer. In such preparations, the protein's native structure and function are preserved. Electron crystallography, a technique that uses an electron beam instead of X-rays to obtain a diffraction pattern for the protein, and atomic force microscopy, which can achieve a resolution of 10 pm (0.1 Å), can be applied to such two-dimensional crystals to acquire structural data.

Molecular biology techniques are widely used in the study of membrane proteins. Analysis of the amino acid sequence can be used to predict protein structure (see Section 6.4.5), which can then be verified by other indirect methods. For example, antibodies can be raised against synthetic peptide sequences corresponding to different parts of the polypeptide and used to determine how the protein associates with the membrane. Antibodies that recognize particular structures (epitopes) on the extracellular part of a membrane protein will bind to the protein in intact cells, whilst antibodies that recognize epitopes in the cytosolic part will only bind if the cells are first made permeable. Those antibodies that recognize epitopes in the transmembrane part of the protein will not be able to bind to the protein in situ in the membrane. Similar 'surface-labelling' strategies using membrane-impermeable protein-specific reagents that are fluorescent or radioactively labelled can be used. Such an approach allows the distribution of a particular protein in the membrane to be determined.

6.4.3 Transmembrane proteins

Transmembrane proteins span the membrane and have portions extending into the extracellular environment and the cytosol. Those in which the polypeptide chain crosses the membrane once only are called **single-pass transmembrane proteins** whilst those that cross more than once are termed **multipass transmembrane proteins**.

α-helical transmembrane proteins

The membrane-spanning portions of transmembrane proteins, which contact the hydrophobic interior of the bilayer, present hydrophobic surfaces composed largely of amino acid residues with non-polar side-chains. The polar peptide bonds are driven to form hydrogen bonds with one another and in most transmembrane proteins this portion of the polypeptide adopts an α-helical conformation. A stretch of α helix structure containing about 20 residues is sufficient to span the lipid bilayer. Most single-pass transmembrane proteins contain a single α helix spanning the membrane. For example, glycophorin A is a protein located in the erythrocyte plasma membrane that forms dimers. It consists of three domains: an extracellular N-terminal domain, a largely hydrophobic α-helical transmembrane domain and a cytoplasmic C-terminal domain (Figure 6.21).

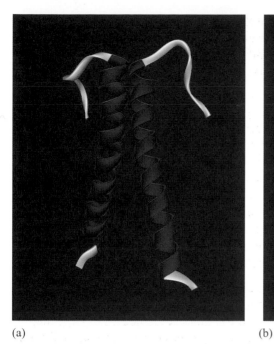

(a)

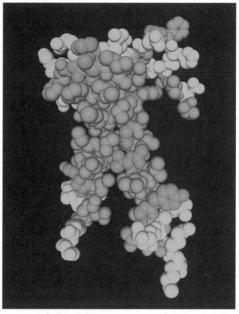

(b)

Figure 6.21
Partial structure of human glycophorin A dimer (pdb file 1afo) represented (a) in ribbon format to highlight the α-helical content (in red) and (b) in space-filling format with strongly hydrophobic residues shown in orange and polar or charged hydrophilic residues shown in green. (For clarity, H atoms are not shown.) Glycophorin A is a single-pass transmembrane protein found in erythrocyte plasma membrane. The α helix spans the membrane. This model does not include the entire N- and C-terminal domains.

Most multipass transmembrane proteins in eukaryotic and bacterial plasma membranes contain transmembrane α helices. These helices are connected by loops on either side of the membrane. The connecting loops, which are exposed to the aqueous environment, are short and consist of residues with polar side-chains.

Bacteriorhodopsin, the major protein component of the membrane of halobacteria, is an example of an α-helical multipass transmembrane protein. The structure of bacteriorhodopsin (Figure 6.22) was determined by electron crystallography. This light-driven proton pump has seven α-helical membrane-spanning segments and belongs to a large family of structurally similar receptors known as the 7-helix transmembrane receptors. You will meet these receptors again when we discuss signal transduction (Chapter 13). The α helices in multipass transmembrane proteins can move relative to each other, and such conformational changes are often critical to the protein's function, as in the case of receptors or ion channels.

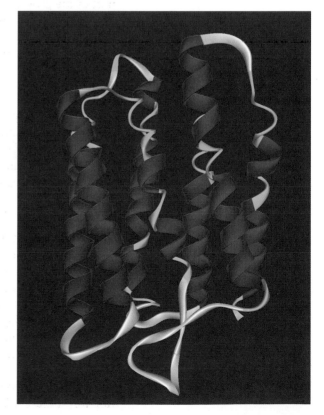

Figure 6.22 Bacteriorhodopsin from *Halobacterium salinarium* (pdb file 1ap9) is a multipass transmembrane protein containing seven membrane-spanning α helices. The protein is shown here in ribbon format and coloured according to secondary structure (α helix, red; turn, green; random coil, white).

(a) Single transmembrane helix

(b) Four-helix bundle

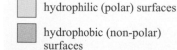

hydrophilic (polar) surfaces

hydrophobic (non-polar) surfaces

Figure 6.23 Hydrophobic and hydrophilic surfaces on α-helical transmembrane proteins. (a) A single-pass transmembrane protein has mainly hydrophobic residues in the membrane-spanning helix. (b) In helical multipass transmembrane proteins, the association of several α helices can create a hydrophilic pore. In the hydrophobic interior of the lipid bilayer, the α helices associate such that polar side-chains point towards the centre of the assembly whilst non-polar side-chains project out into the lipid environment.

Whilst single α helices spanning the membrane have mainly hydrophobic residues, in proteins with several transmembrane helices, the helices are typically bundled and only the side-chains that are presented on the outside of the bundle need be hydrophobic (Figure 6.23). Often, such bundles of helices create a central channel lined with polar residues, which are screened off from the hydrophobic membrane, and the resulting structure may function as a pore.

β barrel transmembrane proteins

In other transmembrane proteins, the membrane-spanning portion of the polypeptide adopts a β barrel conformation (Figure 6.20). In this conformation, hydrogen bonds can form between the polar peptide bonds of neighbouring strands as in β pleated sheet. Note that β barrel transmembrane proteins are necessarily multipass proteins. They are often transport proteins, enzymes or receptors and are abundant in the outer membrane of mitochondria, chloroplasts and many bacteria.

The β barrel structure in transmembrane proteins has hydrophobic side-chains projecting into the lipid bilayer and polar residues pointing towards the centre of the barrel. In **porins**, a family of pore-forming proteins, this arrangement creates a channel in the membrane for selective passage of hydrophilic solutes. Figure 6.24a and b shows the structure of maltoporin in ribbon format. This transmembrane protein consists of three subunits, each with a β barrel conformation. The interior of the barrel forms a channel for the selective passage of small sugar molecules. The selectivity of porins derives from the conformation of loops of the polypeptide chain which extend into the channel. In Figure 6.24c, the maltoporin structure has been represented in space-filling format and the

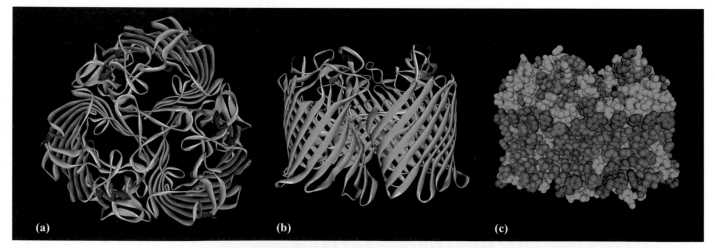

(a)　　　　(b)　　　　(c)

Figure 6.24 Maltoporin (pdb file 1mpm) is a member of the porin family of membrane proteins and consists of three subunits, each adopting a β barrel conformation. (a) Top view, looking down towards the membrane surface (β sheet shown in cyan). (b) Side view, in the plane of the membrane. (c) Space-filling representation (side view) in which hydrophobic residues are shown in orange and polar or charged hydrophilic residues are shown in green.

residues have been coloured according to whether they are hydrophobic or hydrophilic. A band of hydrophobic residues (shown in orange) around the protein corresponds to the part of the protein that is exposed to the hydrophobic interior of the lipid bilayer. Note the predominance of hydrophilic polar and charged residues (shown in green) on the parts of the protein that extend either side of the membrane.

Note that the distribution of hydrophobic and hydrophilic residues in the β barrel of porins is virtually the reverse of that in globular cytosolic proteins with similar folding patterns (Table 3.4, Chapter 3).

6.4.4 Other integral membrane proteins

Integral membrane proteins that do not span the membrane fall into three categories (Figure 6.20):

1   They are anchored at the cytosolic surface of the membrane by means of an α-helical segment. This α helix typically has a hydrophobic central stretch, bound at either end with hydrophilic segments. An example of such a protein is the electron transfer protein cytochrome b_5 which is located in the ER membrane (Figure 6.25).

2   They are anchored at the cytosolic surface of the membrane by means of a covalently attached lipid group (fatty acyl or isoprenoid group) (Figure 6.26). This protein modification was described in Chapter 3. For some proteins, covalent linkage to the fatty acid palmitic acid is reversible. This reversibility provides an important way in which the localization of such proteins, and their activity, can be regulated. Many fatty-acylated and prenylated proteins participate in intracellular signalling processes through protein–protein interactions, a subject that we will discuss further in Chapter 13.

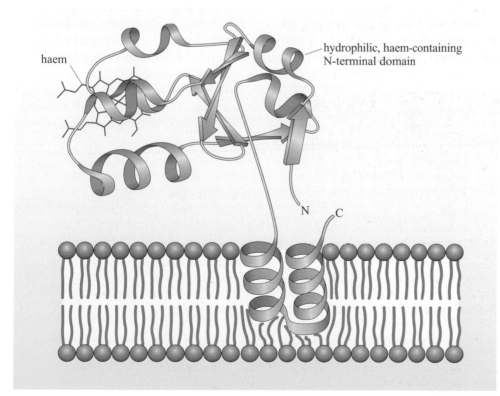

Figure 6.25
Representation of liver cytochrome b_5 in association with a lipid bilayer. Hydrophilic parts of the protein are highlighted in green and hydrophobic parts are coloured orange. Notice that the part of the protein that is located amongst the head groups of the lipids is hydrophilic. The structure of the catalytic N-terminal domain has been determined by X-ray diffraction, whilst the structure of the hydrophobic anchor has been deduced from the amino acid sequence.

Figure 6.26
Some membrane proteins are anchored in the lipid bilayer by a covalently attached lipid group such as a fatty acyl group (a), or a prenyl group (b).

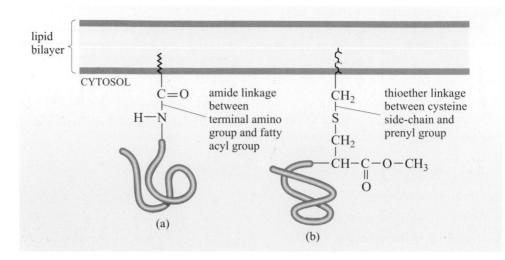

3   They are anchored at the extracellular surface by means of covalent linkage to glycoinositol phospholipids (see Chapter 3). GPI-linked proteins are synthesized in the ER as single-pass transmembrane proteins, but the transmembrane segment is removed when the GPI anchor is added. GPI-anchored proteins are diverse in function and include enzymes and receptors. The GPI anchor can direct the protein to lipid rafts within the plasma membrane, with consequences for the protein's activity, as we shall see later. In some cases, GPI-linked proteins are released from the cell surface when the link to the GPI anchor is cleaved by a specific phospholipase.

6.4.5 Hydropathy plots

The amino acid sequences of many membrane proteins have been deduced from DNA sequence data, and the same data have revealed functional and evolutionary relationships between proteins. From the amino acid sequences, it is possible to predict how polypeptide chains might fold, as discussed in Chapter 3. In the case of proteins that contain membrane-spanning α-helical segments, it is possible to identify these segments on the basis of sequence information. In such an analysis, different residues are assigned a value as an index of hydrophobicity. This value is a measure of the free energy required for transfer of the amino acid side-chain from an organic solvent to water, i.e. replacing an organic solvation shell with a water solvation shell. Thus hydrophobic residues have positive values and hydrophilic residues have negative values. For a particular residue (n) in the sequence, a **hydropathy index** is calculated as the mean hydrophobicity value over a prescribed number of residues to either side of n (e.g. $n - 9$ to $n + 9$). The hydropathy index is then plotted on the y-axis as a function of its location in the polypeptide (n), to give a **hydropathy plot**. Sharp peaks in the plot indicate sequences that would be unusually hydrophobic for a soluble protein. In a membrane protein, these peaks are used to identify the parts of the polypeptide that are likely to constitute a transmembrane section. Figure 6.27 shows hydropathy plots for a single-pass and a multipass transmembrane protein.

○   From Figure 6.27b, try to predict the number of α-helical transmembrane segments that this multipass transmembrane protein contains.

●   The four peaks indicate that this protein contains four membrane-spanning α helices.

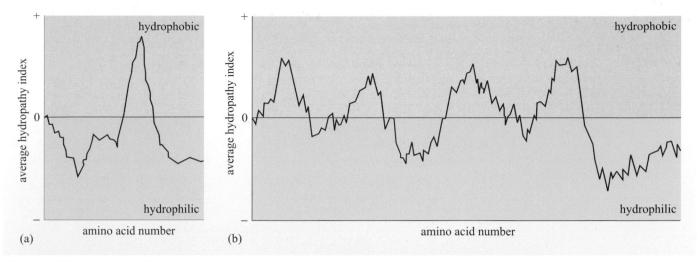

Figure 6.27 Examples of hydropathy plots for α-helical transmembrane proteins. (a) A single-pass protein such as glycophorin A. (b) A multipass protein, e.g. connexin.

Proteins that contain four membrane-spanning α helices (also known as tetraspan proteins) include a family of proteins called **connexins**. Six connexin proteins assemble to form a channel at gap junctions between cells (see Section 6.6.2).

Whilst hydropathy plots can help with the prediction of α-helical transmembrane segments, this analysis is uninformative in the case of proteins with β sheet transmembrane domains, such as the porins. This is because the length of extended β strand required to span the membrane is no more than ten residues and only alternate residues are hydrophobic. Clearly, compared with α-helical transmembrane segments, typically consisting of a stretch of around 20 largely hydrophobic residues, transmembrane β sheet is not readily identifiable by this technique.

○ In transmembrane proteins with β barrel conformations, why are hydrophobic residues required only at alternate positions in the β strand sequence?

● In β sheet, the side-chains of neighbouring residues point in opposite directions, above or below the sheet (see Figure 3.11a, Chapter 3). In the β barrel, therefore, alternate side-chains point towards the inside of the barrel, or outside, away from the barrel. In membrane proteins with this conformation, only those residues that point outwards, into the membrane, need to be hydrophobic.

6.4.6 Membrane proteins are asymmetrically associated with the membrane

Biological membranes are asymmetric with respect to the distribution of all integral membrane proteins. In the plasma membrane, each protein has a single specific orientation with respect to the cytosolic and extracellular surfaces of the membrane and all molecules of any particular protein are oriented the same way. Those proteins that locate to one side of the membrane are *always* located to the same surface. Importantly, asymmetry of membrane proteins is required for most functions (e.g. transport, signal transduction, recognition). The asymmetry of membrane proteins is established during their synthesis (discussed in Chapter 11) and maintained throughout their lifetimes. As mentioned earlier, all the oligosaccharide groups linked to glycoproteins and glycolipids are on the extracellular surface of the plasma membrane. In the ER, where they are synthesized, they are found on the lumenal membrane surface.

Note that membrane proteins have never been observed to flip-flop from one side of the membrane to the other in the way that lipids do. Such a movement would necessitate overcoming the prohibitively large energy barrier associated with moving the large hydrophilic cytosolic or extracellular domains across the lipid bilayer. Lateral movement of proteins in the plane of the membrane does occur and is often important to protein function. This property, of course, is an important feature of the fluid-mosaic model of membrane structure. However, some membrane proteins are connected, directly or indirectly, to the cytoskeleton of the cell and they tend to be relatively restricted in their mobility (see Section 6.6).

Summary of Section 6.4

1   Integral and peripheral membrane proteins are distinguished on the basis of how readily, and under what conditions, they can be extracted from the lipid bilayer.

2   Integral proteins can associate with the lipid bilayer in a number of different ways. Transmembrane proteins span the lipid bilayer and others are embedded in or anchored at only one surface of the membrane. Integral membrane proteins that do not span the membrane include those that are anchored at the cytosolic surface by means of an α-helical segment, those anchored at the cytosolic surface by means of a covalently attached lipid group (fatty acyl or isoprenoid group) and GPI-anchored proteins at the extracellular surface.

3   Peripheral proteins have no well-defined hydrophobic surface and associate with the membrane via hydrogen bonds and electrostatic interactions with the head groups of membrane phospholipids or with other membrane proteins.

4   Transmembrane proteins have portions extending into the extracellular environment and the cytosol. The polypeptide chain may cross the membrane once only (single-pass) or more than once (multipass).

5   The membrane-spanning portions of transmembrane proteins that contact the hydrophobic interior of the bilayer present hydrophobic surfaces composed largely of amino acid residues with non-polar side-chains. The polar peptide bonds are driven to form hydrogen bonds with one another and in most transmembrane proteins this portion of the polypeptide adopts an α-helical conformation. α-helical multipass transmembrane proteins include receptors and ion channels.

6   In β barrel transmembrane proteins, the membrane-spanning portion of the polypeptide adopts a β barrel conformation. These transmembrane proteins are often transport proteins, enzymes or receptors.

7   Hydropathy plots are used to predict α-helical transmembrane segments.

8   In the plasma membrane, each protein has a single specific orientation with respect to the cytosolic and extracellular surfaces of the membrane and all molecules of any particular protein are oriented the same way. Membrane proteins have never been observed to flip-flop from one side of the membrane to the other in the way that lipids do.

6.5 Lipid rafts

Singer and Nicolson's fluid-mosaic model of membrane structure proposed a homogenous distribution of proteins, uniformly soluble in the lipid bilayer. This view has been revised in recent years following the development of the **lipid raft hypothesis**. According to this hypothesis, membranes are not entirely in the liquid-crystal phase but contain microdomains (rafts) that are highly ordered (Figure 6.28). These rafts are enriched in lipids such as sphingolipids with saturated (high T_m) fatty acyl chains and also contain high levels of cholesterol. Interactions between these lipids drive formation of the rafts. Cholesterol tends to interact with sphingolipids and saturated fatty acyl chains because they accommodate its rigid structure more readily than do unsaturated chains in glycerophospholipids. There is also the potential for hydrogen bonding interactions between the oligosaccharide groups of glycosphingolipids, further enhancing the cohesive property of the microdomain.

Though many sphingolipids have a T_m higher than normal physiological temperatures, the true gel-state (described in Section 6.3.1) is avoided in lipid rafts by the presence of cholesterol which prevents tight packing of the sphingolipid fatty acyl chains. As you learned in Section 6.3.1, this intermediate state, between liquid-crystal and gel, is described as liquid-ordered. Thus lipid rafts are envisaged as liquid-ordered islands in a sea of fluid liquid-crystal phase membrane.

One of the most important properties of lipid rafts is that they can include or exclude proteins to variable extents. Lipid rafts are enriched in GPI-anchored and fatty-acylated membrane proteins as the hydrophobic anchors that locate these proteins in the membrane are generally saturated and therefore interact preferentially with the lipids in the raft. Prenylated membrane proteins, having unsaturated hydrocarbon chains, tend to be excluded from lipid rafts. Some transmembrane proteins have also been identified in lipid rafts. The association of proteins with lipid rafts has important consequences for their function. Among those proteins that co-isolate with lipid rafts are many that are involved in signal transduction, e.g. G proteins, kinases of the Src family, Ras-related GTPases and protein kinase C, suggesting that lipid rafts act as signalling hotspots.

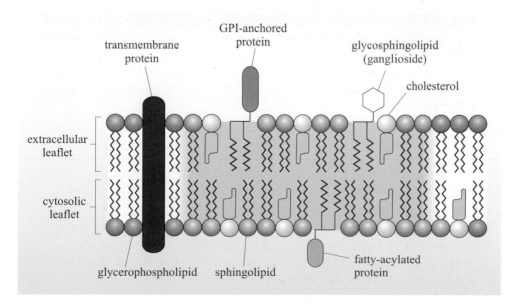

Figure 6.28
Lipid rafts. Sphingolipid and cholesterol molecules form highly ordered clusters or microdomains (shown here shaded green) within the fluid membrane. GPI-anchored and fatty-acylated proteins concentrate in these lipid rafts but many proteins are excluded.

○   What advantage might there be in co-locating signalling proteins in this way?

●   Co-location of signalling proteins in lipid rafts would facilitate their interactions and allow integration of different signalling processes.

Lipid rafts include a very specific subtype known as **caveolae**. Caveolae contain caveolins, which belong to a family of multipass integral membrane proteins. Caveolae form flask-shaped invaginations in the plasma membrane (Figure 6.29) and they have been implicated in endocytosis and in the transport of molecules across endothelial cells. These structures will be discussed further in Chapter 12. As with rafts in general, caveolae play a part in signal transduction.

Figure 6.29
Caveolae in the plasma membrane of a fibroblast. Caveolae are a special type of lipid raft distinguished by their flask-like structure and the presence of the protein caveolin.

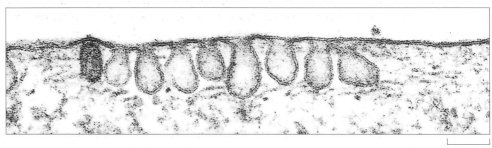

0.15 µm

The particular lipid composition of lipid rafts makes them, and their constituent proteins, resistant to solubilization with non-ionic detergents. Such treatment effectively extracts the liquid-crystal part of cell membranes but does not disrupt the rafts. Their resistance to extraction under these conditions has led to lipid rafts being known as detergent-resistant membranes (DRMs) and this property is exploited in their isolation. Due to their lipid composition, the rafts have a low density. Thus a mixture of detergent-soluble and insoluble membrane fractions can be resolved by sucrose density gradient ultracentrifugation (Figure 6.30).

Although isolation of detergent-resistant membranes for biochemical analysis is straightforward, the identification of lipid rafts in living cells has proved more problematic and has led to controversy regarding the nature of lipid rafts – indeed, has raised questions as to whether they really exist. Lipid rafts can not be identified by conventional microscopy techniques, their size being less than the lower limit (300 nm) for detection. A variation of a technique known as fluorescence resonance energy transfer technique (FRET; Box 6.3) has been used to determine the

Figure 6.30
Isolation of lipid rafts can be achieved by sucrose density gradient ultracentrifugation of membrane preparations following treatment with a non-ionic detergent (e.g. Triton X-100) at 4 °C. The lipid rafts are resistant to solubilization under these conditions and due to their low density, they float to near the top of the gradient.

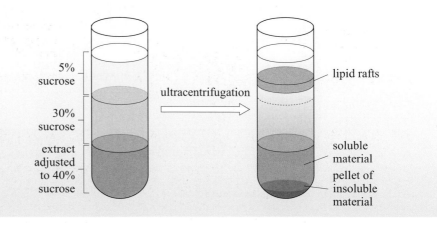

distribution and proximity of GPI-anchored proteins and glycosphingolipids that have been 'tagged' with fluorescent molecules called *fluorophores*. This experimental approach indicates when two differently tagged proteins or lipids are within 10 nm of each other. From such studies it has been determined that lipid rafts are about 70 nm in diameter. It is clear also from these studies that lipid rafts are very dynamic structures, with proteins moving into and out of them and rafts coalescing and splitting.

Box 6.3   Fluorescence resonance energy transfer (FRET)

FRET is used to determine the proximity of two molecules on a cell surface. The two molecules are labelled with distinct fluorophores. Labelling can be achieved directly, e.g. by covalent attachment or expression as a fusion protein (i.e. tagged using recombinant DNA techniques), or indirectly, using specific fluorescently labelled antibodies. One of the fluorescent tags is termed the donor and the other is termed the acceptor and these fluorophores are chosen according to their excitation and emission wavelengths. In Figure 6.31, protein A has been labelled using an antibody conjugated to the fluorophore fluorescein (the donor) and protein B has been labelled with an antibody conjugated to a different fluorescent molecule, rhodamine (the acceptor). The cells are illuminated at a wavelength that excites the donor, which emits at a specific wavelength. If proteins A and B are sufficiently close to each other (< 10 nm apart), energy from the donor emission is transferred to the acceptor, resulting in emission at a specific wavelength. In the case of rhodamine, the acceptor in this example, the emission is visible red light.

The general principle of this technique can be applied for a variety of different experimental purposes; for example, to demonstrate the interaction between proteins or nucleic acids, as well as demonstrating proximity.

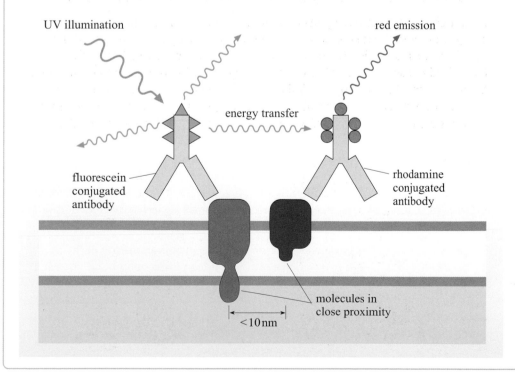

Figure 6.31
Fluorescence resonance energy transfer (FRET). In the example shown here, the acceptor fluorophore (rhodamine) emits red light when it is excited by the donor (fluorescein) emission (caused by excitation with UV light). This event requires the two fluorophores to be in close proximity.

Summary of Section 6.5

1   Lipid rafts are cohesive liquid-ordered microdomains within the fluid membrane phase. They are enriched in sphingolipids with saturated fatty acyl chains and in cholesterol.

2   There is a selective partitioning of certain membrane proteins to lipid rafts. Lipid rafts are enriched in GPI-anchored and fatty-acylated membrane proteins whilst prenylated membrane proteins are generally excluded.

3   Lipid rafts act as signalling hotspots.

4   Caveloae are a type of lipid raft associated with the protein caveolin.

6.6 The plasma membrane

In multicellular organisms, different cells in different tissues are often specialized to perform particular functions. At the same time, there are cellular processes common to all cells (e.g. metabolism). The plasma membranes of different cell types crucially reflect and contribute to this diversity of function, primarily by means of the proteins that they contain. All communication with the extracellular environment is via the plasma membrane, and proteins associated permanently or transiently with the cytosolic surface are key mediators in communication in both directions.

The very different shapes (morphologies) of different cell types are conferred by the cytoskeleton of the cell rather than the membrane. Thus the cytoskeleton acts like the scaffolding for the cell. The plasma membrane is not independent of the rest of the cell but is connected to the cytoskeleton by means of structural proteins. These connections are regulated and are an important aspect of the cell's response to extracellular signals, particularly with respect to adhesion and migration or the changes in cell shape and organization that occur in cell division and differentiation. The importance of the cytoskeleton and its links to the plasma membrane will be evident when we go on to look at these different cellular processes in later chapters.

In the previous sections, most of our considerations of membrane structure and function apply to all biological membranes (i.e. the plasma membrane and the intracellular membranes). We will now consider specific aspects of the plasma membrane.

6.6.1 Connecting the plasma membrane to the cytoskeleton

The human erythrocyte plasma membrane has been studied extensively due to the relative ease with which these cells can be obtained and the plasma membrane isolated. The erythrocyte plasma membrane is also much less complex than other cell membranes. For these reasons, the human erythrocyte has become a model system for the study of the plasma membrane.

Figure 6.32 shows the proteins of the erythrocyte membrane resolved by SDS–PAGE. Band 3 and glycophorin are both integral transmembrane proteins. However, most of the other proteins associated with the erythrocyte plasma membrane are peripheral proteins associated with the cytosolic surface. Most abundant is **spectrin**, a long, thin rod-like protein (Figure 6.33). Spectrin is a heterodimer of two long subunits that associate to form tetramers 200 nm in length.

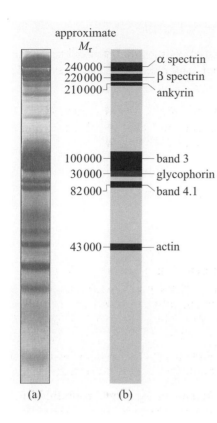

(a)　　　(b)

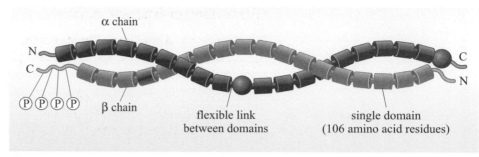

Figure 6.33　Schematic of spectrin showing the intertwined α and β subunits. Two such heterodimers associate end-to-end via the phosphorylated heads to form a tetramer.

Figure 6.32　SDS–PAGE of the proteins in the human erythrocyte membrane. (a) The proteins in the gel are stained with Coomassie blue (not shown in colour). (b) The positions of some of the major proteins are indicated alongside their approximate M_r values. Note that glycophorin is highly glycosylated, so it migrates much more slowly than an unglycosylated protein of the same M_r.

Spectrin is the principle component of the **cell cortex**, the network of proteins that connect with actin filaments of the cytoskeleton and which lie under the plasma membrane (Figure 6.34). Four or five spectrin dimers are linked to each other at one end by means of a number of other proteins in a **junctional complex**. The other proteins include short actin filaments and a protein called band 4.1. At intervals along its length, spectrin is also linked to the cytosolic domains of band 3 and glycophorin, the major transmembrane proteins of the erythrocyte plasma membrane. Band 4.1 links spectrin to both these proteins whilst a protein called **ankyrin** links spectrin to band 3.

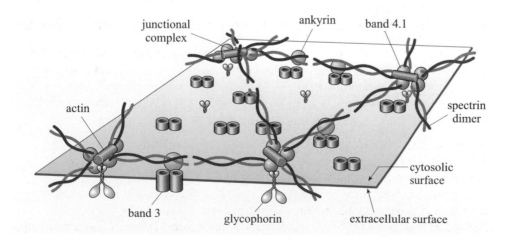

Figure 6.34
Schematic showing cytoskeletal connections on the cytosolic surface of the erythrocyte plasma membrane.

6.6.2 Cell polarity and intercellular junctions

Cells are rarely symmetrical. Contacts with different cells, with different types of extracellular matrix or with extracellular fluids can vary greatly over the surface of even a single cell. The variations in the contacts that a cell makes are often reflected in the shape of the cell and, inevitably, in the composition of the plasma membrane. Thus the plasma membrane of a neuron can have very different lipid and protein compositions in the cell body, the axon and the terminals. Where neighbouring cells in a tissue contact each other or contact the extracellular matrix, different types of cell junction can be observed by electron microscopy. Cell junctions are areas of specialized membrane structure and function.

> The different types of intercellular junctions are dealt with in some detail in S204, Book 3 *The Core of Life*, Vol. I, so will be discussed only briefly here, by way of illustrating the structure–function relationships in cell membranes.

In some highly *polarized* cells such as gut epithelial cells (Figure 6.35), there can be a very clear demarcation between different parts of the plasma membrane. In epithelial cells, the two distinct parts of the plasma membrane are known as the **apical** and the **basolateral** domains. These domains not only look different and have a different composition, but they also have very different activities and functions. The apical domain is exposed to the contents of the intestine and is the site of absorption of nutrients, facilitated by the microvilli which increase the surface area. This part of the membrane is particularly rich in sphingolipids. The basolateral domain contacts other cells and the extracellular matrix and is rich in glycerophospholipids. The apical and basolateral domains of the epithelial cell plasma membrane are separated by a particular type of junction between

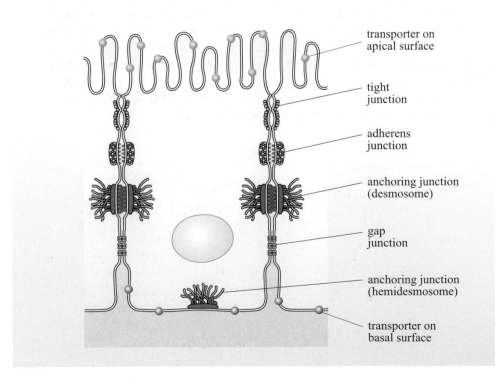

Figure 6.35
Schematic of an epithelial cell from the intestine illustrating the different types of intercellular junctions and the polarized distribution of transporter proteins between the apical and basolateral domains. Note that other types of cell may have some, but not all, of these junctions.

transporter on apical surface

tight junction

adherens junction

anchoring junction (desmosome)

gap junction

anchoring junction (hemidesmosome)

transporter on basal surface

neighbouring epithelial cells, known as a **tight junction**. Tight junctions are cell junctions with a barrier function. In gut epithelial cells, they prevent leakage of the gut contents and restrict the lateral movement of plasma membrane proteins between the apical and basolateral domains. In this way, the characteristic polarized distribution of transporters is maintained in these cells and the unidirectional transport of the products of digestion from the gut to the bloodstream is possible. The major transmembrane proteins in tight junctions are the claudins, and different members of this protein family occur in different tight junctions.

The epithelial cell represented in Figure 6.35 is a good example of a cell that contains a number of other junctions. Other cells may have some, but not all, of these different junctions. As well as tight junctions, which act as a barrier to the movement of small molecules between cells, there are **anchoring cell junctions**, which mechanically attach cells to each other and to the extracellular matrix, and **gap junctions**, which mediate passage of signals from one cell to another. Many variations occur in different cells, comprising different membrane proteins and involving various connections with the cytoskeleton.

Anchoring cell junctions connect the cytoskeleton of a cell to that of its neighbour or to the extracellular matrix (Figure 6.36). Specific anchoring proteins connect actin filaments or intermediate filaments of the cytoskeleton to the cytoplasmic domains of transmembrane adhesion proteins at the site of the junction. Depending on the nature of the junction, the extracellular part of the adhesion proteins interacts either with other adhesion proteins on the neighbouring cell or with the extracellular matrix. Adherens junctions and desmosomes are anchoring junctions between cells and they contain transmembrane adhesion molecules belonging to a family of proteins called the **cadherins**. Focal adhesions and hemidesmosomes are anchoring junctions between a cell and the extracellular matrix. In these junctions, the adhesion proteins are of the **integrin** family (discussed in Chapter 16).

Most cells in animal tissue communicate with their neighbours via gap junctions. These junctions contain connexins, which you have encountered earlier in this chapter. Six connexin proteins assemble to form a channel known as a connexon, and two such channels, one on each cell, connect to form the gap junction. The extracellular portions of the connexin proteins bridge a narrow gap of 2–4 nm between the membranes of adjacent cells, and ions and small water-soluble molecules can pass directly between the cells via these channels. Thus gap junctions couple cells both metabolically and electrically.

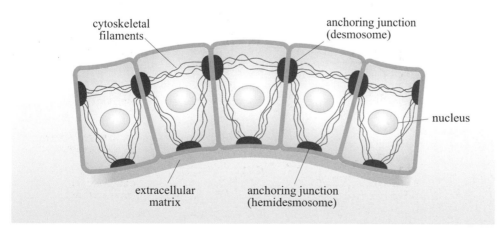

Figure 6.36
Anchoring cell junctions, which connect the cytoskeleton between neighbouring cells and between a cell and the extracellular matrix.

Summary of Section 6.6

1   The plasma membrane is not independent of the rest of the cell, but is connected to the cytoskeleton of the cell by means of structural proteins. The cell cortex is the network of proteins that connect with actin filaments of the cytoskeleton and lies under the plasma membrane.

2   The composition and organization of the proteins in the cell cortex of the human erythrocyte have been studied extensively.

3   Epithelial cells of the gut are an example of a highly polarized cell type. These cells have two distinct plasma membrane domains, the apical and the basolateral. The domains are separated by tight junctions between neighbouring epithelial cells. Tight junctions have a barrier function.

4   Anchoring cell junctions connect the cytoskeleton of a cell to that of its neighbour or to the extracellular matrix.

5   Most cells in animal tissues communicate with their neighbours via gap junctions. Gap junctions form a channel that permits the passage of ions and small water-soluble molecules between the cells.

Conclusion

The essential role of biological membranes in all living things cannot be overemphasized, as they define the boundary of every living cell. Membranes also permitted compartmentalization of cellular functions, a key stage in evolution of eukaryotic cells, as discussed in Chapter 1.

In this chapter we have outlined the basic structural features of biological membranes, described their physical properties and related these to the chemical properties of their constituents. The relationship between structure and function in membranes has been discussed in rather general terms here. You should bear in mind however, that biological membranes from many different organisms and from different compartments within a single cell actually demonstrate huge variety in form and specialized function. As you progress through this course, you will inevitably encounter many specific examples of membrane function, since these structures feature prominently in virtually every cellular process.

In this first book of S377, we have explored key aspects of the molecular composition and organization of the cell, placing particular emphasis on the relationship between structure and function. At this stage in the course, you will be beginning to appreciate how cellular organization and function are explained in terms of fundamental physical and chemical principles. Cell membranes, as discussed in Chapter 6, illustrate this point very well. In the next book, we begin to look at basic processes in the life and death of the cell. To appreciate the molecular basis of these cellular processes you will, of course, draw on what you have learned in Book 1.

Learning outcomes for Chapter 6

When you have studied this chapter, you should be able to:

6.1 Define and use each of the terms printed in **bold** in the text.

6.2 Describe the structures of the different types of membrane lipids.

6.3 Describe the general properties and characteristics of biological membranes.

6.4 Relate the biochemical and biophysical properties of membranes to their function.

6.5 Describe, using examples, the different types of membrane protein.

6.6 Discuss the significance of lipid rafts and caveolae.

6.7 Describe distinctive features of the plasma membrane.

Questions for Chapter 6

Question 6.1

Draw a schematic to illustrate the amphipathic nature of the different types of membrane lipids.

Question 6.2

How does the melting temperature, T_m, of fatty acids vary with (a) their chain length and (b) the number of double bonds they contain?

Question 6.3

Sketch a graph to illustrate the relationship between lipid bilayer permeability and solubility in oil for compounds diffusing passively across a lipid bilayer. This relationship does not strictly apply to the permeability of real membranes for some compounds. Why is this?

Question 6.4

How do some helical multipass transmembrane proteins create a hydrophilic pore through the membrane?

Question 6.5

What characterizes lipid rafts in terms of (a) their lipid composition and (b) their physical properties?

References

Becker, W. M., Kleinsmith, L. J. and Hardin, J. (2000) *The World of the Cell*, Addison-Wesley Longman, Inc.

Rothman, J. E. and Lenard, J. (1977) Membrane asymmetry, *Science*, **195**, pp. 743–753.

Silvius, J. R. (1982) Thermotropic phase transitions of pure lipids in model membranes and their modification by membrane proteins, in *Lipid–Protein Interactions,* John Wiley & Sons Inc., New York.

Singer, S. J. and Nicolson, G. L. (1972) The fluid mosaic model of the structure of cell membranes, *Science*, **175**, pp. 720–731.

Further sources

Brown, D. A. and London, E. (2000) Structure and function of sphingolipid- and cholesterol-rich membrane rafts, *Journal of Biological Chemistry*, **275**(23), pp. 17221–17224.

Sackman, E. (1995) Biological membranes – architecture and function, in *Handbook of Biological Physics*, Vol. 1, R. Lipowsky and E. Sackman (eds), Elsevier Science.

Werten, P. J. L., Rémigy, H.-W., de Groot, B. L., Fotiadis, D., Philippsen, A., Stahlberg, H., Grubmüller, H. and Engel, A. (2002) Progress in the analysis of membrane protein structure and function, *FEBS Letters*, **529**, pp. 65–72.

ANSWERS TO QUESTIONS

Question 1.1

The cytoskeleton has a role in cell division and intracellular transport. Going beyond the more basic cellular function, the cytoskeleton is involved in shaping specialized, differentiated cells and is required for cell motility.

In terms of cellular evolution, the cytoskeleton, since it helped maintain cell shape and integrity, could support larger cells. Evolution of the cytoskeleton enabled the development of the intracellular transport functions necessary in compartmentalized cells.

Question 1.2

In complex multicellular organisms, cells can differentiate, a property that is based on selective expression of different sets of genes in different types of cell. Sophisticated intercellular signalling systems are required to coordinate the differentiation pathways and the interactions between groups of cells in the adult. Hence these cells require appropriate sets of receptors and have the capacity to secrete their own signalling molecules. Cells within a complex organism cooperate with each other, rather than compete. Ultimately this may mean that a cell dies (by apoptosis), thereby allowing the development or functions of the organism to proceed normally.

Question 2.1

Water molecules are polar and can form hydrogen bonding networks where the O atom in each molecule can form two hydrogen bonds with two other molecules and each H atom participates in one such bond. The high level of hydrogen bonding means that water is cohesive and has a large temperature-stabilizing capacity, since heat energy is absorbed to break the hydrogen bonds rather than elevating temperature.

Question 2.2

Leucine has one chiral carbon atom; isoleucine has two chiral carbon atoms.

L-leucine (flying-wedge format)

Question 2.3

(a) A buffer is a solution of an acid and its conjugate base (or a solution of a base and its conjugate acid), which upon the addition of either acid or base does not change significantly in pH. It is very important that biological systems use buffers to maintain the pH, so that protein structure is maintained and the chemical reactions can proceed without any detrimental effect.

(b) HCO_3^- and HPO_4^{2-} fulfil a particularly important role in buffering intracellular and extracellular pH. Intracellular pH is maintained around pH 7.4. Hydrogen carbonate also acts as a carrier for carbon dioxide, and phosphate serves many cellular functions as part of phosphorylated coenzymes and metabolic intermediates.

Question 2.4

(a) Negatively charged. At pH 7.4 the N-terminal amino group is positively charged and the C-terminal carboxyl group is negatively charged. These charges balance each other, but the aspartate residue is also negatively charged, giving the peptide a net negative charge.

(b) Positively charged. The arginine and lysine residues are strongly basic and each ionizes to $-NH_3^+$, and these two positive charges exceeds the single negative charge on the glutamate. (The positive charge on the N-terminus and the negative charge on the C-terminus balance each other.)

Question 2.5

At pH 7.4, glutamic acid is predominantly in its fully ionized form (glutamate), as shown below.

glutamate

Question 2.6

The hormone binds more strongly than the inhibitor.

$$R + I \rightleftharpoons RI$$

where R is the receptor, I is the inhibitor and RI is the receptor–inhibitor complex. 50% of the receptor has ligand bound. So [RI] = [R].

$$\frac{[R][I]}{[RI]} = K_D = 10^{-8} \, \text{mol} \, l^{-1}$$

$$[I] = 10^{-8} \, \text{mol} \, l^{-1}$$

When 50% of the receptor has inhibitor bound, the concentration of free inhibitor is $10^{-8} \, \text{mol} \, l^{-1}$. Since the peptide has an M_r of 1200, this concentration corresponds to $1200 \times 10^{-8} \, \text{g} \, l^{-1} = 12 \, \mu\text{g} \, l^{-1}$.

Question 3.1

Secondary structure describes the conformation adopted by the polypeptide backbone and can be either α helix, β pleated sheet (parallel, antiparallel or mixed), loops and turns or random coil. Supersecondary structure is intermediate between secondary and tertiary structure (the arrangement of elements of secondary structure in the folded polypeptide). Supersecondary motifs are characteristic arrangements of two or three elements of secondary structure and can be identified in many different proteins. Folds are more extensive structural arrangements that combine elements of secondary and supersecondary structures.

Question 3.2

A Ramachandran plot indicates the values of the torsion angles ϕ and ψ that are sterically permissible for a particular residue. In other words, it allows us to identify those conformations (i.e. for a particular value of ϕ and ψ) that are sterically favourable or unfavourable. Such a plot is generated from data on the minimal permitted distance between atoms, which depends on the van der Waals radii of the atoms. Those values of ϕ and ψ that give conformations such that the distances between non-bonding atoms of the peptide are greater than or equal to the allowed distances can then be plotted against each other. Experimental observations of torsion angles in polypeptide structure can also be used to generate a Ramachandran plot.

Question 3.3

Src is a tyrosine kinase with four domains. Two of these domains can be thought of as subdomains, as they correspond to two lobes of the kinase fold. The other two are an SH2 and an SH3 domain, which are critical to the regulation of the kinase activity. Intramolecular interactions between the SH2 domain and a phosphorylated tyrosine residue in the C-terminal tail and between the SH3 domain and an internal peptide sequence stabilize the enzyme in an inactive conformation. Activation of Src occurs when specific ligands disrupt these intramolecular interactions. As a result, the inhibitory phosphate is removed and phosphorylation of another tyrosine residue, this time in what is known as the activation loop, occurs. This phosphorylated tyrosine stabilizes the active conformation of the enzyme so that it is able to bind its substrates, i.e. a specific peptide sequence and ATP. Thus the interactions of regulatory domains with other proteins or with internal sequences determine the conformation of the protein as a whole and the activity of the kinase domain.

Question 3.4

The different types of covalent modification of proteins include the following: addition of a lipid group (lipidation); addition of sugar residues and oligo-saccharides (glycosylation); phosphorylation; methylation and acetylation.

Question 3.5

Phosphorylation of proteins may alter their activity in a number of ways. (1) The phosphorylated residue may be recognized by other proteins and thereby elicit formation of a protein–protein complex. (2) The phosphoryl group may prevent the interaction of the protein with a substrate or other ligand, either by offering steric hindrance or, by virtue of its negative charge, disrupting electrostatic interactions. (3) The phosphorylation event may result in a conformational change in the protein.

Question 3.6

The two-hybrid system entails screening of libraries of genes against a specific bait protein. When an interaction is demonstrated, the gene encoding the interacting protein is available for expression or manipulation. Expression of the gene greatly facilitates the characterization of the protein, which can be more readily purified in large quantities. Biochemical methods, such as affinity chromatography, generally yield a small amount of interacting protein, which is pulled out from a biological sample (e.g. a cell or tissue extract). Large amounts of material may be necessary to get a sufficiently high yield of the interacting protein for biochemical characterization.

Question 3.7

Generally, in SDM the residue is replaced with one of similar or smaller overall size, with different chemical properties (e.g. a glutamate for a glutamine, or vice versa). The intention is to avoid any gross disruption of the structure of the protein.

Question 4.1

By definition, ΔG is the free energy change for the reaction, so $\Delta G = -2870\ \text{kJ mol}^{-1}$.

Question 4.2

The value of ΔG for the synthesis of ATP under physiological conditions is 46–55 kJ mol^{-1}. The return of one proton across the inner mitochondrial membrane, to the mitochondrial matrix, typically generates ~22 kJ mol^{-1}. Therefore the movement of a minimum of three protons is needed to generate one molecule of ATP, in an interaction that is coupled by the F_0-F_1 ATP synthase.

Question 4.3

$$\Delta G = \Delta G^{\circ\prime} + RT \ln \frac{[\text{ADP}]\,[P_i]}{[\text{ATP}]}$$

$$= -30.5 + 8.314 \times 10^{-3} \times 298 \times \ln \frac{[0.25 \times 10^{-3}]\,[1.65 \times 10^{-3}]}{[2.25 \times 10^{-3}]}$$

$$= -51.8\ \text{kJ mol}^{-1}$$

Question 4.4

If there is a fall in demand for ATP, the level of ATP in the cell will start to rise. The increase in ATP concentration in the mitochondrion will lead to a back-up in the proton flow through the F_0-F_1 ATPase. Thus the proton motive force will increase, until compensated by decreased proton transfer by the ETC.

ΔG for ATP synthesis is given by the equation:

$$\Delta G = \Delta G^{\circ\prime} + RT \ln \frac{[\text{ATP}]}{[\text{ADP}][P_i]}$$

Therefore an increase in the concentration of ATP results in an increase in ΔG for ATP synthesis.

Question 4.5

ΔG for the binding of Y to X, will decrease, i.e. less energy will be required to dissociate X and Y.

Question 5.1

When ethidium bromide intercalates into duplex DNA, it results in an unwinding of the helix through disruption of the base-stacking interactions that contribute to its structure. This untwisting of the helix reduces the energy available for supercoiling. Hence, supercoiled DNA, when incubated with ethidium bromide, becomes less supercoiled.

Question 5.2

The chromosomal location of the gene could be determined by FISH, where the DNA is labelled and hybridized to metaphase chromosomes. The position of the fluorescent signal on the chromosome should indicate the position of the gene. The expression pattern can be determined in one of two ways. Firstly, the DNA can be used to perform ISH on tissue sections. Secondly, it could be used as a probe against a Northern blot of mRNA taken from various human tissues.

Question 5.3

Chromatin packaging serves (1) to compact the large amounts of DNA in a small space, (2) to protect DNA from damage, and (3) as a platform for DNA processing.

Question 5.4

Histone tails are rich in positively charged lysine residues, many of which are subject to modification by acetylation (and also phosphorylation and methylation). Removal of acetyl groups from the tails exposes the positive charge on the tails, which in turn allows the tails to counteract the repulsion of negatively charged DNA backbones, hence permitting closer packing of the DNA.

Question 5.5

Two left-handed super-helical turns are introduced to the DNA, so that it adopts a solenoid-like structure around the core.

Question 5.6

Modifications of core nucleosomal proteins include covalent modification of the tails of core histones by acetylation, methylation or phosphorylation. Acetylation or methylation of lysine residues in the histone tails reduces the net positive charge associated with this part of the protein and affects its ability to neutralize the repulsive forces between regions of the DNA backbone. As a result, compaction of the DNA is decreased. Modification of histones can also affect chromatin compaction and transcriptional activity by recruiting regulatory proteins to specific regions.

Question 6.1

As Figure 6.3b, highlighting the non-polar (hydrophobic) tail portion and polar (hydrophilic) head, which are common features of all membrane lipids.

Question 6.2

(a) T_m of fatty acids increases with increasing chain length. (b) T_m of fatty acids decreases with increasing number of double bonds. The degree of unsaturation has a much more dramatic effect on the T_m of a fatty acid than does the chain length.

Question 6.3

For substances that diffuse passively across a lipid bilayer, there is a linear relationship between their permeability in the bilayer and their solubility in oil (see Figure 6.37 below).

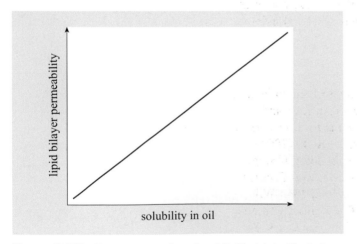

Figure 6.37   For answer to Question 6.3. Sketch to illustrate the relationship between lipid bilayer permeability of a substance and its solubility in oil.

Real membranes have a variety of different carrier and channel proteins, which selectively transport substances, and pores which facilitate the diffusion of substances across the lipid bilayer. Such transport mechanisms obviate the need for the substance to contact the hydrophobic interior of the membrane and their transport is not therefore related to the solubility of the substance in lipid.

Question 6.4

Transmembrane proteins with multiple α helices spanning the membrane can create a hydrophilic pore by association of the transmembrane helices to form a bundle. Hydrophilic side-chains on individual transmembrane helices are turned away from the hydrophobic interior of the lipid bilayer and towards the centre of the structure. The side-chains presented on the outside of the bundle of helices are non-polar and can interact with the hydrophobic core of the lipid bilayer.

Question 6.5

(a) Lipid rafts are characterized by a high cholesterol and saturated glycosphingolipid content. (b) Lipid rafts are cohesive liquid-ordered microdomains which can move around in the fluid-phase lipid bilayer. Lipid rafts can coalesce and divide. GPI-anchored and acylated proteins tend to partition in lipid rafts whilst prenylated proteins are excluded. Their lipid composition makes lipid rafts resistant to solubilization in non-ionic detergent (e.g. Triton X-100) at low temperatures (4 °C).

ACKNOWLEDGEMENTS

Every effort has been made to contact copyright holders. If any have been inadvertently overlooked, the publishers will be pleased to make the necessary arrangements at the first opportunity. Grateful acknowledgement is made to the following sources for permission to reproduce material within this book.

Chapter 1

Figure 1.1 (top) Mary Evans Picture Library; *Figure 1.1 (bottom)* Frank Cloystein.

Chapter 2

Figure 2.11a Johnson, C. W. Jr. (1990) 'Information content in the circular dichroism of proteins', *Proteins; Structure, Function and Genetics*, Vol. 7, John Wiley and Sons Inc.; *Figure 2.11b* Riazance, J. H. *et al.* (1985) in *Nucleic Acids Research*, copyright © 1985 IRL Press Ltd, Oxford University Press; *Figure 2.26* Edgar Fahs Smith Collection, University of Pennsylvania Library; *Figures 2.27, 2.28* Texas A & M University-Kingsville.

Chapter 3

Figures 3.3, 3.5 3.7, 3.40, 3.41 Voet, D. and Voet, J. G. (1995) *Biochemistry*, 2nd edn, copyright © 1995 John Wiley & Sons Inc.; *Figures 3.4, 3.8, 3.9a, 3.10, 3.14, 3.24, 3.25a,c* Voet, D. and Voet, J. G. (1995) *op. cit.*, illustration Irving Geis, rights owned by Howard Hughes Medical Institute, reproduced by permission; *Figures 3.11b, 3.17, 3.18, 3.22, 3.28, 3.37, 3.50, 3.51* Alberts, B. *et al.* (2002) *Molecular Biology of the Cell*, 4th edn, Garland Science, Taylor and Francis Group; *Figure 3.21c* Dr Andreas Merdes, University of Edinburgh; *Figure 3.29* Huse, M. and Kuriyan, J. (2002) 'The conformational plasticity of protein kinases', *Cell*, **109**(3), copyright © 2002 Elsevier; *Figure 3.30* Protein sequence data was obtained from the Swiss-Prot database http://www.ebi.ac.uk/swissprot/index.html; *Figures 3.32a, 3.46* Stryer, L. (1981) *Biochemistry*, 2nd edn, W. H. Freeman & Co.; *Figure 3.32b* Baldwin, J. and Chothia, C. (1979) *Journal of Molecular Biology*, **192**, copyright © 1979 Academic Press Inc. (London) Ltd; *Figure 3.53* Joanne Mathers, Dundee University.

Chapter 4

Figure 4.4 Harris, D. A. (1995) 'Gibbs free energy – measurement and application', *Bioenergetics at a Glance,* Blackwell Science Ltd; *Figure 4.8* Frey, T. G. and Manella, C. A. (2000) 'Internal structure of mitochondria', *Trends in Biochemical Sciences*, **25**(7), copyright © 2000 Elsevier; *Figure 4.11* Murphy, K. P. (2001) 'Calorimetry', *Encyclopaedia of Life Sciences*, April, Nature Publishing Group; *Figure 4.12* Devlin, T. M. (1992) *Enzymes: Classification, Kinetics and Control, Textbook of Biochemistry with Clinical Correlation*, Wiley-Liss Inc., John Wiley & Sons Inc. publication; *Figure 4.15* Jen-Jacobson, L. *et al.* (2000) 'Structural and thermodynamic strategies for site-specific DNA binding proteins', *Structure*, **8**, p.1016, copyright © 2000 Elsevier.

Chapter 5

Figure 5.1a courtesy Robert Saunders; *Figure 5.1c* Mark Hirst and David Shuker/Open University; *Figure 5.1d* Dr Thomas Broker; *Figure 5.1e* Dr George Palade; *Figure 5.1f* Fedoroff and Botstein (1992) 'The plural of heterochromatin', *The Dynamic Genome*, Cold Spring Harbor Laboratory; *Figures 5.7a,d, 5.8a,b, 5.33b* Mark Hirst/Open University; *Figure 5.8c* Ruth Akhter/Open University; *Figure 5.14* Teicher, B. A. (ed.) (1997) 'DNA topoisomerase II inhibitors', *Cancer Therapeutics: Experimental and Clinical Agents*, Humana Press Inc.; *Figure 5.16* courtesy Peter Lansdorp, Terry Fox Laboratory, B. C. Cancer Research Center, UBC, Vancouver, Canada; *Figure 5.17c* Brown, V. P. *et al.* (2001) 'Microarray identification of FMRP-associated brain mRNAs …', *Cell*, **107**, Cell Press; *Figure 5.18a,c* Rich, A. *et al.* (1973) 'Three-dimensional structure of yeast Phe tRNA', *Science*, **179**, copyright © American Association for the Advancement of Science; Ladner, J. *et al.* (1975) 'Structure for yeast Phe tRNA', *Proceedings of the National Academy of Sciences*, **12**, National Academy of Sciences, reprinted with permission from *Nature*, **250**, copyright © 1974; *Figures 5.18b, 5.19* Moss, E. G. 'MicroRNAs: hidden in the genome', *Current Biology*, **12**, copyright © 2000 Elsevier; *Figure 5.23c* Bulyk, M. L. *et al.* (2001) 'Exploring the DNA-binding specifications of zinc fingers with DNA microarrays', *Proceedings of the National Academy of Sciences*, **98**, June 19, copyright © 2001 National Academy of Sciences; *Figure 5.29b* photograph kindly provided by Barbara Hamkalo; *Figure 5.29c* Wolffe, A. (1995) *Chromatin Structure and Function*, 2nd edn, copyright © 1995 Elsevier; *Figure 5.34* Bulger, M. *et al.* (2002) 'ChIPs of the β-globin locus …', *Current Opinion in Genetics and Development*, **12**, copyright © 2002 Elsevier; *Figure 5.36* Boggs, B. A. *et al.* (2002) 'Differentially methylated forms of histone H3 …', *Nature Genetics*, **30**, January, Nature Publishing Co.; *Figure 5.37* Grewal, S. and Elgin S. C. R. (2002) 'Heterochromatin: new possibilities for the inheritance of structure', *Current Opinion in Genetics and Development*, **12**, copyright © 2002 Elsevier; *Figure 5.38* Pereira, S. L. *et al.* (1997) 'Archaeal nucleosomes', *Proceedings of the National Academy of Sciences*, **94**, Nov., copyright © 1997 National Academy of Sciences; *Figure 5.41* courtesy Joseph G. Gall; *Figure 5.42a* Boyle, S. *et al.* (2001) 'The spatial organization of human chromosomes …', *Human Molecular Genetics*, **10**(3), by permission of Oxford University Press; *Figure 5.42b* Lemke, J. *et al.* (2002) 'The DNA-based structure of human chromosome 5 in interphase', *American Journal of Human Genetics*, **71**, The American Society of Human Genetics; *Figure 5.43* adapted from Purves, W. K. *et al.* (1998) *Life, the Science of Biology*, 5th edn, Sinauer Associates Inc.

Chapter 6

Figure 6.1 Heather Davies/Open University; *Figures 6.4, 6.27* Becker *et al.* (2000) 'Membranes: their structure, function and chemistry', *The World of the Cell*, 4th edn, Pearson Education Inc.; *Figure 6.6* courtesy Richard Pastor, FDA, Washington, D.C.; *Figure 6.7* Richard Pastor, FDA, Washington, D.C.; *Figures 6.9a–c, 6.11, 6.15, 6.16, 6.20, 6.29, 6.32, 6.34, 6.36* Alberts, B. *et al.* (2002) *op. cit.*; *Figure 6.25* Voet, D. and Voet, J. G. (1995) *op. cit.*; *Figure 6.28* Ilangumaran, S. *et al.* (2000) 'Microdomains in lymphocyte signalling …', *Trends in Immunology*, **21**, copyright © 2000 Elsevier; *Figure 6.31* Male, D. (1998) 'Immunology techniques', *Immunology – An Illustrated Outline*, 3rd edn 1998 by Mosby, an imprint of Mosby International.

Tables

Tables 3.1 and 6.2 Voet, D. and Voet, J. G. (1995) *op. cit.*

INDEX

Note: Entries in **bold** are key terms. Page numbers referring to information that is given only in a figure or caption or a table are printed in *italics*.